Basic Tags for Inserting Java into JSPs

Scriptlet Tags

Purpose: Used for embedding blocks of Java code into your JSPs.

Syntax:

```
<% //embed Java Code %>
```

Declaration Tags

Purpose: Used for declaring variables and methods.

Syntax:

```
<%! variable declaration;
    method declaration;  %>
```

Expression Tags

Purpose: Used for inserting a Java expression into your JSPs.

Syntax:

```
<%= Java Expression %>
```

Directives for JSPs

General syntax of directives:

```
<%@ directive_type directive_attributes %>
   directive_type::= page | include | taglib
   directive_attributes::= dependent on the directive_type
```

include *Directive*

Purpose: Used to include the text of another file.

Syntax:

```
<%@ include file="Relative_URL_to_File" %>
```

taglib *Directive*

Purpose: Used to extend the functionality of your JSP by importing custom action tags.

Syntax:

```
<%@ taglib uri="URI_to_Tag_Library" prefix="Custom_actions" %>
```

page *Directive*

Purpose: Used to set properties of the JSP, such as what packages it imports, if it is part of a session, and if there is an error page.

Syntax:

```
<%@ page page_attributes %>
   page_attributes::=    { language="scriptingLanguage"  }
                         { extends="className"            }
                         { import="importList"            }
                         { session="true|false"           }
                         { buffer="none|sizekb"           }
                         { autoFlush="true|false"         }
                         { isThreadSafe="true|false"      }
                         { info="info_Text"               }
                         { errorPage="errorPageURL"       }
                         { isErrorPage="true|false"       }
                         { contentType="contentMIMEtype"  }
```

Predefined Action Tags

The general syntax of the action tags:

```
<jsp:action_Name action_attributes /> or
<jsp:action_Name action_attributes></jsp:action_Name>
   action_Name::=useBean | getProperty | setProperty
                 include | forward | plugin
```

SAMS

Teach Yourself JavaServer Pages in 24 Hours

useBean *Action*

Purpose: Used to access a JavaBean utility class on the server.

Syntax:

```
<jsp:useBean id="name" scope="page|request|session|application"
             class="type_Spec" />
```

or

```
<jsp:useBean id="name" scope="page|request|session|application"
             class="type_Spec">
   //body
</jsp:useBean>

type_Spec::=class="className" |
            class="className" type="typeName" |
            type="typeName" class="className" |
            beanName="beanName" type="typeName" |
            type="typeName" beanName="beanName" |
            type="typeName"
```

setProperty *Action*

Purpose: Used to set the attributes of a JavaBean class.

Syntax:

```
<jsp:setProperty name="beanName" property_expression />
  property_expression::=property="*" |
                        property="propertyName" |
                        property="propName" param="paramName" |
                        property="propName" value="valueName"
```

getProperty *Action*

Purpose: Used to get the value of an attribute of a JavaBean class.

Syntax:

```
<jsp:getProperty name="beanName" property="propName" />
```

include *Action*

Purpose: Used to include the output of another JSP.

Syntax:

```
<jsp:include page="Relative_URL" />
```

forward *Action*

Purpose: Used to forward the request to another JSP.

Syntax:

```
<jsp:forward page="Relative_URL" />
```

plugin *Action*

Purpose: Used to insert a Java applet or a JavaBean component (for client side presentation).

Syntax:

```
<jsp:plugin type="bean|applet" code="objectCode"
            codebase="objectCodebase"
            { align="alignment"          }
            { archive="archiveList"      }
            { height="height"            }
            { hspace="hspace"            }
            { jreversion="jreversion"    }
            { name="componentName"       }
            { vspace="vspace"            }
            { width="width"              }
            { nspluginurl="url"          }
            { iepluginurl="url"          } >
  <params>
    <param name="name" value="paramValue" />
  </params>
  <fallback>text</fallback>
</jsp:plugin>
```

Jose Annunziato
Stephanie Fesler Kaminaris

SAMS
Teach Yourself

JavaServer Pages™

in 24 Hours

SAMS

201 West 103rd St., Indianapolis, Indiana, 46290

Sams Teach Yourself JavaServer Pages™ in 24 Hours

Copyright © 2001 by Sams Publishing

International Standard Book Number: 0-672-32023-1

Library of Congress Catalog Card Number: 00-104401

Printed in the United States of America

First Printing: November 2000

03   02   01   00   4   3   2   1

Trademarks

Warning and Disclaimer

ASSOCIATE PUBLISHER
Michael Stephens

ACQUISITIONS EDITORS
Steve Anglin
Heather Goodell

DEVELOPMENT EDITOR
Heather Goodell

MANAGING EDITOR
Matt Purcell

PROJECT EDITOR
George E. Nedeff

COPY EDITOR
Maryann Steinhart

INDEXER
Sandy Henselmeier

PROOFREADER
Candice Hightower

TECHNICAL EDITORS
Alexandre Pereira Calsavara
Venkat S.R. Krishna Chaganti
Al Saganich

TEAM COORDINATOR
Pamalee Nelson

MEDIA DEVELOPER
Matt Bates

INTERIOR DESIGNER
Gary Adair

COVER DESIGNER
Aren Howell

PRODUCTION
Lizbeth Patterson

Contents at a Glance

Contents

About the Authors

JOSE ANNUNZIATO received his Master's and Doctor of Science degrees in computer science from the University of Massachusetts Lowell. He taught at the university for several years while completing his doctorate. Although content in academia, he was lured into private industry, working on a range of Internet-related projects for several years. Dr. Annunziato has consulted for several companies working on many distributed systems projects for the Department of Defense. He then found a nice blend of academic rigorousness and private-industry challenges at BEA Systems, developing courseware for the industry's leading application server products such as WebLogic Server, WebLogic Commerce Server, and WebLogic Enterprise. His other interests include 3D graphics animation, robotics, virtual reality, artificial intelligence, and classical piano. In his spare time he enjoys wrestling with his three children, and the company of his wife.

STEPHANIE FESLER KAMINARIS has several years of experience in software development training. She has split her time between the classroom and writing course materials. In that time she has written hundreds of pages of course materials on Web development, such as HTML, JavaScript, Active Server Pages, VBScript, and CGI programming. She has also written course materials for BEA's WebLogic Server courses, such as WebLogic as a Web Server, JavaServer Pages, Servlets, and Web Applications. In the classroom she has taught courses in software programming languages, including Java and C++, and Java Enterprise technologies such as EJBs, JSPs, Servlets, JNDI, JDBC, and much more. She also teaches courses on running BEA's WebLogic Server and Administrating BEA's WebLogic Server.

Dedications

I would like to dedicate this book to my wife, Alexandra, who has been so caring, loving, and patient with me, and has brought us the joy of our three beautiful children, Katerina, Rafael, and Victoria. Thank you, this is for you.

This book is also dedicated to the loving memory of my parents Pasquale and Emilia Annunziato. Thank you and I wish you were here.

—Jose Annunziato

There are many people who have helped me get to where I am today. I would like to thank my family and especially my mother and father for always supporting me and believing that I can do anything that I put my mind to. Thanks to my Grandma Fesler and Grandma Corneau for being proud of me and making me feel like I have wings to fly. I am also dedicating this book to my grandfather, John F. Fesler, who was truly a great man; it is an absolute honor when people compare me to him. Also thanks to my sister, Kristy: you have always been a great big sister and have always been there when I needed you. I would also like to mention my puppies, Mickey and Minnie, who have added so much joy and laughter to my life.

Last, but definitely not least, I am dedicating this book to my husband, Chris. I love you more and more each day, thanks for loving me, believing in me, supporting me, and most importantly just being you. You are the sweetest man.

—Stephanie Fesler Kaminaris

Acknowledgments

Although not directly involved in the production of this book, I would like to thank Margarita Turcotte for helping our family through several ordeals. Also Dr. Charles Kosta for sponsoring and mentoring me while in school. Thank you to the staff at UMass Lowell for their support, especially Professor Charlie Steele, Professor William Moloney, Dr. Mariam Williams, and Dr. James Canning. Also thanks to Dr. Haim and Dr. Ethel Levkowitz for their insights, subjectivity, and guidance.

It was a pleasure to work with my co-author Stephanie Fesler Kaminaris. I love the way she jumps at the occasion to help and volunteer in some of the most adverse scenarios. Good for you. I would like to thank the people at Sams Publishing, especially Heather Goodell, for doing a wonderful job at keeping everything on track.

—*Jose Annunziato*

It has been such a pleasure writing this book and having the opportunity to work with absolutely wonderful individuals. The book author is just one piece of the puzzle, but there are so many people working behind the scenes to make a book a success. So thanks to Heather Goodell, who kept the book on track and oversaw the development of the material. Thanks also Al Saganich, who tech edited the book and made sure that all code listings were in tip-top shape. Thanks also to all the other people at Sams Publishing who worked on this book to make it the way it is.

—*Stephanie Fesler Kaminaris*

Tell Us What You Think!

As the reader of this book, *you* are our most important critic and commentator. We value your opinion and want to know what we're doing right, what we could do better, what areas you'd like to see us publish in, and any other words of wisdom you're willing to pass our way.

As an Associate Publisher for Sams Publishing, I welcome your comments. You can fax, email, or write me directly to let me know what you did or didn't like about this book— as well as what we can do to make our books stronger.

Please note that I cannot help you with technical problems related to the topic of this book, and that due to the high volume of mail I receive, I might not be able to reply to every message.

When you write, please be sure to include this book's title and authors as well as your name and phone or fax number. I will carefully review your comments and share them with the authors and editors who worked on the book.

Fax: 317-581-4770
Email: java@mcp.com
Mail: Michael Stephens
Associate Publisher
Sams Publishing
201 West 103rd Street
Indianapolis, IN 46290 USA

Introduction

Welcome to Sams Teach Yourself JavaServer Pages in 24 Hours!

You have decided that you want to learn how to write JavaServer Pages. Well, you have come to the right place. This book introduces you to the basics of JSPs, such as their structure, their application models, and how they can be used to create dynamic content on the Web. You also will learn about some advanced topics such as connecting to a database from within a JSP and using JavaBeans to access a database. Finally, you are going to write a Web application that models a human resources Web site for a company's intranet. Sound like a lot? It is, and you will accomplish it all in 24 one-hour lessons. Good luck, work hard, and have fun.

Who Is This Book's Intended Audience?

This book is aimed at individuals who are familiar with HTML and Java. You do not need to be an expert in HTML, but you should be familiar with the common tags and be able to create a simple HTML document. Also, you do not need to be an expert Java programmer, although experience with programming in any language will help you work through the activities.

What You'll Learn in the Next 24 Hours

You will learn what JSPs are and how they fit into Sun Microsystems Java 2 Enterprise Edition Platform. You'll also see how JSPs compare to other similar technologies such as CGI programs and Active Server Pages (ASPs).

First, we'll show you the basics of JSPs, such as the tags that allow you to embed Java in HTML pages and how to divide the work among several JSPs. This book also goes into advanced features such as connecting to a database from your JSP, using a JavaBean or server-side class, and extending the functionality of your JSPs using a custom tag library. You will complete the book with a project, writing a human resources Web site for a company's intranet. There is a lot to do, so buckle up and enjoy the ride.

What You Need

There are a few things you need before starting your journey. You need a text editor, such as Notepad in the Windows operating environment. You also need a Java Development Kit, JDK, from Sun Microsystems. The JDK can be downloaded from Sun's Web site, `http://java.sun.com/products/jdk/1.2/index.html`. Under the Production Releases heading you can choose what platform to download for. The best JDK to select is version 1.2.2. It is very easy to download and install and should only take a few minutes. You will download a zip file, typically named `jdk1_2_2-win.zip`, that contains the necessary files. All you need to do to deploy is unzip it to your root directory, such as `c:\`.

Conventions Used in This Book

This book uses different typefaces to differentiate between code and regular English, and also to help you identify important concepts. Therefore, code lines, commands, statements, variables, and any text you type or see onscreen appear in a `computer typeface`.

Do not type any line numbers that appear at the beginning of lines in code listings! The line numbers are used to reference the lines of code during explanation of the listing.

Placeholders for variables and expressions appear in a `monospace italic` font. You should replace the placeholder with the specific value it represents.

A Note presents interesting pieces of information related to the surrounding discussion.

A Tip offers advice or teaches an easier way to do something.

A Caution advises you about potential problems and helps you steer clear of disaster.

New Term:
A New Term provides a clear definition of a new, or essential term.

PART I
Overview

Hour

HOUR 1

Introduction to Web Applications

Our story begins with a young lady, Marian, who is interested in going to
Florida for her upcoming vacation. Marian is Internet savvy, so she visited an
airline's Web site and entered in her destination, Florida. A list of flights to
Florida was returned and displayed in an easy-to-read fashion in her browser.
Her business partner, John, was also planning his upcoming vacation, but he
wanted to go to Hawaii. Because he was Internet savvy as well, he went to
the same airline's Web site, entered in his destination, and received a listing
of flights to Hawaii. How was it possible that they received such different
information from the same Web site? The airline's Web site has an application, called a *Web application*, that accepted their requests and generated a
response pertaining to each particular query. Because the Web application
created these documents on-the-fly, it is considered to return dynamic content. That means the response from these sites, such as flights to various parts
of the country, are dynamically created when the particular query is entered.

> **New Term: Web Application**
>
> A Web application is a program that runs on a Web server.

Marian and John found their flights and off on vacation they went. Our story about Marian and John has come to an end, but our adventure is just beginning. You are going to delve into Web structures and understand how Web applications can generate different responses to various queries. This book focuses on Sun Microsystems technology JavaServer Pages (JSP) to deliver dynamic content to Web clients. So, let the adventure begin.

In this hour, you are going to understand

- What JavaServer Pages are
- The evolution of the Web
- The reason the Java 2 Enterprise Edition (J2EE) platform was created
- What application servers are

What Are JavaServer Pages (JSPs)?

JavaServer Pages (JSPs) are a technology defined by Sun Microsystems to create dynamic content on the Web. They are HTML documents that are interleaved with Java, which provides the dynamic content. JSPs are a server-side application; they accept a request and generate a response. Generally the requests are made from a Web client, and the response is a generated HTML document that gets sent back to the Web client. Because JSPs are a server-side application, they have access to the resources on the server, such as Servlets, JavaBeans, EJBs, and databases. In Hour 5, "Understanding the JSP Application Models," you will take a look at various design patterns that JSPs can implement, as defined in the Sun specification.

> **New Term: Web Client**
>
> A Web client is a client that interacts with a Web server using the HTTP protocol. The client runs a Web browser, such as Internet Explorer or Netscape Navigator, and requests documents by specifying a URL in the browser.

There are many benefits to using JavaServer Pages. Because JSPs utilize the Java programming language, they follow the write-once, run-anywhere policy. This means that a JSP can be run on any application server that supports JSPs without any modifications to

1

the code. (Application servers will be discussed in the section "What Are Application Servers?") Another benefit of JSPs is that the specification is written in a way that promotes integration with integrated development environments (IDEs).

> JSPs can be written in any text editor; just be sure to save the document with a .jsp extension. This means you can write JSPs in Notepad on a Windows operating system, or emacs on a UNIX operating system. An IDE that supports writing JSPs is Dreamweaver, which is part of the WebGain Studio.

Another benefit of JSPs is the use of tag libraries. JSPs use tags, which are similar to HTML and XML, to insert dynamic content. It is possible to add additional functionality to a JSP by importing a tag library. The tag library defines additional tags that can be used to replace sections of code.

Another major benefit of JSPs is the separation of roles. The specification for JSPs allows for the workload to be separated into two categories: the graphical content of the page and the dynamic content of the page. The creative team that has no knowledge of the Java programming language can create the graphical content of the page. A Java programmer then inserts Java into the HTML document to achieve the dynamic content.

> When writing a JSP, it is easier to write the HTML code and then insert the Java code to create your dynamic content. So, if you don't plan to write the HTML, have your graphical artists work their magic to create a beautiful page and then insert your Java code to make the JSP dynamic.

Listing 1.1 is a simple JSP that shows how Java code is inserted into a JSP. All this JSP does is insert the current time and date into an HTML page (see Figure 1.1). Don't worry if you don't understand what the parts are right now—this book goes into great detail about generating JSPs. In Hour 2, "Building Your First JSP," you are going to create and deploy your first JSP.

LISTING 1.1 A Simple JSP That Inserts the Current Time and Date into an HTML Document

```
1:    <HTML>
2:    <HEAD><TITLE>A Simple JSP</TITLE></HEAD>
3:    <BODY>
4:      <FONT COLOR="blue" FACE="Trebuchet">
5:      <CENTER>
6:        The Current Date and Time is: <%= new java.util.Date()%>
```

LISTING 1.1   continued

```
 7:        </CENTER>
 8:        </FONT>
 9:    </BODY>
10:    </HTML>
```

FIGURE 1.1

The simple JSP is viewed in a browser.

Evolution of the Web

The technology of the Web has evolved enormously in the last few years. It was not so long ago that the Web consisted of only static documents. Now, programs are embedded in HTML and dynamic content can be added to the HTML documents at runtime. Take a look at the evolution of the Web.

The Static Web

The Static Web is the simplest Web structure. Figure 1.2 shows a diagram of the Static Web.

The Web client connects to the Web server using TCP/IP and makes requests using HTTP. The server sends an already-made HTML document to the Web client. This HTML document contains text, possibly hyperlinks, and the formatting tags. It does not contain any dynamic content, nor does it contain a way for the user to interact with it. Basically, in this structure HTML documents are stale and provide no interaction to the client.

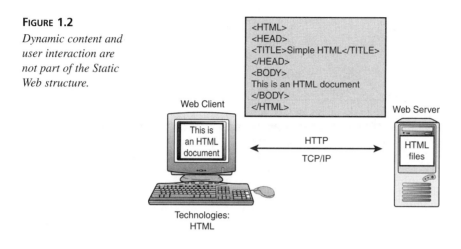

FIGURE 1.2
Dynamic content and user interaction are not part of the Static Web structure.

The Plug-In Web

As technology evolved, people wanted more capabilities in their Web pages. The Plug-In Web, diagrammed in Figure 1.3, allowed users to add small programs to HTML documents.

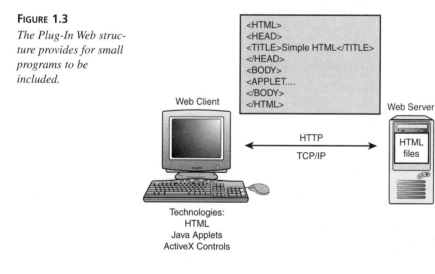

FIGURE 1.3
The Plug-In Web structure provides for small programs to be included.

The addition of small programs meant new HTML tags were needed and browsers would have to understand how to handle the new tags. Two types of programs that can execute in a browser are Java applets and Microsoft's ActiveX controls.

Java applets are small programs written in the Java programming language that are inserted into HTML documents to add more functionality. Since applets are written in the Java programming language, they are very portable. Java programs are compiled into bytecode, which is executed on a Java virtual machine. Applets can execute within browsers that have a built-in virtual machine.

New Term: Java Virtual Machine

A Java virtual machine takes the compiled bytecode and translates it into your machine language to execute. There are Java virtual machines for almost every type of computer available today. Internet Explorer and Netscape Navigator have built-in Java virtual machines.

Applets run in an environment called a *sandbox*. When you think of a sandbox, you think of a safe haven for children that serves a couple of purposes: It makes the children feel safe and keeps the sand in. The sandbox for the applets is very similar; it should keep the users feeling safe with the knowledge that it cannot harm their machines, and it provides a working environment for the applet. Java applets have a very strict security code. They cannot touch your local files or your hard drive, and they can create a socket connection only back to the server they came from. This means the applet cannot become vicious and start creating network connections all over the world. Listing 1.2 is an example of a Java applet, called in HTML, that allows the user to input a decimal number; it then computes the binary and hex equivalent numbers.

LISTING 1.2   An HTML Document That Has a Java Applet Embedded in It

```
1:   <HTML>
2:   <HEAD><TITLE>Java Applet Example</TITLE></HEAD>
3:   <BODY>
4:   <CENTER>
5:     <H1>A Number Converter Applet</H1>
6:     This applet takes a decimal number
7:     <BR>
8:     and converts it to its hex and binary numbers
9:     </BR><BR>
10:    <APPLET CODE="com.sams.hourOne.NumberConverter.class"
11:           WIDTH="300" HEIGHT="200">
12:    </APPLET>
13:   </CENTER>
14:   </BODY>
15:   </HTML>
```

The output of Listing 1.2 is shown in Figure 1.4.

ActiveX controls are small programs that can be inserted into an HTML document to add more functionality. These small programs are typically written using the Visual Basic programming language. They are executable programs that are downloaded onto your hard drive and registered into your Windows Registry file. Because they are on your hard drive, they have full access to your system. Therefore, they can touch files on your hard drive and create as many network connections as they want. The main benefit of ActiveX controls is that they run faster than Java applets because they are compiled to your machine's language and do not run on a virtual machine. Listing 1.3 is an example of an ActiveX control embedded in an HTML document.

FIGURE 1.4

You can view the Number Converter Applet in a browser.

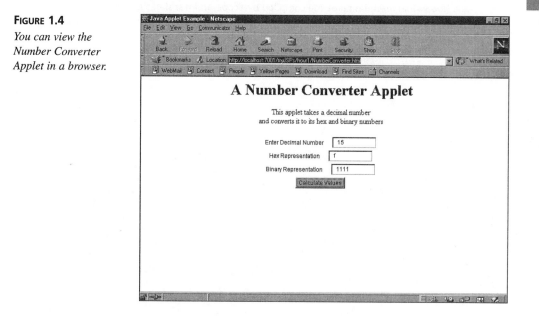

LISTING 1.3 An HTML Document That Has an ActiveX Control Embedded in It

```
 1:   <HTML>
 2:   <HEAD><TITLE>ActiveX Control Example</TITLE></HEAD>
 3:   <BODY>
 4:   <CENTER>
 5:   <OBJECT classid="clsid:8E27C92B-1264-101C-8A2F-040224009C02"
 6:     id="Calendar1"
 7:   width="288" height="192">
 8:     <param name="_Version" value="524288">
 9:     <param name="_ExtentX" value="7620">
10:     <param name="_ExtentY" value="5080">
11:     <param name="_StockProps" value="1">
12:     <param name="BackColor" value="-2147483633">
13:     <param name="Year" value="2000">
14:     <param name="Month" value="7">
15:     <param name="Day" value="13">
16:     <param name="DayLength" value="1">
17:     <param name="MonthLength" value="2">
18:     <param name="DayFontColor" value="0">
19:     <param name="FirstDay" value="1">
```

LISTING **1.3**   continued

```
20:        <param name="GridCellEffect" value="1">
21:        <param name="GridFontColor" value="10485760">
22:        <param name="GridLinesColor" value="-2147483632">
23:        <param name="ShowDateSelectors" value="-1">
24:        <param name="ShowDays" value="-1">
25:        <param name="ShowHorizontalGrid" value="-1">
26:        <param name="ShowTitle" value="-1">
27:        <param name="ShowVerticalGrid" value="-1">
28:        <param name="TitleFontColor" value="10485760">
29:        <param name="ValueIsNull" value="0">
30:    </OBJECT>
31:    </CENTER>
32:    </BODY>
33:    </HTML>
```

The output of the ActiveX control in an HTML document is shown in Figure 1.5.

FIGURE **1.5**

*Use a browser to view
the HTML document
with an ActiveX control.*

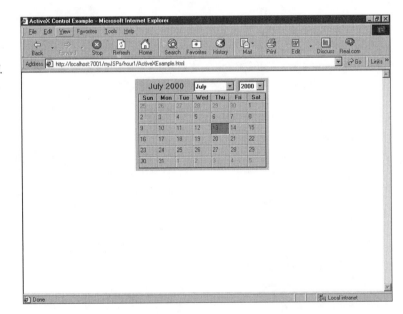

The Dynamic Web

Although the Plug-In Web increased functionality by adding Java applets or ActiveX controls, the users were still requesting predefined HTML documents. Applets provided a way to access a database and get dynamic data, but they were slow and inefficient. The Dynamic Web solved that problem by introducing common gateway interface (CGI) programs. Figure 1.6 shows a diagram of the Dynamic Web.

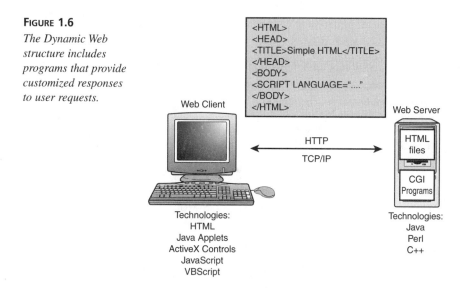

FIGURE 1.6

The Dynamic Web structure includes programs that provide customized responses to user requests.

```
<HTML>
<HEAD>
<TITLE>Simple HTML</TITLE>
</HEAD>
<BODY>
<SCRIPT LANGUAGE="..."
</BODY>
</HTML>
```

Web Client

Web Server

HTTP

TCP/IP

HTML files

CGI Programs

Technologies:
HTML
Java Applets
ActiveX Controls
JavaScript
VBScript

Technologies:
Java
Perl
C++

The CGI programs reside on the server and they accept requests, use the server-side resources, and generate an HTML page as a response. They can be written in a variety of languages, such as Java, C++, Perl, and Visual Basic. Examples of CGI programs are JSPs, Servlets, and Active Server Pages (ASPs). Because these programs are defining the HTML document that gets sent back, the users get responses that are tailored to their particular request. Remember our friends Marian and John? They both visited the same Web site, but Marian got information about flights to Florida and John got flight information for Hawaii. This was made possible by a CGI program accessing a database and executing particular queries.

Another technology that was introduced in the Dynamic Web structure was client-side scripting.

New Term: Scripting Languages

Scripting languages are interpreted languages. They do not get compiled before execution; instead, they are understood, or *interpreted*, one line at a time. Two examples of scripting languages are JavaScript and VBScript.

Client-side scripting took some workload off of the server because it allowed small business applications, such as form validation, to occur on the client. When the client tries to submit a form, a script can be executed to make sure that all required fields are filled in. If a field is missing a value, a message can be given to the client to let the user know that it is a required field. This can be done on the client so that the server does not get bogged down doing simple form validation. Netscape's scripting language is called JavaScript, and Microsoft's is called VBScript.

JavaScript's syntax is very much like C++ and Java. However, it is not an object-oriented language, although there are intrinsic objects that it can use. JavaScript can be used in Netscape Navigator and Internet Explorer.

VBScript is a subset of the Visual Basic programming language. For that reason it is very easy to learn. VBScript's major drawback is that it works only in Internet Explorer.

Listing 1.4 is an HTML document that is using JavaScript to validate the form.

LISTING 1.4   An HTML Document That Utilizes JavaScript to Do Form Validation

```
 1:  <HTML>
 2:  <HEAD><TITLE>Using JavaScript for Form Checking</TITLE></HEAD>
 3:  <BODY>
 4:  <FORM NAME="MyForm" ACTION="SomeCGIProgram" METHOD="POST">
 5:  First Name:
 6:  <INPUT TYPE="text" NAME="txtFirstName" VALUE="Christos">
 7:  <BR>
 8:  Last Name:
 9:  <INPUT TYPE="text" NAME="txtLastName" VALUE="">
10:  <BR>
11:  <INPUT TYPE="button" NAME="btnSubmit" VALUE="Submit Form"
12:  onClick="checkForm();">
13:  <BR>
14:  <SCRIPT LANGUAGE="JavaScript">
15:  <!--
16:  function checkForm()
17:  {
18:    if (document.MyForm.txtFirstName.value == "")
19:    {
20:      alert("Please enter your first name");
21:      document.MyForm.txtFirstName.focus();
22:    }
23:    else if (document.MyForm.txtLastName.value == "")
24:    {
25:      alert("Please enter your last name");
26:      document.MyForm.txtFirstName.focus();
27:    }
28:    else
29:    {
30:      document.MyForm.submit();
31:    }
32:  }
33:  //-->
34:  </SCRIPT>
35:  </FORM>
36:  </BODY>
37:  </HTML>
```

Figure 1.7 shows the output of the HTML document in Listing 1.4.

FIGURE **1.7**
*A browser displays
JavaScript working in
an HTML form.*

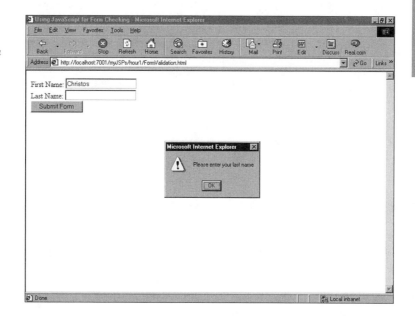

The N-Tier Web

Technology has evolved to a point where Web applications are very complex and have
many parts. Figure 1.8 shows the structure called the N-tier Web. The N-tier Web, also
known as distributed systems, is where the Web is today in its evolution.

FIGURE **1.8**
*The N-tier Web struc-
ture looks complicated,
but it is just made of
smaller, less scary
pieces.*

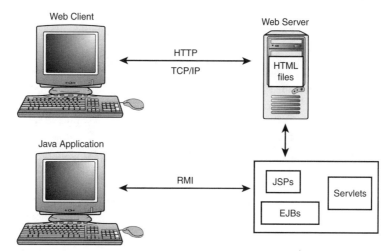

Although Figure 1.8 looks rather scary, you can separate the figure into three sections: the client layer, the application logic level, and the data level.

Let's begin dissecting this structure starting with the client layer. Different kinds of clients can be in this structure. For example, a Web client is accessing a Web server using TCP/IP and making requests with HTTP. Another type of client, a Java application, also can access the application server through other communication protocols such as Remote Method Invocation (RMI) and Internet Inter-Orb Protocol (IIOP) .

The application logic can be spread over a Web server and an application server. The Web server can handle requests from Web clients and service simple HTML documents. If the request is for an application, it can forward the request on to the application server. The application server can handle larger programs than the Web server can. Later in this hour, you will take a closer look at other services an application server provides in the "What Are Application Servers?" section.

The last layer in this structure is the data level. The data level can be made up of one or more databases, and it can also include legacy systems, such as mainframes.

Why are there so many pieces? Well, the philosophy is that if you concentrate on one thing, you should do it well, and that is the philosophy being employed here. If a Web server concentrates on serving Web pages, it should be able to optimize that process and serve them efficiently. If an application server focuses on serving applications, it should be able to offer services that almost all applications use, such as security. Finally, if a database is responsible for handling data, it can focus on providing services, such as caching, to access data faster. Another benefit of breaking up the responsibilities is that it is easier to write and maintain smaller components than large, bulky applications.

What Is the Java 2 Enterprise Edition (J2EE) Platform?

Many companies are placing their products on the Web and building enterprise systems. Today's thought is that it should be easier to program these systems now than it was a few years ago. That is where the Java 2 Enterprise Edition (J2EE) comes into play.

Who Developed This Specification?

The J2EE specification was written by Sun Microsystems. Sun Microsystems accepted input from the industry (what it actually used is not known) when creating the enterprise system that includes specifications for messaging, database support, and distributed components.

1

What Does the Specification Define?

The specification defines the parts of an enterprise application and the services they require. Also defined are how these parts communicate.

Who Benefits from This Specification?

Many benefit from this specification. Most enterprise applications represent or use data from a database. The data in that database is persistent over time. Also in these applications transactions need to be monitored. A transaction is a group of steps that need to all operate without error or not happen at all. For example, if you transfer $100 from your savings account to your checking account, a couple steps need to happen. The money is withdrawn from your savings and then deposited to your checking account. If an error occurs after the money is withdrawn and it is not deposited, you want that transaction to roll back, or go back to the original state, with the $100 in your savings account. Because the specification defines the services that enterprise applications need, application server vendors are able to implement many primary services—such as transactional support, security, and persistence—so the programmer does not need to worry about programming these services into his or her code. So, this specification allows companies or individuals to create products that can help application developers decrease the development time while building a scalable application.

What Technologies Make Up This Platform?

The J2EE is made up of 13 technologies:

- JavaServer Pages (JSPs)
- Servlets
- Java Messaging Service (JMS)
- Java Database Connectivity (JDBC)
- Java Naming and Directory Interface (JNDI)
- Java Transaction Service (JTS)
- Java Transaction API (JTA)
- JavaMail
- JavaBeans Activation Framework (JAF)
- Remote Method Invocation (RMI)
- Enterprise JavaBeans (EJB)
- Extensible Markup Language (XML)
- Java Integrated Definition Language (Java IDL)

Sun has also recently added J2EE Connector Architecture to the J2EE.

As you saw earlier in the hour, JSPs are HTML documents that are embedded with Java
to provide dynamic content.

Servlets are Java classes that accept a request and generate a response. A more specific
Servlet, called `HttpServlets`, handles HTTP requests and generates HTTP responses.
For our purposes, we are most interested in `HttpServlets`. It is important to understand
the relationship between JSPs and Servlets, and Hour 3, "Introduction to Servlets," will
go into more detail about Servlets.

JMS allows applications to send messages to each other. There are a couple of types of
messaging: Point-to-Point and Publish/Subscribe. Point-to-Point messaging is one producer
and one consumer. This is much like someone sending an email. The producer writes the
email and the consumer receives it. Publish/Subscribe messaging is similar to a newsgroup.
A message gets published to a topic and many consumers can receive that message.

JDBC provides an API that allows a Java programmer to access any type of database
without knowing the particular implementations of that database. This is helpful because
it means you are not locked in to one database vendor. The database can change with
little or no effect in your Java code.

JNDI is much Java Naming and Directory Interface (JNDI)like the JDBC spec in that it
allows you to access naming services and directory services without knowing of the implementation of the particular service. This is very useful because naming services and directory services handle their services—such as binding, lookup, and listing—very differently.
An example of a naming server is a Domain Name Server (DNS). A DNS maps IP
addresses to hostnames, which allows you to enter `http://www.bea.com` and communicate
to the BEA Web site. This is very much like looking up a phone number for an individual.
You look up the name in your phone book and it provides you with the phone number.

JTS and JTA work together to allow users to control their own transactions. A *transaction*
is a set of commands that need to execute as if they were one. They need to all execute
without failure, or none execute. EJBs, JMS, and JDBC are just some of the technologies
that use transactions.

JavaMail and JAF work together to allow programmers to send emails from Java applications. The JavaMail API provides methods that access mail servers and the JAF helps
integrate MIME types.

RMI allows Java objects to invoke methods on remote Java objects. After it obtains a reference to that object, a Java object can call a method on another Java object that may
even be on a different host.

EJB is a component architecture that defines how local and distributed Java components can
communicate. EJBs execute within an environment called a *container* on application servers.
The specification defines the relationship between the application server and the container, the

1

container and the EJB, and the client and the container. This helps the container supplier to provide the primary services—such as transactions, security, and persistence—that EJBs use. If the container handles the primary services, this code is taken out of the component itself.

XML is a meta-language used to define other tag-based languages. This allows you to create a language to model your business concepts. J2EE uses XML documents for deployment descriptors. EJBs need deployment descriptors that let the application server know how to handle them. JSPs and Servlets are now able to use XML deployment descriptors that define relationships between JSPs and Servlets within an application.

The Java IDL allows Java objects to communicate to CORBA objects. Since CORBA is very abundant it is helpful for your Java objects to be able to use CORBA objects.

What Are Application Servers?

Application servers are pieces of software that handle the processing of programs and applications. The application server can handle larger processing chores than a Web server can. Large applications that exist on application servers could consist of EJBs, Servlets, and JSPs.

The Need for an Application Server

Recall from the discussion of the N-tier architecture the advantages of separating the workload between a Web server and an application server. The Web server can focus on serving Web pages so it could optimize the process. The application server can then concentrate on serving applications so it can provide many primary services that applications need, such as transactional support, security, and persistence to a database. With the application server handling these services, the application can focus on the business model.

What Does It Mean to Be Compliant with the J2EE?

A compliant application server supports all the technologies defined in the J2EE. This helps developers because they can write applications to the specification and then choose what application server to deploy on. An application written to the specification can be deployed on various compliant application servers without modifying any code. This is valuable because you do not get locked into one vendor. As the technology changes and application servers change, you know that you can change your application server to fit your needs and you don't have to change your code.

A Listing of Application Server Vendors

More and more vendors are coming out with application servers. If you write your applications to the specification, you will be able to change vendors to suit your needs. Table 1.1 lists some of the application vendors available to you.

TABLE 1.1   Application Server Vendors

Company	Application Server
Allaire Corp.	ColdFusion
Apple Computer	WebObjects
BEA Systems, Inc.	WebLogic Server
Bluestone Software	Total-e-Server
Delano Technology Corp.	Delana e-Business Interaction Suite
Esemplare Development	Galileo Application Server
Haht Software	HAHTsite
IBM	WebSphere
Intertop	Intertop Server
Lotus	Lotus Domino
Oracle Corp.	Oracle Application Server
Pervasive Software, Inc.	Tango 2000
Silver Stream, Inc.	SilverStream
Sun Netscape Alliance	NetDynamics
Sun Netscape Alliance	Netscape Application Server
Sybase, Inc.	Sybase Enterprise Server
Versata	Versata Business Logic Server

Summary

JSPs are HTML documents embedded with Java code that help produce dynamic content to clients on the Web. Because they are on the server, JSPs have access to other server-side resources, such as Servlets, EJBs, and databases.

The Simple Web was the minimal Web structure that you looked at. The Web client requested a predefined HTML document from a Web server, and the Web server responded by sending it back. The HTML documents were very stale and dry. More functionality was added to HTML documents in the Plug-In Web when small programs were embedded in the HTML document. Examples of the executable programs that were embedded are Java Applets and ActiveX controls. Recall that Java Applets were more secure because they did not have access to your hard drive, but ActiveX controls ran faster because they were compiled to your machine language. Dynamic HTML documents were introduced with the Dynamic Web because CGI programs were on the server dynamically creating HTML documents based on the user's query. Client-side scripting was introduced in the Dynamic Web as a way to take some of the workload off the server

1

and put it on the client. The two kinds of scripting are JavaScript and VBScript. Recall that VBScript cannot work in Netscape Navigator, and JavaScript works in both Netscape Navigator and Internet Explorer. Finally, the Web evolved into the N-tier Web, which is the structure that is most prevalent today. So many pieces exist to allow each of the pieces to focus on what it does and to do it well. The separation of roles helps smaller companies play a part in the evolution of enterprise applications.

J2EE helps define the technologies that exist in distributed applications. Having the specification allows application servers to write primary services that all distributed applications use, such as transactional support, security, and persistence to a database. The application developers will not need to worry about programming these primary services into their applications because the application server will handle them.

Application servers are pieces of software that are used to process larger programs /applications. If they follow the J2EE specification, an application written to the specification will be able to be deployed on the server without modifying the code. This makes sure you do not get locked into a specific vendor so that as technology changes, your application server can change to meet your demands.

Q&A

Q What application server will I use for my environment in this book?

A You will use Apache's Tomcat and BEA System's WebLogic Server 5.1. Apache's Tomcat is a small Web server that supports JSPs, but it cannot handle large applications, such as EJBs. BEA WebLogic Server is the most prominent application server in the market today. It is fully compliant with the J2EE specification and is the only independent application server to pass the J2EE certification tests.

Q Why should I understand the evolution of the Web?

A It is always beneficial to see how the Web has evolved and where it is today. When concerned with JSPs, it is helpful to see where they fit in the picture and why they came to be.

Workshop

The quiz questions and activities are provided for your further understanding. See Appendix A, "Answers," for the answers to the quiz.

Quiz

1. What are the four types of Web structures?

2. Why are there so many parts to the N-tier Web?

3. What are the two types of client-side scripting languages, and what can they do?

Activities

1. Explain the different types of the Web to a friend or relative. Explaining them to someone will help solidify your understanding.

2. Describe a JSP to a friend or relative who has minimal technical experience. Explain the need for JSPs and the pros and cons of using JSPs.

Hour **2**

Building Your First JSP

The moment has finally arrived when you are going to create your first JavaServer Page. I know you cannot wait to start typing away and see your beautiful work, but there is preparation to be done. Before you jump in, let's take a comparative look at JSPs and Active Server Pages (ASPs) and at JSPs and common gateway interface (CGI) programs. Get your swimwear ready because the water is fine.

In this hour you are going to learn

- The basic HTML tags
- How JSPs compare to ASPs
- How JSPs compare to CGI programs
- The basic setup of Apache's Tomcat server
- Running your first JSP on Tomcat

A Review of HTML

The layout of a JSP is an HTML document that is embedded with Java code. Special tags are used to insert the Java code into the HTML document. Throughout this book, tags will be introduced and you will see how they can be used to increase the functionality of your JSP. Right now let's do a brief review of HTML documents and their structure.

Hypertext Markup Language (HTML) is a markup language. HTML documents are text documents formatted with tags. Listing 2.1 is an example of an HTML document that outputs to the Web page HTML is Easy.

HTML is not case sensitive, so the tag <HTML> is the same as <html>, which is the same as <HtMl>. However, using all capital letters makes the tags stand out in the document and makes it easier to debug.

LISTING 2.1 A Simple HTML Document (ExampleHTML.html)

```
1: <HTML>
2: <HEAD><TITLE>This is a simple HTML</TITLE></HEAD>
3: <BODY>
4: HTML is Easy
5: </BODY>
6: </HTML>
```

The output of the simple HTML document is shown in Figure 2.1.

FIGURE 2.1

You can view the simple HTML document in a browser.

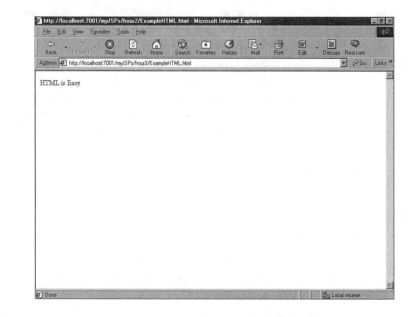

Comparing JSPs and CGI Programs

Let's take a moment and see how JSPs compare to CGI programs.

CGI programs are the most general term used to describe programs on the server that provide dynamic content. These programs can be written in C, C++, Perl, or Java.

JSPs are a type of CGI program. They allow access from Web clients, use server-side resources, and generate dynamic responses to the Web clients. CGI is just a general term used to describe programs such as ASPs, JSPs, and others written in languages such as C and Perl.

Comparing JSPs and ASPs

ASP technology, developed by Microsoft, embeds VBScript in HTML documents to create dynamic content for Web clients. Sound familiar? ASPs and JSPs are very similar in their mission—to create dynamic content for Web clients. ASPs use VBScript, and JSPs use Java embedded in the HTML documents. They are server-side programs, which means that they have access to all server-side resources, such as databases. Even their syntax for embedding their respective languages is similar. Listing 2.2 is an example of an ASP that embeds the current date and time, and Listing 2.3 is an example of a JSP that embeds the current date and time. In line 8 of Listing 2.2, you can see that the tags <%= and %> are used to embed the VBScript function 'Now'. Now take a look at line 6 of Listing 2.3 and you will see the same tags used to insert the Java code 'new java.util.Date()'. These tags, which will be covered in more detail in Hour 8, "Inserting Java Expressions in a JSP," are used to insert expressions.

LISTING 2.2   A Simple ASP That Outputs the Current Date and Time (Date.asp)

```
 1: <%@ Language=VBScript %>
 2: <HTML>
 3: <HEAD>
 4: <TITLE>A Simple ASP</TITLE>
 5: </HEAD>
 6: <BODY>
 7:   <CENTER>
 8:     The Current Date and Time is: <%= Now %>
 9:   </CENTER>
10: </BODY>
11: </HTML>
```

ASPs, like JSPs, can be written in any text editor and are saved with an .asp extension. A popular editing tool that highlights text and helps with syntax is Microsoft's Visual Interdev. This tool helps organize large applications that involve many HTML and ASP pages.

The output of the ASP is shown in Figure 2.2.

FIGURE 2.2

A simple ASP outputing the current time and date.

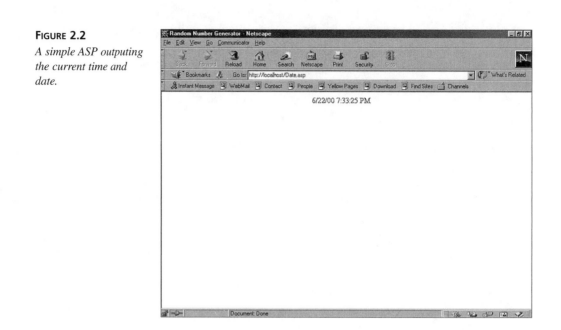

The equivalent JSP code is in Listing 2.3.

LISTING 2.3   A Simple JSP That Outputs the Current Date and Time (Date.jsp)

```
 1: <HTML>
 2: <HEAD><TITLE>A Simple JSP</TITLE></HEAD>
 3: <BODY>
 4: <FONT COLOR="blue" FACE="Trebuchet">
 5: <CENTER>
 6: The Current Date and Time is: <%= new java.util.Date()%>
 7: </CENTER>
 8: </FONT>
 9: </BODY>
10: </HTML>
```

Java combines similar classes into packages. The Date class is located in the java.util package and allows you to use its constructor to get the current date and time. A *constructor* is a method that creates and instantiates an object.

The output of the JSP is shown in Figure 2.3. Notice that the format of the dates between the two pages is different. VBScript and Java each return a different format of the current date and time.

FIGURE 2.3

A simple JSP outputs the current time and date in a different format than the simple ASP does.

2

Although ASPs and JSPs are similar, there are several differences. A major difference is that ASPs can run only on Microsoft platforms. JSPs, however, follow the write-once, run-anywhere philosophy and can run on any server that provides a Java virtual machine. Because a Java virtual machine is available for almost any platform, this should not be a problem. Another JSP benefit is that it uses the powerful programming language of Java to create its dynamic content. This means that hundreds of classes and methods are at your disposal.

Creating Your First JSP

The time is here to set up your working environment and get going on your first JSP. I know your heart is pounding with excitement, so let's jump right in.

Setting Up Apache's Tomcat

Before you can write your JSP, you need an environment in which to run your JSP. In this section you are going to set up Apache's Tomcat as your JSP server. Apache Tomcat is a free Web server that can handle requests for HTML, JSPs, and Servlets. In Hour 4, "Configuring Application Servers," you are also going to set up another working environment called BEA WebLogic Server. WebLogic Server can be downloaded off the Web and has an evaluation period of 30 days. This will give you experience running JSPs on multiple servers and give you experience with the most popular application server today—BEA WebLogic Server. So, without further ado, let us begin:

1. In order to install Apache's Tomcat, you need to get a copy of the zip file jakarta-tomcat.zip. This is for Windows NT and the following instructions are Windows

centric. There is a copy of this on the CD in the book, or you can download it from their Web site. If you are using the version from the CD go to step 5. Or continue with these steps. Go to Apache's Web site to download Tomcat: `http://jakarta.apache.org` (see Figure 2.4).

FIGURE 2.4

Download Tomcat from Apache's home page.

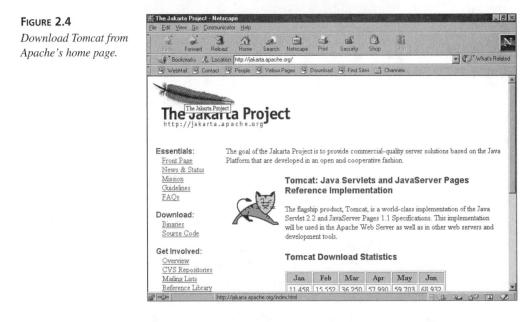

2. Under Download, select the `Binaries` link to download (see Figure 2.5).

FIGURE 2.5

Download from the Binary Downloads Web page.

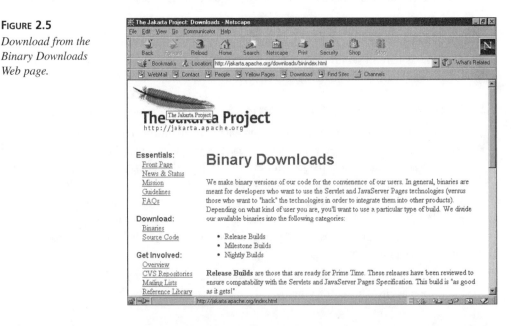

3. Scroll down the Binary Downloads Web page to select a release (see Figure 2.6). You want to download the newest release edition.

FIGURE 2.6

You can choose which release to download.

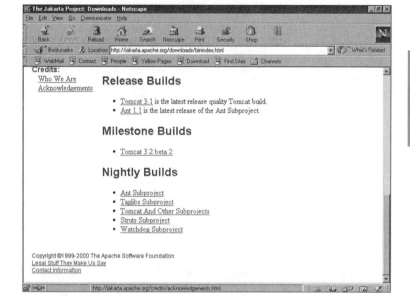

4. Now you are at the index of downloads (see Figure 2.7). Select the jakarta-tomcat.zip file to download. Save it to a temp directory on your hard drive. This zip file is used to install Tomcat on a Windows platform; downloads are also available for other operating systems such as Linux.

5. Unzip the file to c:\tomcat on your machine. Create this directory if it does not already exist. After extracting the files, your directory structure should be c:\tomcat and the folders bin, conf, doc, lib, src, webapps.

6. Edit the tomcat.bat file and correct the JAVA_HOME variable to point to the root of your JDK install. The tomcat.bat file is found in c:\tomcat\bin. For example, mine pointed to d:\jdk1.2.2.

7. Now it is time to start Tomcat. In a DOS prompt, go to c:\tomcat\ bin. Then type in the command **tomcat start**. Another way to start Tomcat is to type **startup**, which will start Tomcat in a new DOS window.

8. Test to see whether Tomcat is working properly by viewing the home page in your browser (see Figure 2.8). View the home page at http://localhost:8080.

FIGURE 2.7

Find the
`jakarta-tomcat.zip`
file in the index of
downloads for Tomcat.

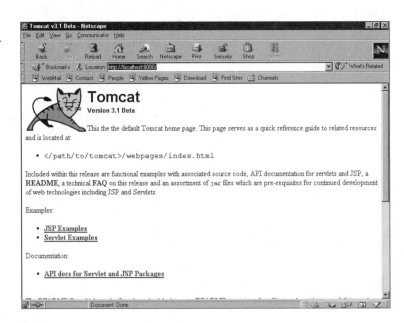

FIGURE 2.8

View the home page of
Tomcat running on
your machine.

9. Now that you know Tomcat is working, make sure it is serving up JSPs properly by clicking JSPExamples and executing one of the listed examples. Figure 2.9 shows the Number Guess JSP executing.

FIGURE 2.9

Use Tomcat to serve up the Number Guess JSP.

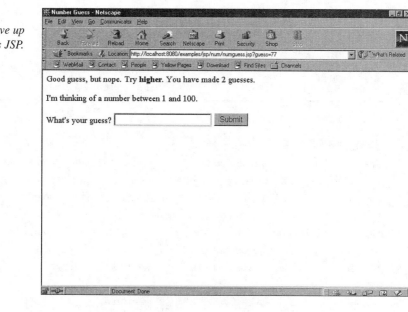

2

If you did not get the proper JSP, make sure your JAVA_HOME, in the tomcat.bat file, is pointing to the root of your correct JDK installation.

10. You are now all set. You have Apache's Tomcat up and running and now you can write your first JSP.

Type the JSP into a Text Editor

JSPs can be written in any text editor. If you are working on a Windows operating system, you can use Notepad. The first JSP you are going to write will calculate the sine of several angles and display the result in a table. Type the code from Listing 2.4 into a text editor now.

LISTING 2.4   Your First JSP (MyFirstJSP.jsp)

```
1: <HTML>
2: <HEAD><TITLE>My First JSP</TITLE></HEAD>
3: <BODY>
4: <%! int angles[] = {0, 30, 45, 75, 90}; %>
5: <TABLE BORDER="2" ALIGN="center">
6:   <TH>Angle</TH><TH>Sine of Angle</TH>
7:   <% for (int i=0; i<5; i++) { %>
8:    <TR><TD><%= angles[i]%></TD>
9:       <TD><%= Math.sin(Math.toRadians(angles[i]))%>
```

LISTING 2.4   continued

```
10:    </TR>
11:    <% } //end for loop %>
12: </TABLE>
13: </BODY>
14: </HTML>
```

Save with a .jsp Extension

After you have typed the preceding code into Notepad, you need to save it with a .jsp extension. The .jsp extension lets your Web server or application server know that it is dealing with a JSP. Save this file in the directory c:\tomcat\webapps\myJSPs\Hour2. If this directory structure does not exist, create it. When saving your JSP, make sure you save it as a text document and when typing in your name, surround it with double quotes and add your extension. An example of this is shown in Figure 2.10. Now save this file with the name "MyFirstJSP.jsp" in the directory specified earlier.

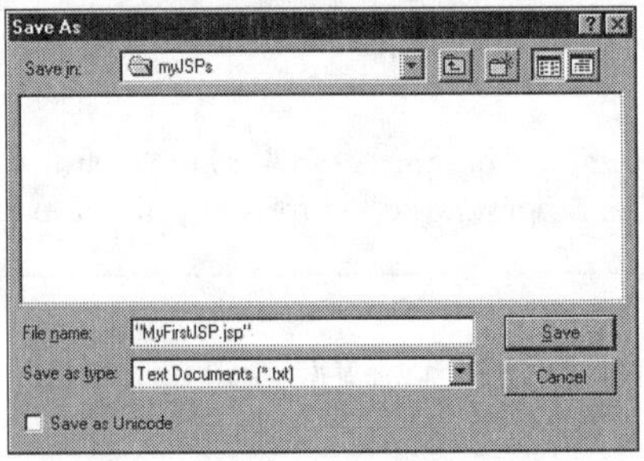

FIGURE 2.10

Save your JSP as a text file.

View the Page in a Browser

To look at your first beautiful JSP, open up your browser of choice and type in the following URL:http://localhost:8080/myJSPs/Hour2/MyFirstJSP.jsp. This tells the server to use the local host listening on port 8080, and the rest is the path to your JSP file (see Figure 2.11).

You have now created and run your first JSP. How does it feel? Hopefully, you are feeling charged and ready to tear through the rest of the book—enjoy the ride.

FIGURE 2.11

Your browser displays your first JSP.

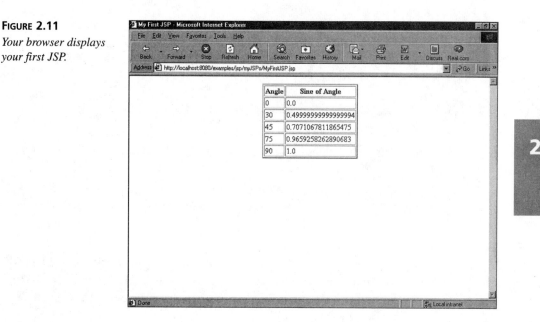

Summary

A CGI program is a server-side program that accepts requests and generates responses. They can be written in many languages—C, Perl, or Java. JSPs and ASPs are types of CGI programs. JSPs and ASPs are HTML documents that are embedded with Java and VBScript respectively.

In this hour you installed Apache's Tomcat on your machine and wrote your first JSP. Congratulations on your achievement thus far, however there is much to do. Throughout the rest of the book you are going to learn what the tags mean in the JSP you typed in and learn about many other tags. Work hard and have fun.

Q&A

Q I wrote a JSP and then changed the code, but it still appears the same in the browser. Why?

A Try stopping Tomcat and then starting it up again. Tomcat does not support Servlet reloading, and sometimes your JSP will not get updated.

Q Am I going to learn more about the setup of Apache's Tomcat and its directory structure?

A Yes, you are. In Hour 4 you are going to cover Apache's Tomcat in more detail, along with BEA WebLogic Server.

Workshop

The quiz questions and activities are provided for your further understanding. See Appendix A, "Answers," for the answers to the quiz.

Quiz

1. What is a CGI program?
2. What are the similarities between ASPs and JSPs? What are some of the benefits of JSPs?
3. What extension do you save JSPs with and how do you specify it when saving in a text editor?

Activity

Now that you have your environment set up, go back through the first and second hours, type in the sample JSPs, and view them in your browser. Save them in the same directory as your first JSP and use a similar URL to locate them, typing in the appropriate filename.

Hour 3

Introduction to Servlets

Talking about Servlets may seem out of place to you in a book about JSPs. However, the underlying implementation of JSPs is via Servlets. That is right: JSPs get translated into Servlets before they are executed. You may be wondering how this impacts performance. It may hurt performance on the first hit, but you are going to see ways to avoid this performance decrease on subsequent hits. Throughout this book you will learn new JSP tags and you will also see how those tags get translated into the equivalent Servlet code. Understanding the translation into Servlet code will help deepen your understanding of the behind-the-scenes activities of JSPs.

In this hour you are going to learn

- What a Servlet is
- The JSP/Servlet lifecycle
- The translation of JSPs into their Servlet equivalent code

What Is a Servlet?

A Servlet, in the most general case, is a Java class that implements the `Servlet` interface and accepts requests and generates responses. The requests can come from Java classes, Web clients, or other Servlets.

When you implement an interface you are saying that your class provides implementations for the methods declared in the interface. Therefore, when you implement the Servlet interface you are declaring that your code will provide implementations for the methods in the Servlet interface.

For example, if you are writing a banking example and you have many classes that need to provide a definition for methods withdraw() and deposit(), you can write an interface that declares these methods. The other classes would implement the banking interface and will guarantee that they provide definitions for the behavior of the methods withdraw() and deposit().

Since this book concentrates on JSPs and the Web, the focus on Servlets will be on a specific type of Servlet, the HttpServlet. The HttpServlet accepts HTTP requests and generates HTTP responses. When you write your HttpServlet, you do not implement the Servlet interface directly; instead you extend the HttpServlet class.

Extending a Java class creates a class hierarchy, much like a family tree. The class that is being extended from is called a superclass, or parent class. The class that declares it is extending another class is called the subclass, or child class.

You are an extension from your parents and you inherit certain attributes and behaviors from them. The same is true for Java classes. The child class inherits the attributes and behaviors of the parent class, but has other attributes and behaviors that make it unique.

You will see the methods that make up an HttpServlet a little later in this hour, but first it is helpful to see how JSPs translate into Servlets and to see the lifecycle of a JSP/Servlet.

How JSPs Become Servlets

The underlying implementation of JSPs is Servlets, so why use one over the other? JSPs have a big advantage over Servlets because JSPs offer the separation of roles. The Web artists can create the aesthetic feature of the Web page and the Java programmer can add the dynamic content. Also, the programmers do not need to be sophisticated Java programmers and be aware of creating classes and inheritance like they would when writing Servlets. You may be concerned that the performance of your application will decrease if you use JSPs since they get translated, but you will see why this is not always true. Now take a look at the lifecycle of JSPs/Servlets and also the translation between JSPs and Servlets.

The JSP/Servlet Lifecycle

Since the underlying implementation of JSPs is via Servlets, the lifecycle of both are the same. Figure 3.1 shows the lifecycle of a JSP/Servlet.

FIGURE 3.1

The lifecycle of JSPs/Servlets is pretty straightforward.

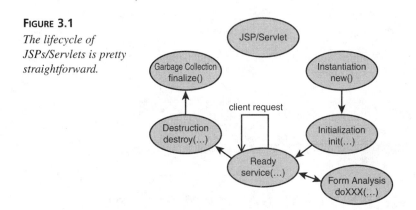

You start with a JSP or a Servlet class. The server is responsible for instantiating the JSP/Servlet and it uses the new() method to accomplish this. This new() method is the Java method for creating space in memory for an object.

After the JSP/Servlet is instantiated, the init(...) method is invoked for initialization purposes. The init(...) method will be looked at in more detail in a few minutes.

Then the JSP/Servlet moves into the Ready state and is prepared to handle client requests. You can write a service(...) method to handle your business logic or you can write a doGet(...) or doPost(...) method for your business logic. These methods will be discussed shortly.

The JSP/Servlet is then destroyed when the server invokes the destroy() method (container invoked). The garbage collector finally comes around and cleans up the memory with the finalize() method.

The JSP Translation Process

The JSP is translated into the appropriate Servlet code, which is a .java file. Many application servers provide the option of keeping the generated .java files. Once it is translated into the .java file it is compiled into the bytecode file (.class). The .class file is executed and the output HTML document is generated and sent back to the client. Figure 3.2 shows a diagram of this process.

Now you may think that this is a large process and that the performance will take a large hit. Well, after the first invocation of a JSP, subsequent requests will not go through the translation phase but will go to the already compiled .class file. Many application servers allow you to dictate how long an application server should wait before it checks if your JSP has changed and needs to be recompiled. Many application servers also provide a compiler for JSPs so the first hit on the JSP will not notice a performance decrease.

3

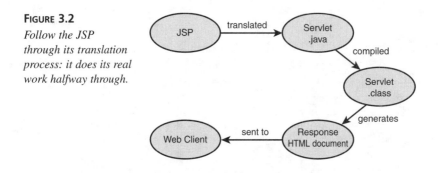

Figure 3.2
Follow the JSP through its translation process: it does its real work halfway through.

The Basic Structure of an `HttpServlet`

There are several methods that you commonly override when you write an `HttpServlet`. These methods are

```
void init(ServletConfig sc) throws ServletException;
void service(HttpServletRequest request, HttpServletResponse response)
            throws ServletException, IOException;
void doGet(HttpServletRequest request, HttpServletResponse response)
          throws ServletException, IOException;
void doPost(HttpServletRequest request, HttpServletResponse response)
           throws ServletException, IOException;
```

You can see where these methods fit into the lifecycle of the JSP/Servlet, if you refer back to Figure 3.1. Recall the `init(...)` method is used for initialization purposes. You will override this method to handle your own particular initialization of the Servlet. The `service(...)` method can be overridden to handle your business logic, if your business logic does not care if the request came over `POST` or `GET`. If your logic differs depending if the HTML form is sent by `POST` or `GET`, then you will want to override the `doPost(...)` or `doGet(...)` methods.

The `init(...)` Method

You saw in the lifecycle of a JSP/Servlet that the `init(...)` method is called to initialize your JSP/Servlet. The syntax of the `init(...)` method is:

```
void init(ServletConfig sc) throws ServletException;
```

The parameter that is passed into the `init(...)` method is a `ServletConfig` object. The `ServletConfig` object gives you access to initial parameters. Initial parameters allow you to specify global variables for your Servlet. Many times these parameters are used to specify the maximum or minimum number for your Servlet. For example, if you have a banking account, there is typically a minimum amount required to maintain the account. The initial parameter could be set to this minimum number and then your Servlet could access it to check the object's value. Hour 13, "Configuring and Initializing JSPs," shows you how to use the `ServletConfig` object in your JSPs.

The `service(...)` Method

The `service(...)` method can be used to implement your business logic. The syntax of the `service(...)` method is:

```
void service(HttpServletRequest request, HttpServletResponse response)
          throws ServletException, IOException;
```

Typically a Servlet developer overrides the `doPost(...)` or `doGet(...)` methods of a Servlet, assuming the Servlet contains different logic, depending on the type of request. However in practice, the same code is often written for both methods. You could just override the `service(...)` method, rather than write the code twice.

The type of business logic your Servlet is executing depends on your application. Consider an order processing example, where the user fills in an HTML form that accepts their name, phone number, address, and various other personal information. The user also fills in the products he wants to buy. The product information could contain the product ID and the quantity the user wants to purchase. The business logic in the Servlet could do several things. Maybe it checks to see if the client is already in the database and if not adds them. It could also check to see if the product is in stock. If it is in stock, then it subtracts the amount the client wants from inventory and sets up the shipping information for the order.

The parameters that are passed in are `HttpServletRequest` and `HttpServletResponse` objects. These objects allow you to parse the request coming in and generate the response going back to the client. Hour 10, "Processing Requests from the User," and Hour 11, "Generating a Dynamic Response for the User," show you how to use these objects in your JSP.

The `doPost(...)` and `doGet(...)` Methods

The `doPost(...)` and the `doGet(...)` methods handle requests from the appropriate HTML form and execute your business logic. The syntax of the `doPost(...)`and the `doGet(...)`methods are:

```
void doPost(HttpServletRequest request, HttpServletResponse response)
          throws ServletException, IOException;
void doGet(HttpServletRequest request, HttpServletResponse response)
          throws ServletException, IOException;
```

An HTML form has an attribute called "METHOD" that defines how the data will be sent to the server. The `GET` method appends the data to the URL and sends it to the server that way. The `POST` method bundles the data in a packet and sends the packet of data to the server. Listing 3.1 is an HTML document that contains two forms. One of the HTML forms uses `GET` and the other form uses `POST` to send the data to the server.

LISTING 3.1   An HTML Document Containing Two Forms (`ExampleForms.html`)

```
 1: <HTML>
 2: <HEAD><TITLE>Form Examples</TITLE></HEAD>
 3: <BODY>
 4: <CENTER>
 5: <FORM NAME="getForm" ACTION="SomeJSP.jsp" METHOD="GET">
 6:     Name:
 7:         <INPUT TYPE="text" NAME="txtName" VALUE="Jon">
 8:         <BR>
 9:     Password:
10:         <INPUT TYPE="password" NAME="txtPassword" Value="">
11:         <BR>
12:         <INPUT TYPE="submit" NAME="btnSubmitGetForm" Value="Submit GET Form">
13: </FORM>
14: <BR>
15: <BR>
16: <FORM NAME="postForm" ACTION="SomeJSP.jsp" METHOD="POST">
17:     Name:
18:         <INPUT TYPE="text" NAME="txtName" VALUE="Katherine">
19:         <BR>
20:     Please Select Your Favorite Ice Cream Flavors:
21:         <BR>
22:         <SELECT NAME="sltIceCream" SIZE="5" MULTIPLE>
23:             <OPTION>Mint Chocolate Chip</OPTION>
24:             <OPTION>Rocky Road</OPTION>
25:             <OPTION>Strawberry Cheesecake</OPTION>
26:             <OPTION>Chocolate</OPTION>
27:             <OPTION>Vanilla</OPTION>
28:         </SELECT>
29:         <BR>
30:         <INPUT TYPE="submit" NAME="btnSubmitPostForm" Value="Submit POST Form">
31: </FORM>
32: </CENTER>
33: </BODY>
34: </HTML>
```

The output of the HTML document in Listing 3.1 is shown in Figure 3.3.

The parameters that are passed in to the do*XXX*(...) methods are the same as the service(...) method: HttpServletRequest and HttpServletResponse objects. Hours 10 and 11 show you how to use these objects in your JSP.

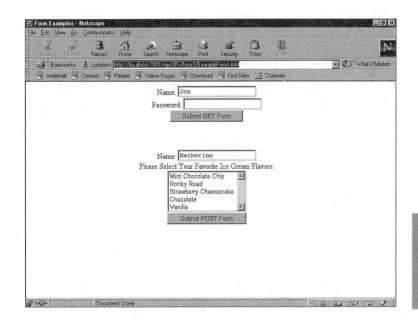

FIGURE 3.3

*The HTML document
with two forms.*

Translating a Simple JSP into a Servlet

Since the underlying implementation of a JSP is a Servlet, let's take a look at a JSP and then look at the equivalent Servlet code. The equivalent Servlet code does the same output as the JSP, but you will see there is much more work to do. Throughout the book when you are shown new JSP tags, the equivalent Servlet code will also be shown to deepen your understanding of the inner workings of the JSP.

Writing a Simple JSP

Listing 3.2 is a JSP that creates a table of the powers of 2. This is very similar to the first JSP that you created in Hour 2, "Building Your First JSP."

LISTING 3.2   A Simple JSP (PowersOf2.jsp)

```
 1: <HTML>
 2: <HEAD><TITLE>Powers of 2</TITLE></HEAD>
 3: <BODY>
 4: <CENTER>
 5:   <H2>Behold The Powers Of 2</H2>
 6: </CENTER>
 7: <TABLE BORDER="2" ALIGN="center">
 8:   <TH>Exponent</TH><TH>2^Exponent</TH>
 9:   <% for (int i=0; i<10; i++) {%>
10:   <TR><TD><%= i%></TD>
11:       <TD><%= Math.pow(2, i)%></TD>
```

LISTING **3.2**   continued

```
12:    </TR>
13:    <% } //end for loop %>
14: </TABLE>
15: </BODY>
16: </HTML>
```

You will be learning about the various tags used by JSPs throughout the book, but let's take a moment and see what is happening in this JSP.

Line 1 and 16 are the opening and closing <HTML> tags that specify this page to be an HTML document. Line 2 creates the head section of the document and creates a title to be Powers of 2. The <BODY> tag starts on line 3 and closes on line 15, which wraps around the content of the page. Lines 4–6 create a heading on the page in level 2 heading that is centered on the page. The heading is Behold The Powers Of 2. The output of this page is going to be a table, with the exponent in one column and the result of 2 raised to that exponent in the second column. Line 7 creates the table, with a border of size 2 pixels that is centered on the page. The table headings are created in line 8 using the <TH> tags.

Now for the Java embedded in the HTML document. Line 9 uses a JSP tag called a scriptlet tag, <%, which is closed by %>. The scriptlet tag allows you to insert Java code into your JSP. Line 9 uses this tag to insert the for loop into the page. Hour 9, "Controlling JSPs with Java Scriplets," will explain these tags in more detail.

During the for loop, this page creates rows in the table and adds the exponent number followed by the evaluation of 2, raised to the exponent. Line 10 creates the table row with the <TR> tag and specifies the first column data to be the exponent, which is simply the value of the variable i. Notice there is a new tag inserting the value of i; it is not the scriptlet tag that you saw in line 9. This new tag, <%=, is called an expression tag. This allows you to insert a Java expression that will be evaluated and the result is inserted into your JSP. The expression tag will be covered in more detail in Hour 8, "Inserting Java Expresions in a JSP."

After the exponent is inserted into the page, the power of 2 raised to the exponent is inserted, again using the expression tags. This is shown in line 11. Line 12 simply ends the table-row definition. The for loop needs to be closed. The scriptlet tags can be used to insert the final close curly brace to end the for loop. Line 13 contains this scriptlet.

The output of the JSP can be seen in Figure 3.4.

Now let's take a look at the equivalent Servlet code. This is the code that will produce the same output as the JSP. Earlier you learned that JSPs are translated into Servlets. The JSP code would be translated to this Servlet code.

FIGURE 3.4

View PowersOf2.jsp *in a browser.*

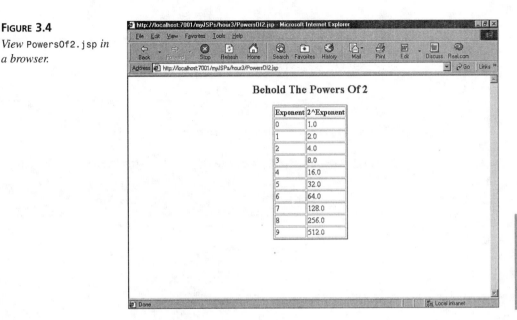

LISTING 3.3 A simple Servlet ( )

```
 1: package com.sams.jspin24hrs.hour3;
 2: import java.io.*;
 3: import javax.servlet.*;
 4: import javax.servlet.http.*;
 5: public class PowersOf2 extends HttpServlet
 6: {
 7:     public void service(HttpServletRequest request,
 8:                         HttpServletResponse response)
 9:                           throws IOException, ServletException
10:     {
11:         response.setContentType("text/html");
12:         ServletOutputStream out = response.getOutputStream();
13:         out.print("<HTML>");
14:         out.print("<HEAD><TITLE>Powers of 2</TITLE></HEAD>");
15:         out.print("<BODY>");
16:         out.print("<CENTER>");
17:         out.print("<H2>Behold The Powers Of 2</H2>");
18:         out.print("</CENTER>");
19:         out.print("<TABLE BORDER='2' ALIGN='center'>");
20:         out.print("<TH>Exponent</TH><TH>2^Exponent</TH>");
21:         for (int i=0; i<10; i++)
22:         {
23:             out.print("<TR><TD>" + i + "</TD>");
24:             out.print("<TD>" + Math.pow(2, i) + "</TD>");
25:             out.print("</TR>");
26:         } //end for loop
```

LISTING 3.3   continued

```
27:          out.print("</TABLE></BODY></HTML>");
28:          out.close();
29:   }
30: }
```

The output of the Servlet is shown in Figure 3.5.

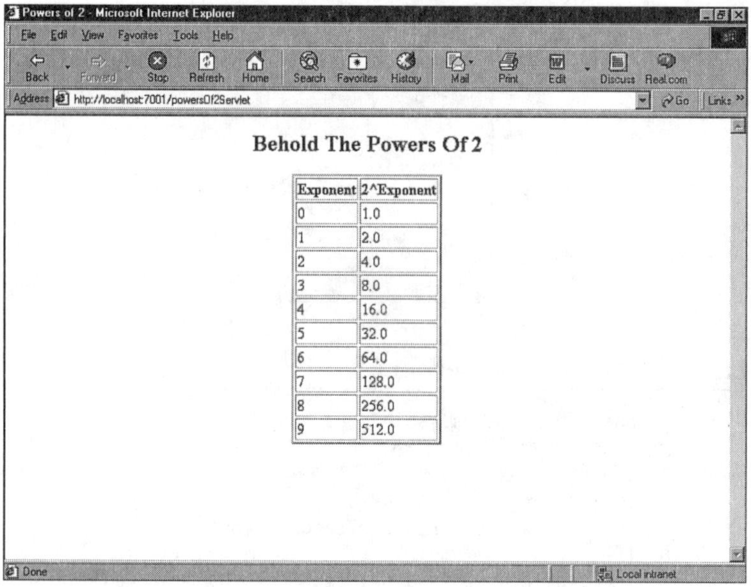

FIGURE 3.5

The JSP equivalent Servlet looks the same in a browser.

Notice that the output is the same as the output of the JSP. Although the output is the same, it required more work for the Servlet, making JSPs more desirable. You do not need a deep understanding of Java in order to write your JSPs as you do with Servlets.

Summary

A Servlet is a Java class that accepts a request and generates a response. The Servlets that we are interested in are called HttpServlets. The HttpServlet accepts HTTP requests and generates HTTP responses. It is important to understand Servlets because they are the underlying implementation of JSPs. The correlation between the JSP code and the Servlet code will be pointed throughout this book to deepen your understanding of JSPs.

Q&A

Q What are the benefits of using JSPs over Servlets?

A There are several benefits of using JSPs. One of the major benefits of using JSPs over Servlets is that you don't have to be a very experienced Java programmer. You only need to understand the basics of Java in order to add the dynamic content. Also, JSPs are easier for presentation purposes. You can create your HTML page and make it look pretty, or your graphical department at work can do this. Then you can add the dynamic content. A great benefit of JSPs over Servlets is the separation of roles.

Q Is it possible to keep the generated Servlet code?

A Many application servers provide the option to keep the generated Servlet code. When you configure BEA WebLogic Server in Hour 5, "Understanding the JSP Application Models," you will see how to keep the generated code.

3

Workshop

The quiz questions and activities are provided for your further understanding. See Appendix A, "Answers," for the answers to the quiz.

Quiz

1. What method, in the lifecycle of a JSP/Servlet, is used for initialization?

2. What kind of Servlet accepts HTTP requests and generates HTTP responses?

3. Describe the do*XXX*(. . .) methods.

Activity

Describe the lifecycle of the JSP/Servlet to a relative or friend. This will help solidify your understanding of the process.

HOUR 4

Configuring Application Servers

You have already been introduced to application servers, but you have not seen how to set one up. In this hour you are going to install and configure BEA WebLogic Server (WLS).

In this hour you will learn

- Why you need to configure an application server
- How to setup BEA WebLogic Server
- How to deploy JSPs on BEA WebLogic Server

How to Configure BEA WebLogic Server

BEA WebLogic Server is the most popular application server today. It is the only independent application server that is J2EE certified from Sun Microsystems. Each application server handles requests for JavaServer Pages differently. BEA uses a Servlet called the JSPServlet to handle JSP requests. You can set initial arguments for this Servlet, such as your Java Development

Kit (JDK), your working directory, and whether or not you want to keep the generated
.java Servlet files. In just a short amount of time you will be setting up the JSPServlet
and configuring its initial arguments.

> The JDK can be downloaded from Sun Microsystems Web site, http://java.
> sun.com. The latest version of the JDK is 1.3. However, WLS 5.1 does not sup-
> port JDK 1.3, so download the 1.2.2 version of the JDK. The 1.2.* versions of
> the JDK provide better garbage collection than their predecessors, 1.1.*.

Installing BEA WebLogic Server

Before you can start using WebLogic Server, you need to install the software. The following steps show you how to install on Windows NT or Windows 98.

1. On the CD-ROM provided in this book, locate the weblogic510.exe file. This is
   an install shield program, so double-click the file now.

2. The install shield provides instructions on what to do. You are prompted for the
   following:

   - Name of a directory to install to. c:/weblogic is a good choice. Remember
     where this is installed because you will need this information later. Whenever
     directories are discussed, I am assuming you installed to c:/weblogic. If you
     install to another directory, from here on in substitute that directory when
     you see c:/weblogic.

   - A system password. The system password must be at least 8 characters long;
     a good choice would be "weblogic." If you forget this password, you can find
     it in the properties file later.

> WebLogic Server 5.1 uses a properties file for configuration information. This
> file is named weblogic.properties and you will find it in the c:/weblogic direc-
> tory. This file contains name value pairs for configuration data. If you forget
> your system password you can look in the weblogic.properties file and search
> for weblogic.password.system. This will be your system password. Throughout
> the book you will see other properties that go in this properties file.

3. Now that the program is installed you need to start WebLogic Server running.
   There are several ways to start WebLogic Server.

   - Through the Start Menu: Select Start, Programs, WebLogic 5.1.0, WebLogic
     Server.

- Run a pre-made batch file called startWebLogic.bat located in the c:/ weblogic directory. Just double-click the batch file or type its name in a DOS prompt from the c:/weblogic directory.

4. After you start WebLogic Server, a DOS prompt appears with text scrolling. When the scrolling stops, you should see the words, "WebLogic Server Started." Another way to test whether WebLogic Server started is to go to a browser and type in the following URL: **http://localhost:7001**. A Web page that looks like the one in Figure 4.1 should appear.

FIGURE 4.1

The welcome page for WebLogic Server running on your machine appears.

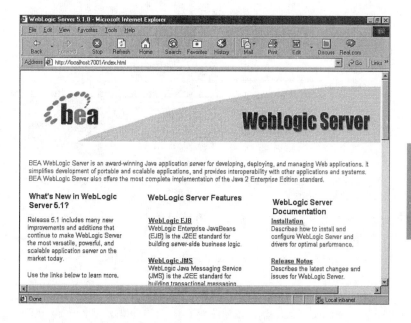

The WebLogic Server Directory Structure

The home directory of your WebLogic Server is c:\weblogic (or whatever directory you installed to). The subdirectories under c:\weblogic are

```
bin
classes
lib
license
myserver
```

The bin folder contains shared and dynamic link libraries.

The classes folder contains Java classes that WLS uses and utility tools, such as a console that allows you to monitor your WLS instance.

> **New Term: WLS instance**
>
> When you started WLS running earlier, you started an instance of WebLogic Server. An instance is one particular running of WLS on a machine. It is possible to have multiple instances of WLS running on a machine.

The `lib` folder contains the `weblogicaux.jar` file that includes all the J2EE classes from Sun Microsystems.

WLS cannot be run without a valid license. There are two forms of the license: a Java class or an XML file. Either one can be used as long as it is valid. The license dictates how many clients can connect to your server, the database drivers you can use, and other aspects of WLS. A valid license to run WLS and execute your JSPs is on your CD-ROM.

The `myserver` directory is your server-specific directory. In it there is a `weblogic.log` file that contains all the text that was written to your screen when WLS started up. If an error occurred during startup, you can go to this file and read the description. The `public_html` folder in the `myserver` directory is where you place your HTML and JSP files. For use with this book, you are going to create a directory under the `public_html` folder called `myJSPs` and under that a folder for each hour, such as hour1, hour2, and so on through hour19. You will need just one folder called `project` for Hours 22 and 23. In these hours you are going to create a human resources Web site and all files will be located in the `project` directory.

Create this directory structure now for maintaining your work throughout the book.

The `weblogic.properties` File

The `weblogic.properties` file is located in the `c:/weblogic` directory. This is the global properties file and would be valid for all instances of servers on your machine. The file is read when WLS starts and not at any other time. If you make a change to your `weblogic.properties` file, you need to stop WLS and restart it. Listing 4.1 shows some excerpts from the `weblogic.properties` file.

LISTING 4.1   Excerpts from WebLogic Server's (`weblogic.properties`)

```
1: # REQUIRED: The system password MUST be set in order to start the
2: # WebLogic Server. This password is case-sensitive, at least 8
3: # characters.
4: # The username for the privileged user is ALWAYS "system".
5: # This username and password also includes httpd access (see
6: # HTTPD properties below).
7: weblogic.password.system=weblogic
8:
```

LISTING 4.1   continued

```
 9: # TCP/IP port number at which the WebLogic Server
10: # listens for connections
11: weblogic.system.listenPort=7001
12:
13: # Enable SSL
14: # (default if property not defined is false)
15: weblogic.security.ssl.enable=\
16:     true
17: #
18: # SSL listen port
19: weblogic.system. SSLListenPort=7002
```

ANALYSIS   There are many points to make about the excerpts from the weblogic.properties file. Many of the lines begin with a # symbol, that signifies the line to be a comment.

Recall from an earlier note that the property to set the system's password is weblogic.password.system. Line 7 shows this property in an excerpt from the weblogic.properties file.

Line 11 is the property that sets the TCP/IP listen port for the server. The default for the listen port is 7001. Most Web servers listen to port 80, so if you were setting up WLS as a Web server you would set this property to 80.

Another property that you can set is if you are going to allow SSL (Secure Sockets Layer) communications. Lines 15 and 16 show the property to allow SSL communications. Notice at the end of line 15 there is a backslash, this allows the name/value pair to continue on the next line.

> Since a backslash is used to allow code to continue on the next line, they cannot be used in directory structures. To represent a directory structure use two backslashes, \ \, or one forward slash, /.

If you enable SSL communications you need to specify a port that WLS will listen on for SSL requests. Line 19 shows the command, weblogic.system.SSLListenPort, which is default at 7002.

Since you will only have one instance you will use the weblogic.properties file in the c:/weblogic directory to configure your application server.

It is possible to run multiple instances of WebLogic Server on one machine. The `weblogic.properties` file in the `c:/weblogic` directory is the global configuration file and pertains to all instances of WLS on the machine. If you want to configure a specific instance, then you would place a `weblogic.properties` file in that server-specific directory (`myserver` directory is an example of a server-specific directory).

As you saw from Listing 4.1 this file contains information such as the listening port, the system password, and Servlet registrations. The `weblogic.properties` file also contains name/value pairs, although it may not look like it since the names tend to be long and the values tend to be long. There are a few rules to this file:

- A # denotes a line as a comment.
- There cannot be any spaces in your name/value pairing.
- A backslash is used to continue to the next line so you must use a forward slash or two backslashes in your directory structures. An example of a directory structure would be, `c:/weblogic/myserver/classfiles`, or `c:\\weblogic\\myserver\\classfiles`.

Registering the `JSPServlet`

WebLogic Server uses Servlets as the underlying implementation of how it handles different types of files. WLS uses the `JSPServlet` to handle the serving of JSPs. You need to register this Servlet in the `weblogic.properties` file.

At the top of your `weblogic.properties` file, type in the following:

```
weblogic.httpd.register.*.jsp=weblogic.servlet.JSPServlet
```

This lets WebLogic Server know that all files with the `.jsp` extension are handled with the `JSPServlet`.

Setting the Initial Arguments for the `JSPServlet`

The `JSPServlet` takes some initial arguments, such as the JDK compiler to use and the number of seconds WLS should wait before checking whether the JSP has been updated. Listing 4.2 is one common way to configure the `JSPServlet` in the `weblogic.properties` file:

LISTING 4.2 Configuring the `weblogic.properties` File

```
1: weblogic.httpd.initArgs.*.jsp=\
2:      pageCheckSeconds=1,\
3:      compileCommand=c:/jdk1.2.2/javac.exe,\
```

LISTING 4.2   continued

```
4:      workingDir=/weblogic/myserver/classfiles,\
5:      keepgenerated=true,\
6:      verbose=true
```

ANALYSIS The pageCheckSeconds argument, in line 2, specifies the number of seconds WLS waits until it checks whether the JSP has been changed. A value of 0 specifies to always check it, and a value of -1 specifies never to check it.

Line 3 sets the compileCommand, which is the fully qualified path to your Java compiler. In this example the java compiler is located in c:/jdk1.2.2/javac.exe. WLS works with JDK 1.1.* and JDK 1.2.*.

The workingDir argument, in line 4, is the directory where WLS will keep the generated Servlet code—weblogic/myserver/classfiles, in this example.

The keepgenerated argument, in line 5, specifies to keep the generated Servlet code. The values it can take are true and false. A value of true states that you want to keep the generated .java files, and false tells WLS not to keep the .java Servlet code.

The verbose argument, in line 6, tells WLS to be descriptive if it comes across errors. This property can take true or false as values. A value of true tells WLS to give you debugging information, a value of false tells WLS not to give you debugging information.

Deploying a JSP on WLS

Once you have registered the JSPServlet and set up the initial arguments, you are ready to write a JSP and run it on WLS. Type the content of Listing 4.3 into a text editor and save it with a .jsp extension. Save it as OrderForm.jsp. Do not type in the line numbers. They are there for reference purposes only.

LISTING 4.3   Deploying a JSP on BEA WebLogic Server (OrderForm.jsp)

```
1: <HTML>
2: <HEAD><TITLE>A Catalog Order Form</TITLE></HEAD>
3: <BODY>
4: <H1 ALIGN="center">An Order Form</H1>
5: <%! String item[] = {"toaster", "CD", "diskette"};
6:     double price[] = {19.99, 12.99, 1.99};
7:     int quantity[] = {2, 9, 24};
8: %>
9: <TABLE ALIGN="center" BGCOLOR="yellow" BORDER="1" WIDTH="75%">
10:    <TR><TD>Item</TD>
11:        <TD>Price</TD>
12:        <TD>Quantity</TD>
```

LISTING 4.3 continued

```
13:        <TD>Total Price</TD>
14:    </TR>
15:    <% for (int i=0; i<3; i++) { %>
16:    <TR><TD><%= item[i] %></TD>
17:        <TD><%= price[i] %></TD>
18:        <TD><%= quantity[i] %></TD>
19:        <TD><%= price[i] * quantity[i] %></TD>
20:    </TR>
21:    <% } //end for loop %>
22: </TABLE>
23: </BODY>
24: </HTML>
```

Remember to save this file in the directory structure `c:/weblogic/myserver/public_html/myJSPs/hour4`. This JSP creates a table that lists items, their prices, and quantities, and calculates their total price dynamically. In Hour 7, "Declaring Variables and Methods in a JSP," you are going to learn about the declaration tag that is used in line 5 to declare variables in the JSP. The scriptlet tag in line 15 is explained in great detail in Hour 9, "Inserting Java Code in a JSP." Finally, the expression tags in lines 16-19 are covered in Hour 8, "Inserting Java Expressions in a JSP." Until then, just know these are a couple of the tags used to insert Java code into your JSPs. Figure 4.2 shows the output of this JSP.

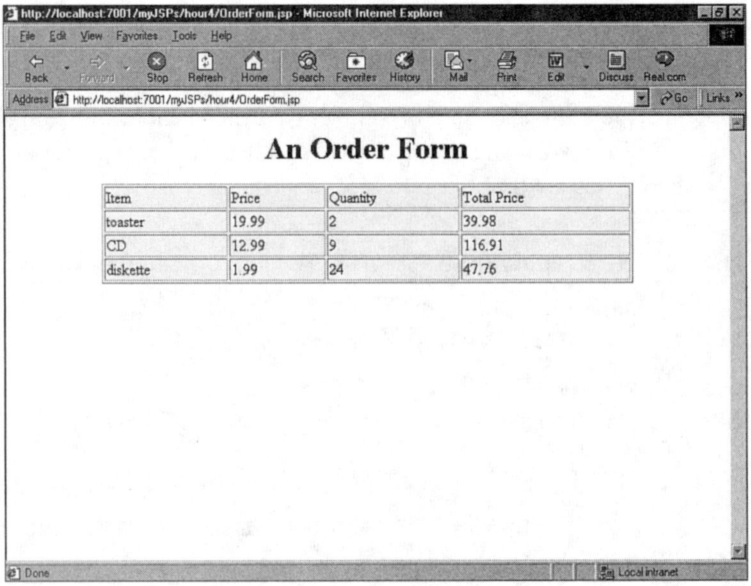

FIGURE 4.2

Your first JSP on WebLogic Server should look like this.

Congratulations on running your first JSP on BEA WebLogic Server.

Summary

In this hour you got to work with the most popular application server today, BEA WebLogic Server. Throughout the rest of this book you can run your JSPs on WLS or Apache's Tomcat. The rest of the examples in the text and the URLs that are shown are running on BEA WebLogic Server.

Q&A

Q Which server should I use for the rest of the book?

A The examples you will see are going to be run on BEA WebLogic Server. You can run your code on whichever you prefer. Since WLS is the most popular application server you may want to get experience using it. Also, Tomcat is not a production server, it does not provide security and Servlet reloading. The final project will be done on WLS, so you can set security on the Web application.

Q What directory structure should I use if I am using Tomcat?

A If you decide to use Tomcat for some of the examples, you will want to use the directory structure c:\tomcat\webapps\myJSPs\Hour*XX*. This type of directory structure helps you keep your files organized.

Q Does it matter where I register the `JSPServlet` and configure its initial arguments in the `weblogic.properties` file?

A No, it does not matter. You can register the Servlet anywhere and configure the initial arguments anywhere. If you put your configuration and arguments at the top of the file, it will be easy for you to locate them.

Workshop

The quiz questions and activities are provided for your further understanding. See Appendix A, "Answers," for the answers to the quiz.

Quiz

1. What happens if you set the initial argument property `pageCheckSecs` equal to `0`?

2. Where do you place you JSP files for this book? How does that correlate to the URL you use to request them?

4

Activity

Have some fun with the initial arguments for the JSPServlet: Have WLS check every 3 seconds for modifications to your JSP, do not keep the generated Servlet code, and do not have WLS be descriptive if errors happen. Your challenge is to match these requirements to the appropriate initial argument, and to set them appropriately.

PART II

Building Simple JSPs

Hour

HOUR 5

Understanding the JSP Application Models

In this hour you look at how JSPs can interact with each other. It is important to understand how JSPs interact before you start coding JSPs. Sometimes you want a JSP to accept the request and pass it along to another JSP, or you might just want to include the output of another JSP in your JSP. There are many ways that JSPs can interact with each other, and this hour you are going to see various models that the specification defines.

In this hour you learn

- What an application model is
- How to do JSP chaining
- How JSPs include output from other JSPs

What Are Application Models?

An application model is a description of how JSPs can interact with each other. The JSP 1.1 specification defines many models that describe how your

JSPs can interact. Your application model could be as simple as a single JSP accepting the request and generating the response, or it could be a JSP that includes output from another JSP. The following sections explain each of the application models in more detail.

The Simple Model

The Simple Model consists of a single JSP. Figure 5.1 shows the request coming into the JSP and the response being generated from the same JSP.

FIGURE 5.1

In the Simple Model, the JSP handles the request and the response to it.

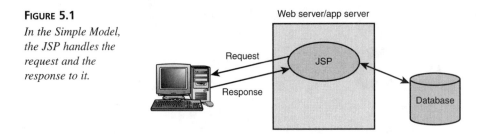

In this model there is one JSP that accepts the request and generates the response. It hits the database or legacy system to get the data for its dynamic content. This model was aimed at replacing CGI scripts. Recall from Hour 1, "Introduction to Web Applications," that a CGI script was a program written in C, C++, or Perl that created dynamic content on the Web. Until now, all the examples in this book have been Simple Model JSPs, although none have needed to access a database. Accessing a database or legacy system is an option that provides this model with some of the dynamic content it needs. Listing 5.1 is another example of the Simple Model illustrating the JSP accessing the database (in this example the JSP retrieves book information). Don't get too hung up with the syntax of how it is accessing the database; Hour 17, "Accessing a Database from a JSP," explains that.

LISTING 5.1 A JSP that Pulls Book Information from a Database
(SimpleBookTable.jsp)

```
 1: <HTML>
 2: <HEAD><TITLE>An Example of a Simple Model</TITLE></HEAD>
 3: <BODY>
 4: <CENTER>
 5:   <FONT COLOR="blue" SIZE="6">
 6:     A Listing Of Books
 7:   </FONT>
 8: </CENTER>
 9: <BR><BR>
10: <%@ page import="java.sql.*" %>
```

LISTING 5.1   continued

```
11: <TABLE WIDTH="100%" BORDER="2" BGCOLOR="silver">
12:   <TR><TH WIDTH="50%">Title</TH>
13:       <TH WIDTH="25%">Author</TH>
14:       <TH WIDTH="25%">ISBN</TH>
15:   </TR>
16:   <%
17:     try{
18:       Class.forName("COM.cloudscape.core.JDBCDriver").newInstance();
19:       Connection conn =
20:         DriverManager.getConnection("jdbc:cloudscape:c:\\BookDB");
21:       Statement statement = conn.createStatement();
22:       String sql = "SELECT * FROM BOOKDATA";
23:       ResultSet rs = statement.executeQuery(sql);
24:       while (rs.next()) {
25:   %>
26:     <TR><TD><%= rs.getString("TITLE") %></TD>
27:         <TD><%= rs.getString("AUTHOR") %></TD>
28:         <TD><%= rs.getString("ISBN") %></TD>
29:     </TR>
30:     <%
31:       }
32:     %>
33: </TABLE>
34:   <%
35:     if (statement != null)
36:       statement.close();
37:     if (conn != null)
38:       conn.close();
39:     } // end try block
40:     catch (Exception e) {out.print(e);}
41:   %>
42: </BODY>
43: </HTML>
```

5

Figure 5.2 shows the output of SimpleBookTable.jsp. The book information was pulled from the database and formatted in an easy-to-read table format.

An advantage to this model is its simplicity to program. The page author can very easily create dynamic content based on the user's request.

A disadvantage to this model is it does not scale easily when the number of clients increases. The JSP can use potentially scarce or expensive resources, such as a connection to a database. Each client must either establish this resource or share one, which can hurt performance when you get many clients.

FIGURE **5.2**

`SimpleBookTable.jsp` *produces a very readable table of information.*

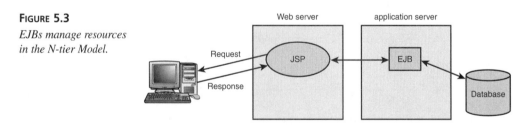

The N-Tier Model

The N-tier model adds server-side resources such as Enterprise JavaBeans. Figure 5.3 shows the structure of the N-tier Model.

FIGURE **5.3**

EJBs manage resources in the N-tier Model.

In this model the JSPs interact with backend systems such as databases and legacy systems via Enterprise JavaBeans. Since the EJBs are handling the access to the backend resources, this model scales easier than the Simple Model in which the JSPs were managing their resources. Listing 5.2, later in this hour, is an example of a JSP that uses an EJB to retrieve the book information from the database.

Recall from Hour 1 that the EJB specification describes how to write components in the Java programming language. The specification defines how the components communicate with each other. They represent business logic and business data.

The advantage of this model is its scalability because the EJBs are managing your resources. Also, the EJBs can be used by many JSPs for common functionality so you don't have to keep repeating common code in all your JSPs.

A disadvantage to this model is that you are still using only one JSP, so it will have quite a bit of work within it.

The Loosely Coupled Model

The Loosely Coupled Model allows JSPs on remote systems to act as peers or have a client/server relationship. Figure 5.4 shows the interaction of the JSPs in this model.

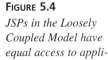

FIGURE 5.4

JSPs in the Loosely Coupled Model have equal access to applications.

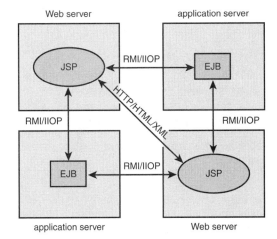

This model represents two applications that can be on the same intranet, or communicating over an extranet or Internet.

New Term: Extranet

An extranet is a company's intranet that allows customers access to certain applications within that intranet.

Each JSP application is isolated from changes in the other JSP application by communicating over HTTP using HTML or XML. An example of a loosely coupled model is a supply chain application between vendors. An example of this is when JSP *X*, on Intranet *Y*, communicates with JSP *Z*, on Intranet *Q*, using the HTTP communication protocol.

5

The Including Requests Model

Sometimes it is helpful to distribute the work of your application among multiple JSPs. Figure 5.5 shows one way to split up the work.

FIGURE 5.5

One JSP can do the work with input from another JSP in the Including Requests Model.

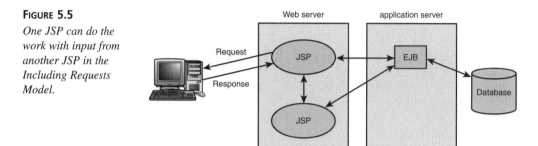

One JSP could be responsible for the request and the response, but includes the output of other JSPs. This is accomplished by using the `include` action. Hour 20, "Using Multiple JSPs to Handle the Request," covers this action in much more detail. Listing 5.2 is a JSP that includes the output of other JSPs, whose code is shown in Listings 5.3 and 5.4.

LISTING 5.2   A JSP that Manages a Request and Includes the Output of Other JSPs (`IncludeActionExample.jsp`)

```
 1: <HTML>
 2: <HEAD><TITLE>Example Of The include Action</TITLE></HEAD>
 3: <BODY>
 4:    Include the First File:
 5:      <jsp:include page="PowersOf2.jsp"/>
 6:    <BR>
 7:    Include the Second File:
 8:      <jsp:include page="OrderForm.jsp"/>
 9: </BODY>
10: </HTML>
```

LISTING 5.3   A JSP that Calculates the Powers of 2 (`PowersOf2.jsp`)

```
 1: <HTML>
 2: <HEAD><TITLE>Powers of 2</TITLE></HEAD>
 3: <BODY>
 4: <CENTER>
 5:    <H2>Behold The Powers Of 2</H2>
 6: </CENTER>
 7: <TABLE BORDER="2" ALIGN="center">
```

LISTING 5.3   continued

```
 8:    <TH>Exponent</TH><TH>2^Exponent</TH>
 9:    <% for (int i=0; i<10; i++) {%>
10:      <TR><TD><%= i%></TD>
11:        <TD><%= Math.pow(2, i)%></TD>
12:      </TR>
13:    <% } //end for loop %>
14:  </TABLE>
15:  </BODY>
16:  </HTML>
```

LISTING 5.4   A JSP that Has a Table Containing Item Price, Quantity, and Total Price (OrderForm.jsp)

```
 1: <HTML>
 2: <HEAD><TITLE>A Catalog Order Form</TITLE></HEAD>
 3: <BODY>
 4: <H1 ALIGN="center">An Order Form</H1>
 5: <%! String item[] = {"toaster", "CD", "diskette"};
 6:      double price[] = {19.99, 12.99, 1.99};
 7:      int quantity[] = {2, 9, 24};
 8: %>
 9: <TABLE ALIGN="center" BGCOLOR="yellow" BORDER="1" WIDTH="75%">
10: <TR><TD>Item</TD>
11:      <TD>Price</TD>
12:      <TD>Quantity</TD>
13:      <TD>Total Price</TD>
14: </TR>
15: <% for (int i=0; i<3; i++) { %>
16: <TR><TD><%= item[i] %></TD>
17:      <TD><%= price[i] %></TD>
18:      <TD><%= quantity[i] %></TD>
19:      <TD><%= price[i] * quantity[i] %></TD>
20: </TR>
21: <% } //end for loop %>
22: </TABLE>
23:
24: </BODY>
25: </HTML>
```

5

Figure 5.6 shows the output of IncludeActionExample.jsp. As you can see, that page includes the output of the other JSPs.

An advantage to using the Including Requests Model is that one JSP is responsible for handling the request and the response, but there are other JSPs doing the work. The workflow is easy to see in this model: one JSP manages the whole application.

FIGURE 5.6

The output of
IncludeActionExample.
jsp *includes the output
of two other JSPs.*

Include the First File:

Behold The Powers Of 2

Exponent	2^Exponent
0	1.0
1	2.0
2	4.0
3	8.0
4	16.0
5	32.0
6	64.0
7	128.0
8	256.0
9	512.0

Include the Second File:

An Order Form

The Forwarding Requests Model

Another way to break up work among JSPs is the Forwarding Requests Model, also
known as the Redirecting Requests Model. Its diagram is shown in Figure 5.7.

FIGURE 5.7

*Forwarding the User's
Request to Another JSP
utilizing the Forwarding
Request Model.*

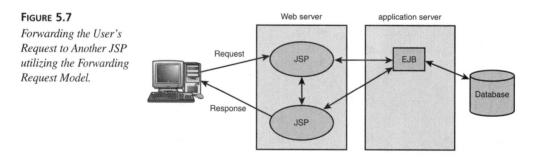

In this model the JSPs are *chained* together by forwarding the request and response
objects. The forwarding is accomplished with the forward action. Hour 20 will go in great
detail about the forward action. The first JSP accepts the request and the last JSP in the
chain is responsible for sending the response back to the user, the JSPs in between the
first JSP and the last JSP can handle some of the business logic (see listings 5.5 and 5.6).

LISTING 5.5 A JSP that Forwards Request to One of Two JSPs Based on a Random Number (ForwardActionExample.jsp)

```
 1: <HTML>
 2: <HEAD><TITLE>Example Of The forward Action</TITLE></HEAD>
 3: <BODY>
 4: <% if (Math.random() > .5) { %>
 5: <jsp:forward page="FibonacciComputation.jsp"/>
 6: <% }else { %>
 7: <jsp:forward page="FactorialComputation.jsp"/>
 8: <% } %>
 9: </BODY>
10: </HTML>
```

LISTING 5.6 A JSP that Calculates the Fibonacci Number for the Numbers 0-19 (FibonacciComputation.jsp)

```
 1: <HTML>
 2: <HEAD><TITLE>Calculating the Fibonacci Numbers</TITLE></HEAD>
 3: <BODY BGCOLOR="navy" TEXT="yellow">
 4: <%! int [] fib; %>
 5: <CENTER>
 6: <H1>Calculating the Fibonacci Numbers of 0-19</H1>
 7: <br>
 8: The fibonacci number of 0 is 0
 9: <BR>
10: The fibonacci number of 1 is 1
11: <BR>
12: <% fib = new int[20];
13:     fib[0] = 0;
14:     fib[1] = 1;
15:     for (int i=2; i<20; i++) {
16: %>
17: The fibonacci number of <%= i%> is <% fib[i] = fib[i-1] + fib[i-2]; %>
18: <%= fib[i] %>
19: <br>
20: <% }%>
21: </CENTER>
22: </BODY>
23: </HTML>
```

> The Fibonacci numbers function is a recursive function that is used to simulate rabbit reproduction patterns. It is just a fun way to play with numbers.

5

LISTING 5.7   A JSP that Calculates the Factorial Number for the Numbers 0-19
(FactorialComputation.jsp)

```
 1: <HTML>
 2: <HEAD><TITLE>Calculating the Factorial Numbers</TITLE></HEAD>
 3: <BODY BGCOLOR="purple" TEXT="white">
 4: <CENTER>
 5: <H1>Calculating the Factorial Numbers for 0-19</H1>
 6: <BR>
 7:
 8: <%! long numbers[];
 9:      long fact[];
10:      int i,j;
11: %>
12: <%
13: numbers = new long[20];
14: fact = new long[20];
15: numbers[0] = 1;
16: numbers[1] = 1;
17: for (i=2; i<20; i++){
18: numbers[i] = i;
19: }
20: for (i=0;i<20;i++){
21: fact[i] = 1;
22: }
23: for (i=0; i<20; i++){
24:   for (j=0; j<=i; j++){
25:     fact[i] *= numbers[j];
26:   }
27: }
28:
29: for (i=0; i<20; i++) {
30: out.print("The factorial of " + i + " is " + fact[i] + "<BR>");
31: }
32: %>
33: </CENTER>
34: </BODY>
35: </HTML>
```

The ForwardingActionExample.jsp determines a random number and then forwards it to one of the other JSPs. Figure 5.8 shows the output if the number is forwarded to the FibonacciComputation.jsp, and Figure 5.9 shows the output of the FactorialComputation.jsp.

A disadvantage to this model is diagramming the workflow of the JSPs. Since there is no one JSP responsible for managing the work of the others, it gets more complicated following the flow of work in large applications.

FIGURE 5.8

The other output of the Forwarding Requests Model is from the Fibonacci JSP.

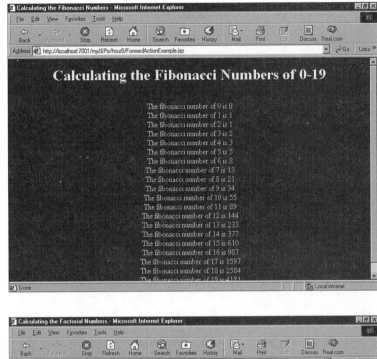

FIGURE 5.9

One output of the Forwarding Requests Model is from the factorial JSP.

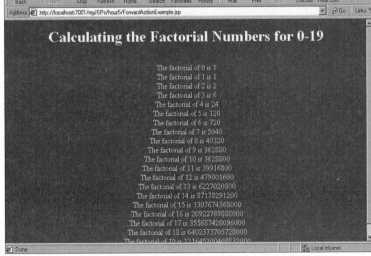

5

Summary

There are many ways to build your applications with JavaServer Pages technology. The specification gives guidelines on how to build these applications and ways that your JSPs can communicate. Hour 20 contains much more detail about the actions that help you build your applications to these guidelines.

Q&A

Q Why is it helpful to know these application models?

A The application models can guide you in designing your application. They describe how the work of your application can get done with one JSP or multiple JSPs.

Q What are the actions that are referred to in this hour?

A JSPs have tags that allow you to do an action, such as using a JavaBean, including requests from other JSPs, and forwarding requests to another JSP. By simply using these tags you can do an action that would typically take multiple lines of code to perform.

Workshop

The quiz questions and activities are provided for your further understanding. See Appendix A, "Answers," for the answers to the quiz.

Quiz

1. What application model describes using server-side resources such as EJBs to manage your backend resources?

2. What actions are used in the Including Requests Model and the Forwarding Requests Model, respectively?

3. If your application follows the Loosely Coupled Model and one JSP changes, does it affect the other JSP application?

Activity

Describe the various application models to a friend and/or relative. Explaining these models in your own words furthers your understanding of these topics.

Hour **6**

Understanding the Layout of a JSP

This hour covers general concepts that will be useful as they are expanded in the following hours. The different parts of a JSP are listed and described briefly, deferring details to the appropriate hour in the book.

In this hour you will learn

- Using tags and their attributes
- Adding HTML, JSP, and Java comments
- Writing HTML code
- Embedding Java with JSP tags
- An introduction to the JSP built-in objects
- Using JavaBeans

Using Tags and Attribute Values

Everything in a JSP source code is either a single tag, a pair of tags, or simple text. Tags have attributes that configure their behavior. Tags can either be HTML tags or JSP tags. This hour provides some general information and conventions about JSP tags and their attributes that you will find useful throughout the book.

Understanding Single and Paired Tags

Like HTML tags, JSP tags can be single tags or paired tags. An example of a tag that has both versions and is used a lot throughout the book is `<jsp:useBean>`. As a single tag it can instantiate a Java class and associate a name to it. Here is an example of its use as a single tag:

```
<jsp:useBean name="myClass" class="SimpleClass" scope="page"/>
```

As a single tag, `<jsp:useBean>` either succeeds in instantiating the class or not. If the tag fails to instantiate the class and the name is used to reference the instance, it is likely that a null pointer exception will be thrown. The paired tag version allows you to execute code contingent on the successful instantiation of the Java class. Here is the paired tag version of the `<jsp:useBean>` tag:

```
<jsp:useBean...>
...some HTML or JSP code...
<jsp:useBean/>
```

Many other HTML and JSP tags have the same configuration in that they can be used as a single tag or paired with a closing tag. When used as a paired tag, the first of the pair is referred to as the *begin* tag and the second as the *end* tag. The general meaning of paired tags is that whatever content is within the tags is affected by the containing tags.

Configuring Tags with Attributes

Tags have attributes that configure their behavior. For instance, the HTML anchor tag used to declare hyperlinks has an HREF attribute that declares the URL to which the hyperlink points. The following is an example declaration of a hyperlink that points to www.bea.com:

```
<A HREF="http://www.bea.com">Click Here</A>
```

When the user clicks on the hyperlink, the browser will load the page pointed to by the HREF attribute.

JSP tags also have plenty of attributes to configure. The earlier `<jsp:useBean>` example used the attributes name, class, and scope. Here it is again:

```
<jsp:useBean name="myClass" class="SimpleClass" scope="page"/>
```

The attributes configure the useBean tag to instantiate a class called SimpleClass, name it myClass, and then discard it when the JSP is done creating the page.

Adding Comments to the Code

Comments are sentences and phrases inserted by programmers to document the JSP source code. Comments are useful for explaining what the code does in plain English. Explanations can be very helpful especially when revising the code after an extended period of time, or if it is being reused by other developers. Comments do not affect what is displayed in a browser but help a user understand the HTML and JSP source that generated the page. There are three types of comments: HTML, JSP, and Java.

Adding HTML Comments

HTML comments are created using the tags `<!--` and `-->`. When these tags appear in a JSP, they are added to the response of the JSP unchanged, and they will appear in the resulting HTML code that is sent out to the browser. The browser is then responsible for ignoring the comments. Comments can have dynamic content embedded in them since they are not simply ignored by the JSP. JSP expressions within an HTML comment will be evaluated and inserted in the response to the browser. Here are examples of a simple HTML comment and one that includes a JSP expression:

```
<!-- This is a simple comment -->

<!-- 2 + 2 = <%= 2 + 2%> -->
```

The resulting HTML code would be the following:

```
<!-- This is a simple comment -->

<!-- 2 + 2 = 4 -->
```

Both comments will be ignored by the browser.

Adding JSP Comments

HTML comments are used to document the HTML content generated by the JSP. JSP comments are used to document the JSP code itself. JSP comments are not included in the resulting response sent back to the browser. They are created using the tags `<%--` and `--%>`. The following is a simple example:

```
<%-- This comment won't go to the browser--%>
```

So unlike HTML comments, JSP comments are ignored by the JSP and do not appear in the source code of the Web page in the browser.

Adding Java Comments

Java comments are used to comment the Java code embedded in a JSP. One-line Java comments are preceded by `//`. The pair `/*` and `*/` can comment a whole section of code.

6

Here is a simple example where the /* and */ are used to comment a function and the //
comment is used to comment one of two possible values of variable discount.

```
/*
 * This function returns
 * the value of the discount
 */
double getDiscount(){
    double discount = 20;
 // double discount = 30;
    return discount;
}
```

The extra * characters in the first comment are purely aesthetical.

> Although JSPs are primarily developed using HTML as the static layout lan-
> guage for the page and Java as the programming language to control the
> page, the JSP specification does not preclude other languages to be used as
> well. Anything that is not within JSP tags is considered to be static text that
> is sent to the browser unchanged. This means that the static source code can
> be anything that the requesting client is meant to understand. If the client is
> a Web phone it may understand WML (Wireless Markup Language) instead
> of HTML. The programming language can also be something other than
> Java, like Perl or Visual Basic. Each of these languages has its own develop-
> ment details. For instance, the one-line comment in a Visual Basic script is a
> single quote instead of two forward slashes. This book will focus on the two
> most widely used languages for developing JSPs: HTML for the static layout
> and content and Java for the scripting and flow control of the page.

Dissecting a JSP

The JSPs presented throughout this book contain some or all of the following parts:

1. HTML code—for laying out the overall layout and look and feel of the page

2. JSP tags—for scriptlets, expressions, declarations, actions, and directives

3. JSP implicit objects—the request object, response object, session object, and
   config object, for example

4. JavaBeans—for implementing the business logic

The following sections present each of the elements of a JSP; they'll be covered in detail
in later hours.

Writing HTML Code

Usually Web page developers use specialized software to create Web pages in standard HTML. Some of these tools are aware of other technologies that enhance regular HTML and provide some support for Java applets, JSP, and plug-ins. But for the most part the development of HTML consists of creating the static portion of the Web pages and determining which portion of the page is dynamic. The dynamic content is then implemented by inserting JSP tags.

Understanding JSP Tag Elements

JSP tags allow Web page developers to dynamically generate pages using program logic.

JSP tags come in two flavors: They can be created using several versions of the paired tags <% and %> or with XML equivalent tags <jsp:*tagid*> and </jsp:*tagid*>.

> All JSP tags have an XML version and a shorthand equivalent version. The XML version allows JSPs to be forward compatible with the industry's fast adoption of XML as a standard. However, it is impractical to use XML until appropriate tools are available to easily create JSPs with XML. In the meantime, JSPs are still better developed by hand and the shorthand version of the tags are best.

Using the JSP Declaration Tags

Declaration statements list variables and methods that are available throughout the rest of the JSP code. JSP declarations are created using the following JSP syntax:

```
<%!
    declaration_statement(s)
%>
```

or the XML equivalent

```
<jsp:declaration>
    declaration_statement(s)
</jsp:declaration>
```

Listing 6.1 is an example of a JSP that declares two variables (variableA and variableB) and two methods (methodX(), methodZ()).

LISTING 6.1 A JSP that Declares Variables and Methods (declarations.jsp)

```
1: <HTML><HEAD><TITLE></TITLE></HEAD><BODY>
2: <%! String variableA = "This is a string variable";
3:     int variableB = 123;
```

6

LISTING **6.1**   continued

```
 4:     int methodX(int newInteger){
 5:       variableB = newInteger;
 6:       return variableB;
 7:     }
 8:     String methodZ(String newString){
 9:       variableA = newString;
10:       return variableA;
11:     }
12: %>
13: </BODY></HTML>
```

ANALYSIS   This JSP declares a string variable variableA and sets its value to "This is a string variable" in line 2. Then it declares an integer variable, variableB, and initializes it to 123 in line 3. Lines 4–6 declare methodX(), which takes an integer as an argument, modifies the value of variableB, and returns its new value. Lines 8–11 declare methodZ(), which takes a string as an argument, changes the value of variableA, and returns its new value.

When the JSP is requested by the browser, it does not generate any output. The variables and methods don't get evaluated until they are referenced from either a JSP expression tag or a scriptlet tag. The following two sections introduce these tags, and Hour 7, "Declaring Variables and Methods in a JSP," covers declarations in more detail.

Using the JSP Expression Tags

Expressions are a combination of constants, references to variables and methods with operators. Expressions are evaluated to a single value by evaluating the individual elements in the expression and then combining them according to the operators.

Expressions can exist either inside JSP scriptlets or on their own in a JSP expression tag. If in a scriptlet, expressions are usually part of an assignment statement or method call. That is, the expression is evaluated and assigned to some other variable or passed on to some method. When they are in a tag, the expressions are evaluated, their result converted to a string representation, and the strings are included in the resulting HTML code generated by the JSP.

The syntax for declaring a JSP expression tag is

```
<%= expression %>
```

or, using the XML equivalent:

```
<jsp:expression> expression </jsp:expression>
```

An example of a simple expression based on the variables declared in the previous example is referencing a declared variable as follows:

```
<%= variableA %>
```

When the JSP executes, the expression evaluates to "This is a string variable" and is part of the resulting HTML code. If the variable is anything other than a string variable, it is automatically converted to a string representation and inserted in the HTML code. Hour 8, "Inserting Java Expressions in a JSP," covers JSP expressions in great detail.

Using the JSP Scriptlet Tags

Scriptlets allow Web developers to embed Java code in their JSPs. What this means is that Web developers can take advantage of a powerful programming language to create dynamic Web content and layout.

Scriptlets provide several flow control structures like decision and iteration control structures. The following sections introduce these concepts. Hour 9, "Controlling JSPs with Java Scriptlets," covers scriptlets in more detail.

Using Decision Control Structures

Decision control structures allow developers to program decision-making criteria into Web pages to decide among several possibilities. For instance, a JSP could check a user's identity and password and decide to either greet the user as an authenticated user or politely ask the user to properly register with the Web site. Decision control is programmed in scriptlets by using the Java if and switch statements. The JSP in Listing 6.2 shows an example of using an if statement to check the credentials of an imaginary user and decide whether to greet the user or ask the user to log in.

LISTING 6.2   A JSP that Uses the if Statement (decisions.jsp)

```
 1: <HTML><HEAD><TITLE></TITLE></HEAD><BODY>
 2: <%! boolean isPasswordAnyGood(String password){
 3:        return false; // really go to database to find out
 4:      }
 5: %>
 6: <%  if(isPasswordAnyGood("somePhoneyPassword")){
 7: %>    <H1> Welcome </H1>
 8: <%  } else {
 9: %>    <H1> Please Login </H1>
10: <%  }
11: %>
12: </BODY></HTML>
```

6

Using Iteration Control Structures

Iteration control structures allow developers to progressively handle a collection of data or objects. For instance, a JSP could iterate through the items in a shopping cart and calculate the total cost of the shopping cart by accumulating the individual costs of each item.

Listing 6.3 is a JSP that lists imaginary items from some online shopping cart and computes the total purchase amount.

LISTING 6.3   A JSP that Uses a for Loop (`iteration.jsp`)

```
 1: <HTML><HEAD><TITLE></TITLE></HEAD><BODY>
 2: <%! String itemName  = ["Item 1", "Item 2", "Item 3"];
 3:     double itemCost  = [123.00,    234.50,    345.50  ];
 4:     double totalCost = 0.0;
 5: %>
 6: <UL>
 7: <%  for(int j=0; j<itemName.length; j++){
 8: %>    <LI> Item = <%=itemName[j]%>, $<%=itemCost[j]%>
 9: <%    totalCost = totalCost + itemCost[j];
10:     }
11: %>
12: </UL>
13: Total = <%=totalCost%>
14: </BODY></HTML>
```

ANALYSIS   Lines 2 and 3 of the JSP declare two arrays that contain information for each item, `itemName` and `itemCost`. Line 4 declares and initializes the `totalCost` of the items in the shopping cart. Line 7 uses a `for` loop to iterate through each of the items in the arrays to print out the item names and their costs in line 8. Line 9 accumulates the total cost of the shopping cart and then prints it in line 13.

Declaring JSP Directive Tags

Directive tags are used to command JSPs to perform certain functions or to behave in a particular way.

For instance, the following directive imports all classes under the package `com.macmillan.jspIn24`:

```
<%@ page import="com.macmillan.jspIn24.*" %>
```

There are three directives—`page`, `include`, and `taglib`—that will be covered in other hours in the book.

Declaring JSP Action Tags

Action tags are used to extend the functionality of JSPs. There are actions that allow JSPs to use objects created in Java, include other JSPs, forward requests to other JSPs, and interact with a Java plugin. There are six JSP action tags: useBean, setProperty, getProperty, include, forward, and plugin.

As an example, the following action tag instantiates a JavaBean implemented by the class ShoppingCart in the package com.macmillan.jspIn24.hour16 and associates it with the name shoppingCart:

```
<jsp:useBean name="shoppingCart"
             class="com.macmillan.jspIn24.hour16.ShoppingCart">
```

The JSP code can then use the identifier shoppingCart to call methods on the object instance.

You'll find more information on JSP action tags in appropriate places throughout this book.

Using the JSP Built-in Objects

JSPs have access to several objects that provide functionality to process a request from a browser and then generate a dynamic response. These objects are

request	out
response	pageContext
session	application
config	page

Understanding the request Object

JSPs have direct access to the request from a browser through the request object. The request object implements the HttpServletRequest interface, which represents the request from a browser through a defined set of methods. The request object's methods allow JSP programmers to access information about the user, HTTP headers, the client's machine, cookie information, request URL, and parameters. Hour 10, "Processing Requests from the User," provides several examples of how to create requests through simple URLs and forms and how to access the information within the JSP.

Understanding the response Object

JSPs also have direct access to the response object to generate dynamic content as HTML code. The response object implements the HttpServletResponse interface, which represents the response of the JSP to the browser's request. The response object's methods allow JSP programmers to set HTTP headers, set cookies, and encode session information into URLs, among other things. Hour 11, "Generating a Dynamic Response for the User," has several examples of how to use the response object to generate dynamic content like dynamic HTML tables, dynamic HTML forms, and a configurable Web page.

6

Understanding the `session` Object

HTTP is a stateless protocol and therefore a JSP is not able to remember anything specific about a particular client. However, the `session` object together with cookies allows JSPs to associate information that is specific to a unique client request. The `session` object implements the `HttpSession` object, which is also accessible through the `request` object. Methods of the `session` object allow you to bind objects to string names so that the objects can be retrieved by name across several interactions with client browsers. Hour 12, "Keeping Track of the User Session," shows examples of how to use cookies to remember user preferences and how to use the `session` object to keep track of the content of a shopping cart.

Understanding the `config` Object

The `config` object implements the `javax.servlet.ServletConfig` interface. The `config` object gives access to configuration data for initializing the JSP. Hour 13, "Configuring and Initializing JSPs," will cover the `config` object in detail.

An Overview of the Other JSP Built-in Objects

The other objects available in a JSP—`out`, `pageContext`, `application`, and `page`—will be covered throughout the book with no specific hour devoted to them. A short description of each follows.

The `out` object is an instance of the class `javax.servlet.jsp.JspWriter` and provides methods to generate output to the browser as well as methods to control the behavior of the output being generated.

The `pageContext` object is an instance of the class `javax.servlet.jsp.PageContext`. This class gives access to several page attributes and allows you to forward or include the `request` object to or from other application components.

The `application` object implements the `javax.servlet.ServletContext` interface for communicating with the `servlet` container. The `servlet` container manages the lifecycle and information of all Servlets.

The `page` object represents the `servlet` instance generated from having compiled the JSP. It is essentially equivalent to the keyword `this` in Java; that is, a reference to the current instance object you are in.

Understanding JSPs and JavaBeans

JavaBeans are Java classes that adhere to the JavaBean specification. The specification establishes guidelines for developing Java code that is easy to reuse as modular functional blocks in a variety of scenarios. Hour 16, "Using JavaBeans in a JSP," will go into a lot of detail on the aspects of developing and using JavaBeans from a JSP but here are some of the highlights.

The Motivation Behind JavaBeans

Since JSPs allow developers to mix HTML and Java code in one unified source, you might ask why we need JavaBeans at all. There is no inherent reason that you should use JavaBeans. Technically, you could do all the work of a JavaBean in a JSP. But the reality is that JSPs were designed to be used as the presentation layer. The presentation layer is the portion of an application (any application) that deals with the direct interaction with the user. This task is complex enough.

There is still another complex aspect of developing applications: the computations and business logic that must occur to fulfill some request from some interaction with the user. And the general rule of thumb gathered from the collective experience of computer science engineers in the field developing tons of applications is that it is best to divide the presentation layer and the computation or business logic. Sure, there is quite a lot of computation that goes on in a JSP. But the computation in a JSP usually accomplishes some aspect of laying out the content of the page according to some preferences, dynamically including other pages, inserting messages, and creating HTML tables with a dynamic number of rows, all aspects of how data is presented to the user. The heavy computation that occurs behind the scenes should be handled by some dedicated computation mechanism like JavaBeans.

There are, of course, other computation structures available for implementing business logic—like Enterprise Java Beans, interfacing to some C++ DLL through JNI, and using RMI to use a remote object, for instance—but these escape the scope of this book.

The JavaBean Specification

The Java class that implements the JavaBeans will usually have a number of variables. These variables are referred to as the properties of the JavaBean. For each of the variables the JavaBean specification requires, developers must provide matching set and get methods to set the value of the variable and to get the value of the variable. The names of the methods are derived from the name of the variable, for instance if the variables name is abc then the name of the methods would be setAbc() and getAbc(). Note the capitalization of the first letter of the name of the variable in the name of the method.

Instantiating a JavaBean

The JSP action tag <jsp:useBean> is used to instantiate a JavaBean. The following tag instantiates a JavaBean of the class Circle and associates it with the name circle1 in the JSP. The JSP then goes on to set and get several properties of circle1.

```
<jsp:useBean name="circle1" class="com.macmillan.jspIn24.hour06.Circle">
```

6

Here is an example implementation of a JavaBean:

```
package com.macmillan.jspIn24.hour06;
public class Circle {
  double radius;
  double area;
  public void    setRadius(double r){radius = r;}
  public double getRadius(){return radius;}
  public void    setArea(double a){area = a;}
  public double getArea(){return area;}
}
```

Note that the Circle JavaBean declares two variables, radius and area, and then declares set and get methods for each of the variables. When the JavaBean is instantiated and associated with a name, it can be used to make method calls to the instance. If the class adheres to the JavaBean specification then the values of the variables can be set and accessed using the JSP tags setProperty and getProperty.

Using the set and get Property Tags

By following the JavaBeans naming conventions to set and get properties, JSPs can provide special tags to modify and access the properties of JavaBeans. The <jsp:setProperty> tag is used to set the value of a property and the <jsp:getProperty> tag is used to get the value of the property. The value of having tags for setting and accessing JavaBean properties is that it allows developers of tools like HTML GUI editors to provide special draggable and configurable icons to represent JavaBeans.

A Quick Example of Using JavaBeans

The following simple example illustrates the use of a JavaBean from a JSP using the circle example listed earlier in this section.

```
<HTML><HEAD><TITLE>A Simple JavaBean Example</TITLE><BODY>
<jsp:useBean name="circle1" class="com.macmillan.jspIn24.Circle">
<jsp:setProperty name="circle1" property="radius" value="2">
Area = <jsp:getProperty name="circle1" property="area">
</BODY></HTML>
```

When the above JSP executes in a browser, the result is the string Area = 12.5664.

Summary

This hour presented several general concepts that will be covered in greater detail in the following hours. It served as a quick overview of all the parts and pieces of a JSP. Tags and their attributes were covered first. Then, comments in HTML, JSP, and Java were presented. Finally, you got a rundown of each of the parts of a JSP, like HTML code, JSP tags, JSP built-in objects, and JavaBeans.

Q&A

Q **What is the difference between a JSP declaration tag and the JSP scriptlet tag? I understand that you can declare variables in the declaration tag but can you declare them in the scriptlet tag?**

A As far as variable declaration and initialization is concerned, declaration and scriptlet tags are identical. The difference lies in the declaration of methods. You can only declare methods in a JSP declaration tag. These methods are not executed until referenced from within JSP scriptlet tags. Declaring variables in a JSP declaration tag is just a good programming practice of organizing your code so that it is easier to read.

Q **I don't understand the need for JavaBeans. What can you do with JavaBeans that you can't do with JSPs?**

A JSPs can basically do everything a JavaBean can do, but these technologies were designed to complement one another and are specialized in their particular domain. JSPs are meant to quickly create dynamic content and interact with users at the presentation layer. JavaBeans used from JSPs are meant to process requests from the presentation layer and translate them into actions that affect the underlying infrastructure of a business, such as databases, other machines, other services, printers, and so on.

Workshop

The quiz questions and activities are provided for your further understanding. See Appendix A, "Answers," for the answers to the quiz.

Quiz

1. What are four of the implicit or built-in objects available to a JSP?
2. What is the JSP declaration tag used for?

Activity

6

This activity gives you a chance to grasp the complexity involved in the design of a Web site. You will choose a Web site and draw a diagram that identifies the presentation implemented with JSPs and the business logic implemented with JavaBeans. Diagrams like these are usually used in early development and planning of Web sites.

Choose a Web site that you are familiar with, preferably one that sells something online, and browse it with attention. As you browse the site, annotate the different pages that are involved in the purchase of a particular product. Starting from the home page, draw a diagram with rectangles that represent the pages. Draw arrows from every page to any other page that you can get to from that page. These arrows identify the transitions of the Web site. If the Web site allows multiple shopping scenarios, then choose one particular scenario and stick to it.

After you have drawn the diagram, annotate for every arrow the actions that you think are happening behind the scenes. Actions might include things like "registered me with their database," "searched database for item or category," and "accessed my credit card information."

When you are done, come up with a list of names for JSPs that can represent the Web pages. Then come up with names of JavaBeans that could implement the actions that occur in the transitions between pages. Names for the JSPs might be things like `home.jsp`, `about.jsp`, `help.jsp`, `search.jsp`, and `catalog.jsp`. Names for the JavaBeans might be things like `RegisterUserWithDatabase.java`, `SearchItemInCatalog.java`, and `VerifyCreditCard.java`.

Hour 7

Declaring Variables and Methods in a JSP

This hour shows you how to declare variables and methods in a JSP. Although you are probably familiar with the Java programming language and how to declare and use variables and methods, this hour covers the basics to get you up to speed, so that you are able to work through the examples and activities. If you are a savvy Java programmer, you might want to skim through the next couple of hours just to familiarize yourself with the syntax of declaring variables and methods in JSPs.

This hour covers:

- Declaring variables in a JSP
- Understanding data types
- Initializing variables
- Working with arrays, `Vectors`, and `Enumerations`
- Declaring methods in a JSP
- Invoking methods
- Understanding method overloading

Using the Declaration Tags

Declaring variables and methods consists of listing them within the JSP declaration tags <%! and %>. Declarations state the existence of variables and methods that are available throughout the rest of the JSP code. Declared variables and methods are referenced by using their declared name. First, you will see how to declare variables and then how to declare methods.

Declaring Variables in a JSP

Variables consist of placeholders for data items. Data comes in all shapes and sizes and it requires some underlying piece of physical memory to be stored. Variables allow you to refer to the content of a particular chunk of memory by name. The structure and size of the data is referred to as its *data type* or simply *type*. In object-oriented jargon, variables are often called *objects* or *object instances*, and data types are called *classes*. The term *object* is more often used when referring to a variable that has been declared using a Java class as a data type.

You declare variables by declaring the type of the variable and the variable name within the <%! %> tags following this general syntax:

dataType variableName [= initialization];

In this example, initialization is optional and will be covered later this hour. In the meantime, Listing 7.1 declares three variables:

LISTING 7.1   Declaring Variables (declaringVariables.jsp)

```
1: <HTML>
2: <HEAD><TITLE> Variable Declaration Example </TITLE></HEAD>
3: <BODY>
4: <%!  int myIntegerVariable;
5:      String myStringVariable;
6:      float myFloatingPointVariable;
7: %>
8: </BODY>
9: </HTML>
```

Line 4 of the preceding code declares a variable called myIntegerVariable of type int that can hold an integer number. Line 5 declares a variable called myStringVariable of type String that can hold a concatenated series of characters. Line 6 declares a variable called myFloat of type float that can hold a floating-point number. Data types are covered in just a minute, but first a word on variable and method names.

It is a good programming practice to choose descriptive, meaningful names for your variables and methods. In a professional environment, your code will often be read or reused by someone other than yourself who will try to make sense out of what you wrote in the past, and you may not be around. Meaningful names help to make the code more readable, increasing its value and its chances of not ending up in the garbage.

Understanding Data Types

Data is usually structured in some standard format. This structure is called the data type of the variable. Simple data types such as `int` and `float` represent integer and floating-point numbers. More complex data types such as arrays and vectors handle collections of data. And custom data types can even be declared by the user.

New Term: Data Type

Data type, or just type, is a classification of data into categories that describe the characteristics of the data. For instance, numbers are considered data, and they can be classified into several types of numbers, such as integers and floating-point numbers. Hence, programming languages provide data types such as `int` and `float` to declare variables that can either hold integers or floating-point numbers. Characters and concatenation of characters are another form of data. The data types `char` and `String` are used to declare variables or objects that can hold a single character or a set of characters.

The data type of a variable also determines the operations that are allowed on the data represented by the variable. For instance, integer data types allow operations such as addition and multiplication but do not generally allow an operation such as concatenation, like a `String` data type might allow. Some of the more common data types used in this book are listed in Table 7.1.

TABLE 7.1 Common Data Types

Data Type	Description
int	A primitive data type that can hold integer numbers
float	A primitive data type that can hold floating-point numbers
double	A primitive data type that can hold double precision numbers
long	A primitive data type that can hold large numbers
char	A primitive data type that can hold characters
String	A Java class that can hold a concatenation of characters
Vector	A Java utility class that can hold a collection of objects of different types
Enumeration	A Javautility interface for inspecting collections of objects sequentially

7

> **New Term: Primitive Data Type**
>
> Primitive data types are types that are directly supported by a programming language. These data types can't generally be taken apart or represented in terms of other data types. Programming languages support primitive data types by providing automatic memory allocation and operators. The int data type is an example of a primitive data type. In contrast, programmers can create custom data types by declaring Java classes. Java classes are made up of a collection of data types which can themselves be primitive data types or other custom data types. Operations on custom data types are implemented by declaring methods in the Java class definition.

When you declare a variable, memory is allocated to hold the variable's data. Memory can be allocated implicitly or explicitly, depending on the data type you use. Primitive data types such as int, float, double, long, and char allocate memory when you declare the variables. Data types implemented through Java classes need to be allocated explicitly by using the new operator. The String data type is a Java class, but it is so widely used that the Java compiler treats strings as if they were primitive data types. You have seen examples of declaring primitive data types. Listing 7.2 is an example of using the new operator to declare Java objects:

LISTING 7.2   Declaring Java Objects (declaringJavaObjects.jsp)

```
1: <HTML>
2: <HEAD><TITLE>Declaring Java objects</TITLE></HEAD>
3: <BODY>
4: <%!  String myString = new String();     // memory allocated explicitly
5:      String anotherString;               // memory allocated implicitly
6:      Vector myVector = new Vector();      // memory allocated explicitly
7: %>
8: </BODY>
9: </HTML>
```

In Java, primitive data types have class counterparts to be able to treat the data as objects. For instance, the data types int, float, double, and char have class counterparts Integer, Float, Double, and Character. The Java classes have methods that allow conversion from each other.

For an exhaustive coverage of Java data types, you should consult a book on the Java programming language, such as *Java in a Nutshell,* by David Flanagan, published by O'Reilly (ISBN 1565924878).

Initializing Variables

Initializing a variable consists of associating a value with the variable. Initialization can occur either at or after declaration. The data type of the value you want to initialize a variable with must be the same type as the variable. Listing 7.3 is an example of variables being initialized at declaration time:

LISTING 7.3   Initializing Variables with Constants (`initializingVariables.jsp`)

```
 1: <HTML>
 2: <HEAD><TITLE> Initializing Variables At Declaration </TITLE></HEAD>
 3: <BODY>
 4: <%!  int myIntegerVariable    = 123;
 5:      String myStringVariable = "hello world";
 6:      float myFloatVariable    = 123.321f;
 7: %>
 8:  <P> myIntegerVariable = <%= myIntegerVariable%>
 9:  <P> myStringVariable  = <%= myStringVariable %>
10:  <P> myFloatVariable   = <%= myFloatVariable  %>
11: </BODY>
12: </HTML>
```

Variables can be initialized with other variables, with expressions containing other variables, and even with the result of method invocations. Listing 7.4 illustrates this.

LISTING 7.4   Initializing Variables With Other Variables And Method Calls (`initializingVariablesWithOtherVariables.jsp`)

```
 1: <HTML>
 2: <HEAD><TITLE> Different ways of initializing variables </TITLE></HEAD>
 3: <BODY>
 4: <%!  int    a = 4;
 5:      int    b = a * 2;
 6:      double c = Math.sqrt(Math.pow(a, 2) + power(b, 2));
 7: %>
 8:  <P> a = <%= a %>
 9:  <P> b = <%= b %>
10:  <P> c = <%= c %>
11: </BODY>
12: </HTML>
```

7

The preceding code declares integers a and b (lines 4 and 5). Integer b is initialized by multiplying a by two. Variable c is declared to be of type double, and it is initialized by using method calls to methods squareRootOf() and power() and referring to the values of variables a and b. The Math class used in line 6 is a standard Java class that is accessible from any JSP. The Math contains several static methods for computing several common math functions. `Math.sqrt()` computes the square root and `Math.pow()` computes the power of the first argument raised to the second argument. The `Math` object is part of the `java.lang` package and it includes many static methods to compute different mathematical functions, and access different constants. You may need to prepend the package name in front the `Math` object like so: `java.lang.Math`. So the call to the square root function would be `java.lang.Math.sqrt(...)`.

Declaring Arrays and Collections

Sometimes it is convenient to handle a set of data as a group or collection. Java provides several data types to handle data as collections, depending on whether the data is all of the same type, whether the size of the collection is fixed, and how you intend to access the data.

The simplest form of a collection of data is the array. Arrays are contiguous data slots that can hold values of a certain type. You can create an array out of any data type by using the array indexing characters [and]. Arrays are declared by appending the [] operator to the data type declaration and then allocating the array with the new operator. This is illustrated in Listing 7.5 where you declare several arrays.

LISTING 7.5   Declaring Arrays (`declaringArrays.jsp`)

```
 1: <HTML>
 2: <HEAD><TITLE> Examples of declaring arrays </TITLE></HEAD>
 3: <BODY>
 4: <%! int[]     orderedQuantities   = new int[3];
 5:     int[]     inStockQuantities   = {1, 2, 2};
 6:     String[] productNames         = {"Screen House", "Rain Flyer", "Tent"};
 7:     String[] productDescriptions = getDescriptions();
 8:     double[] productPrices        = {149.99, 29.99, 129.99};
 9:     String[] getDescriptions(){
10:        String[] descriptions = {"Desc1", "Desc2", "Desc3"};
11:        return descriptions;
12:     }
13: %>
14: <%  for(int i=0; i<3; i++){ %> <HR>
15:        <BR>Name:        <%= productNames[i]         %>
16:        <BR>Description: <%= productDescriptions[i] %>
17:        <BR>Price:       <%= productPrices[i]        %>
18:        <BR>In Order:    <%= orderedQuantities[i]    %>
19:        <BR>In Stock:    <%= inStockQuantities[i]    %>
20: <%  }
21: %>
22: </BODY>
23: </HTML>
```

Line 4 declares an array of three integers. Arrays are indexed from 0 to 2. Line 5 declares an array of 3 integers and initializes the array so that

```
inStockQuantities[0]=1
inStockQuantities[1]=2
inStockQuantities[2]=2
```

Similarly, line 6 declares an array of three strings and initializes the array appropriately. Line 7 declares another array of strings and uses a method to initialize the array. Line 8 initializes an array of double precision numbers. The execution actually begins in line 14 where a for loop is used to access each element of the arrays to create the JSP in Figure 7.1.

FIGURE 7.1

This page was generated by the JSP code in Listing 7.5.

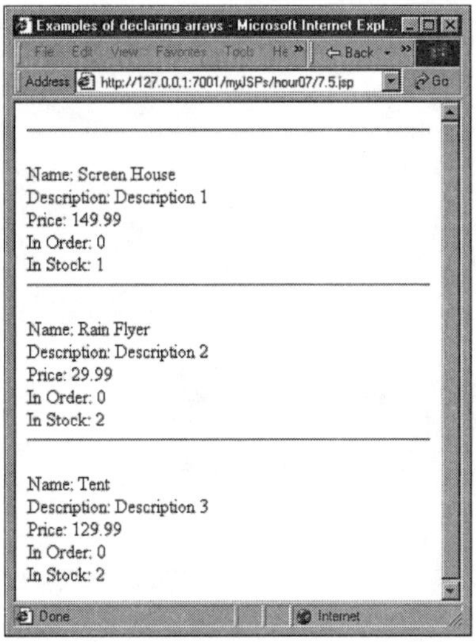

Two other Java data types are useful for managing a collection of data: the Vector class and the Enumeration interface. These are defined in java.util, Java's utility package.

Unlike arrays, which are of a fixed size, data collections of type Vector can grow as needed to accommodate more data. Also unlike arrays, Vectors allow the collection of data of disparate types. In Listing 7.6, a Vector is used to store several objects of different types:

LISTING 7.6   Declaring Vector Objects (declaringVectors.jsp)

```
1: <HTML>
2: <HEAD><TITLE> Example use of Vectors </TITLE></HEAD>
3: <BODY>
4: <%!  String name      = new String("John Doe");
```

LISTING 7.6   continued

```
 5:        Integer ssn     = new Integer(111223333);
 6:        Double salary   = new Double(65432.10);
 7:        Vector employee1 = new Vector();
 8: %>
 9: <%   employee1.addElement(name);
10:      employee1.addElement(ssn);
11:      employee1.addElement(salary);
12: %>
13:      Employee Name:   <%= (Object)employee1.elementAt(0) %>
14:      Employee SSN:    <%= (Object)employee1.elementAt(1) %>
15:      Employee Salary: <%= (Object)employee1.elementAt(2) %>
16: </BODY>
17: </HTML>
```

ANALYSIS   Note that in lines 4 through 6, you are declaring several objects that you will put into the vector employee1. These must be objects because Vectors accept only objects as their elements. Also note that in line 7 you leave out the size of the vector. This causes the vector to be a default size of 10 elements. In lines 9 through 11 you add three elements to the vector, and it would automatically grow if you kept adding elements.

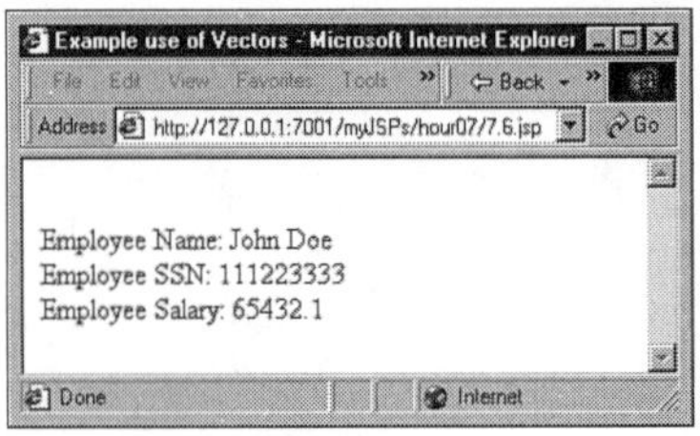

FIGURE 7.2

This is the page generated by the JSP code in Listing 7.6.

The Enumeration interface is another popular mechanism to handle a collection of data elements that are of diverse types. An Enumeration is meant to be accessed as a sequential series of data items. To do this, the Enumeration interface declares just two methods:

- boolean hasMoreElements() —Returns true if there are still elements in the Enumeration and false if there are no more data items.

- Object nextElement() —Returns the next element in the sequence of data items.

The Vector class has a method called elements() that returns all the elements in the Vector as an Enumeration. Listing 7.7 is an example of enhancing Listing 7.6 with the use of Enumeration:

LISTING 7.7   Using Enumerations to Sequentially List All Elements of a Vector
(usingEnumerations.jsp)

```
 1: <HTML>
 2: <HEAD><TITLE> Example use of Vectors </TITLE></HEAD>
 3: <BODY>
 4: <%!  String name        = new String("Jonh Doe");
 5:      Integer ssn        = new Integer(111223333);
 6:      Double salary       = new Double(65432.10);
 7:      Vector employee      = new Vector();
 8:      String[] infoTitles = {"Name", "SSN", "Salary"};
 9: %>
10: <%   employee.addElement(name);
11:      employee.addElement(ssn);
12:      employee.addElement(salary);
13:      int i = 0;
14:      Enumeration employeeInfo = employee.elements();
15:      while(employeeInfo.hasMoreElements()){ %>
16:        <P> Employee <%= infoTitles[i++] %>:
17:           <%= (Object)employeeInfo.nextElement() %>
18: <%   } %>
19: </BODY>
20: </HTML>
```

The output of the preceding JSP is identical to that of Listing 7.6.

The utility package java.util contains a whole assortment of classes and interfaces that are worth becoming familiar with, including Date, Calendar, Hashtable, List, Set, and Dictionary. This section discussed the more commonly used ones: Vector and Enumeration.

Declaring Methods in a JSP

Declaring a method consists of listing the method name, its signature, and the method body within the JSP declaration tags <%! %>. Methods declared in these tags are available throughout the JSP code by referring to the methods by their declared name. A method declaration hasthe following syntax:

returnType methodName (parameterList) { methodBody }

The *methodName* name is an identifier that is used to refer to the method by name. The *parameterList* consists of a comma-separated list of variables and their types inside a pair of parenthesis. The *methodBody* consists of Java statements that perform some computation and may optionally return a value of type returnType to the method caller.

7

The return type, method name, and parameter list make up the signature of the method. Method signatures will be covered in detail in the section "Understanding Method Overloading," later in this hour. Listing 7.8 is a simple example of a declaration of a method that verifies that a login password is at least of a certain size (HTML tags have been removed for conciseness).

LISTING 7.8   Declaring a Method

```
1: <%! boolean verifyPasswordLength(String password){
2:          if(password.length() < MIN_PSWD_LEN) return false;
3:          return true;
4:      }
5: %>
```

Methods can be used by other methods. Listing 7.9 is an example of a method declaration that uses two other method declarations.

LISTING 7.9   Declaring a Method that Uses Another Method

```
 1:  <%! boolean verifyPasswordHasDigit(String password){
 2:          for(int i=0; i<password.length(); i++)
 3:             if(Character.isDigit(password.charAt(i))) return true;
 4:          return false;
 5:      }
 6:      boolean verifyPasswordPolicy(String password){
 7:          if(verifyPasswordLength(password) &&
 8:            verifyPasswordHasNumber(password))
 9:            return true;
10:          return false;
11:      }
12: %>
```

Method `verifyPasswordPolicy()` in line 6 makes use of methods `verifyPasswordHasDigit()` and `verifyPasswordLength()` to accomplish its task of verifying that the password meets security policies. Method `verifyPasswordHasDigit()` in line 1 verifies that the password has at least one digit.

Invoking Methods

Methods don't do anything until they are actually invoked. JSP Java code execution begins with the first occurrence of the JSP tags `<%` and `%>`. From within executing code, you can invoke the methods. When methods are invoked, they execute their method body, which might involve invoking other methods. As an example you are going to create a login page that accepts a login username and password. The JSP will verify that the password meets some security policy using the methods in Listings 7.8 and 7.9. Listing 7.10 shows the HTML code that implements the login page login.html.

LISTING 7.10 HTML Code that Creates a Simple Login Page (login.html)

```
 1: <HTML>
 2: <HEAD><TITLE>A Simple Login Page</TITLE></HEAD>
 3: <BODY>
 4: <P>Please Login:
 5: <FORM ACTION=login.jsp METHOD=POST>
 6: <P>User Name: <INPUT TYPE=TEXT NAME=usernameField>
 7: <P>Password: <INPUT TYPE=TEXT NAME=passwordField>
 8: <P><INPUT TYPE=SUBMIT VALUE=Submit>
 9: </FORM>
10: </BODY>
11: </HTML>
```

The login page uses HTML forms to gather user information and invoke the JSP. You will take a look at HTML forms and how to process them from a JSP in Hour 10, "Processing Requests from the User." The JSP code in Listing 7.11 has two main parts to it. The first part declares three methods that can verify the integrity of a password. The second part defines the main executing Java code that implements the logic of the page. The logic consists of checking the result of invoking the method verifyPasswordPolicy with the password as argument. Listing 7.11 shows the code of login.jsp:

LISTING 7.11 JSP That Verifies Login Password (login.jsp)

```
 1: <HTML>
 2: <HEAD><TITLE>A Simple JSP That Verifies Password Policy</TITLE></HEAD>
 3: <BODY>
 4: <%! final static int MIN_PSWD_LEN = 8;
 5:      boolean verifyPasswordLength(String password){
 6:       if(password.length() < MIN_PSWD_LEN) return false;
 7:       return true;
 8:      }
 9:      boolean verifyPasswordHasDigit(String password){
10:       for(int i=0; i<password.length(); i++)
11:         if(Character.isDigit(password.charAt(i))) return true;
12:       return false;
13:      }
14:      boolean verifyPasswordPolicy(String password){
15:       if(verifyPasswordLength(password) &&
16:          verifyPasswordHasDigit(password))
17:         return true;
```

7

LISTING 7.11 continued

```
18:          return false;
19:      }
20: %>
21: <%  String password = request.getParameter("passwordField");
22:      if(verifyPasswordPolicy(password)){ %>
23:        <P> Thankyou -
24:        <P> Your password meets the security policy
25: <%  } else {%>
26:        <P> Sorry -
27:        <P> Your password does not meet the security policy
28:        <P> <A HREF="7.11.html"> Please try again </A>
29: <%  }%>
30: </BODY>
31: </HTML>
```

Figure 7.3 shows the login page and the resulting JSP when the user clicks the Submit button.

FIGURE 7.3

Clicking the Submit button produces the login page and the resulting JSP.

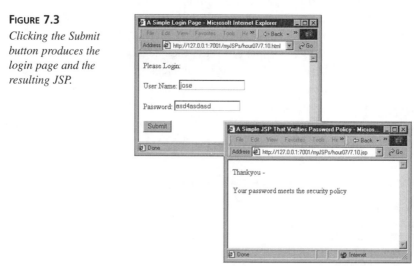

ANALYSIS In the HTML code for the login page login.html, you have declared an HTML form in lines 5 to 9. The form declares two text input fields, one for the username and another for the password (lines 6 and 7). Note that the input fields are named usernameField and passwordField, respectively. These names can be used from within the JSP to retrieve the value of these fields—that is, what the user types into these fields. In line 8, you declare a Submit button that, when clicked, will cause the browser to package the content of the form into a request and forward it to the JSP declared in line 5 in the ACTION parameter login.jsp.

In the JSP code that verifies the login information, `login.jsp`, you first declare the variables password and `MIN_PSWD_LEN in line 4`. Then the three methods covered in Listings 7.3 and 7.4 are declared in lines 5 through 19. Line 21 initializes the password variable with the value of the `passwordField` parameter embedded in the request from the browser. Note that this is the name given to the input field in the HTML form. Hour 10 will cover parameters in the `request` object in detail. The `MIN_PSWD_LEN` variable was initialized to 8 and represents the lower limit for the length of acceptable passwords. Lines 21 through 28 implement the logic of the JSP. The logic consists of a single `if` statement that uses the result of the `verifyPasswordPolicy()` method to decide whether the password is acceptable. If the password is okay, the JSP says thank you in line 23; otherwise, it says sorry in line 26 and lets the user try again.

Understanding Method Overloading

The names of declared methods need not be unique. What needs to be unique is the signature of the method. When you declare methods that have the same name, it is called overloading the method.

New Term: Method Signature

The signature of a method consists of the name of the method as well as the parameter list and return data type.

Listing 7.12 is an example of a method that has been overloaded.

LISTING 7.12   `overloading1.jsp`—An Overloaded Method Declaration

```
 1: <%! int month = 1, day = 1, year = 2000;
 2:    void setTodaysDate(int mm, int dd, int yyyy){
 3:      month = mm;
 4:      day   = dd;
 5:      year  = yyyy;
 6:    }
 7:    void setTodaysDate(Date date){
 8:      month = date.getMonth();
 9:      day   = date.getDay();
10:      year  = date.getYear();
11:    }
12: %>
```

Note that both method declarations have the same name, (`setTodaysDate()`), but have distinct parameter lists. By the name of the methods, you can guess that the methods accomplish the task of setting today's date. One accomplishes it accepting integer values for the month, day, and year. The other one accomplishes the same by accepting a Date object. The month, day, and year information is accessible from the Date object through several get methods.

Overloading a method allows the programmer to focus on the logic and worry less about the data types involved.

It is often good programming practice for one overloaded method to reuse another version of the same method to avoid rewriting code. For instance, in the example of the methods for setting today's date, you can write the method that accepts a Date object in terms of the one that accepts the three integers. Listing 7.13 shows the new methods.

LISTING 7.13   An Overloaded Method Declared in Terms of Another (overloading2.jsp)

```
 1: <%! int month = 1, day = 1, year = 2000;
 2:     void setTodaysDate(int mm, int dd, int yyyy){
 3:         month = mm;
 4:         day   = dd;
 5:         year  = yyyy;
 6:     }
 7:     void setTodaysDate(Date date){
 8:         setTodaysDate(date.getMonth(), date.getDay(), date.getYear());
 9:     }
10:  %>
```

The general rule here is that you declare a method that accepts the lowest common data types and then write any overloaded methods in terms of the first.

This is also a good programming practice because if you want to change the logic, you minimize the changes to the code. In the example of setting today's date, any changes in code would occur only in the method that accepts the three integers; whereas in Listing 7.12 you would have to change the logic in both method declarations.

Summary

In this hour I showed you how to use the JSP declaration tags <%! and %>. First you learned how to declare variables, and then you learned how to declare methods. You looked at the more common data types that are used in this book, and I suggested that you refer to a Java programming book for a more in-depth coverage of Java data types, classes and objects. You learned how to initialize variables, how to refer to them from within JSP code, and how to declare arrays, Enumerations and Vectors. You then focused on declaring methods and how to use them from the main JSP code. Finally you learned about method overloading.

Q&A

Q What happens if several browsers try to access my JSP all at once?

A Each browser request will be handled by a separate thread, and they will all try to execute the Servlet code generated from compiling the JSP. Variables and methods in declarations have class scope. This means that objects that you declare in a declaration are shared between multiple threads executing in the same Servlet instance. If you are knowledgeable about thread programming, you should synchronize class scope objects. If you are not thread-programming savvy, I suggest that you declare your JSP as not threadsafe by using the following directive within your JSP:

```
<%@ page isThreadSafe=false %>
```

By default, a JSP is set to be threadsafe—that is, `isThreadSafe=true`. Declaring your JSP as not threadsafe forces the corresponding Servlet to implement the `SingleThreadModel` interface, which prevents multiple threads to execute in the same Servlet instance.

Q Can I use recursive methods in JSPs?

A Yes; everything you can do Java, you can do in JSPs. At certain times, a solution to a problem is best expressed in terms of the solution to smaller instances of the same problem.

Q How do I declare my own data types?

A You can declare your own data types by creating a class that best represents the data you want to handle and then using the class within your JSP code. For instance, the following class declares a new data type called `Employee` that captures the data typically associated with an Employee:

```
public class Employee {
  protected String lastName, firstName, midInitial, title;
  protected int ssn;
  protected Date birthDate, hireDate;
  protected float salary;
}
```

In addition to all the data associated with an `Employee` object, you would typically declare several `get` and `set` methods that give you access to the data, as well as a constructor that initializes the object. From within a JSP you can declare employee objects, initialize them, and reference them:

```
<HTML>
<HEAD><TITLE>A JSP that uses the Employee class</TITLE></HEAD>
<BODY>
<%! Employee john = new Employee("John","", "Doe"); %>
<P> Employee Last Name  <%= john.getLastName()%>
<P> Employee First Name <%= john.getFirstName()%>
</BODY>
</HTML>
```

Workshop

The quiz questions and activities are provided for your further understanding. See Appendix A, "Answers," for the answers to the quiz.

Quiz

1. What is method overloading?

2. What is a data type?

3. How are `Enumerations` and `Vectors` related to one another?

Activities

1. Choose any three JSPs and examine the equivalent Servlets generated by the application server you are using. Make sure you understand how declarations in the JSP correspond to declarations in the Servlet.

2. Leonardo Fibonacci published an influential book in 1202 called *Book of the Abacus (Liber Abaci)*. The book contained the following problem: "How many pairs of rabbits can be produced from a single pair in one year if it is assumed that every month each pair begets a new pair which from the second month becomes productive?" The solution to this problem gave rise to the famous infinite sequence of integers generally referred to as the Fibonacci numbers. The sequence is useful for describing certain natural phenomenon and it is well known among academics. The sequence is described mathematically as follows:

```
Fib(0) = 0
Fib(1) = 1
Fib(n) = Fib(n-2) + Fib(n-1)
```

The first twelve values of the sequence are

```
    n = 0   1   2   3   4   5   6    7    8    9   10  11   12
Fib(n) = 0   1   1   2   3   5   8   13   21   34   55  89  144
```

Write a JSP that computes the *n*th Fibonacci number using recursive method calls. In Java, a recursive method is one that references itself within its method body.

Hour 8

Inserting Java Expressions in a JSP

This hour introduces the JSP expression tags <%= %> that allow you to evaluate Java expressions and embed the resulting text within HTML code. This feature allows you to programmatically control the dynamic content at a very fine granularity. For instance, a JSP that prints payroll information might query a database for all the employees, which meet some criteria. The result of the query would be a collection of objects including the names and salary of each of the employees that meets the query criteria. To print the output, a JSP might use an iteration control structure like a for loop, or while loop (more on loops in Hour 9 "Controlling JSPs with Java Scriptlets"). Inside the iteration each name of the employees is accessed from the query result and stored temporarily in a variable called employeeName. The output of the JSP will likely be an HTML table with a row for each employee. Mixed in with the HTML code for the table, the JSP has to insert the name of the employee in the employeeName variable in the right table cell. Inserting dynamic content, like the value of the variable employeeName, is accomplished by evaluating the variable with the JSP expression tags <%= and %>.

Later hours will show how to control the overall layout of a Web page using Java control
and decision structures.

The following topics are covered in this hour:

- Understanding the JSP expression tag
- Referencing variables from a JSP expression
- Calling local methods from a JSP expression
- Calling methods on a JavaBean from a JSP expression
- Overriding the toString() method

The JSP Expression Tags

JSP expressions are pieces of JSP code that can be evaluated to strings and be interlaced
within HTML code. JSP expressions are declared using the syntax:

```
<%= expression %>
```

The equal sign (=) in the left tag means that the expression *expression* should be evaluated and the tags should be replaced with the string equivalent of the resulting value.
Consider the following JSP code:

```
<%! int kids = 2 %>
Dante has <%= kids %> kids
```

The code above evaluates to the string Dante has 2 kids. In this case the expression
happens to be a simple reference to a variable which evaluates to 2.

The expression inside the tags can be arbitrarily complex, and the result is ultimately
converted to a string representation. Expressions can be a combination of the following:

1. Numeric and string literal values like 2 and "hello"
2. Mathematical operators such as +, -, *, and /
3. Variables of a primitive data types
4. Object instances of a custom class
5. Local method calls declared in the JSP
6. Method calls of an object created from a custom class

The following sections provide examples that utilize all of the above elements.

Referencing a Variable from an Expression

The JSP in Listing 8.1 declares several variables of different primitive data types.
The JSP compiler knows how to convert primitive data types to a string representation.

This example shows how JSPs convert numeric values into strings and concatenate them with other strings. Also, the example demonstrates how to convert the result of a mathematical expression into a string. Although the example only shows how to use the plus (+) operation, you can use any mathematical operation in an expression, as long as the operation is defined for the arguments it takes. For instance, the plus operator is defined for strings, numbers, and combination of strings and numbers. For strings, the plus operator concatenates the strings into a single resulting string. For numbers, the plus operator acts as the numeric addition. For combination, the plus operator converts the numbers to strings and then concatenates them into a string. Other mathematical operators like minus (−), multiplication (*), and division (/) are only meant to be used with numeric arguments.

The result of the JSP is shown in Figure 8.1. Note how the plus operation is smart enough to combine a string and a number as a string concatenation and combines two numbers as numeric addition.

LISTING 8.1 A JSP that References a Variable to Print Out Its Contents (referencingVariables.jsp)

```
 1: <HTML><HEAD><TITLE>Referencing Variables</TITLE></HEAD><BODY>
 2: <%! String stringVar = "This is string variable";
 3:      int integerVar = 123;
 4:      double doubleVar = 234.345;
 5: %>
 6: <UL>
 7: <LI>     stringVar = <%=stringVar%>
 8: <LI>     integerVar = <%=integerVar%>
 9: <LI>     doubleVar = <%=doubleVar%>
10: <LI>     stringVar + integerVar = <%=stringVar + integerVar%>
11: <LI>     stringVar + doubleVar = <%=stringVar + doubleVar%>
12: <LI>     integerVar + doubleVar = <%=integerVar + doubleVar%>
13: </UL>
14: </BODY></HTML>
```

ANALYSIS Lines 2 through 4 declare variables of different types. Lines 7 through 9 evaluate each of the variables and prints them out. Lines 10 through 12 show how each variable can be combined with the other, using the plus (+) operation.

FIGURE 8.1

JSP expressions can be used to print out the values of variables.

Being able to use numeric operators like + and * is important because they let you compute numeric expressions on the spot and insert the dynamic result in the HTML code. Consider the earlier example of the payroll. One of the columns might list the monthly contribution of the employee to their 401K retirement plan. The contribution is usually some percentage of the employee's salary where each employee chooses their own percentage and each has a different salary. If the percentage is stored in a variable called `contribution401K` (as a %) and their salary is stored in a variable called `salary`, then the expression to compute their contribution could be computed with the following expression:

```
<%=contribution401K * salary%>
```

The expression can be inserted among the HTML tags that create the table row and cell for each employee.

Overriding the toString( ) Method

The JSP compiler knows how to convert standard data types like `int`, `float`, and `double` to strings. If the expression evaluates to a value representable by a standard data type, then the JSP compiler knows how to convert the value into a string representation. However, if the resulting expression evaluates to a custom data type created from a user-defined class, JSP will try to use a `toString()` method for that object. If the `toString()` method has not been defined for that object, then the JSP determines what superclass of the user-defined class has a `toString()` method that could be used. If no `toString()` method can be found in the class's hierarchy tree, the `toString()` method of the `Object` class will be used since all objects inherit from the `Object` class. This might mean that the resulting string is a string representation of the binary representation of the object in memory—which would be gibberish to most of us. Therefore, if you intend for a custom data type to have a meaningful string representation, you must override the `toString()` method in the custom data type that creates and returns a string representation of the object.

> The `Object` class is the root of the class hierarchy. All other classes are derived directly or indirectly from the `Object` class. In object-oriented programming a class that is derived from another class inherits their methods and variables. So if a class `myObject` inherits from the class `Object`, `myObject` inherits the method `toString()`. Within the source code of `myObject.java` the method `toString()` can be overridden and tailored to the needs of the `myObject` class. If the `toString()` method is not overridden and an instance of `myObject` is printed, then the method `toString()` inherited from the `Object` class is used.

Listings 8.2 and 8.3 implement an example in which a custom data type is declared that overrides the `toString()` method. The method is then used from within a JSP to print out the string representation of the object. This example uses JavaBeans, which will discussed in more detail in Hour 16, "Using JavaBeans in a JSP."

LISTING 8.2 A JavaBean that Overrides the `toString()` Method (`OverridingToString.java`)

```
1: package jspin24hrs.hour08;
2: public class OverridingToString{
3:   String message = "Default Message";
4:   public OverridingToString(){}
5:   public OverridingToString(String msg){message = msg;}
6:   public String toString(){ return message; }
7: }
```

LISTING 8.3 A JSP that Uses a JavaBean that Overrides the `toString()` Method (`overridingToString.jsp`)

```
1: <HTML><HEAD><TITLE>Overriding toString() Method</TITLE></HEAD><BODY>
2: <%@ page import="com.macmillan.jspIn24.OverridingToString"%>
3: <%! OverridingToString ots1 = new OverridingToString();
4:     OverridingToString ots2 = new OverridingToString("New Message");
5: %>
6: <UL>
7: <LI>ots1 = <%=ots1%>
8: <LI>ots2 = <%=ots2%>
9: </UL>
10: </BODY></HEAD>
```

ANALYSIS Listings 8.2 and 8.3 consist of a JavaBean that overrides the `toString()` method and a JSP that uses the JavaBean to demonstrate how it's used from the JSP. Line 3 of the JavaBean declares a default message string. Lines 4 and 5 declare constructors with and without arguments. The argument of the second constructor is used to initialize the message variable. Line 6 overrides the `toString()` method which just returns the message. The JSP creates two instances of the JavaBean in lines 3 and 4 using either constructor. Lines 7 and 8 print out the objects, causing their `toString()` methods to get called and then substituting the tags with the resulting string from `toString()`. The result is shown in Figure 8.2.

FIGURE 8.2

A JSP can use a JavaBean that overrides the `toString()` method.

Calling Methods from an Expression

JSP expressions can contain variables and method calls. Methods can be declared either locally within the JSP code or in a Java class. The following sections present examples of these two scenarios.

Calling a Local Method

JSP expressions can reference methods declared locally in the JSP. The methods are declared using the JSP declaration tags `<%!` and `%>` covered in Hour 7, "Declaring Variables and Methods in a JSP." The methods can return any data type; they will be converted into a string representation, and the entire JSP expression will be replaced by the string representation. Again, if the method returns a standard Java data type, the JSP compiler knows how to convert it to a string. If the method returns a custom data type, the appropriate `toString()` method will be used as discussed earlier in this hour.

The JSP in Listing 8.4 demonstrates how a JSP expression can reference methods that have been declared locally using the JSP declaration tags. The methods return values of different data types and are converted into strings by the JSP expression tags so that they can be inserted in the resulting HTML code.

LISTING 8.4   A JSP that Calls Methods Within a JSP Expression
(`callingLocalMethods.jsp`)

```
1: <HTML><HEAD><TITLE>Calling Local Methods</TITLE></HEAD><BODY>
2: <%! String stringVar = "This is a string variable";
3:     int integerVar = 123;
4:     double doubleVar = 234.345;
5:     String getStringVar(){return stringVar;}
6:     int getIntegerVar(){return integerVar;}
7:     double getDoubleVar(){return doubleVar;}
8: %>
9: <UL>
10: <LI> getStringVar()  = <%=getStringVar() %>
11: <LI> getIntegerVar() = <%=getIntegerVar()%>
12: <LI> getDoubleVar()  = <%=getDoubleVar() %>
13: <LI> getStringVar() +getIntegerVar()=<%=getStringVar() +getIntegerVar()%>
14: <LI> getStringVar() +getDoubleVar() =<%=getStringVar() +getDoubleVar() %>
15: <LI> getIntegerVar()+getDoubleVar() =<%=getIntegerVar()+getDoubleVar() %>
16: </UL>
17: </BODY></HTML>
```

ANALYSIS   The preceding listing declares three methods using the JSP declaration tags in lines 5–7. Several JSP expression tags are used to reference the methods by themselves in lines 10–12 and then combined with one another in lines 13–15. The output of the JSP is shown in Figure 8.3. Note that the JSP compiler knows how to combine several data types. Lines 13 and 14 combine strings and numbers into a resulting concatenated string. Line 15 combines the individual values into a resulting number. This is all handled automatically by Java's automatic casting mechanism.

New Term: Casting

Casting is the process of transforming one data type into another. Throughout this hour, several examples have shown how numeric variables like integers and doubles are converted automatically to strings. This transformation is possible because Java has rules for how to transform or cast some types to other types. For strings, the casting occurs implicitly since it is just a matter of the compiler calling the `toString()` method of the variable to get its string representation. On other data types it is not as simple; casting must be done explicitly. Consider a variable of type `Vector` that can hold a collection of objects of disparate types. The objects are stored in the variable as types `Object` since every object directly or indirectly inherits from the class `Object`. Information about their original type is discarded. When the objects are retrieved from the vector variable, the objects must be casted back to their original data types explicitly. The casting cannot occur automatically (or implicitly) because information about their original type was discarded when the elements were stored in the vector variable.

FIGURE 8.3

A JSP expression can reference methods that have been declared locally by using the JSP declaration tags.

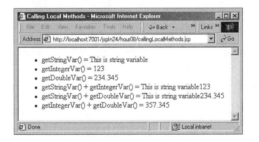

Calling a Method of an Object

Not only can JSP expressions reference methods declared locally within the JSP but they can also reference methods of an object declared in Java classes. The example in Listings 8.5 and 8.6 shows how a JSP creates an instance of a JavaBean and then calls several methods on the instance, printing out the string representation of the results of each of the method calls. The first listing declares the JavaBean with several methods, and the second declares the JSP that uses the JavaBean.

Being able to reference methods both locally in the JSP, and from a JavaBean is important because computations in a JSP expression can quickly get out of hand, especially if the computation is complex. It is often better to declare a method that accomplishes the computation, give it a descriptive name, and then reference it from the JSP expression.

LISTING 8.5   A JavaBean that Declares Methods that Return Different Data Types
(callingJavaBeanMethods.java)

```
 1: package com.macmillan.jspIn24;
 2: public class CallingJavaBeanMethods {
 3:   String stringVar;
 4:   int    intVar;
 5:   double doubleVar;
 6:   public CallingJavaBeanMethods(){}
 7:   public void setStringVar(String s){ stringVar = s; }
 8:   public String getStringVar() { return stringVar; }
 9:   public void setIntVar(int i){ intVar = i; }
10:   public int getIntVar(){return intVar; }
11:   public void setDoubleVar(double d){ doubleVar = d; }
12:  public double getDoubleVar(){return doubleVar; }
13: }
```

LISTING 8.6   A JSP that Calls Methods of a JavaBean (callingJavaBeanMethods.jsp)

```
 1: <HTML><HEAD><TITLE>Calling Java Bean Methods</TITLE></HEAD><BODY>
 2: <H1>Using Properties</H1>
 3: <jsp:useBean class="com.macmillan.jspIn24.CallingJavaBeanMethods" id="cm1">
 4: <jsp:setProperty name="cm1" property="stringVar" value="String Value 1"/>
 5: <jsp:setProperty name="cm1" property="intVar"    value="123"/>
 6: <jsp:setProperty name="cm1" property="doubleVar" value="345.456"/>
 7: </jsp:useBean>
 8: <UL>
 9: <LI>cjbm1.stringVar = <jsp:getProperty name="cm1" property="stringVar"/>
10: <LI>cjbm1.intVar    = <jsp:getProperty name="cm1" property="intVar"/>
11: <LI>cjbm1.doubleVar = <jsp:getProperty name="cm1" property="doubleVar"/>
12: </UL>
13: <H1>Using Methods</H1>
14: <% com.macmillan.jspIn24.CallingJavaBeanMethods cm2 =
15:       new com.macmillan.jspIn24.CallingJavaBeanMethods();
16:    cm2.setStringVar("String Value 2");
17:    cm2.setIntVar(234);
18:    cm2.setDoubleVar(567.678);
19: %>
20: <UL>
21: <LI>cm2.getStringVar() = <%=cm2.getStringVar()%>
22: <LI>cm2.getIntVar()    = <%=cm2.getIntVar()%>
23: <LI>cm2.getDoubleVar() = <%=cm2.getDoubleVar()%>
24: </UL>
25: </BODY></HTML>
```

ANALYSIS   These listings consist of a declaration of a JavaBean and a JSP that uses the
JavaBean. The JavaBean declares three variables of different types in lines 3–5.

Then a constructor with no arguments is declared. Finally the JavaBean declares set and get methods for each of the class variables. The JSP references the JavaBean using the <jsp:useBean> tag in line 3. Then the class variables are initialized using the <jsp:setProperty> tag in lines 4–6. After the class variables have been initialized, lines 9–11 access the values of the class variables using the <jsp:getProperty> tag. Lines 14–23 do the same but using method calls. Line 14 creates an instance of the JavaBean. Then lines 16–18 call the set methods for each of the class variables. Once the variables are set, lines 21–23 use the get methods for each of the class variables to print out the values. Figure 8.4 shows a sample of the output of the JSP.

FIGURE 8.4

A JSP can call JavaBean methods.

Summary

This hour showed how to use JSP expression tags to evaluate Java expressions and include their values as dynamic text within HTML code. Several examples were provided to demonstrate how to evaluate variables, objects, and method calls. JavaBeans were used to illustrate how to evaluate method calls declared in custom classes and how to override the toString() method.

Q&A

Q **It seems that the JSP expression tags are limited to evaluating to a string. What if the result of some method call consists of a vector of values or some collection of objects—how could they be properly printed in HTML?**

A JSP expressions are meant to be used to generate dynamic content inserted in HTML code. Nonetheless, you could conceive of a complex resulting string that contains HTML code that formats a vector of values into a table or items in a numbered list. Normally you would first obtain the collection of objects, perhaps as an enumeration, and then use a `for` loop or a `while` loop to iterate through each of the elements in the collection using JSP scriptlet tags. You would then use JSP expression tags to evaluate each element of the collection individually to its string representation.

Workshop

The quiz questions and activities are provided for your further understanding. See Appendix A, "Answers," for the answer to the quiz.

Quiz

1. What happens when a JSP evaluates a JavaBean instance?

Activity

Create a JSP that declares a string array with the names of five (5) people you know, and another integer array that holds their telephone numbers. Then have the JSP create an HTML table with two columns and five rows. Use the JSP expression tags to retrieve the contents of the arrays to fill in the rows of the table. The names should go on the first column and the phones on the second column.

Hour 9

Controlling JSPs with Java Scriptlets

HTML is a language for describing the layout and content of Web pages.
Browsers read an HTML document and render the page on the screen as
they read it from left to right, top to bottom. The order or flow in which the
page is interpreted is fixed. HTML does not provide mechanisms to program
decisions, do computations, or alter the flow of rendering of a page.

Java, like many other programming languages, provides control mechanisms
to program decisions, evaluate expressions, and control the flow of execution,
among other things.

JSPs combine both HTML and Java languages into a powerful and easy way
to create dynamic Web pages. Examples throughout the book have shown
you JSP code that generates HTML content with embedded Java code. In
the last couple of hours I have covered embedded Java declarations and
expressions and their associated tags. You have seen how to declare Java
variables and methods, you have seen how to use these in expressions, and,
although not formally, you have seen examples of scriptlets.

In this chapter you will learn you how to

- Use scriptlets to control the flow of execution of a JSP
- Use selection control statements `if` and `switch` to program decision-making procedures
- Use iteration control statements `for` and `while` to handle individual elements of a set of data

Scriptlets

Scriptlets consist of embedded Java code within two special JSP tags, `<%` and `%>`. The Java code consists of a set of declarations, expressions, and statements that programmatically control the content of the JSP.

Scriptlets define the main thread of execution that controls the dynamic behavior of a Web page. When a JSP loads, execution begins with the first occurrence of a scriptlet. The scriptlet can then make use of declared variables and methods.

Java provides two flow control structures: selection and iteration.

Selection Control Structures

Selection control structures allow you to program or encode decisions when the JSP is executed. Decisions are programmed by evaluating Boolean expressions and then selecting a course of action based on the result. For instance, a JSP may evaluate whether a registered user is logged in or not and decide to welcome the user or demand that the user log in. There are two selection control structures available in Java: the `if` statement and the `switch` statement.

Using `if` Selection Statements

The `if` selection statement allows you to select different courses of action depending on the outcome of a Boolean conditional expression. `if` statements provide the basis for encoding a decision-making procedure. The syntax of an `if` statement is

```
if(booleanExpression)
  javaCodeBlock
```

If the *booleanExpression* evaluates to `true`, *javaCodeBlock* is executed. Otherwise execution continues after the *javaCodeBlock*. Boolean expressions can be combined with Boolean operators `&&` (and), `||` (or), and `!` (not). Listing 9.1 is a JSP that uses an `if` statement to print an appropriate message if a user is not logged on.

LISTING 9.1 Example of Using an `if` Statement (`ifStatement.jsp`)

```
 1: <HTML><HEAD><TITLE>Example Use of The if Statement</TITLE></HEAD>
 2: <BODY>
 3: <%  boolean userIsLogged = false;
 4:     boolean securityOn   = true;
 5:     if(!userIsLogged && securityOn) {%>
 6:        <H1>Warning</H1>
 7:        You have not yet logged onto the system.
 8:        <A>Please click here to log on</A>
 9: <%  }  %>
10: </BODY></HTML>
```

The actual code that would determine the real value of `userIsLogged` in Listing 9.1 would consist of some mechanism that compares the values of `username` and `password` of some user against some database. Databases will be covered in Hour 17, "Accessing a Database from a JSP."

An `if` statement can be followed by an optional `else` statement to choose between two possible actions depending on whether the Boolean expression is `true` or `false`. When an `else` statement accompanies an `if` statement, it is often referred to as an `if/else` statement. Here is the syntax of the `if/else` statement:

```
if(booleanExpression)
  javaCodeBlock1
else
  javaCodeBlock2
```

If the *booleanExpression* evaluates to `true` then *javaCodeBlock1* is executed, otherwise (else) *javaCodeBlock2* is executed and then execution continues after the `if/else` statement. Listing 9.2 is an example JSP that prints one of two messages depending on whether the user is logged in or not:

LISTING 9.2 Example of `if/else` Statement (`ifElseStatement.jsp`)

```
 1: <HTML><HEAD><TITLE>Example Use of The if/else Statement</TITLE></HEAD>
 2: <BODY>
 3: <%  boolean userIsLogged = true;
 4:     if(userIsLogged) { %>
 5:        <H1>Welcome</H1>
 6:        You have successfully logged onto the system.
 7:        Please click <A HREF=nowhere.html>here</A> to continue
 8: <%  } else { %>
 9:        <H1>Warning</H1>
10:        You have not yet logged onto the system.
11:        Please click <A HREF=nowhere.html>here</A> to log on
12: <%  }  %>
13: </BODY></HTML>
```

9

It is often necessary to chain a set of related if statements to choose from a long set of possible outcomes. The outcome of the decision depends on the result of comparing some data to an equally long set of possible values. This can be accomplished by chaining several else statements that start with an if statement. These are generally referred to as if/else if statements. Here is the syntax of such a statement:

```
if(booleanExpression1)
  javaCodeBlock1
else if(booleanExpression2)
  javaCodeBlock2
else if(booleanExpression3)
  javaCodeBlock3
...
else if(booleanExpressionN)
  javaCodeBlockN
else
  defaultJavaCodeBlock
```

The Boolean expressions in this syntax are typically several related comparisons of a particular variable against different value ranges (possible values) of the variable. The if/else statements create a mapping from the possible values of a variable to a corresponding code execution. Listing 9.3 is a JSP that shows different airfare prices depending on the age of a passenger. The output of the listing is shown in Figure 9.1.

LISTING 9.3 Example of if/else if Statement (ifElseIfStatement.jsp)

```
 1: <HTML><HEAD><TITLE>Example Use Of if/else if Statements</TITLE></HEAD>
 2: <BODY>
 3: <H1>Air fare cost is
 4: <%  int    passengerAge = 11;
 5:     double fullPrice = 123.45;
 6:     double discountPercent;
 7:     double finalPrice;
 8:     if(passengerAge <=2)
 9:       discountPercent = 90;
10:     else if(passengerAge <=12)
11:       discountPercent = 50;
12:     else
13:       discountPercent = 0;
14:     finalPrice = fullPrice - fullPrice * discountPercent / 100;
15: %> <%=finalPrice%>
16: </BODY></HTML>
```

ANALYSIS Listing 9.3 declares a chain of if statements in lines 8–13. The if statements compare the age of a passenger (passengerAge) against several values. The outcome of the comparisons is setting the value of the discount on the full price of a plane ticket, discountPercent. The default result of the if statements is the last else statement in lines 12 and 13, that is, if all other if statements fail, the last else statement will execute. The values of the passengerAge and the fullPrice are hard-coded in this example. In a working application these would be parameters dynamically read from a database or an HTML form filled out by the user. Databases and HTML forms are covered in Hour 10, "Processing Requests from the User."

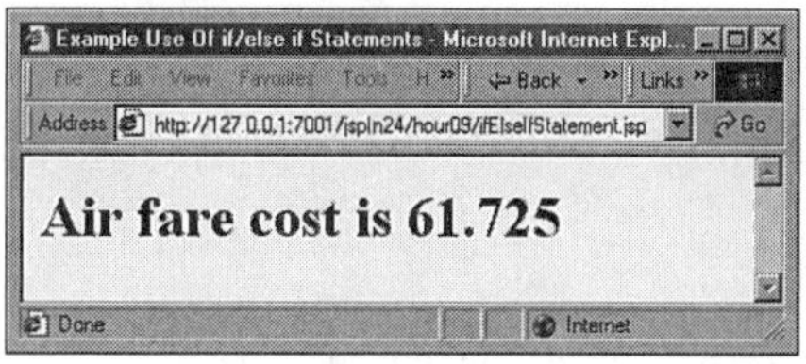

FIGURE 9.1

View the result of ifElseIfStatement. jsp *in a browser.*

Air fare cost is 61.725

Chained decisions are very common and can become somewhat awkward. The switch statement is a control statement specifically created to handle long decision chains.

Using switch Statements

A switch statement is an elegant version of a series of if/else if statements. Chained series of decisions occur so often that the scenario merits its own selection statement, the switch statement. The general syntax of a switch statement is as follows:

```
switch(argument){
   case value1 :
      javaCode1
   case value2 :
      javaCode2
   case value3 :
      javaCode3
   ...
   case valueN :
      javaCodeN
   default:
      javaCodeD
}
```

The *argument* to a switch statement must be an integer, a character, or an expression that evaluates to an integer or character.

The body of the switch statement consists of a series of case statements with their respective values. The values must be constant integer or constant character values. Each case statement is associated to a block of Java code.

The argument value is compared against each of the values in the case statements. If the values match, the Java code that follows the case statement up to the closing curly

bracket "}" is executed. If none of the values match, the optional default case is
executed. For instance, if the value of the argument matches value2, then the code
javaCode2, javaCode3, all the way to javaCodeD is executed. Listing 9.4 is an example
of using the switch statement; its output is shown in Figure 9.2.

LISTING 9.4   Example of switch Statement (switchStatement.jsp)

```
 1: <HTML><HEAD><TITLE>Example switch statement</TITLE></HEAD>
 2: <BODY>
 3: <% final int LOGGED_OFF=0, LOGGED_ON=1;
 4:    int userType=LOGGED_ON;
 5:    switch(userType){
 6:      case LOGGED_ON :    %>
 7:        <H1>Welcome !</H1>
 8:        You are now logged onto the system<BR>
 9:        You have access to the system
10: <%     break;
11:      case LOGGED_OFF :   %>
12:        <H1>Sorry !</H1>
13:        You need to log onto the system before<BR>
14:        granting you access to the system
15: <%     break;
16:      default:           %>
17:        <H1>Error !</H1>
18:        The system is unable to determine whether<BT>
19:        the user is logged on or not.
20: <%   }                  %>
21: </BODY></HTML>
```

ANALYSIS   The JSP in listing 9.4 uses a switch statement to decide between three possible
greetings based on whether the user accessing the page is logged in or not. The
JSP hard codes two state variables in line 3 as well as the login status of the user in line
4. In a working application these values would be gathered from some user session information stored either in a database or an object representing the user (not hard coded as
shown in the listing). The switch statement in line 5 takes the login status of the user as
an argument, and compares it to the state variables in the case statements in lines 6 and
11. If none of the case statements succeed then the default case statement in line 16 executes. If the value of userType is LOGGED_ON then the user is greeted positively. If the
value of userType is LOGGED_OFF then the user is greeted negatively. If neither, the JSP
prints an error message.

You might have expected that if the value of the argument matched value2, the code that
would be executed would be just javaCode2. Indeed, many programmers force this type of
behavior by "breaking" out of the switch statement at the end of the code of each of the
case statements. This is accomplished by using the break statement (line 15 in Listing 9.4).

FIGURE 9.2

Use your browser to view the output of the example JSP using switch *statements.*

Using the break Statement

The break statement is used to stop the flow of execution and jump to the end of a segment of code. You can use the break statement to change the behavior of the switch statement. One might expect that only the Java code block of the matching case statement would be executed when speculating the behavior of the switch statement, but this is not the case. Without a break statement at the end of each Java code block, all of the Java code blocks after the first case statement that match the value of the argument are executed. The following code snippet is the syntax of the switch statement with break statements added to the end of each Java code block. This forces execution to halt at the end of the Java code block of the case statement that matches the value of the argument. The break statement forces execution to continue after the switch statement, skipping any other Java code blocks that would be executed.

```
switch(argument){
  case value1 :
    javaCode1
    break;
  case value2 :
    javaCode2
    break;
  case value3 :
    javaCode3
    break;
  ...
  case valueN :
    javaCodeN
    break;
  default:
    javaCodeD
}
```

Now the switch statement behaves the way you might have expected.

break statements can be used anywhere you want to disrupt the normal flow of execution and jump out of the current code block to the containing code block.

The break statement can also be used to break out of iterative control structures like for and while loops to break out of the loop prematurely, as well as in selection statements

to break out of an if or switch statement and continue right after the conditional statement. You will see more examples of the break statement throughout this hour and the
rest of the book.

Iteration Control Structures

A common solution to a great many problems consists of repeatedly applying some
methodology to individual elements of an ordered data set. This action is called *iteration*.
As a simple example, consider the problem of computing the total of an invoice whose
items have an associated price. To compute the total you repeatedly accumulate the price
of each of the items one at a time. When you have iterated through each of the items, you
will have computed the total.

Java provides two basic types of iterative control structures. Their difference lies on
whether the limit of the iteration is a known fixed limit or a conditional limit. Although
each can be programmed to behave as the other, the syntax suggests their intended use.
The for loop is mainly used to iterate through a fixed set of elements. The while loop
and do/while loop are intended to iterate until a conditional statement determines the
end of the loop.

Using for Loops

for loops allow you to repeatedly execute a chunk of Java code a given number of times.
The for loop typically uses a variable to keep track of the progress of the iteration. The
variable is usually referred to as "the iteration variable" and the for loop "iterates over"
the variable. The for loop initializes the variable, repeatedly updates the value of the
variable at each iteration, and checks to see if its value has reached a specified bound.
The syntax of a for loop is the following:

```
for(initStatement; booleanExpression; updateExpression)
  javaCodeBlock
```

The *initStatement* is a statement used to initialize the iteration variable, such as j=0. At
the beginning of the iteration, the *booleanExpression* is evaluated. If the expression
evaluates to true, the *javaCodeBlock* is executed once. Otherwise execution continues
after the *javaCodeBlock*. The *javaCodeBlock* is referred to as the body of the for loop
and consists of an arbitrarily long set of Java declarations and statements that use the
iteration variable to reference a particular element of some ordered set or data. The
Boolean expression is usually used to determine whether the loop has reached its limit,
for example j<=10. After *booleanExpression* is evaluated, *updateExpression* is evaluated to update the value of the variable you are iterating on, which is j=j+1. Listing 9.5
is a simple example of a for loop that repeats an opinion of mine several times:

LISTING 9.5   A Simple `for` Loop (`forStatement.jsp`)

```
1: <HTML><HEAD><TITLE></TITLE></HEAD>
2: <BODY>
3: <%  int j;
4:     for(j=1; j<=10; j++) { %>
5:        JSPs are great !!! : <%=j%><BR>
6: <%  }  %>
7: </BODY></HTML>
```

ANALYSIS   The `for` loop initializes the iteration variable j to 1 in line 4. It then checks to see if the value of j is less than or equal to 10, which is true the first time around. The update of j is postponed until the end of the loop by using the post increment operator (j++). The first time around, j is 1 throughout the entire code block. At the end of the `for` loop, j is incremented to 2 and the loop is repeated. The second time around, j is not initialized but it is compared to 10 and incremented at the end of the loop. The loop then executes 10 times until j is equal to 10. The last time around, when j is equal to 10, j is incremented to 11 at the end of the loop and so the expression j<=10 is no longer true, and the loop ends.

The JSP in Listing 9.6 shows a more interesting example. The JSP prints out a table (shown in Figure 9.3) from an imaginary order. The order contains 4 fixed items.

LISTING 9.6   A JSP that Prints Out a Checkout Order (`checkoutOrder.jsp`)

```
 1: <HTML><HEAD><TITLE>Example using for loops</TITLE></HEAD>
 2: <BODY>
 3: <H1> Your Order: </H1>
 4: <%!  String[] items ={"Music CD", "Book", "Software", "Video"};
 5:      double[] prices={ 12.95,     6.90,   29.99,     17.97  };
 6:      double   total =0; %>
 7:      <TABLE BORDER=1 CELLSPACING=0 CELLPADDING=2>
 8:      <TR><TD>Item Name</TD>
 9:          <TD>Price</TD>
10:      </TR>
11: <%   for(int i=0; i<items.length; i++){%>
12:        <TR><TD><%= items[i]%></TD>
13:            <TD>$<%=prices[i]%></TD>
14:        </TR>
15: <%     total += prices[i];
16:      }  %>
17:      <TR><TD>Total</TD>
18:          <TD>$<%=total%></TD>
19:      </TR>
20: </TABLE>
21: </BODY></HTML>
```

ANALYSIS   In Listing 9.6, lines 4 and 5 declare arrays `items` and `prices`. The `for` loop in line 11 iterates through the arrays. The loop causes the code in lines 12–15 to execute several times. The code will execute exactly `items.length` times; that is, for the number of items in the items array. The loop inserts a table row with two columns for each iteration. One of the columns has the item name and the other has its price. The fixed portion of the table is declared around the `for` loop in lines 7–10 and lines 17–20. These fixed portions consist of a row of headings for the columns at the top and the last row that shows the total price summed up from all the items.

FIGURE 9.3

A table is generated by the `for` loop in Listing 9.6.

Your Order:

Item Name	Price
Music CD	$12.95
Book	$6.9
Software	$29.99
Video	$17.97
Total	$67.81

Arrays are a means for programming languages to manage a collection of items as one single entity, the array. The items of an array are usually of the same type. Each takes up the same amount of space in memory, and the amount of items is usually well known and fixed. Therefore the items are usually created or allocated contiguous to one another. The individual items are then accessed using an index number together with the name of the array, as in `myArray[i]`. Using arrays has its pros and cons. On the one hand, accessing items of an array is very fast, since their location in memory and space is very easy to predict. Changing the size of the array or the data type of items on the other hand is difficult, since this would complicate indexing. Arrays can be created from any data type by using the square brackets `[` and `]`. To declare an array, use the syntax

```
MyDataType[] myArray = new MyDataType[howManyItems];
```

where `howManyItems` is the number of contiguous elements of the same type in the array.

In the previous example the items and their prices are shown hard-coded to keep the example simple. In a more realistic scenario, this information would be dynamically read from a database. You will learn how to access a database from a JSP in Hour 17.

Using while Loops

Like for loops, while loops repeatedly execute the Java code in their bodies. Unlike for loops, while loops are not intended to iterate for a fixed amount of time but to loop as long as a certain Boolean condition holds true.

The syntax of a while loop is the following:

```
while(booleanExpression)
  javaCodeBlock
```

This can be read as "while booleanExpression is true, execute javaCodeBlock". The booleanExpression is an expression that evaluates to true or false. The javaCodeBlock is executed repeatedly as long as the booleanExpression evaluates to true. Otherwise execution continues after the while loop.

while loops are equivalent to the following for loop:

```
for(;booleanExpression;)
  javaCodeBlock
```

The reason to use a while loop instead of a for loop is that intuitively a for loop would want to go through the whole list of items, whereas the while loop searches the list until the item is found. The JSP in Listing 9.7 searches for an item, and Figure 9.4 shows the results of both a successful and a failed search.

LISTING 9.7   A JSP that Searches an Inventory for an Item (searchingWithWhile.jsp)

```
 1: <HTML><HEAD><TITLE>Example using while loops</TITLE></HEAD>
 2: <BODY>
 3: <%!  String[] itemsInInventory  = {"qwe123", "asd234", "zxc456", "fgh567",
 4:                 "cvb789", "hjk345", "sdf765", "jhg432", "fgh876", "hgf234"};
 5:      String   itemBeingSearched = "hjk345";
 6:      boolean  found = false;
 7:      int      foundIndex = -1;  %>
 8: <H1>Searching for <%=itemBeingSearched%> in database:
 9: </H1>
10: <UL>
11: <%   int i=0;
12:      while(!found && i<itemsInInventory.length){%>
13:        <LI> Searching index <%= i %>: <%= itemsInInventory[i] %>
14: <%      if(itemsInInventory[i] == itemBeingSearched){
15:          found = true;
16:          foundIndex = i;
17:        }
18:        i++;
19:      }  %>
20: </UL>
21: <H2>
22: <%    if(found){   %>
```

LISTING 9.7   continued

```
23:        Found at index = <%=foundIndex%>
24: <%  } else {    %>
25:        Sorry, <%=itemBeingSearched%> not found in database
26: <%  }           %>
27: </H2>
28: </BODY></HTML>
```

ANALYSIS Lines 3 and 4 declare a string array representing the IDs of items in an inventory. Line 5 declares the ID of the item you are looking for. The found flag is initialized to false and the index to -1 (not found) in lines 6 and 7. The while loop in line 12 declares that the search should continue as long as the item has not been found (!found) and (&&) the end of the array has not been reached (i<itemsInInventory.length). The integer i is used as the current index to the array of items; that is, itemsInInventory[i] references the current item. Line 13 prints each item searched as an unnumbered HTML list (<UL>, <LI>, and </UL>). Line 14 checks to see if the ID of the current item is the same as the one being searched for. If so, the found flag is raised to true, and the index at which you found the item is recorded. Otherwise index i is incremented in line 18 and the while loop goes on to the next item through the loop. If the found flag is raised, it causes the while loop to end and terminate the search. On the other hand, if the item is not found, the while loop will go through all the items until index i is no longer within the range of the array. In any case the reason for the termination of the loop is checked in line 22. If the loop terminated because found is true, a success message is printed along with the index at which the item was found. Otherwise, a failure message is printed.

FIGURE 9.4

Different messages are printed for successful and failed searches.

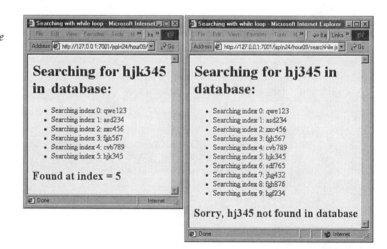

Using the `continue` Statement

The `continue` statement is a close relative of the `break` statement. It is used only in iteration loops. Like the `break` statement, `continue` is used to break the normal flow of execution by jumping to the end of the block of code it is in. Unlike the `break` statement, the `continue` statement does not leave the block; rather, it forces a new iteration. Listing 9.8 is an example JSP that illustrates the use of the `continue` statement.

LISTING 9.8   Using the `continue` Statement (`continueStatement.jsp`)

```
 1: <HTML><HEAD><TITLE>The continue Statement</TITLE></HEAD>
 2: <BODY>
 3: <%  for(int j=0; j<20; j++){
 4:         if(isEven(j)) continue;
 5: %>      j=<%=j%>
 6: <%  }   %>
 7: <%! boolean isEven(int j){
 8:         if(Math.IEEEremainder(j,2)==0)
 9:           return true;
10:         return false;
11:     }  %>
12: </BODY></HTML>
```

The code in Listing 9.8 prints out all of the odd numbers between 0 and 20. The `IEEEremainder` method of the `Math` class returns the remainder of dividing the first argument by the second. If the remainder of dividing j by 2 is equal to zero, then j must be even. If j is even, the `if` statement executes a `continue` statement that forces the iteration to start over without printing the value of j. That is, only when j is odd will its value be printed to the Web page.

> The `Math` class used is part of the standard set of classes that make up the Java Development Kit or JDK. The JDK contains several packages that categorize these classes according to their functionality. All fundamental classes that constitute the Java language itself is the `java.lang` package of which `Math` is part. So the full name of the class is `java.lang.Math`.

New Term: Packages

A package is a logical and hierarchical organization of classes according to their functionality. Some of the packages that Sun Microsystems distribute with their JDK include `java.net`, for network functionality; `java.io`, for input/output and `java.awt`, for graphical user interface. Packages use a dot (.) notation to organize the names used to name the

9

packages. The dots are synonymous to the slash (/) or backslash (\) character used in determining a path of a file or directory in a computer's directory structure. Classes that belong to a package must declare so at the beginning of their source using the package keyword. For instance the Math class declares that it is part of the java.lang package, with the statement package java.lang; at the beginning of its source. To organize the packages not only logically but also physically, Java imposes the convention that a compiled class belonging to a package must be in a directory structure that parallels the package name. For instance the compiled class for Math, Math.class, must be in a directory called java\lang\ in Windows or java/lang/ in Unix. The full name of the class is used to search for the class in the appropriate directory. The starting point of where to start the search for a class is determined by the CLASSPATH environment variable. The CLASSPATH must contain all the directories that can be searched for classes using their full name. So if the Math class is in directory d:\myJdk\classes\java\lang\Math.class then the directory d:\myJdk\classes must be listed in the CLASSPATH. The full name of the class, java.lang.Math will be used to search for the class starting at the classes directory.

Using do/while Loops

The do/while loop is very similar to the while loop. Like the while loop, do/while allows you to define conditional iterations of a block of Java code. Unlike the while loop, do/while loops check whether to continue looping at the end of the loop instead of at the beginning of the loop. This is quite useful when the iteration should normally execute at least once. The syntax of the do/while loop is

```
do
   javaCodeBlock
while(booleanExpression)
```

The code javaCodeBlock executes at least once before the booleanExpression is evaluated. If booleanExpression evaluates to true, the loop is repeated until it evaluates to false. The example in Listing 9.9 uses a do/while loop to implement a popular sorting algorithm called Quicksort. The JSP sorts some imaginary search results based on an imaginary level of confidence. Figure 9.5 shows the resulting sorted list.

LISTING 9.9   Sorting with the while and do/while Statements (sortingWithDoWhile.jsp)

```
1: <HTML><HEAD><TITLE>Quicksorting with the do/while loop</TITLE></HEAD>
2: <BODY>
3: <%! void quickSort(String[] titles, int[] conf, int p, int r){
4:       if(p<r){
5:          int q = partition(titles, conf, p, r);
6:          quickSort(titles, conf, p,   q);
7:          quickSort(titles, conf, q+1, r);
8:       }
```

LISTING 9.9   continued

9

```
 9:    }
10:
11:    int partition(String[] titles, int[] conf, int p, int r){
12:      int x = conf[p];
13:      int i = p - 1;
14:      int j = r + 1;
15:      while(true){
16:        do{
17:          j = j - 1;
18:        } while(conf[j]>x);
19:        do{
20:          i = i + 1;
21:        } while(conf[i]<x);
22:        if(i < j){
23:          String temp1 = titles[i];
24:          titles[i] = titles[j];
25:          titles[j] = temp1;
26:          int temp2 = conf[i];
27:          conf[i] = conf[j];
28:          conf[j] = temp2;
29:        } else {
30:          return j;
31:        }
32:      }
33:    }
34: %>
35:
36: <% String[] searchResultTitles =       { "Teach Yourself Internet Game
37:                                           Programming With Java In 21 Days",
38:                                          "Teach Yourself Java In 21 Days",
39:                                          "Graphic Java, Mastering The AWT",
40:                                          "Ready-To-Run Java 3D",
41:                                          "Advanced Java Networking",
42:                                          "Java Network Programming" };
43:    int[]    searchResultConfidence = { 23,
44:                                          56,
45:                                          27,
46:                                          67,
47:                                          34,
48:                                          78    };
49:    quickSort(searchResultTitles, searchResultConfidence, 0, 5); %>
50:    <H1>Search result sorted by confidence factor:</H1><BR>
51: <% for(int j=searchResultTitles.length-1; j>=0; j--){  %>
52:      <%= searchResultConfidence[j] %>% --
53:      <%= searchResultTitles[j] %><BR>
54: <%  }  %>
55: </BODY></HTML>
```

ANALYSIS The details of how the Quicksort algorithm works is beyond the scope of this book, but here are the basics. Execution of the JSP code begins with the scriptlet in line 36. Two arrays are declared to hold the results of some query. One of them holds the titles and the other the confidence factors, from 0 to 100%, for each of the results. The confidence factor is a measurement of how certain the search engine is in finding matches for item queries. These would of course be generated as a result of some dynamic query or search from a database (see Hour 17). Both arrays are passed to a method called quickSort(), which takes as arguments both arrays and two indices. The indices are referred as p and q from within the quickSort() method declared in lines 3–9. They refer to the portion of the arrays that must be sorted, so for the first pass these are 0 and 5 (6 elements). When quickSort is done, the arrays are sorted from least to maximum confidence, and the for loop in line 51 prints them in reverse order. As for the quickSort() method, it repeatedly splits the arrays in two by calling the partition() method, which returns the index q where the split should occur. When the array can't be split any further (r>=p in quickSort()), the arrays have been sorted in ascending order. The sorting is accomplished in partition() by choosing a pivot point, that is, an arbitrary index of the array. The partition() method exchanges the elements of the array so that all elements less than the pivot element are to the left of the pivot and all those that are greater than the pivot are to the right of the pivot. Hence the pivot is in the correct ascending order. And since all possible pivot points are eventually chosen when quickSort() partitions the array, and all pivot points are in their correct ascending order at the end of a call to partition(), the array is therefore sorted when the arrays can't be partitioned any further.

FIGURE 9.5

sortingWithDoWhile. jsp *produces a list of items sorted with the Quicksort algorithm implemented with* while *and* do/while *loops.*

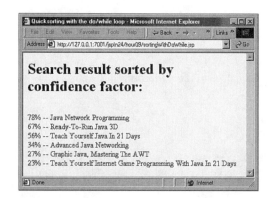

Quicksort is one of the fastest sorting algorithms. For a more in-depth analysis of this and other interesting algorithms, refer to *Introduction to Algorithms* by Thomas H. Cormen, Charles E. Leiserson, and Ronald L. Rivest.

Summary

In this hour you were introduced to Java scriptlets and how they can be used to declare the main thread of execution. You used scriptlets to employ the selection control structures if and switch. You also learned how to use the iterative control structures for loops and while loops. Finally you learned how to use the break and continue statements to alter the normal flow of execution.

9

Workshop

The quiz questions and activities are provided for your further understanding. See Appendix A, "Answers," for the answers to the quiz.

Quiz

1. What are the differences and similarities of the break and continue statements?

2. How would you implement a for loop using a while loop?

Activity

Add a "Quantity" column to the order table of Listing 9.6. The total should be the summation of the multiplication of the item dollar value and the item quantity.

HOUR 10

Processing Requests from the User

In this hour you will learn how to gather and process user requests. User requests consist of messages that contain information that can be gathered about users and their interaction with the browser. Requests are generated by the browser and sent to the JSP for processing as a result of actions taken by users as they interact with their browser—for example, clicking a hyperlink or submitting a form. The information in a request contains information about the user, the remote and local machine, HTTP headers, the invoking URL, hard-coded parameters in the Web page, and HTML form fields. All this information is accessible by the JSP through the implicit request object when the JSP is invoked.

First, you will learn the details of how requests are represented and how they are created. The information contained in a request is categorized, and then you see the API used to access the information. You will also learn how to process the invoking URL and extract path information. Next, you'll see how to obtain meta information about the request itself and the machines involved in the request. Finally, you will look at how to use HTML forms to generate and process requests with parameters.

This hour covers:

- Understanding the `ServletRequest` and `HttpServletRequest` interfaces and the implicit JSP `request` object
- Creating a request
- Parsing the invoking URL
- Obtaining server information
- Creating and parsing a query string
- Declaring HTML forms
- Processing HTML forms

Understanding User Requests

A user request consists of information that a client provides to a JSP. As you may remember from Hour 3, "Introduction to Servlets," user requests are represented in a JSP by two interfaces: `ServletRequest` and `HttpServletRequest`.

The `ServletRequest` interface models user requests that do not depend on the underlying protocol or infrastructure used to communicate the requests. The functionality provided by the `ServletRequest` interface includes

- Providing access to attributes and parameters
- Obtaining information about the remote and local machines and protocol being used
- Obtaining information about the content of the request

`ServletRequest` attributes are usually used when redirecting a request to another JSP in conjunction with the `RequestDispatcher` interface. Attributes and the `RequestDispatcher` interface are covered in Hour 20, "Using Multiple JSPs to Handle the Request."

The `HttpServletRequest` interface extends `ServletRequest`, adding functionality that assumes the underlying use of the Hypertext Transfer Protocol (HTTP). The `HttpServletRequest` interface adds the following functionality:

- Provides access to HTTP headers
- Provides access to user session information with cookies, URL encoding, and the `HttpSession` interface
- Allows parsing the invoking URL
- Allows managing user security

From within a JSP, the implicit `request` object implements the `HttpServletRequest` interface. The JSP uses the `request` object to obtain information from the browser, cookies, headers, and user session.

HTTP headers and user session management are covered in Hour 11, "Generating a Dynamic Response for the User," and Hour 12, "Keeping Track of the User Session."

The following sections explain how a request is generated from a user interaction with a browser. The URL generated by the browser will be dissected and several methods will be introduced for obtaining information about the invoking URL, the remote and local machines. Then you will see how to include arguments or parameters in a request and how to process them. Finally, HTML forms are introduced to gather information from the user and JSP code is shown for processing the information.

Creating User Requests

A request contains information that is passed from a user to a JSP. Part of the process of generating a request is to declare or generate a URL that represents the invocation of the JSP. It is useful to first describe the different parts of a URL and its syntax.

10

The Anatomy of a URL

A URL has the following general syntax:

`protocol://host:port/virtualPath?queryString`

- *protocol*—Declares the underlying mechanisms for transferring information between remote machines. Valid protocols include `http`, `https`, `ftp`, `rmi`, and `corba`. For the purpose of this book, you will be using the `http` protocol.

- *host*—Identifies the remote machine name or IP address of the machine to which the request will be forwarded.

- *port*—Declares the machine port number on which the host server machine will be listening for requests. For the `http` protocol the port is usually 80, and it is the default value if you leave out this parameter. In this section you will be using WLS as the server, and it is usually configured to listen to port 7001.

- *virtualPath*—Contains a set of identifiers delimited by the slash character (/) that is used by the server to map to a physical path and the location of the JSP.

- *extraPathInformation*—The *virtualPath* may optionally contain several identifiers that don't map to any physical path. The identifiers can serve as an argument to the JSP to configure its behavior.

- *queryString*—A list of name/value pairs passed to the JSP as an argument.

The following is an example of a URL that invokes a JSP with a query string:

`http://alice:7001/myJSPs/hour10/request.jsp?p1=val1&p2=val2`

The virtual path in the preceding URL is everything after the port declaration and before the query string:

```
myJSPs/hour10/request.jsp
```

The query string is everything after the question mark (?):

```
p1=val1&p2=val2
```

The query string is a list of name/value pairs delimited by an ampersand character (&). The query string can be thought of as an argument list that gets passed to the target JSP very much like a function call.

Generating Requests with a Hyperlink

The browser generates requests when a user either clicks a hyperlink or submits an HTML form. HTML forms are covered at the end of this hour. Let's concentrate on the easier way of generating a request—with a hyperlink. The HTML code shown in Listing 10.1 declares a hyperlink.

LISTING 10.1 Declaration of a Hyperlink with a Hard-Coded Query String (request.html)

```
1: <HTML>
2: <HEAD><TITLE>Request JSP</TITLE>
3: <BODY>
4: Click
5: <A HREF="request.jsp?p1=v1&p2=v2">here</A>
6: to send a request to the JSP
7: </BODY>
8: </HTML>
```

When the user clicks the Here hyperlink, the browser generates a request that is forwarded to request.jsp. The JSP will have access to the information in the request through the implicit request object. First you will learn how the JSP can use the request object to get information about the invoking URL, the server machines, and ports. Then you will see how to process query strings and how they can be used with HTML forms.

 Requests generated by hyperlinks are static requests; that is, they are hard-coded at development time in a static URL. Requests generated by HTML forms are dynamic in the sense that the developer provides the user with fields that the user fills out. When the form is submitted, the URL is generated with the values of the fields set by the user; that is, the URL is not hard-coded—it is created dynamically at runtime when the form is submitted.

Extracting Path and URL Information

The request object provides methods to process the different parts of the URL used to invoke the JSP. Table 10.1 lists the methods and a brief description.

TABLE 10.1   Path- and URL-Related Methods

Method	Description
String getPathInfo()	Returns portion of the URL after the name of the Servlet and before the query string
String getPathTranslated()	Converts the URL to a physical path location of the JSP
String getContextPath()	Returns portion of the URL that indicates the context of the request
String getQueryString()	Returns portion of the URL following the question mark (?)
String getRequestURI()	Returns portion of the URL from the protocol name up to the query string. Depends on method POST or GET

10

The JSP in Listing 10.2 declares a link that points to the JSP itself. When the user clicks the link, the browser creates a request and invokes the JSP in the URL. The JSP uses request object's several methods to print out different portions of the URL.

LISTING 10.2   A JSP that Uses Path- and URL-Related Methods (pathInformation.jsp)

```
 1: <HTML>
 2: <HEAD><TITLE>Path Related Request Methods</TITLE>
 3: <BODY>
 4: Click
 5: <A HREF="pathInformation.jsp">here</A>
 6: to send a request to the JSP <BR>
 7:   getPathInfo()       = <%= request.getPathInfo() %>        <BR>
 8:   getPathTranslated() = <%= request.getPathTranslated() %><BR>
 9:   getContextPath()    = <%= request.getContextPath() %>     <BR>
10:   getQueryString()    = <%= request.getQueryString() %>     <BR>
11:   getRequestURI()     = <%= request.getRequestURI() %>      <BR>
12:   getServletPath()    = <%= request.getServletPath() %>     <BR>
13: </BODY>
14: </HTML>
```

Figure 10.1 shows the output generated by the JSP after the user has clicked the hyperlink here.

FIGURE 10.1

This JSP uses path- and URL-related methods of the request *object.*

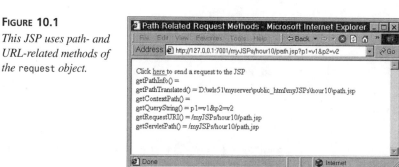

Extracting Host and Port Information

The request object provides methods to obtain some information about the machine from which the request originated, as well as to determine some meta information about the request itself. This information can be used to implement some simple security policies that consider the originating host as a safe machine. Table 10.2 lists methods useful for determining machine and request information.

TABLE 10.2 Machine-Related Methods of the Request Object

Method	Description
String getRemoteAddr()	Returns the IP address of the client machine that generated the request; for example, 127.0.0.1
String getRemoteHost()	Returns the name of the machine of the client that generated the request; for example, whiterabbit
String getServerName()	Returns the name of the local server that received the request; for example, alice
int getServerPort()	Returns the port number that the local server is listening to for incoming requests from client machines; for example, 7001
String getScheme()	Returns the name of the scheme used to create the request; for example, HTTP, HTTPS, or FTP
String getProtocol()	Returns the name and version of the protocol used to communicate the request; for example, HTTP/1.1
String getMethod()	Returns the name of HTTP method with which the request was made; for example, GET, POST, or PUT
String getCharacterEncoding()	Returns the character encoding of body of the request; for example, Cp1252
boolean isSecure()	Returns whether request was made through a secure channel such as HTTPS
int getContentLength()	Returns the length of the body in bytes
String getContentType()	Returns the MIME type of the body

To illustrate the use of the methods listed in the preceding table, the JSP in Listing 10.3 uses all the methods to determine where the request came from and how long it is, among other things.

LISTING 10.3   A JSP That Uses Machine and Request-Related Methods (machineInformation.jsp)

```
 1: <HTML>
 2: <HEAD><TITLE>Host Machines Related Request Methods</TITLE>
 3: <BODY>
 4: Click
 5: <A HREF="machineInformation.jsp"> here </A>
 6: to send a request to the JSP <BR>
 7:    getRemoteAddr()       = <%= request.getRemoteAddr() %>        <BR>
 8:    getRemoteHost()       = <%= request.getRemoteHost() %>        <BR>
 9:    getScheme()           = <%= request.getScheme() %>           <BR>
10:    getProtocol()         = <%= request.getProtocol() %>         <BR>
11:    getMethod()           = <%= request.getMethod() %>           <BR>
12:    getCharacterEncoding() = <%= request.getCharacterEncoding() %><BR>
13:    isSecure()            = <%= request.isSecure() %>            <BR>
14:    getContentLength()    = <%= request.getContentLength() %>    <BR>
15:    getContentType()      = <%= request.getContentType() %>      <BR>
16:    getServerName()       = <%= request.getServerName() %>       <BR>
17:    getServerPort()       = <%= request.getServerPort() %>       <BR>
18: </BODY>
19: </HTML>
```

When the user clicks the Here hyperlink, the JSP generates the HTML page shown in Figure 10.2.

FIGURE 10.2

A JSP that uses server- and request-related methods produces this page.

Parsing Parameters in the Query String

User requests cancontain a list of name/value pairs as an argument to the JSP being invoked. Each of the arguments in the argument list is referred to as a *parameter*. Parameters are passed as part of the URL that invokes the JSP. This is accomplished by declaring a query string by appending a question mark (?) after the JSP invocation and then an ampersand-delimited parameter list. The general syntax of a URL for invoking a JSP with an argument list is the following:

URL?queryString

where *queryString* has the following syntax:

```
name1=value1[,value2,...valueN1][&name2=value1[,value2,...valueN2]]
```

Notice that the [value2,...valueN1] part in the preceding code means that optionally a parameter can have more than one value. Also notice that each name/value pair is delimited by ampersands (&) and the question mark denotes the beginning of the parameter list.

The following is an example of a JSP being passed through two parameters, lastName and firstName, with their respective values, Doe and John:

```
http://alice:7001/myJSP/hour10/name.jsp?lastName=Doe&firstName=John
```

Multivalued parameters are declared by providing several values delimited by commas for a given parameter. For instance, the following example assigns three values for the parameter named colors:

```
http://localhost:7001/myJSPs/hour10/myFlag.jsp?
       colors=yellow&color=blue&color=red&country=venezuela
```

The parameter list is passed to a JSP within the HttpServletRequest object, and it is made available to a JSP through the standard JSP request object. The request object provides three methods to access parameters passed to it. These are

- String getParameter(String *paramName*)—Returns the value of a parameter named *paramName*.
- Enumeration getParameterNames()—Returns all the parameter names as an enumeration of String objects. You can then navigate the enumeration extracting each String object. The extracted String can then be used as an argument to getParameter(String) method to retrieve the value of the parameter.
- String() getParameterValues(String *paramName*)—Returns all the values of a multivalued parameter.

To illustrate the process of passing to and processing parameters from a JSP, create a simple HTML page that invokes a JSP with some parameters; then the JSP just prints out the parameters and their values. Listing 10.4 shows the HTML page that invokes the JSP.

LISTING 10.4 An HTML Page That Generates a Request with Parameters in the Query String (myFlag.html)

```
1: <HTML>
2: <HEAD> <TITLE> Link Invoking a JSP with parameters </TITLE> </HEAD>
3: <BODY>
4: <A HREF="myFlag.jsp?country=venezuela&
5:    &colors=yellow&colors=blue&colors=red">Invoke myFlag.jsp</A>
6: </BODY>
7: </HTML>
```

When the user clicks the link Invoke JSP, parameters country and colors will be bundled into an HttpServletRequest object and made available to the JSP through the request object. The JSP can then access the parameters and their values by using the request object methods. Listing 10.5 shows a JSP that processes the parameters using the getParameter() and getParameterValues() methods.

LISTING 10.5 A JSP that Processes Parameters (myFlag.jsp)

```
1: <HTML>
2: <HEAD> <TITLE> JSP that processes parameters in a link </TITLE> </HEAD>
3: <BODY>
4: Parameters
5: <UL>
6: <LI>Country = <%= request.getParameter("country") %>
7: <LI>Colors:
8:    <UL>
9:    <%! String[] colorValues = request.getParameterValues("colors"); %>
10:   <LI> Color 1 = <%= colorValues[0]%>
11:   <LI> Color 2 = <%= colorValues[1]%>
12:   <LI> Color 3 = <%= colorValues[2]%>
13:   </UL>
14: </UL>
15: </BODY>
16: </HTML>
```

Using HTML Forms

Requests generated by hyperlinks have the query string hard-coded at development time using the anchor tag <A>. HTML forms allow you to create a URL with a query string generated dynamically when the user submits the form. The names and values of the query string are extracted from the form, and the name/value pair list is generated and appended to the URL.

HTML forms provide several types of graphical user interface (GUI) components that serve as fields you can use to create forms for the user to fill out and then submit to a JSP for processing. HTML forms are the topic of books that cover HTML in general, and so here I will just remind you of the essentials.

Forms are declared using the FORM HTML tag as follows:

```
<FORM ACTION="action" METHOD=method>
...form GUI elements...
</FORM>
```

The ACTION parameter of the FORM tag declares the action to be taken when the form is submitted. For JSPs, you use the URL of the JSP to be invoked. A query string is appended to the URL. The names and values of the name/value pairs in the query string are created dynamically from the names of the GUI elements and the input the user fills out in the form.

The METHOD parameter of the FORM tag declares the HTTP method used to post the request to the JSP. The value for the METHOD parameter can be either GET, POST, or PUT. For JSPs, use the POST method.

Within the form tags, you can declare any number of form elements by using the HTML tags INPUT, TEXTAREA, and SELECT. The simplified syntax for the INPUT tag is

```
<INPUT TYPE=type NAME=name VALUE=defaultValue>
```

The TYPE parameter of the INPUT form element allows you to choose from one of several input types. These can be any of the following: TEXT, CHECKBOX, RADIO, IMAGE, RESET, and SUBMIT. Although the names for the TYPE parameter are self-explanatory, you might want to refer to *Sams Teach Yourself Web Publishing with HTML 4 in 21 Days, Professional Reference Edition*, by Laura Lemay (ISBN 0672318385),for full coverage of these form elements.

The syntax for the TEXTAREA tag is

```
<TEXTAREA NAME=name ROWS=rows COLS=columns VALUE=defaultText>
```

The TEXTAREA tag declares just that—a text area where the user has several rows to type. The value of this tag is the text the user types.

The SELECT tag declares a list of options from which the user can choose either one or multiple options. The value of this tag is the option selected by the user. Here is the syntax of the SELECT tag:

```
<SELECT NAME=name [SIZE=size MULTIPLE]>
  <OPTION [SELECTED]>option</OPTION>
  ...
```

```
<OPTION [SELECTED]>option</OPTION>
</SELECT>
```

Notice that each of the form elements has a parameter called NAME. Also, each of the form elements has a value associated with it that is either set by the users when they fill out the form elements or by the developer with a default value set by the VALUE parameter. The names and values associated with the fields are used to construct the query string.

All forms must declare a Submit button that informs the browser that the form has been filled and that the JSP should be invoked with the URL specified in the FORM tag's ACTION parameter. To declare the Submit button, you use the INPUT tag with the TYPE parameter set to SUBMIT. Listing 10.6 shows a simple HTML form that declares two text fields and a submit button and is shown in Figure 10.3.

LISTING 10.6   A Simple Form (simpleForm.html)

```
 1: <HTML>
 2: <HEAD><TITLE>A Simple Form</TITLE></HEAD>
 3: <BODY>
 4: <FORM ACTION="simpleForm.jsp" METHOD=POST>
 5:   Last Name:  <INPUT TYPE=TEXT NAME=lastName  VALUE="Shakespeare"> <BR>
 6:   First Name: <INPUT TYPE=TEXT NAME=firstName VALUE="William"> <BR>
 7:   <INPUT TYPE=SUBMIT VALUE="Click here to submit">
 8: </FORM>
 9: </BODY>
10: </HTML>
```

FIGURE 10.3

View your simple form in a browser.

If the user clicks the Submit button without editing the fields (leaving the default values), the browser invokes the JSP called simpleForm.jsp using the following URL:

```
simpleForm.jsp?lastName=Shakespeare&firstName=William
```

Of course, if the user types something else into the fields, the URL reflects the values of the fields with whatever was typed into the fields.

The query string is packaged into a request and shipped off to the JSP. The JSP is able to process the request with the request object and parse the parameters in the query string as described in the section "Parsing Parameters in the Query String," earlier in this hour.

An HTML Form and JSP That Process Credit Card Information

To illustrate how to process forms with a JSP, it's time to develop a form that accepts credit card information and is then submitted to a JSP. The JSP will process the form data and create a page that contains the information the user submitted for confirmation.

Figure 10.4 shows the form that you are going to create.

FIGURE 10.4

Create a form for gathering credit card information.

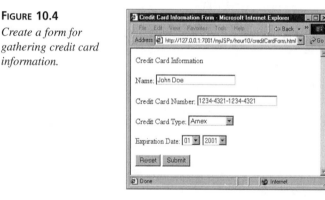

Although you can add a lot of HTML code to make the form look more appealing, the code in Listing 10.7 is stripped to the bare minimum to make it easier to understand how to generate the form in Figure 10.4.

LISTING 10.7   HTML Code That Declares Form for Submitting Credit Card Information (creditCardForm.html)

```
1: <HTML>
2: <HEAD><TITLE>Credit Card Information Form</TITLE></HEAD>
3: <BODY>
4: <FORM ACTION="creditCardForm.jsp"
5:       METHOD="POST">
6: Credit Card Information
7: <P> Name: <INPUT TYPE="TEXT" NAME="name" SIZE="25">
8: <P> Credit Card Number: <INPUT TYPE="TEXT" NAME="number" SIZE="25">
9: <P> Credit Card Type:
10:    <SELECT NAME="type">
11:      <OPTION>Visa</OPTION>
```

LISTING 10.7 continued

```
12:        <OPTION>Master Card</OPTION>
13:        <OPTION SELECTED>Amex</OPTION>
14:      </SELECT>
15: <P> Expiration Date:
16:      <SELECT NAME="month">
17:        <OPTION SELECTED>01</OPTION>   <OPTION>02</OPTION>
18:        <OPTION>03</OPTION>            <OPTION>04</OPTION>
19:        <OPTION>05</OPTION>            <OPTION>06</OPTION>
20:        <OPTION>07</OPTION>            <OPTION>08</OPTION>
21:        <OPTION>09</OPTION>            <OPTION>10</OPTION>
22:        <OPTION>11</OPTION>            <OPTION>12</OPTION>
23:      </SELECT>
24:      <SELECT NAME="year">
25:        <OPTION>2000</OPTION> <OPTION SELECTED>2001</OPTION>
26:        <OPTION>2002</OPTION> <OPTION>2003</OPTION>
27:        <OPTION>2004</OPTION> <OPTION>2005</OPTION>
28:      </SELECT>
29: <P>
30:      <INPUT TYPE="RESET"  NAME="Reset"  VALUE="Reset">
31:      <INPUT TYPE="SUBMIT" NAME="Submit" VALUE="Submit"></TD>
32: </FORM>
33: </BODY>
34: </HTML>
```

ANALYSIS Line 4 declares the form and configures it so that it will be submitted to `processCreditCard.jsp` using the POST method. Lines 7 and 8 declare two input fields for the user to type in the name on the credit card and the credit card number. Lines 9 through 14 declare a pull-down list for choosing the type of the card. "Amex" card type is selected as the default. In a similar fashion, lines 15 through 28 declare two pull-down lists that allow the user to select the expiration month and year. The default values are 01 for the month and 2001 for the year. Finally, lines 30 and 31 declare a pair of buttons for resetting and submitting the form. Resetting the form clears all fields and sets their default values (if any). The Submit button creates the query string from the names and values of the form elements and appends it to the URL declared in the ACTION parameter of the FORM tag.

> Notice that although two INPUT fields of TYPE=TEXT are declared in lines 7 and 8, they are differentiated by the NAME parameter. The field for the name of the cardholder has NAME set to "name" and the credit card number field has NAME set to "number." These parameters allow you to look up the values of these INPUT fields by the given "name" and "number" and retrieve the value that the user types in these fields. The same holds for the SELECT form elements.

Now you are going to write the JSP that processes the form. The names of the fields being submitted are name, number, type, month, and year. You can get a hold of the values of the parameters by passing the names of the parameters to the `getParameter()` method of the `request` object. Listing 10.8 is the JSP code.

LISTING 10.8 JSP Code that Processes Form that Gathers Credit Card Information (`creditCardForm.jsp`)

```
1: <HTML>
2: <HEAD> <TITLE>Credit Card Processing JSP</TITLE>
3: </HEAD>
4: <BODY>
5:    Verify Credit Card Information:
6: <UL>
7:    <LI>Name   = <%= request.getParameter("name") %>
8:    <LI>Number = <%= request.getParameter("number") %>
9:    <LI>Type   = <%= request.getParameter("type") %>
10:   <LI>Date   = <%= request.getParameter("month") %>/
11:              <%= request.getParameter("year")%>
12: </UL>
13: </BODY>
14: </HTML>
```

When the user submits the form, the JSP generates the HTML page shown in Figure 10.5.

FIGURE 10.5

The simple credit-card processing JSP generates this page.

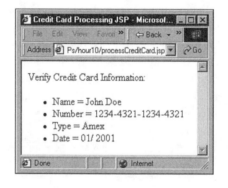

In a real production environment where real credit cards were being processed there would be several security issues that would need to be considered. For one, your application server should support encryption of any sensible information to deter snooping.

Summary

In this hour you learned how to generate and process requests with JSPs. You first took a look at what requests are and how the browser generates them. Then you dissected the different parts of a URL used to invoke a JSP. Next, you learned different methods for processing information about the path, the URL, the machines, and the request. Finally, you saw how to use HTML forms to dynamically create query strings and how to process forms.

Q&A

Q Can JSPs share the request from a browser?

A JSPs can share the request object by forwarding it to other JSPs, as well as with included JSPs. Hour 20, "Using Multiple JSPs to Handle the Request." will show you how a JSP can include and share the request with the included JSPs.

Q The query string in the request is just a list of name/value pairs. This seems to have its limitations on what can be passed around between browsers and JSPs, or even between JSPs. Is there a way to overcome this limitation?

A Yes, a limitation exists in the amount and type of data that browsers and JSPs send to each other. The limitation is imposed by HTTP. Once you extract the parameters and their values, you can create objects that represent the data in an object-oriented form. These objects can then be stored permanently in hard drives, or temporarily in a user session to be shared between JSPs and other server side application components. Once the request parameters have been converted into objects, the limitation disappears on the server side.

Q HTML FORMS are great for gathering lots of information, but processing all those parameters and their values as strings seems to have its drawbacks. Is there a more appropriate way of processing HTML FORMS?

A Yes there is. You can create a JavaBean that has class variables with the same names as the parameter names and then use the special tag `<jsp:setProperty property="*">` to automatically initialize the class variables of the JavaBean. Hour 16, "Using JavaBeans in a JSP" covers JavaBeans in detail.

Workshop

The quiz questions and activities are provided for your further understanding. See Appendix A, "Answers," for the answers to the quiz.

10

Quiz

1. What are the methods used to process parameters in a query string?

2. What are the different parts of a URL?

3. When is a request generated and how can the JSP process it?

Activities

1. The JSPs that you have seen in this hour assume that the names of the parameters in a query string are well known. It is often useful to have a JSP that can print all the parameters and their value or values without needing to know the parameter names *a priori*. To accomplish this, the request method `getParameterNames()` is useful. This method returns all the names of the parameters in a query string as a `java.util.Enumeration`. The names can then be used one at a time to query the `getParametersValues()` method to get all the values of the parameter (even if it's just one).

2. Write a JSP that uses the `getParameterNames()` and `getParameterValues()` methods to navigate through the parameters and their values of an arbitrary HTML page that invokes it.

HOUR 11

Generating a Dynamic Response for the User

Hour 10, "Processing Requests from the User," explained how to process user requests using the request object. This hour will show you how use a response object to generate a dynamic response for the user.

The topics covered in this hour are

- Creating a response for the user
- Generating dynamic tables
- Generating dynamic HTML forms
- Creating a configurable Web page

Generating Dynamic Content

One of the main advantages of JSPs is the ability to generate dynamic content. JSPs generate dynamic HTML pages by using Java control structures like for loops and if statements. For instance, a JSP can generate a fixed text message several times by wrapping the message with a for loop.

Similarly JSPs can generate tables with a dynamic number of rows and columns by wrapping the appropriate tags within an iteration. Forms can be generated dynamically following some specified logical layout.

Generating dynamic content in Web applications is important when the content must reflect the most current and available data and personalized information. An example of such an application is an online stock portfolio. A stock portfolio allows users to keep track of their stock information online, including options, stock listings, current stock prices, and comprehensive daily high and low prices. One of the typical Web pages of such an application might include a table that lists a variety of stock information in separate rows, generated by a JSP. Each stock would have a single row, and the information would be tabulated in columns. Every time the user comes to the page, the table will be different, because the JSP accesses the latest information and generates the table on-the-fly. The page might also provide links and buttons to edit the table, like adding and deleting a row, or sorting the table by column. Other examples of applications that use dynamic content include news outlets, weather information, and personalized Web sites.

The following sections present how JSPs can be used to dynamically generate HTML.

Dynamic Titles

Consider the simple task of generating a string repeatedly. This can easily be done by putting the string inside a `for` loop.

Listing 11.1 is a simple example of a JSP that generates a dynamic response to the user. This illustrates how a JSP can generate dynamic formatting like font size and font color. The example consists of generating several progressively smaller HTML headers (see Figure 11.1). Each header is lighter in color than the preceding one. The example illustrates how a `for` loop can be used to generate lots of similar HTML code.

LISTING 11.1   Dynamic Titles (`dynamicTitles.jsp`)

```
1:  <HTML><HEAD><TITLE>Dynamic Titles</TITLE></HEAD>
2:  <BODY>
3:  <CENTER>
4:  <%  String[] colorArray = { "00", "11", "22", "33",
5:                              "44", "55", "66", "77",
6:                              "88", "99", "AA", "BB",
7:                              "CC", "DD", "EE", "FF"};
8:      for(int j=1; j<5; j++){
9:          String fgColor = colorArray[j*3]+colorArray[j*3]+colorArray[j*3];%>
10:         <H<%=j%>>
11:         <FONT COLOR=<%=fgColor%>>
12:         JSPs are great !!!
13:         </FONT>
```

LISTING 11.1   continued

```
14:         </H<%=j%>>
15: <%  }   %>
16: </CENTER>
17:   </BODY></HTML>
```

ANALYSIS   Line 4 declares a `colorArray` containing a hexadecimal color string. Color in HTML is defined as the combination of the colors red, green, and blue. Each of these has hexadecimal values from `00` to `FF` (`0` to `255` in decimal), and the three are combined by concatenating their values. So purple would be `FF00FF`, black would be `000000`, white `FFFFFF`, and so on. These colors are combined in the `fgColor` string in line 9. Since all three color components are the same, the resulting colors are several shades of gray. The index `j` of the `for` loop in line 8 is used to reference the `colorArray` in line 9 and then in line 10 to declare progressively smaller headers (`H1`, `H2`, ..., `H4`). The color of the header `JSPs are great !!!` (line 12) is set using a `FONT` tag in line 11.

FIGURE 11.1

dynamicTitles.jsp *produces a set of progressively smaller and lighter HTML headers.*

Dynamic Tables

Many Web sites depend on the ability to generate tables dynamically, which consists of controlling the TR and TD tags within a TABLE.

The example of the online stock portfolio mentioned earlier is a good example of an application in which dynamic tables are useful.

The following simple example shows how to generate five rows without having to code each one of them:

```
<TABLE>
<% for(int row=1; row<=5; row++) { %>
    <TR>
    </TR>
<% } %>
```

11

```
</TABLE>
```

Ten columns can be added for each row by nesting another `for` loop within the TR tag as follows:

```
<TABLE>
<% for(int row=1; row<=5; row++) { %>
    <TR>
      for(int col=1; col<=10; col++) { %>
        <TD>  (<%=col%>, <%=row%>)
        </TD>
    </TR>
<% } %>
</TABLE>
```

Each cell contains its row and column numbers as the tuple (`col`, `row`).

Listing 11.2 shows how tables can be generated dynamically. The JSP provides two INPUT fields to define the width and height of the dynamic table. When the user submits the form, the JSP processes the request and generates the table on-the-fly. Each cell of the table has a unique background color and text based on the row and column of the cell. (In the activity at the end of this hour, you will enhance the JSP in Listing 11.2 by adding hyperlinks to dynamically add and remove rows and columns. You will need to wait until you take a look at the JSP of Listing 11.4 to learn a bit about URL rewriting before you tackle that exercise.) Take a look at Listing 11.2 and the analysis that follows.

LISTING 11.2   Generating a Dynamic Table (`dynamicTable.jsp`)

```
 1: <HTML><HEAD><TITLE>A Colorful and Dynamic Table</TITLE></HEAD>
 2: <BODY>
 3: <CENTER>
 4: <H1>Colorful and Dynamic Table</H1>
 5: <FORM METHOD=POST ACTION=dynamicTable.jsp>
 6: Table Width  (<16) = <INPUT TYPE=TEXT NAME=WIDTH  VALUE=15 SIZE=2>,
 7: Table Height (<16) = <INPUT TYPE=TEXT NAME=HEIGHT VALUE=5  SIZE=2>,
 8: <INPUT TYPE=SUBMIT VALUE="Do it !">
 9: </FORM>
10: <HR>
11: <%  String w = request.getParameter("WIDTH");
12:     String h = request.getParameter("HEIGHT");
13:     if(w == null) w = "5";
14:     if(h == null) h = "15";
15:     int width  = Integer.parseInt(w);
16:     int height = Integer.parseInt(h);
17:     if(width>15)  width  = 15;
18:     if(width<0)   width  = 0;
19:     if(height>15) height = 15;
20:     if(height<0)  height = 0;
21:     String[] colorArray  = { "00", "11", "22", "33",
```

LISTING 11.2   continued

```
22:                                   "44", "55", "66", "77",
23:                                   "88", "99", "AA", "BB",
24:                                   "CC", "DD", "EE", "FF"   };   %>
25: <TABLE BORDER=0 CELLPADDING=0 CELLSPACING=0>
26: <%  for(int y=0; y<=height; y++){      %>
27:            <TR>
28: <%         for(int x=0; x<=width; x++){
29:               String bgColor = "AA" + colorArray[y] + colorArray[x];    %>
30:               <TD BGCOLOR=<%=bgColor%>>
31:               (<%=x%>, <%=y%>)
32:               </TD>
33: <%         }                          %>
34:            </TR>
35: <%  }                                 %>
36: </TABLE>
37: <HR>
38: </CENTER>
39: </BODY></HTML>
```

ANALYSIS   Lines 5–9 declare a FORM to set the width and height of the table. They have been limited to less than 16 since these values are then used to choose a hexadecimal-based color system. The input fields declare a default table size of 5 rows of 15 columns each. The values of the fields are then accessed from the request object in lines 11 and 12. If they are not null, the value is used to set the values of variables width and height. Lines 17–20 make sure the values are within 0 and 15. Line 21 declares a colorArray based on hexadecimal values from 00 to FF. Line 25 declares the table. The for loop in line 26 declares a height number of rows. For each row, the for loop in line 28 declares a width number of columns. Each cell is declared with a unique background color. The background color, bgColor, is created in line 29 and the cell's color is defined in line 30. The cell contains the string (x, y) where x is the current column and y is the row.

Figure 11.2 shows the output of dynamicTable.jsp with a width and height of 15.

Dynamic Forms

HTML forms can be generated dynamically by following some layout specification that a JSP code can use to create the form. This is especially useful when forms are used to gather information as part of a collection of data or a sequence.

An example use of dynamic forms, together with dynamic tables, is an online shopping cart. A shopping cart lists the items a user intends to purchase and information such as individual prices, short descriptions, quantities, subtotals, and a grand total of the purchase. The shopping cart can be created by combining HTML forms and tables. The table would be used to tabulate the items in separate rows, with the information for each item filling different columns. The form would be used to gather the quantities for each item, so that

11

subtotals can be computed for each item in the shopping cart. The user can input the quantities for each item (default would be 1) and click on a button that would refresh the cart when a change is made. The rows of the table would be created using a `for` loop, and an `INPUT` field (`TYPE=TEXT`) would be inserted in the appropriate column for each of the items.

Figure 11.2

Although it's a little hard to tell in a black-and-white picture, `dynamicTable.jsp` *produces a dynamically colorful table.*

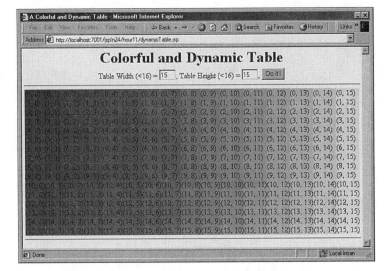

A form's selection elements are an example of a sequence of choices. These typically consist of a long list of choices of the same data type. For instance, if the choices are consecutive years then these can be easily generated within a `for` loop.

The example JSP in Listing 11.3 shows how forms can be generated dynamically. The form (see Figure 11.3) gathers typical billing information like credit card type, number, and expiration date. In real life the information would be processed by a secure server, which is beyond the scope of this book. An example is given for several `FORM` elements. For instance, the `SELECT` element for the expiration date of the credit card contains ten distinct years from which to choose. Instead of hard-coding each choice, a `for` loop is used to dynamically generate the choices.

Listing 11.3 Generating a Dynamic Form (`dynamicForm.jsp`)

```
1: <HTML><HEAD><TITLE>Dynamic Form</TITLE></HEAD>
2: <BODY>
3: <B>Form</B>
4: <FORM ACTION=dynamicForm.jsp METHOD=POST>
5: <TABLE BORDER=0 CELLSPACING=0 CELLPADDING=0>
6: <% String[] textFields = {"FirstName","LastName","Address","City","Zip"};
```

LISTING **11.3**   continued

```
 7:     for(int j=0; j<textFields.length; j++){      %>
 8:     <TR>    <TD> <%=textFields[j]%>:                        </TD>
 9:             <TD> <INPUT TYPE=TEXT NAME=<%=textFields[j]%>> </TD>
10:     </TR>
11: <%  }   %>
12:     <TR>    <TD> State  </TD>
13:             <TD> <SELECT NAME=State>
14: <%  String[] states = {"AZ", "CA", "NM", "MA", "ME", "MD", "..."};
15:     for(int s=0; s<states.length; s++) {     %>
16:                 <OPTION><%=states[s]%></OPTION>
17: <%  }   %>
18:                 </SELECT></TD>
19:     </TR>
20:     <TR>    <TD> Card Number  </TD>
21:             <TD> <INPUT TYPE=TEXT NAME=cNumber></TD>
22:     </TR>
23:     <TR>    <TD> Card Type  </TD>
24:             <TD> <SELECT NAME=CardType>
25: <%  String[] cTypes = {"Amex", "Visa", "Master Card", "Discovery", "..."};
26:     for(int t=0; t<cTypes.length; t++) {     %>
27:                 <OPTION><%=cTypes[t]%></OPTION>
28: <%  }   %>
29:                 </SELECT></TD>
30:     </TR>
31:     <TR>    <TD> Expiration Date (MM/DD/YYYY) </TD>
32: <TD> <INPUT TYPE=TEXT NAME=cMonth SIZE=2><INPUT TYPE=TEXT NAME=cDay SIZE=2>
33:             <SELECT NAME=cYear>
34:             <%  int startYear = 2000;
35:                 int endYear = 2010;
36:                 for(int y=startYear; y<endYear; y++) {      %>
37:                     <OPTION><%=y%></OPTION>
38:             <%  }   %>
39:             </SELECT></TD>
40:     </TR>
41: </TABLE>
42:     <INPUT TYPE=SUBMIT VALUE=Submit>
43: </FORM>
44: <HR>
45: <B>Form Content</B><BR>
46: <TABLE>
47: <%  Enumeration parameters = request.getParameterNames();
48:     while(parameters.hasMoreElements()){
49:         String parameterName = (String)parameters.nextElement();
50:         String parameterValue = request.getParameter(parameterName); %>
51:         <TR>
52:             <TD><%=parameterName%></TD>
53:             <TD><%=parameterValue%></TD>
54:         </TR>
55: <%  }   %>
56: </BODY></HTML>
```

11

ANALYSIS Line 4 declares the FORM and directs its request to itself. The fields of the form are laid out using the TABLE declared in line 5. Lines 6–11 create 5 INPUT TEXT fields. Lines 12–19 declare a pull-down selection field for the states. Lines 20–22 declare a single text field for the card number. Lines 23–30 declare another selection field for the card type. Lines 31–40 declare fields for the month, day, and year of expiration. The year field is another selection field. Lines 45–56 print out the content of the request generated by the form.

Figure 11.3 depicts the Web page after submitting the form.

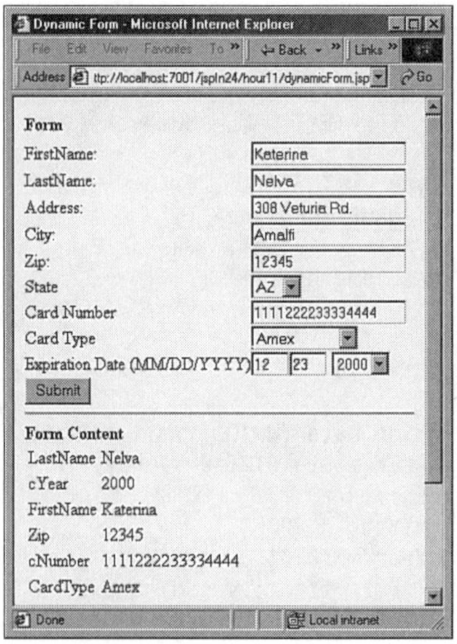

FIGURE **11.3**

The form after it has been submitted.

A Configurable Home Page

Configurable Web pages is currently one of the very hot features Web sites are rushing to provide. They usually consist of keeping track of your personal preferences whenever you visit the Web site. You can configure your personal version of the Web site by rearranging the layout of the site, turning on or off parts of the page, and customizing the look and feel. You will learn how to keep track of the user preferences in Hour 12, but this hour presents you with the aspects of dynamically generating the layout of a simple Web page.

Listing 11.4 shows the implementation of a simple configurable Web page. The page allows users to toggle the position of the navigation menu left and right, turn the footer on or off, and change the background color. See Figure 11.4. The navigation menu, main content section, and footer are included HTML files using the JSP directive <jsp:include> so that you can change these files to customize this example to your own particular implementation. (You'll learn more about including files in Hour 20, "Using Multiple JSPs to Handle the Request)". The example uses URL rewriting to store the state of the page in the URL of the hyperlinks it generates. The state consists of several parameters that keep track of the layout of the page, such as the background color, the position of the navigation menu, and whether the footer is on or off. The activity at the end of this hour asks you to enhance the JSP of Listing 11.2 with hyperlinks that dynamically add/remove rows and columns. You will need to use URL rewriting to remember the number of rows and columns between requests.

LISTING 11.4 A Configurable Home Page (`configurableHomePage.jsp`)

```
 1: <HTML><HEAD><TITLE>A Configurable Home Page</TITLE></HEAD>
 2: <%  String change       = request.getParameter("change");
 3:     String bgColorState = request.getParameter("bgColor");
 4:     String navState      = request.getParameter("nav");
 5:     String footerState  = request.getParameter("footer");
 6:     if(change!=null){
 7:         if(change.equals("footer")){
 8:             if(footerState.equals("on")) footerState = "off";
 9:             else                         footerState = "on";
10:         }
11:         if(change.equals("nav"))
12:             if(navState.equals("left")) navState = "right";
13:             else                        navState = "left";
14:         if(change.startsWith("color"))
15:             bgColorState = change.substring(5);
16:     } else {
17:         bgColorState="yellow";
18:         navState="left";
19:         footerState="on";
20:     }
21:     String state = "&footer="+footerState+"&nav="+navState+
22:                    "&bgColor="+bgColorState;
23: %>
24: <BODY BGCOLOR=<%=bgColorState%>>
25: <TABLE WIDTH=100% CELLSPACING=0 CELLPADDING=0>
26: <%  String leftPercent, rightPercent;
27:     if(navState.equals("left")){
28:         leftPercent="30%"; rightPercent="70%";
29:     } else {
30:         leftPercent="70%"; rightPercent="30%";
31:     }
32: %>
33:     <TR><TD WIDTH=<%=leftPercent%>>
34:         <%  if(navState.equals("left")){    %>
35:             <jsp:include page="nav.html" flush="true"/>
36:         <%  } else {                        %>
37:             <jsp:include page="content.html" flush="true"/>
38:         <%  }                               %>
39:     </TD>
```

11

LISTING 11.4   continued

```
40:            <TD WIDTH=<%=rightPercent%>>
41:            <%  if(navState.equals("left")){     %>
42:                    <jsp:include page="content.html" flush="true"/>
43:            <%  } else {                          %>
44:                    <jsp:include page="nav.html" flush="true"/>
45:            <%  }                                  %>
46:        </TD></TR>
47: </TABLE>
48: <%  if(footerState.equals("on")) {  %>
49:            <jsp:include page="footer.html" flush="true"/></TD>
50: <%  }    %>
51: <HR>
52: <TABLE BORDER=0 CELLPADDING=0 CELLSPACING=1>
53: <TR><TD><A HREF="configurableHomePage.jsp?change=footer<%=state%>">
54:        <IMAGE SRC="images/footerToggle.gif"></A><BR>footer<BR>on/off</TD>
55:     <TD><A HREF="configurableHomePage.jsp?change=nav<%=state%>">
56:     <IMAGE SRC="images/navToggle.gif"></A><BR>nav bar<BR>left/right</TD>
57:        <TD><A HREF="configurableHomePage.jsp?change=colorblue<%=state%>">
58:     <IMAGE SRC="images/bgColorBlue.gif"></A><BR>bg color<BR>to blue</TD>
59:        <TD><A HREF="configurableHomePage.jsp?change=coloryellow<%=state%>">
60:     <IMAGE SRC="images/bgColorYellow.gif"></A><BR>bg color<BR>to yellow</TD>
61:        <TD><A HREF="configurableHomePage.jsp?change=colorgreen<%=state%>">
62:     <IMAGE SRC="images/bgColorGreen.gif"></A><BR>bg color<BR>to green</TD>
63:        <TD><A HREF="configurableHomePage.jsp?change=colororange<%=state%>">
64:     <IMAGE SRC="images/bgColorOrange.gif"></A><BR>bg color<BR>to orange</TD>
65: </TR>
66: </TABLE>
67: </CENTER>
68: </BODY></HTML>
```

ANALYSIS Lines 2–5 retrieve the values of parameters change, bgColor, nav, and footer and store them in state variables bgColorState, navState, and footerState. These parameters are kept in the query string to remember the state of the page from request to request. The change parameter is used to determine whether the user has changed the color of the background, toggled the position of the navigation bar, or toggled the footer on or off. If the change is not null in line 6, then the JSP determines what type of change. If it is "footer", then lines 8 and 9 toggle the state of the footer depending on what it was in the previous request. If the change is to the navigation bar, then in lines 12 and 13 the position is toggled between left and right. If the change is to the color of the background, then the color is set in line 15 to whatever color the user chose. If the change is null, then the default values for the state variables are chosen in lines 17–19. Line 21 generates a state variable that contains the concatenation of all the state variable's names and their values separated by &.

The state variable will be used as part of the query string in hyperlinks to the JSP itself. This way the state of the current page will be preserved in subsequent requests and the page can be generated as stipulated in the query string. Line 24 declares the BODY tag with the background color set to the bgColorState. A table is used in line 25 to lay out the different parts of the Web page. If navState is left, the navigation bar will be on the left and the content of the page on the right. Lines 27–46 set the percentages and contents of two columns. One contains the navigation bar and the other the content of the page. JSP includes are used in lines 35, 37, 42, and 44 to include other HTML pages that make up the navigation bar and content. Lines 48–50 check to see whether the footer should be included as well.

Lines 52–66 declare a table with several hyperlinks. Each hyperlink points to the JSP itself. Note that the query string of each URL in the hyperlinks contains a change parameter followed by the state variable. The hyperlinks use icons and some text to describe their purpose.

Figure 11.4 shows the Web page at several stages of interaction with the user.

FIGURE 11.4

The configurable Web page at several stages of its life: (a) shows all the components of the page in their default state; (b) shows the Web page with the navigation menu toggled to the left; *and (c) shows the Web page with the footer toggled off.*

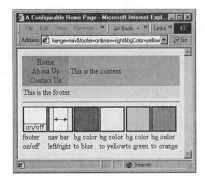

a

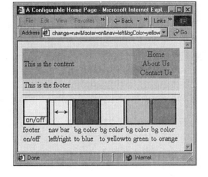

b

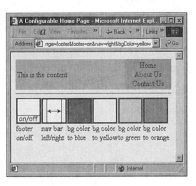

c

Summary

This chapter showed many examples of using JSPs to generate dynamic content. Examples of how to generate tables and forms were provided, as well as showing how to format simple text and headings. The last example showed how to configure a Web page according to a user's preference. The example highlighted the importance of dynamic content creation in controlling the overall layout of a page.

Q&A

Q The example of the configurable Web page seemed to use a convoluted way of keeping track of a user's preferences by including parameters in the query string of hyperlinks. Is there an easier way to do this?

A Yes, there is an easier way to keep track of a user's preference that will be shown in Hour 12, "Keeping Track of the User Session." The technique shown in this example is actually not convoluted, since keeping track of a user's session will most likely make some use of parameters in the query string. The examples in the next hour will show how the query string can be generated automatically, by using forms, or by using a session object that keeps track of user information.

Workshop

The quiz questions and activities are provided for your further understanding. See Appendix A, "Answers," for the answer to the quiz.

Quiz

1. The JSP listed below was written to create a contact list from the data stored in the string and integer arrays. Find what is wrong with the source code and fix it.

```
1: <HTML><HEAD><TITLE></TITLE></HEAD><BODY>
2: <%  String names = {"Katerina Lozada", "Rafael Greco", "Pasquale
    Marotta",
3:                     "Alexander Zahringer"};
4:     int numbers = {1233212, 2344323, 3455434, 4566545};
5:     <TABLE>
6:     <TR><TD>Names</TD><TD>Numbers</TD></TR>
7:     for(int j=0; j<names.length(); j++){ %>
8:        <TR> <TD>names</TD><TD>numbers</TD> </TR>
9: <%  }  %>
10:    </TABLE>
11: %>
12: </BODY></HTML>
```

Activity

The JSP in Listing 11.2 showed you how you can create dynamic tables. Enhance the JSP so that it provides the following four hyperlinks:

1. Add a row to the end

2. Remove the last row

3. Add a column to the end

4. Remove the last column

The goal of each hyperlink is self-explanatory. You will need to use URL rewriting to keep track of the number of rows and columns.

11

PART III

Adding Functionality to Your JSPs

Hour

HOUR 12

Keeping Track of the User Session

Many Web sites depend on keeping track of individual user information and user state. HTTP is the protocol responsible for transporting Web pages and requests back and forth between client browsers and servers. HTTP is not equipped to maintain state information of the clients. Several alternatives such as cookies and user sessions have been devised to circumvent this problem. This hour presents three mechanisms that JSPs provide to maintain a stateful interaction through the use of cookies, session objects, and URL encoding.

The topics covered in this hour are

- HTTP as a stateless protocol
- Storing and retrieving cookies
- Using the user session object
- URL encoding

HTTP Is a Stateless Protocol

The World Wide Web was designed around a simple request/response mechanism. Browsers running on client machines request HTML documents, and servers respond by delivering the documents. The rules and mechanisms for transferring HTML documents are called the Hypertext Transfer Protocol (HTTP). Servers typically receive requests from many different clients, and servers are only aware of a particular client until they fulfill a request with a response. After that, servers forget about the client and go on to fulfill requests from other clients. HTTP does not provide mechanisms to distinguish one client from the next so if any two requests happen to come from the same client, the server is not aware of it. In this sense HTTP is referred to as a stateless protocol. This feature (or lack thereof) posed a limitation on what a Web site could do. Servers could not remember bits of information for a particular user since there was no way to distinguish one user from another.

To illustrate this problem, consider a Web site that has an online catalog from which a user can select several items and put them in an online shopping cart for later checkout. As the user clicks different hyperlinks and buttons he generates distinct requests. At the same time there are other users shopping at the same Web site. The server must be able to keep track of which requests belong to which user so that items can be put in distinct shopping carts. The server must be able to maintain the state of each of the users, and HTTP does not allow this.

To solve this, Netscape invented the notion of a cookie. Cookies are bits of information and related mechanisms to store user-related information on client machines on behalf of the server. The information is then sent to the server every time the browser makes a request to the same server. The information in a cookie can consist of anything but in general the information is used to identify distinct users accessing the same Web server. The cookie can contain username information, a particular ID, personalization information, or anything else that the Web application decides to use to keep track of particular users. The stateful interaction of a client with a Web site is known as a *stateful conversation* or *stateful session*.

A Web application sets a cookie by requesting that the browser creates a cookie on the client machine on which the browser is running. The amount of information in a cookie and the number of cookies allowed are usually limited because a server generally should not be permitted to use a client's machine as a remote storage device. Browsers can be configured to reject cookies, in which case some Web applications, or parts of them, will refuse or deny some of their services that depend on keeping track of their users.

JSPs provide three ways to maintain a stateful conversation between the client side browser and the server application: cookies, sessions, and URL rewriting.

Storing and Retrieving Cookies

Cookies are created by the server-side application—the JSP—and are stored on the client machine on behalf of the JSP. JSPs can add cookies to the client machine by using the addCookie()method of the response object. The response object implements the HttpServletResponse interface and was covered in the last hour. The addCookie() method takes an instance of the Cookie class, which can contain information relevant to the user. You will see the Cookie class shortly.

The client machine stores the cookies on the local hard drive in a directory managed by the browser running on the client machine. Cookies are retrieved by the JSP from the client machine when the client sends a request to the JSP. JSPs access the cookies by using the getCookies() method of the implicit request object. The request object implements the HttpServletRequest object and was covered in Hour 10, "Processing Requests from the User." The getCookies() method returns an array of Cookie objects.

Cookies are represented as class objects on the server side by the Cookie class. Table 12.1 shows the API methods of the Cookie class.

TABLE 12.1 Methods of the Cookie Class

Method	Description
String getName()	Returns the name of the cookie
void setComment(String)	Specifies a comment that describes a cookie's purpose
String getComment()	Returns the comment describing the purpose of this cookie
void setDomain(String)	Specifies the domain within which this cookie should be presented
String getDomain()	Returns the domain name set for this cookie
void setMaxAge(int)	Sets the maximum age of the cookie in seconds
int getMaxAge()	Returns the maximum age of the cookie, in seconds
void setPath(String)	Specifies a path to which the client should return the cookie
String getPath()	Returns the path on the server to which the browser returns this cookie
void setSecure(boolean)	Indicates to the browser whether the cookie should only be sent using a secure protocol, such as HTTPS or SSL
boolean getSecure()	Returns true if the browser is sending cookies only over a secure protocol, or false if the browser can send cookies using any protocol
void setValue(String)	Assigns a new value to a cookie after the cookie is created
String getValue()	Returns the value of the cookie
void setVersion(int)	Sets the version of the cookie protocol this cookie complies with
int getVersion()	Returns the version of the protocol this cookie complies with

12

The following example (Listing 12.1) illustrates the use of cookies. The example consists of a small imaginary Web site that keeps track of the preferences of the user. The Web site contains a small portal that provides information about organic products in several portlets (just four for now). Figure 12.1 shows the portal with its four default portlets. One includes related organic news. Another has the user's contact list. Another contains a to-do list. And the fourth shows weather information.

The portal allows users to customize their own copy of the portal by providing links that turn the portlets on and off. When users click the on/off link below a portlet, the portal JSP turns the portlet on/off and refreshes itself. The portal uses cookies to store the preferences of users on the users' machines. When a user comes back to use the portal, the application retrieves the cookies and shows a customized view of the portal as indicated by the preferences stored in the cookies.

New Terms: Portals and Portlets

Portals are Web sites that are dedicated to a particular topic and try to put a common front end on the disparate information on the Internet. For instance, a portal called `http://www.safety.com` provides categorized information about safety and pointers on where to find more information on your own. These types of sites try to be a one-stop shop for the topic of interest. Many of these sites allow registered users to personalize their view of the Web site by turning on or off portions of the Web page, or by adding and deleting features. This is usually accomplished by *portlets* that together form the portal. For instance, `http://www.msn.com` provides several portlets for stock information, weather, entertainment news, and so on. Each portlet has icons to turn it on or off, depending on the preferences of the user. Some, like the weather portlet, can be customized for the particular area where the user lives. The weather portlet accepts a ZIP code so that the weather information the user gets is pertinent to his or her local area.

The portal JSP in Listing 12.1 includes four other HTML pages that implement the news, weather, contacts, and to-do lists.

LISTING 12.1 Preferences (`preferences.jsp`)

```
 1: <HTML><HEAD><TITLE>Example of Using Cookies</TITLE></HEAD><BODY>
 2: <H1> Organic Portal </H1>
 3: <%  String[] cookieNames  = {"news", "todo", "contacts", "weather" };
 4:     String  cookieName   = null;
 5:     String[] cookieValues = {"on",   "on",   "on",       "on"};
 6:     String  cookieValue  = null;
 7:     Cookie[] cookies      = request.getCookies();
 8:     for(int j=0; j<cookies.length; j++) {
 9:         boolean cookieExists = false;
10:         for(int k=0; k<cookieNames.length; k++) {
```

LISTING 12.1   continued

```
11:              cookieName  = cookies[j].getName();
12:              cookieValue = cookies[j].getValue();
13:              if(cookieName.equals(cookieNames[k])) {
14:                  cookieExists = true;
15:                  cookieValues[k] = cookieValue;
16:              }
17:          }
18:          if(!cookieExists) {
19:              response.addCookie(new Cookie(cookieName, "on"));
20:          }
21:      }
22:      String   togglePage = request.getParameter("togglePage");
23:      if(togglePage != null) {
24:          for(int j=0; j<cookieValues.length; j++) {
25:              if(togglePage.equals(cookieNames[j])) {
26:                  if(cookieValues[j].equals("on")) {
27:                      response.addCookie(new Cookie(togglePage, "off"));
28:                      cookieValues[j] = "off";
29:                  } else {
30:                      response.addCookie(new Cookie(togglePage, "on"));
31:                      cookieValues[j] = "on";
32:                  }
33:              }
34:          }
35:      } %>
36: <TABLE> <TR>
37: <% for(int j=0; j<cookieNames.length; j++) { %>
38:          <TD VALIGN=TOP>
39: <%      if(cookieValues[j].equals("on")){
40:              String pageName = cookieNames[j] + ".html"; %>
41:              <jsp:include page="<%=pageName%>" flush="true"/>
42: <%      } %>
43:          <A HREF=preferences.jsp?togglePage=<%=cookieNames[j]%>>on/off</A>
44:          </TD>
45: <% } %>
46: </TR> </TABLE>
47: </BODY>
48: </HTML>
```

ANALYSIS   Lines 3–6 declare the names of the cookies and their default values. The actual cookies are retrieved from the request object in line 7. Lines 8–17 compare all the cookies stored in the local machine with the four cookies relevant to the example. If they are found, their values are retrieved and stored in array cookieValues[]. Otherwise they are created with an initial value of on. Lines 22–35 handle requests to toggle the portlets on and off. The request parameter name of interest is called togglePage and its value determines which portlet should be toggled on/off. The togglePage value is compared to the names of the cookies and the appropriate cookie is updated in the local machine and in the array cookieValues[]. Lines 36–46 generate a table with the portlets using JSP `include` directives (more on this in Hour 20, " Using Multiple JSPs to Handle the Request"). Each portlet has a hyperlink underneath to notify the JSP to turn the portlet on or off.

FIGURE **12.1**

All the portlets are on in this view of the `preferences.jsp` *page.*

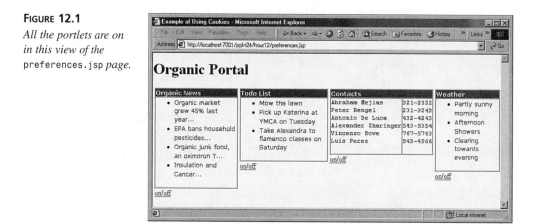

Using cookies can quickly become cumbersome because you need to write special code that processes them and they don't have a useful data structure. A better way of keeping track of user information is to use server-side `session` objects that are unique to each user.

User Sessions

The `HttpSession` interface provides JSPs with the functionality to store and share information about an ongoing interaction with a user. The `HttpSession` interface is accessible through the `getSession()` method of the `HttpServletRequest` interface. You learned about most of the methods of the `HttpServletRequest` interface in Hours 10 and 11, postponing those methods pertinent to session management until this hour.

Within a JSP the implicit `session` object implements an instance of the `HttpSession` interface. The `session` object serves, for example, as a sketch pad for JSPs of an e-commerce application to keep track of temporary data about the user they are interacting with. Data that needs to be stored permanently must be persisted to a database. Hour 17 covers database interaction using JSPs and JDBC.

Table 12.2 lists the methods in the `HttpServletRequest` interface that are relevant to managing sessions.

TABLE 12.2   Session-Related Methods of the `HttpServletRequest` Class

Method	Description
`HttpSession getSession()`	Returns the current session or creates one if it doesn't exist
`HttpSession getSession(boolean)`	Returns the current session or creates one if argument is `true`
`String getRequestedSessionId()`	Returns the session ID
`boolean isRequestedSessionIdValid()`	Returns `true` if session ID is still valid or `false` otherwise
`boolean isRequestedSessionIdFromCookie()`	Returns `true` if the session ID came from a cookie, `false` otherwise
`boolean isRequestedSessionIdFromURL()`	Returns `true` if the session ID came from an encoded URL (discussed in the "Encoding URLs" section), false otherwise

Every distinct user who starts an interaction with any JSP of an application is associated with a unique `session` object. This is accomplished by creating a unique ID for every user that interacts with the application and storing it as a cookie on the client's machine. On every request the client makes to the server application, the cookie that holds the client ID is used to distinguish among potentially many different users. The ID is used to determine the correct `session` instance for the corresponding user. This mechanism allows JSPs to maintain a private conversation with each different user as they jump from page to page. JSPs can store and retrieve temporary data in a session by using the `setAttribute()` and `getAttribute()` methods. These methods allow developers to bind any object containing user data to a string so that they can be retrieved by name. The `session` object is an implementation of the `HttpSession` interface and its API methods are listed in Table 12.3.

12

TABLE 12.3   Methods of the `HttpSession` Session

Method	Description
`Object getAttribute(String)`	Returns the object bound to the string in the parameter
`void setAttribute(String, Object)`	Binds the object to the string in the parameter
`void removeAttribute(String)`	Unbinds the object bound to the string in the parameter
`Enumeration getAttributeNames()`	Returns an enumeration of strings for all bound objects in the session
`long getCreationTime()`	Returns the time when the session was created as milliseconds from January 1, 1970
`long getLastAccessedTime()`	Returns the time when the session was last accessed as milliseconds from January 1, 1970

TABLE 12.3 continued

Method	Description
`int getMaxInactiveInterval()`	Returns the maximum time that the Servlet container will allow a user session to remain in memory without having received requests from the user. After that time the session is marked invalid and is a candidate for garbage collection
`void setMaxInactiveInterval(int)`	Sets the maximum time that the Servlet container will allow a user session to remain in memory without having received requests from the user
`boolean isNew()`	Returns `true` if this is the first time the client has started a session, that is, the first time that client stores a cookie with a session ID
`void invalidate()`	Invalidates sessions and unbinds all objects bound to the session
`String getId()`	Returns the ID of the session

The example in Listing 12.2 illustrates the use of a `session` object to keep track of the content of a shopping cart. The application consists of two JSPs that play the role of two online catalog pages that allow users to select items to add to a shopping cart. The `cds.jsp` shows a listing of CDs and the `toys.jsp` shows a listing of toys. Each of the pages has a link to the other and shows the current contents of the cart to demonstrate how each JSP is aware of the other.

LISTING 12.2 A JSP that Allows Users to Shop for CDs to Illustrate the Use of the session Object (cds.jsp)

```
 1: <HTML><HEAD><TITLE>Example of Using Cookies</TITLE></HEAD><BODY>
 2: [<A HREF=toys.jsp>Shop for Toys</A>]
 3: <H1> Online CD Catalog </H1>
 4: <TABLE>
 5: <% String[] titles = {"Tchaikovsky_Orchestral_Masterpieces",
 6:                       "Mendelssohn_Melodic_Masterpieces",
 7:                       "Haydn_Symphonic_Masterpieces",
 8:                       "Schumann_Romantic_Legends",
 9:                       "Bach_Baroque_Masterpieces"};
10:     for(int j=0; j<titles.length; j++){ %>
11:        <TR><TD><%=titles[j]%></TD>
12:            <TD><A HREF=cds.jsp?itemName=<%=titles[j]%>>
13:                Add to Shopping Cart</A></TD>
14:        </TR>
15: <% } %>
16: </TABLE>
17: <A HREF=cds.jsp?itemName=emptyCart>Empty Shopping Cart</A>
```

LISTING 12.2   continued

```
18: <% String item = request.getParameter("itemName");
19:    if(item != null && item.equals("emptyCart")){
20:       Enumeration attributeNames = session.getAttributeNames();
21:       while(attributeNames.hasMoreElements()){
22:          String attributeName = (String)attributeNames.nextElement();
23:          session.removeAttribute(attributeName);
24:       }
25:    } else if(item != null){
26:       String attributeName = item + "CD";
27:       session.setAttribute(attributeName,item);
28:    }
29: %>
30: <HR>
31: <H1> Content of Shopping Cart </H1>
32: <UL>
33: <% Enumeration attributeNames = session.getAttributeNames();
34:    if(attributeNames != null)
35:    while(attributeNames.hasMoreElements()){
36:       String attributeName = (String)attributeNames.nextElement();
37:       String attributeValue = (String)session.getAttribute(attributeName); %>
38:       <LI><%=attributeValue%>
39: <% } %>
40: </BODY>
41: </HTML>
```

ANALYSIS   Line 2 of cds.jsp declares a link to the toys catalog. The toys catalog declares a similar link to the CD catalog. Lines 4–16 create the catalog by using a table of two columns: one lists the CD titles, and the other contains links directed to the JSP itself. The hyperlink passes in its query string an argument that identifies the corresponding CD. The table is constructed by looping through each of the elements of the titles[] string array and inserting a row for each of the elements. At the end of the table, line 17 declares a hyperlink for emptying the cart. Lines 18–29 process the hyperlinks that add items to the cart and empty the cart. The argument passed to the JSP is stored in the string variable item in line 18. If the item is not null and it contains the string emptyCart then the while loop in line 21 iterates through all of the attributes of the session and removes them all. Otherwise item must contain the name of a CD (or toy) and lines 26 and 27 add the item to the session. Lines 33–39 print out the content of the shopping cart. Line 33 gets all the attributes in the session. Then the while loop in line 35 iterates through the attributes and gets all their values in line 37. Line 38 prints the item as a bullet in a list.

The listing for toys.jsp (listing 12.3) is very similar to cds.jsp. The only differences are the content of the string array titles and the fact that the links are swapped between cds.jsp and toys.jsp.

12

LISTING 12.3   A JSP that Allows Users to Shop for Toys (toys.jsp)

```
 1: <HTML><HEAD><TITLE>Example of Using Cookies</TITLE></HEAD><BODY>
 2: [<A HREF=cds.jsp>Shop for CDs</A>]
 3: <H1> Online Toy Catalog </H1>
 4: <TABLE>
 5: <% String[] titles = {"Rollerskating_Katerina","BMZ_Bike","Doll_House",
 6:                       "FIFA_Soccer_Ball","Radio_Controlled_X5"};
 7:    for(int j=0; j<titles.length; j++){ %>
 8:      <TR><TD><%=titles[j]%></TD>
 9:          <TD><A HREF=toys.jsp?itemName=<%=titles[j]%>>
10:              Add to Shopping Cart</A></TD>
11:      </TR>
12: <% } %>
13: </TABLE>
14: <A HREF=toys.jsp?itemName=emptyCart>Empty Shopping Cart</A>
15: <% String item = request.getParameter("itemName");
16:    if(item != null && item.equals("emptyCart")){
17:      Enumeration attributeNames = session.getAttributeNames();
18:      while(attributeNames.hasMoreElements()){
19:        String attributeName = (String)attributeNames.nextElement();
20:        session.removeAttribute(attributeName);
21:      }
22:    } else if(item != null){
23:      String attributeName = item + "CD";
24:      session.setAttribute(attributeName,item);
25:    }
26: %>
27: <HR>
28: <H1> Content of Shopping Cart </H1>
29: <UL>
30: <% Enumeration attributeNames = session.getAttributeNames();
31:    while(attributeNames.hasMoreElements()) {
32:      String attributeName = (String)attributeNames.nextElement();
33:      String attributeValue = (String)session.getAttribute(attributeName); %>
34:      <LI><%=attributeValue%>
35: <% } %>
36: </BODY></HTML>
```

Figure 12.2 shows what the cds.jsp and toys.jsp page looks like after having added several CDs and toys to the shopping cart.

Objects can be notified when they are bound or unbound to the session object by implementing the HttpSessionBindingListener interface. The method HttpSession. setAttribute() takes as arguments the object to be bound to the session and the name by which it can be retrieved. If the object implements the HttpSessionBindingListener interface, calling the setAttribute() method will cause the Servlet container to notify the object by calling valueBound() on the object being bound. Similarly, when the method HttpSession.removeAttribute() is called to unbind an object from the session

object, the method valueUnbound() is called on the object being unbound. The methods
valueBound() and valueUnbound() are implemented by the object being bound or
unbound as it implements the HttpSessionBindingListener interface. Table 12.4 lists
the API methods of the interface.

FIGURE 12.2

Several CDs and toys have been added to the shopping cart in the cds.jsp *(left) and* toys.jsp *(right) pages.*

TABLE 12.4   Methods of the HttpSessionBindingListener Class

Method	Description
void valueBound(HttpSessionBindingEvent)	Notifies the object listening that it has been bound to a session
void valueUnbound(HttpSessionBindingEvent)	Notifies the object listening that it has been unbound from a session

The methods of HttpSessionBindingListener take as arguments an instance of the
HttpSessionBindingEvent class. This class provides objects with the ability to learn
about the session they are being bound to. For instance, an object being bound or
unbound can query the session object for the name under which the object is bound.
Also, objects can get the session object with which they are being associated or disasso-
ciated. Table 12.5 lists the API methods of the HttpSessionBindingEvent class.

TABLE 12.5   Methods of the HttpSessionBindingEvent Class

Method	Description
String getName()	Returns the name that the object has been bound to
HttpSession getSession()	Returns a reference to the session object that has the object bound to it

12

Encoding URLs

Cookies and sessions only work if users have cookies enabled on their browsers. Many users disable cookies for various reasons, such as not wanting to be monitored or not wanting to leave a trail of what Web sites they have visited in their local machines. Although these are legitimate concerns on the part of the user, the fact remains that some applications are impossible to build without maintaining some state information about the user. Some sites require users to enable cookies on their browsers for particular features of the site to work. Other sites are so bold as to deny some of their services if cookies are not enabled. Web applications generally should not assume cookies are enabled and they should instead use URL encoding to maintain a stateful conversation with client applications. Maintaining state about a user is not an inherently bad practice. What matters is the purpose of keeping track of users and what is done with this information. URL encoding is a less intrusive mechanism that avoids the use of cookies, while maintaining user-state information in URLs generated by the Web site.

For instance, consider two distinct users browsing through an online catalog. The catalog pages are generated by JSPs. The URLs in the hyperlinks on the pages of the catalog can have special parameters and values in the query string. The parameters and values distinguish one user from another without the need for cookies.

The creation of the special parameters and their values is somewhat tricky and therefore JSPs provide several methods in the `response` object to handle URL encoding. The methods are listed in Table 12.6.

TABLE 12.6 URL Encoding Methods of the `response` Object

Method	Description
`String encodeURL(String url)`	If encoding is needed, it encodes the URL by appending the session ID in the query string
`String encodeRedirectURL(String url)`	If encoding is needed, it encodes the URL to be used with the `sendRedirect()` method
`void sendRedirect(String url)`	Sends a redirect response to the client using the URL

The session ID can be stored either in a cookie or in the encoded URL. The resulting encoded URL contains an ID that is used to associate the user with an `HttpSession` object. So even though cookies are not enabled, the Web application can still make use of a `session` object associated with particular users.

Application servers have logic built into them to determine whether cookies are disabled or not on the browser. The method `encodeURL()` uses this logic to decide whether the URL needs to be encoded or not. If cookies are enabled, encodeURL() will not encode the URL and will return the original URL. Otherwise it will encode a session ID into the URL.

The example in Listing 12.4 illustrates the use of encoded URLs. It shows a JSP that generates a hyperlink and a button using encodeURL(). Listing 12.5 shows the resulting HTML code. Note the session ID in the query string of the resulting HREF parameter in the hyperlink and in the ACTION parameter of the form.

LISTING 12.4   Example of a JSP that Encodes the URLs in Case the User Has Disabled Cookies (encodingURLs.jsp)

```
 1: <HTML><HEAD><TITLE>Encoding URLs</TITLE></HEAD>
 2: <BODY>
 3: <B>Example encoded hyperlink: </B>
 4: <%  String link     = response.encodeURL("nowhereLink.html");
 5:     String button   = response.encodeURL("nowhereButton.html");
 6:     String sessionID = request.getRequestedSessionId();
 7: %>
 8: <A HREF="<%=link%>">Click here</A>
 9: <HR>
10: <FORM METHOD=POST ACTION="<%=button%>">
11: <B>Example encoded button: </B><INPUT TYPE=SUBMIT VALUE="Submit">
12: </FORM>
13: <HR>
14: <B>Session ID</B>
15: <%=sessionID%>
16: </BODY>
17: </HTML>
```

ANALYSIS   Lines 4 and 5 compute the encoded version of the URLs nowhereLink.html and nowhereButton.html using the encodeURL() method of the response object. If cookies are disabled in the browser, the resulting URLs will be the same URLs with the session ID parameter and value appended as the query string of the URLs. If you use WLS as the application server, the session ID parameter is called WebLogicSession, and the value is arbitrarily chosen by the server. Line 6 gets the session ID. Line 8 creates a link with the encoded URL in the link variable and lines 10 and 11 create a submit button with the encoded URL in the button variable. Listing 12.5 shows the HTML code generated by WLS; Figure 12.3 shows the result.

LISTING 12.5   Resulting HTML from Having Encoded the URLs (encodingURLs.html)

```
 1: <HTML><HEAD><TITLE>Encoding URLs</TITLE></HEAD>
 2: <BODY>
 3: <B>Example encoded hyperlink: </B>
 4:
 5: <A HREF="nowhereLink.html?WebLogicSession=ObcKi7hsl017jcTklztVyjCIZFCYOLMXl
```

12

LISTING 12.5 continued

```
 6: sbfGIHNqc9dRos2hCZMx40eFNWsHWxkwM2elFw9cQc3|6431910570148531914/2130706433/
 7: 6/7001/7001/7002/7002/7001/-1">Click here</A>
 8: <HR>
 9: <FORM METHOD=POST ACTION="nowhereButton.html?WebLogicSession=ObcKi7hsl017jc
10: TklztVyjCIZFCYOLMXlsbfGIHNqc9dRos2hCZMx40eFNWsHWxkwM2elFw9cQc3|643191057014
11: 8531914/2130706433/6/7001/7001/7002/7002/7001/-1">
12: <B>Example encoded button: </B><INPUT TYPE=SUBMIT VALUE="Submit">
13: </FORM>
14: <HR>
15: <B>Session ID</B>
16: ObcKi7hsl017jcTklztVyjCIZFCYOLMXlsbfGIHNqc9dRos2hCZMx40eFNWsHWxkwM2elFw9cQc
17: 3|6431910570148531914/2130706433/6/7001/7001/7002/7002/7001/-1
18: </BODY>
19: </HTML>
```

Note that the session ID printed to the Web page is the same as the one appended to the query string of the URLs as the value of parameter `WebLogicSession`.

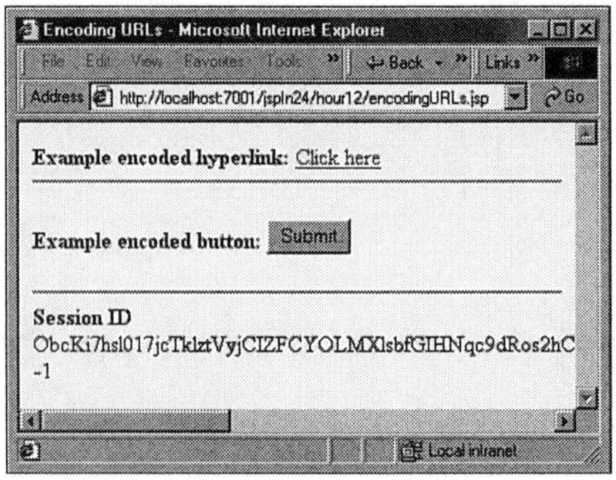

FIGURE 12.3

`encodedURLs.jsp` *produces HTML that results in this page.*

Summary

This hour presented you with techniques to maintain a stateful interaction between Web applications and client browsers. Three JSP mechanisms were covered: cookies, `session` objects, and URL encoding. State information about users is necessary for certain Web applications that must remember particular things about particular users.

Q&A

Q Can I store my own objects in a `session`?

A You can store any Java class in a `session` object. You just have to remember to cast the object back to its original type when you retrieve the object from the `session`.

Q **What are the size limitations of cookies? How many cookies can I use? Where are they stored?**

A Limitations on cookies vary from browser to browser. Cookies are typically 50 to 150 bytes in size. The maximum amount of data a cookie can hold is determined by the maximum size of the cookie header of an HTTP message, which is 4KB.

Netscape browsers impose a maximum number of 20 cookies per server and a total maximum of 300 cookies.

Internet Explorer stores cookies in the `Temporary Internet Files` directory for each user. Netscape stores cookies in a file called `cookies.txt` under its root installation directory.

Workshop

The quiz questions and activities are provided for your further understanding. See Appendix A, "Answers," for the answers to the quiz.

Quiz

1. When would you use URL encoding?
2. How would you create a cookie called `FavoriteColor` with a value of `Blue`?

Activities

Here are a couple of challenging exercises for you to practice what you have learned in this hour.

1. Create a JSP called `allCookies.jsp` that lists the names and values of all the cookies.
2. Create a JSP called `allAttributes.jsp` that lists the names and bound objects of a `session` object.

12

HOUR 13

Configuring and Initializing JSPs

A Web application often needs to carry out tasks that are best accomplished when the application is first started up. Initialization parameters are used to configure the behavior of JSPs as they first execute. This hour will teach you how to configure JSPs to handle start-up procedures.

In this hour you will learn about

- Registering and initializing JSPs
- Compiling JSPs into Servlets
- Using the config objects
- The ServletContext object

Understanding the Registration and Initialization of JSPs

Real-life applications usually have to interact with complex systems like databases, other machines, and services. These systems usually have a setup overhead where the systems need to learn about one another, register, and agree on the services and protocols that will be used. These overheads are best kept hidden from the users since they would be perceived as an overall degradation of performance. Setup overheads are usually best handled when applications first start up and are configured with special initialization parameters.

This hour shows you how to configure JSPs by using parameters that are available when the application first boots up. Boot time is the best time for JSPs and other application components to accomplish tasks that take a long setup time, like initializing and connecting to databases or connecting to other computers.

JSPs cannot be configured or initialized directly. Instead, they must be converted into their equivalent Servlets and then registered and configured by using the `weblogic.properties` file. Registering and initializing a JSP usually consists of the following steps:

1. Write the JSP as you would write any JSP. Optionally, the JSP may use the implicit `config` object to read and process initialization parameters.

2. Compile the JSP into a Servlet using the JSP compiler and place the resulting class in an appropriate directory that the application server can find.

3. Register and name the Servlet with the application server using the appropriate configuration file. You can declare the initialization parameters in the configuration file.

4. Execute the Servlet using a URL that points to the named Servlet. You can use extra path information and query strings as you would with a JSP.

Parameterization of JSPs is useful because it allows you to configure the behavior of JSPs without having to change the source code. This makes the JSPs more portable and reusable across applications.

The next few sections present an example JSP that prints out all of the initialization parameters. The process of compiling a JSP into an equivalent Servlet is detailed. Then the registration and initialization are presented. And finally the API for the `config` object is covered.

A Simple JSP that Prints All Initialization Parameters

The initialization parameters consist of a set of name/value pairs. The parameters are accessed through the JSP implicit object `config`, which will be covered in detail later in this hour. The `config` object provides methods to get all the parameter's names, `getInitParameterNames()`; values of a given parameter, `getInitParameter()`; and other less-used methods.

Listing 13.1 presents a JSP that lists all of the initialization parameters using the `config` object. It first gets the names of the parameters as an `Enumeration` and then uses the names to retrieve the values of each of the parameters.

The initialization parameters and their values are configured in `weblogic.properties`.

LISTING 13.1 A JSP that Prints All the Initialization Parameters
(`printAllParameters.jsp`)

```
 1: <HTML><HEAD><TITLE>JSP Prints All Parameters</TITLE></HEAD><BODY>
 2: <%@ page import="java.util.Enumeration"%>
 3: <H2> Print all initialization parameters </H2>
 4: <UL>
 5: <%  Enumeration parameters = config.getInitParameterNames();
 6:      while (parameters.hasMoreElements()) {
 7:        String name = (String)parameters.nextElement();
 8: %>        <LI> <%=name%> = <%=config.getInitParameter(name)%>
 9: <% } %>
10: </UL>
11: </BODY></HTML>
```

ANALYSIS Line 5 uses the `getInitParameterNames()` method of the `config` object to get all the names of the initialization parameters as an `Enumeration`. Lines 6 and 7 iterate through each of the names, storing them in the variable `name`. Line 8 uses the `name` as an argument to the `getInitParameter()` method to get the value of the initialization parameter named `name`. The name of the initialization parameter and its value are printed as a bulleted list. Figure 13.1 shows example parameters and values configured in the `weblogic.properties` file. The "Registering and Initializing JSPs with the Application Server" section of this hour will detail the process of registering and initializing a Servlet.

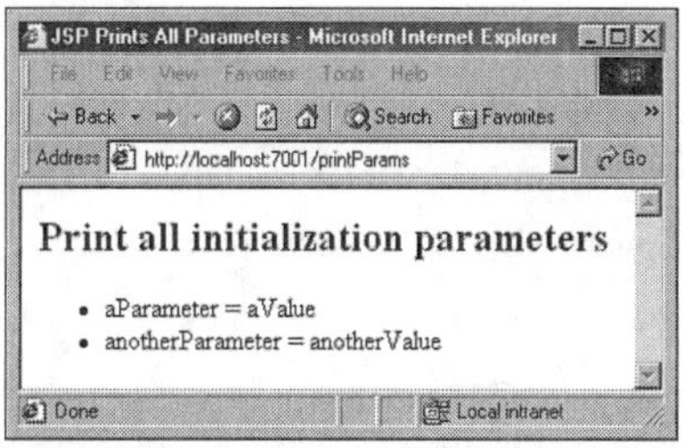

FIGURE 13.1

The JSP creates a bulleted list of the initialization parameters and their values.

13

Compiling JSPs Into Servlets

JSPs can be converted to their Servlet equivalent and compiled by using the `weblogic.jspc` Java class. This class takes as arguments a number of options and a JSP file. The compiler generates the Java source code for a Servlet equivalent to the JSP. Then the compiler uses the javac command to compile the Servlet into a Java class. The javac command is the Java compiler that comes with the JDK. The Servlet can then be registered and initialized in the weblogic.properties file. The compiler can be executed from the command line as follows:

```
c:\> java weblogic.jspc options someJSP.jsp
```

The weblogic.jspc class is located in the classes directory under the WLS root directory. Because of the package name, the class itself is under the weblogic directory under the classes directory. For the java command to find the class, the absolute path to the classes directory should be part of your CLASSPATH environment variable.

Table 13.1 lists the options that can be used with the JSP compiler.

TABLE 13.1   Options Used with the JSP Compiler

Option	Description
-classpath	A semicolon-delimited list of directories used to search for source.
-commentary	Causes the compiler to output helpful comments on what it is doing when working.
-compiler	Sets the compiler to use. Default is javac.
-d	Sets the destination directory of the resulting .class file.
-debug	Turns on debugging.
-deprecation	Causes compiler to warn if source uses deprecated methods.
-docroot	Sets the document root for resolving relative files.
-encoding	Sets the character encoding.
-g	Causes the compiler to generate extra debugging code in the resulting .class file.
-help	Prints out all the flags accepted by the compiler.
-J	Allows you to add compiler specific options.
-keepgenerated	Instructs compiler to keep the .java source of the generated Servlet.
-nowarn	Turns off warning messages from compiler.
-nowrite	Prevents compiler from generating a .class file. When used together with the -keepgenerated option, the compiler will just generate .java source files of the implementing Servlet.
-O	Turns on optimization. Overrides the -g option.
-package	Sets the package for the resulting Servlet source code. Default is jsp_servlet.

TABLE 13.1 continued

Option	Description
-superclass	Sets the superclass extended by the generated Servlet. The superclass must derive HTTPServlet.
-verbose	Causes compiler to print useful messages to the console when working.
-version	Prints the version of the JSP compiler.

To compile the JSP from Listing 13.1, printAllParameters.jsp, use the following command at the command line:

```
c:\> java weblogic.jspc -d d:\wls51\classes
                          -keepgenerated printAllParameters.jsp
```

The command line generates the source code for the Servlet in a file called _printallparameters.java and then compiles it into a Java class called _printallparameters.class. The command line uses the -keepgenerated command-line option to keep the Servlet source code after it is compiled. Otherwise weblogic.jspc will delete the file after it creates the class file. The command-line option -d commands the compiler to generate the class file into the d:\wls51\classes directory. The Servlet source code is by default made part of the jsp_servlet package so the class file will end up in the directory d:\wls51\ classes\jsp_servlet. The fully qualified name of the Servlet is jsp_servlet._printallparameters. The fully qualified name is used to register and configure the Servlet in the weblogic.properties file.

Registering and Initializing JSPs with the Application Server

A JSP's equivalent Servlet, like any other Servlet, is registered and initialized using the weblogic.httpd.register and weblogic.httpd.initArgs properties of the weblogic.properties file. The weblogic.properties file is located in the WebLogic root directory. To register a Servlet, use the following syntax:

```
weblogic.httpd.register.identifier=my.package.name.className
```

The *identifier* is a unique string that names the Servlet and is used to refer to it within the properties file for further configuration and from a URL to execute the Servlet. The registration property declares the class that implements the Servlet using its fully qualified name. The Servlet can be referenced from a browser with a URL as follows:

```
http://localhost:7001/identifier
```

13

The URL will cause the Servlet to execute its `service()` method as described in Hour 3, "Introduction to Servlets."

The `weblogic.httpd.initArgs` declares arguments for a registered Servlet. The arguments consist of a comma-separated list of name/value pairs. The following declares initialization parameters for a Servlet registered with the *identifier* name:

```
weblogic.httpd.initArgs.identifier=paramName1=value1,paramName2=value2,...
```

The initialization parameters are accessible to the JSP through the implicit object `config`. The `config` object is of type `ServletConfig`. The `config` object will be covered in detail in the following section, "Using the `config` Object."

The following two lines in `weblogic.properties` declare the Servlet for the `printAllParameters.jsp` JSP:

```
weblogic.httpd.register.printAllParams=jsp_servlet._printallparameters
weblogic.httpd.initArgs.printAllParams=aParameter=aValue,
                                        anotherParameter=anotherValue
```

Note that the names of the parameters and their values match the ones shown in Figure 13.1.

The next section covers the `config` object in detail.

Using the `config` Object

The `config` object is of type `ServletConfig` and it provides methods to access initialization and configuration for the Servlet. Table 13.2 lists all the methods of the `config` object:

TABLE 13.2   `config` Object Methods

Method	Description
`String getInitParameter (String paramName)`	Returns the value of the initialization parameter `paramName`
`Enumeration getInitParameterNames()`	Returns the names of all the initialization parameters
`ServletContext getServletContext()`	Returns a reference to the `ServletContext` object where the Servlet is executing
`String getServletName()`	Returns the virtual name with which the Servlet is registered in the application server

The `ServletContext` object represents the environment in which the Servlet is executing. This object will be covered shortly in the section "The `ServletContext` Object," but first an example illustrates the use of the `config` object.

A Simple Example: A Configured Login Page

To illustrate the use of initialization parameters, a simple login application is shown that uses initialization parameters to declare a valid username and password. You would not normally put more than a few usernames and passwords as initialization parameters other than a few privileged users or a reference to where a list of users could be found.

Listing 13.2 declares a form that gathers login information from the user and then forwards the request to the `loginCheck.jsp` page in Listing 13.3. The `loginCheck.jsp` page checks the user login information against initialization parameters and informs and either greets the user or invites the user to try again. The valid username and password are declared using the following two lines in the `weblogic.properties` file:

```
weblogic.httpd.register.loginCheck=jsp_servlet._logincheck
weblogic.httpd.initArgs.loginCheck=username=giuseppe,password=bre381sci432a
```

These lines declare the `loginCheck` Servlet and configure two initialization parameters.

LISTING 13.2 A Simple Login Page (`login.jsp`)

```
1: <HTML><HEAD><TITLE>JSP Checks Login Against Parameters</TITLE></HEAD><BODY>
2: <H2> Login </H2>
3: <FORM ACTION=/loginCheck METHOD=POST>
4: Username : <INPUT TYPE=TEXT NAME=usernameFormParam><BR>
5: Password : <INPUT TYPE=TEXT NAME=passwordFormParam><BR>
6: <INPUT TYPE=SUBMIT VALUE=Login>
7: </FORM>
8: </BODY></HTML>
```

LISTING 13.3 A Page that Checks User Login Information Against Initialization Parameters (`loginCheck.jsp`)

```
 1: <HTML><HEAD><TITLE>JSP Checks Login Against Parameters</TITLE></HEAD><BODY>
 2: <H1>Hello</H1>
 3: <%
 4:   String usernameFormParamValue = request.getParameter("usernameFormParam");
 5:   String passwordFormParamValue = request.getParameter("passwordFormParam");
 6:   if(usernameFormParamValue!=null){
 7:     String usernameInitParamValue = config.getInitParameter("username");
 8:     String passwordInitParamValue = config.getInitParameter("password");
 9:     if(usernameFormParamValue.equals(usernameInitParamValue)&&
10:       passwordFormParamValue.equals(passwordInitParamValue)){
11:       // login correct, greetings %>
12:       Welcome !!!
13: <%
14:     } else {
```

13

LISTING 13.3   continued

```
15:              // login incorrect, please try again %>
16:              Sorry but we dont know you <BR>
17:              Would you like to <A HREF=login.jsp>try again</A>
18: <%    }
19: } else {
20:         // login incorrect, please try again %>
21:         Sorry but your login is incorrect <BR>
22:         Would you like to <A HREF=login.jsp>try again</A>
23: <%}
24: %>
25: </BODY></HTML>
```

ANALYSIS Line 3 of Listing 13.2 declares a form that gathers login information and directs the request to loginCheck.jsp. The names of the parameters are tagged usernameFormParam and passwordFormParam in lines 4 and 5 respectively. Lines 4 and 5 of Listing 13.3 get the values of parameters usernameFormParam and passwordFormParam. If any of these values is not null, then lines 7 and 8 get the initialization parameters using the config object. Line 9 checks to see that the initialization parameters are equal to the form parameters. If so, line 12 prints a welcoming message. Otherwise line 16 prints an unfriendly message and suggests the user try again. If the form parameters do not exist, then something must have gone wrong, and line 21 informs the user of the problem and invites the user to try again.

The `ServletContext` Object

Servlets, and therefore JSPs, execute within the context of a Servlet container as described in Hour 3. The ServletContext contains a set of methods that a Servlet can use to communicate with the Servlet container. These methods allow you to configure properties that are accessible and common across all Servlets executing in the Servlet container. Servlets can use the ServletContext to share objects across Servlets, forward requests to other Servlets, log messages to keep track of execution or errors, and find out meta information about the container itself, such as its name and version. Table 13.3 lists the API for the ServletContext class. Many of these methods will be covered in Hour 20, "Using Multiple JSPs to Handle the Request."

TABLE 13.3   ServletContext Object Methods

Method	Description
void setAttribute(String, Object)	Binds object to named attribute in Servlet context
Object getAttribute(String)	Returns object bound to named attribute
Enumeration getAttributeNames()	Returns all the names of the named attributes

TABLE 13.3   continued

Method	Description
void removeAttribute(String)	Unbinds and removes attribute from Servlet context
String getInitParameter(String)	Returns value of context-wide initialization parameter
Enumeration getInitParameters()	Returns all the names of the context-wide initialization parameters
RequestDispatcher getNamedDispatcher (String)	Returns dispatcher that wraps around named Servlet
RequestDispatcher getRequestDispatcher (String)	Returns dispatcher that wraps around resource located in named path
String getRealPath(String)	Returns the real path for the virtual path passed in
ServletContext getContext(String)	Returns Servlet context corresponding to named URL
URL getResource(String)	Returns the URL to the resource in the named path
InputStream getResourceAsStream (String)	Returns the URL to the resource in the named path as an InputStream
String getServerInfo()	Returns the Servlet container's name and version
void log(String)	Writes the message to a log file
void log(String, Throwable)	Writes the message and stack trace for the throwable exception
int getMajorVersion()	Returns the major version of the Servlet API supported by the Servlet container
int getMinorVersion()	Returns the minor version of the Servlet API supported by the Servlet container
String getMimeType(String)	Returns the MIME type of the specified file

Summary

This hour showed you how to register and initialize a JSP. The process of converting a JSP to a Servlet, registering, initializing, and then executing the Servlet was outlined. Several examples were used to illustrate the use of the config object and the JSP compiler. Finally the API for the ServletContext object was presented.

13

Q&A

Q Why are we initializing the Servlets in a configuration file? Why not put the initialization values in the JSP source code and forget the configuration file?

A Putting the initialization parameters in the JSP source code is an alternative to putting them in the configuration file. The benefit of using a configuration file is that the source code does not need to change when the initialization parameters need to change. This makes the source code more portable and reusable. Also note that changes in the source code means that the resulting Servlet needs to be recompiled and redeployed.

Q When I change the source code of a JSP I can usually see the changes right away when I reload the JSP in my browser. This doesn't seem to apply for JSPs that have been converted to Servlets. Why?

A Yes, when you convert a JSP to a Servlet you lose the convenience of being able to change the JSP and see the changes immediately. The reason is that Servlets from a JSP are like any other Servlet—they must be deployed and configured in the configuration file and the classes that implement them are loaded only once by the application server. This means that if you want a change in a JSP to reflect on its corresponding Servlet, you will need to reboot the application server. Some application servers allow hot deployment of some or all of its different services, including Servlets. Hot deployment means that some or all of the pieces of an application can be inserted or modified without shutting down the application server. Hot deployment together with deployment tools help the process of reconfiguring JSPs quickly but can't beat the versatility of just changing the source and having those changes take effect on-the-fly.

Workshop

The quiz questions and activities are provided for your further understanding. See Appendix A, "Answers," for the answers to the quiz.

Quiz

1. How would you change the package name of a Servlet that is compiled from a JSP?

2. From within a JSP how would you find out the name by which the corresponding Servlet is registered in the configuration file?

3. How would you list all the names of the initialization parameters from within a JSP?

Activity

Modify the dynamicForm JSP from Hour 11 and deploy it as a servlet. Modify the JSP so that it uses the config object to set the values of variables startYear and endYear from initialization parameters of the same name. When you register the servlet in weblogic.properties, make sure to also set the initialization arguments for parameters startYear and endYear.

HOUR 14

Creating Error Pages

Errors in an application are inevitable. If not handled properly, they can wreak havoc and often bring an application to a halt. In this hour you will learn mechanisms to properly handle and process errors using Java exceptions and JSP error pages.

The following topics are covered in this hour:

- Creating and using custom exceptions
- Raising and catching exceptions
- Determining and creating error pages
- Using the JSP implicit exception object

Understanding Errors

Web applications naturally strive to provide services that can endure a 24-hour/7-day-a-week work cycle. Part of achieving that goal is handling the unexpected as smoothly as possible. Developers design many scenarios through which users might interact with their application in the "normal" way, following the "rules" of the application. But designers, like everyone else, know that there are always "exceptions" to the rules, and a good Web application should have built-in safety measures to deal with the exceptions.

JSPs, and Java in general, provide a mechanism for dealing with unpredictable scenarios through the use of exception classes and accompanying logic. Handling exceptions appropriately can reduce the chances that an application might hang up and crash.

New Term: Runtime Errors

There are two types of errors of which you need to take care. Some of the errors like syntactical errors are caught by the compiler and it will let you know accordingly. These typically are trivial errors like using a variable that you have not yet declared, or forgetting to pass an argument to a method that expects arguments. There are errors that are not caught by the compiler and only make their presence known when the application executes. These are referred to as runtime errors. Java's exception mechanism is designed to handle runtime errors.

The idea behind controlling errors or exceptions is to write code that contains or catches errors in some predictable and controllable section of the code. In other words, you do not want errors propagating beyond the control of the application, because that usually means that the application enters a state from which it cannot recover—and crashes. The mechanism of processing errors relies on the concepts of throwing (or raising) exceptions and catching exceptions.

By catching errors under a controlled predictable piece of code, applications are able to recover from them gracefully, avoiding a crash.

The Exception and Throwable Classes

Exceptions are Java classes that contain useful information about what went wrong. They capture a small subset of the state of the application that can give you a clue to solving the problem. Exceptions are thrown when an error occurs. The error propagates through the code until it is caught. If the developer's code does not catch an exception, the core Java system will—by which time it is usually too late to be handled properly.

All exceptions in Java extend the Java class Exception. The Exception class does not define any methods of its own; it inherits all its methods from the Throwable class. Table 14.1 lists all the methods of the Throwable class.

TABLE 14.1 Methods of the Throwable Class

Method	Description
`Throwable()`	Constructs object with null error message
`Throwable(String)`	Constructs object with the string error message
`Throwable fillInStackTrace()`	Fills extra information in the stack trace useful when exception is being re-thrown
`String getMessage()`	Returns the string error message
`void printStackTrace()`	Prints the stack trace to the standard error stream
`void printStackTrace(PrintStream)`	Prints the stack trace to the `PrintStream`
`void printStackTrace(PrintWriter)`	Prints the stack trace to the `PrintWriter`
`String toString()`	Returns a string representation of this object

The stack trace mentioned in Table 14.1 is a list of the methods in a chain of nested methods that were pending when the exception occurred. Stack trace will be covered shortly in the "Understanding the Stack Trace" section.

Exceptions are instantiated as any other Java class. Usually a message string is used to provide a description of the circumstances by which the exception was thrown.

Exceptions are thrown using the `throw` statement, which halts execution of the current method and returns by propagating the exception to the method that originated the method call. If the `caller` method does not catch the exception, the exception is propagated to whoever called the method.

A method that throws an exception with the `throw` statement must declare the exception as part of the signature of the method using the `throws` clause. The following syntax describes the `throws` clause:

```
ReturnType methodName(Arguments) throws ExceptionType {
  methodBody
}
```

A method can throw any number of methods as long as each is listed in the `throws` clause. The following syntax illustrates how an exception is instantiated and then thrown with the `throw` statement.

```
ReturnType methodName(Arguments) throws ExceptionType {
  ...
  if(exceptionShouldBeThrown){
    ExceptionType exceptionInstance = new ExceptionType(errorMessageString);
    throw exceptionInstance;
  }
  ...
}
```

14

Notice that an exception is thrown within some logic that determines whether or not the exception should be thrown. For instance, a method or operator that implemented the division operation would need to check that the denominator was not 0. If it were zero, then the implementing method should throw an exception complaining of a division by zero. The following section uses this example to illustrate the concept of a stack trace.

Understanding the Stack Trace

It is often very useful to know how an exception propagated through the code. This is especially so when the exception is raised in the method part of a chain of several nested method calls spanning different objects. If the collection of methods and objects are listed from the origin of the exception to the point where the nested calls began, the list is referred to as a *stack trace*. The listing of the stack trace is useful for tracking down the root cause of a problem. To illustrate the idea of a stack trace, consider the following piece of code where the method divideByZero() intentionally causes an exception to be raised:

```
public class SimpleException {
  public SimpleException(){ callDivideByZero(); }
  public void callDivideByZero(){ divideByZero(); }
  public void divideByZero(){ int infinity = 123/0; }
  public static void main(String args[]){
    SimpleException s = new SimpleException();
  }
}
```

When you compile and execute this class as

```
javac SimpleException.java
java SimpleException
```

the following stack trace is printed to the console:

```
Exception in thread "main" java.lang.ArithmeticException: / by zero
        at SimpleException.divideByZero(SimpleException.java:9)
        at SimpleException.callDivideByZero(SimpleException.java:6)
        at SimpleException.<init>(SimpleException.java:3)
        at SimpleException.main(SimpleException.java:12)
```

Read the stack trace from bottom to top: that order reflects the order in which the methods are called in the class. That is, the main() method is called first, then the constructor (<init>), then the callDivideByZero() method, and finally the divideByZero() method, where the exception is thrown by Java.

Catching Exceptions

Exceptions are caught using the try/catch control structure. The try and catch statements work together to contain and process possible sources of exceptions. The syntax is as follows:

```
try {
  javaCodeBlock0
```

```
} catch(SomeExceptionType1 exceptionObject1){
  javaCodeBlock1
} catch(SomeExceptionType2 exceptionObject2){
  javaCodeBlock2
}...etc...
```

A try/catch block should always be used when the Java code in the try block could potentially throw an exception. In the case of this syntax, the try/catch block attempts to execute the *javaCodeBlock0*, which is some code that is known to potentially throw an exception if something goes wrong. The *javaCodeBlock0* can throw any number of exceptions of different types. If *javaCodeBlock0* throws an exception of type *SomeExceptionType1*, then *javaCodeBlock1* executes to handle the exception. The exception instance can be referenced by the variable *exceptionObject1* inside *javaCodeBlock1*. The methods of object can be used to find out more details about the exception.

Processing Exceptions

Java provides a number of exceptions that it uses to inform developers when something goes wrong. These exceptions have their own logic of when they should be thrown and caught and what messages describe what went wrong. Often the messages are of little help since the errors propagate deep into the inner workings of Java with little relation to the origin of the error. Java allows developers to create their own custom exception classes that can be used to provide more descriptive information to track down errors.

Creating Custom Exceptions

Creating custom exceptions allows developers to create their own mechanisms of determining what could go wrong with their code and to deal with the problems gracefully. The custom exceptions can be tailored to reflect the details of the logic of the application being developed, and the messages describing the error can be made more meaningful.

To illustrate the usefulness of custom exceptions, consider a simple JSP that checks the validity of a username in a string called username. If the JSP is not careful it might not consider that the username string could be null. This error propagates through the JVM (Java Virtual Machine) until a null pointer exception is thrown. Tracking down the original source of the error is often challenging. A more careful logic might check the username against several possible values and policies and throw custom exceptions that describe what the problem is. For instance, a particular exception could be thrown if the username is too short or too long or not defined (null). Each exception could use a custom descriptive message of exactly what went wrong.

The class definition in Listing 14.1 declares a custom exception by extending the Exception class. The custom exception in Listing 14.2 is almost identical except for the name of the class. The exceptions will be used in the following sections to create JSPs

14

that verify login information and throw exceptions when the username or password is invalid based on some criteria.

LISTING 14.1   Declaring a Custom Exception (`InvalidUserNameException.java`)

```
1: package javain24hrs.hour14;
2: import Exception;
3: public class InvalidUserNameException extends Exception {
4:   public InvalidUserNameException(String message){
5:   super(message);
6:   }
7: }
```

LISTING 14.2   Declaring Another Custom Exception
(`InvalidPasswordException.java`)

```
1: package javain24hrs.hour14;
2: import Exception;
3: public class InvalidPasswordException extends Exception {
4:   public InvalidPasswordException(String message){
5:    super(message);
6:   }
7: }
```

ANALYSIS   This analysis is for both Listings 14.1 and 14.2. Line 3 declares the class
(`InvalidUserNameException` or `InvalidPasswordException`) as an `Exception`
by extending the class `Exception`. The constructor in line 4 takes a `message` string as an
argument. The message is usually printed to the console where the application server is
running. Line 5 calls the parent constructor (`Exception`) and passes the `message` argument to it. The custom exception will behave as any other exception when it is thrown.

Raising Exceptions in a JSP

Exceptions can be thrown from any Java code portion, such as within a JSP method declaration, JSP scriptlet, or a method in a Java class. This and the following sections
explore the different possibilities of throwing and catching exceptions.

Listing 14.3 declares two methods that check the validity of a username and its com-
panion password. If these are shorter than expected, corresponding exceptions are
thrown. The exceptions are the custom exceptions declared in Listings 14.1 and 14.2,
`InvalidUserNameException` and `InvalidPasswordException`. The JSP scriptlet that
invokes the methods does not make any attempt to catch the exceptions. This will

illustrate what happens when an exception is not caught. The exception will propagate through the Servlet container and eventually will be reported to the console where the application server is running.

LISTING 14.3   A JSP that Raises an Exception (`raisingExceptionInJSP.jsp`)

```
 1: <HTML><HEAD><TITLE></TITLE></HEAD><BODY>
 2: <%@ page import="com.macmillan.jspIn24.hour14.*"%>
 3: <%!
 4:     void checkUsername(String username) throws InvalidUsernameException {
 5:         if(username.length()<4)
 6:             throw new InvalidUsernameException("The username "+username+
 7:                                             " is too short");
 8:     }
 9:     void checkPassword(String password) throws InvalidPasswordException {
10:         if(password.length()<4)
11:             throw new InvalidPasswordException("The password "+password+
12:                                             " is too short");
13:     }
14: %>
15: <%
16:     String username = request.getParameter("username");
17:     String password = request.getParameter("password");
18:     if(username!=null) checkUsername(username);
19:     if(password!=null) checkPassword(password);
20: %>
21: Please Login
22: <FORM ACTION=raisingExceptionInJSP.jsp METHOD=POST>
23:     Username: <INPUT TYPE=TEXT NAME=username> <BR>
24:     Password: <INPUT TYPE=TEXT NAME=password> <BR>
25:     <INPUT TYPE=SUBMIT VALUE=Login>
26: </FORM>
27: </BODY></HTML>
```

ANALYSIS   Lines 4–8 and lines 9–13 declare methods `checkUsername()` and `checkPassword()`, respectively. These methods take string arguments that represent the username and password. The strings are checked to verify that they are at least 4 characters long. If they are not, an appropriate exception is instantiated and thrown. The methods are called from lines 18 and 19 if the corresponding parameters exist in the `request` object in lines 15 and 17. The request is generated by the form declared in lines 22–26, which declares input fields for the `username` and `password`.

Figure 14.1 shows the output of the JSP when the user submits qwe as the username. Note that the message in the second line is created by the method `checkUsername()`.

14

FIGURE **14.1**

*The exception thrown
by the methods in the
JSP is reflected in the
console where the
application server is
running.*

Catching Exceptions in a JSP

Catching exceptions allows you to create logic to detect the error, notify the user of the error, maybe log the error for maintenance purposes, and recover from the error to an acceptable state of the application.

For instance, consider the billing portion of an online store. It needs to deal with different possible outcomes of authorizing a client's credit card. The transaction might go fine most of the time but once in a while several other things may occur—the server at the financial institution might be down, the local network connection might be down, the user does not have sufficient credit available, and so forth. Different exceptions might be used to handle abnormal conditions.

Listing 14.4 enhances Listing 14.3 by adding a `try/catch`. Since the exceptions are caught in the JSP, they won't be propagated to the JVM and so they will not be reflected in the console.

LISTING 14.4 A JSP that Raises an Exception in a Method and then Catches It
(`raisingAndCatchingExceptionInJSP.jsp`)

```
 1: <HTML><HEAD><TITLE></TITLE></HEAD><BODY>
 2: <%@ page import="com.macmillan.jspIn24.hour14.*"%>
 3: <%!
 4:     void checkUsername(String username) throws InvalidUsernameException {
 5:         if(username.length()<4)
 6:             throw new InvalidUsernameException("The username "+username+
 7:                                             " is too short");  ·
 8:     }
 9:     void checkPassword(String password) throws InvalidPasswordException {
10:         if(password.length()<4)
11:             throw new InvalidPasswordException("The password "+password+
12:                                             " is too short");
13:     }
14: %>
```

LISTING 14.4 continued

```
15: <%
16:     String username = request.getParameter("username");
17:     String password = request.getParameter("password");
18:     try {
19:         if(username!=null) checkUsername(username);
20:     } catch(InvalidUsernameException e) { %>
21:         Sorry but your username <B><%=username%></B> is too short <BR>
22: <%  }
23:     try {
24:         if(password!=null) checkPassword(password);
25:     } catch(InvalidPasswordException e) { %>
26:         Sorry but your password <B><%=password%></B> is too short <BR>
27: <%  }
28: %>
29: Please Login
30: <FORM ACTION=raisingExceptionInJSP.jsp METHOD=POST>
31:     Username: <INPUT TYPE=TEXT NAME=username> <BR>
32:     Password: <INPUT TYPE=TEXT NAME=password> <BR>
33:     <INPUT TYPE=SUBMIT VALUE=Login>
34: </FORM>
35: </BODY></HTML>
```

ANALYSIS Lines 1–17 are the same as in Listing 14.3. They declare methods checkUsername()
and checkPassword() as well as retrieving parameter values username and password
from the request object. The difference between the JSPs begins at line 18 where the if
statements that call the checkUsername() and checkPassword() methods are wrapped inside
a try/catch block. The try statement of line 18 works together with the catch statement of
line 20 to process exceptions of type InvalidUsernameException. If an exception is thrown
by any statement in the try statement body (line 19) then the code in the catch body is executed (line 21). The same goes for the try/catch block in lines 23–27: The try in line 23
works together with the catch in line 25. If an exception of type InvalidPasswordException
is thrown in line 24, the code in line 26 is executed.

Figure 14.2 shows the output of the JSP when the user inputs a bad username and bad
password. Note that the execution of the JSP does not halt when the first exception is
thrown since the catch statement handles it gracefully. Also, no messages are printed to
the console since the exception is handled entirely within the JSP.

14

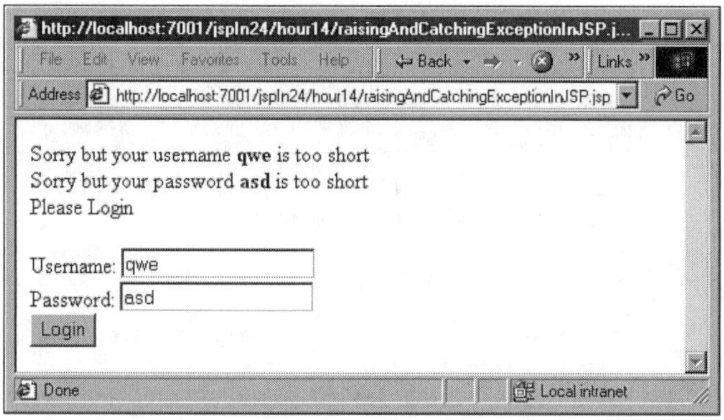

FIGURE 14.2

*The JSP handles the
exceptions internally
by notifying the user
what went wrong.*

Raising Exceptions in a Java Class and Catching Them in a JSP

Although exceptions can be thrown from anywhere, it is more appropriate to throw them from Java classes or JavaBeans. Java classes are more appropriate because JSPs should concern themselves with the presentation layer, that is, the Web page content logic. Low-level details of handling errors are best left to specialized backend Java classes.

Listing 14.5 declares a class that basically wraps the two methods that have been used throughout this hour (`checkUsername()` and `checkPassword()`). The JSP instantiates the Java class as a JavaBean and then invokes the methods within a `try/catch` block. JavaBeans will be covered in detail in Hour 16, "Using JavaBeans in a JSP."

Listing 14.6 declares a JSP that uses the JavaBean of Listing 14.5 and catches and processes the exceptions if any are thrown.

LISTING 14.5   Raising Exceptions from a JavaBean (`RaisingExceptionInClass.java`)

```
 1: package com.macmillan.jspIn24.hour14;
 2: public class RaisingExceptionInClass {
 3:   public RaisingExceptionInClass(){}
 4:   public void checkUsername(String username)
 5:     throws InvalidUsernameException {
 6:     if(username.length()<4)
 7:       throw new InvalidUsernameException("The username "+username+
 8:                                         " is too short");
 9:   }
10:   public void checkPassword(String password)
11:     throws InvalidPasswordException {
12:     if(password.length()<4)
13:       throw new InvalidPasswordException("The password "+password+
14: " is too short");
15:   }
16: }
```

LISTING 14.6 A JSP that Catches Exceptions Thrown by a JavaBean
(raisingExceptionInClass.jsp)

```
 1: <HTML><HEAD><TITLE></TITLE></HEAD><BODY>
 2: <%@ page import="com.macmillan.jspIn24.hour14.*"%>
 3: <jsp:useBean id="validate"
 4:             class="com.macmillan.jspIn24.hour14.RaisingExceptionInClass"/>
 5: <%
 6:     String username = request.getParameter("username");
 7:     String password = request.getParameter("password");
 8:     try {
 9:         if(username!=null) validate.checkUsername(username);
10:     } catch(InvalidUsernameException e) { %>
11:         Sorry but your username <B><%=username%></B> is too short <BR>
12: <% }
13:     try {
14:         if(password!=null) validate.checkPassword(password);
15:     } catch(InvalidPasswordException e) { %>
16:         Sorry but your password <B><%=password%></B> is too short <BR>
17: <% }
18: %>
19: Please Login
20: <FORM ACTION=raisingExceptionInClass.jsp METHOD=POST>
21:     Username: <INPUT TYPE=TEXT NAME=username> <BR>
22:     Password: <INPUT TYPE=TEXT NAME=password> <BR>
23:     <INPUT TYPE=SUBMIT VALUE=Login>
24: </FORM>
25: </BODY></HTML>
```

ANALYSIS Listing 14.5 declares a JavaBean that raises exceptions if the username and/or password are not acceptable. Method checkUsername() in line 4 takes a username string as an argument and checks its length in line 6. If the username is too short, line 7 creates an instance of an exception and throws it. Similarly, method checkPassword() in line 10 checks the length of the password in line 12 and, if it is too short, throws an exception in line 13.

The JSP in Listing 14.6 creates an instance of the JavaBean in line 3, naming it validate. Lines 6 and 7 get the username and password parameters. Line 8 declares a try/catch block that uses the validate JavaBean to validate the username in line 9 if this exists. If the validate JavaBean throws an exception, line 11 is executed, informing the user that the username is too short. Similarly line 13 declares a try/catch block that checks the password, if it exists, and informs the user if the password is too short. The rest of the code declares a form used to gather the login information.

The output of the JSP is exactly the same as the one for Listing 14.4.

14

Implementing Error Pages

An error page is an additional mechanism for processing exceptions when developing Web applications. An *error page* is a Web page that can be used to inform the user of errors and/or document errors that occur in a Web application. It can be used as a catch-all-problems page that could handle unexpected behaviors of the application. For instance, an error page could be defined to handle stale URLs so that if customers click on a hyperlink that points to a page that does not exist anymore, the error page would politely inform the user. This is in contrast to the very rude error message 404, Page Not Found.

Determining the Error Page

Error pages are declared and referenced from JSPs using the errorPage attribute of the page JSP directive with the following syntax:

```
<%@ page errorPage="someErrorPage.jsp "%>
```

A typical arrangement is to have several related JSPs refer to a common error page. If any of the JSPs encounters a problem where an exception is thrown, the error page will be shown. The error page should be smart enough to be able to handle errors from several pages and the pages should be related enough to justify a common error page.

The JSP in Listing 14.7, login.jsp, uses a form to gather login information and sends the request off to goodLogin.jsp (Listing 14.8). goodLogin.jsp uses JavaBean UserNameValidationBean (Listing 14.9) to validate that the username is at least 4 characters long. The JSPs of Listings 14.7 and 14.8 declare badLogin.jsp as their error page. If for any reason an exception is thrown within login.jsp or goodLogin.jsp, the JSPs will redirect the browser to badLogin.jsp.

LISTING 14.7   JSP Gathers Login Information and Ships It to goodLogin.jsp (login.jsp)

```
1: <HTML><HEAD><TITLE></TITLE></HEAD><BODY>
2: <%@ page errorPage="badLogin.jsp"%>
3: <%@ page import="com.macmillan.jspIn24.hour14.UserNameValidationBean"%>
4: <FORM ACTION=goodLogin.jsp METHOD=POST>
5:   <BR>User Name:<INPUT TYPE=TEXT NAME=username>
6:   <BR>Password: <INPUT TYPE=TEXT NAME=password>
7:   <BR><INPUT TYPE=SUBMIT VALUE=Submit>
8: </FORM>
9: </BODY></HTML>
```

LISTING 14.8 JSP that Uses JavaBean to Check Username and Greets User if Successful Login (goodLogin.jsp)

```
1: <HTML><HEAD><TITLE></TITLE></HEAD><BODY>
2: <%@ page errorPage="badLogin.jsp"%>
3: <%@ page import="com.macmillan.jspIn24.hour14.UserNameValidationBean"%>
4: <% UserNameValidationBean validationBean = new UserNameValidationBean();
5:    if(request.getParameter("username")!=null)
6:        validationBean.validateUserName(request.getParameter("username"));
7: %>
8: You have successfully logged in <%=request.getParameter("username")%>
9: </BODY></HTML>
```

ANALYSIS Listing 14.7, login.jsp, declares badLogin.jsp as its error page in line 2. A form is used in lines 4–8 to gather login information and send the request to goodLogin.jsp. goodLogin.jsp in Listing 14.8 also declares its error page to be badLogin.jsp in line 2. Line 4 of goodLogin.jsp creates an instance of UserNameValidationBean and then uses it in line 6 to validate the username parameter from the request object.

Figure 14.3 shows the output of the JSPs when the username is at least four characters long.

FIGURE 14.3

If the username is at least 4 characters long, goodLogin.jsp *is shown.*

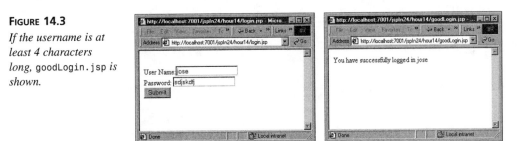

Listing 14.9 declares JavaBean UserNameValidationBean that checks that the username is at least 4 characters long and throws an exception if not. If an exception is thrown within login.jsp or goodLogin.jsp, then badLogin.jsp (Listing 14.10) will be executed informing the user of a problem with the username.

LISTING 14.9 A Class that Validates Usernames (UserNameValidationBean.java)

```
1: package com.macmillan.jspIn24.hour14;
2: public class UserNameValidationBean {
3:    public UserNameValidationBean(){}
4:    public boolean validateUserName(String userName)
5:                   throws InvalidUsernameException {
```

14

LISTING 14.9   continued

```
 6:      if(userName.length()<4)
 7:         throw new InvalidUsernameException("User Name Invalid: " + userName);
 8:   return true;
 9:    }
10: }
```

LISTING 14.10   Declaring a JSP as an Error Page (badLogin.jsp)

```
1: <HTML><HEAD><TITLE></TITLE></HEAD><BODY>
2: There was an error with the login
3: <P><A HREF=login.jsp>Try again</A>
4: </BODY></HTML>
```

ANALYSIS   The JavaBean UserNameValidationBean in Listing 14.9 declares a method called validateUserName() in line 4. The method takes the username from the JSP and makes sure that the username is at least 4 characters long in line 6. If it isn't, the method throws an exception in line 7; otherwise it returns true in line 8. If an exception is thrown, it will cause the JSP that uses the JavaBean to redirect the browser to the badLogin.jsp in Listing 14.10.

Figure 14.4 shows the output of badLogin.jsp after a user submits a username with less than 4 characters.

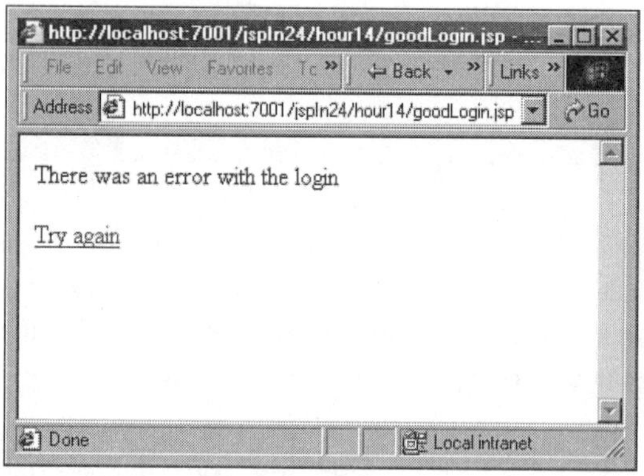

FIGURE 14.4

A simple error page is displayed when the user enters a bad username.

The exception Implicit Object

The example error page badLogin.jsp introduced in the previous section provided a static message that, although it describes the problem, is inadequate in cases where there might be several sources of error. In such cases the error page must have access to

information about the cause of the error. This can be accomplished by using the
isErrorPage attribute of the page directive with the following syntax:

```
<%@ page isErrorPage=true|false %>
```

When an error JSP sets the isErrorPage attribute to true, the JSP has access to the JSP
implicit object exception object in addition to the other implicit objects. The exception
object contains a reference to the exception that was thrown and can be used by the JSP
to find out what went wrong and be more informative. The exception object is of type
JspException, which inherits all its methods and attributes from the class Exception,
which in turn inherits all its methods and attributes from the class Throwable.

Listing 14.11, badLoginWithExceptionObject.jsp, shows a JSP that declares itself to be
an error page and then uses the exception object. The JSP is meant to be used in place of
its simpler version, badLogin.jsp, the example in the previous section. To do the substitu-
tion you need to edit the errorPage attributes of login.jsp and goodLogin.jsp pages so
that they point to badLoginWithExceptionObject.jsp instead of badLogin.jsp.

The JSP in Listing 14.11 illustrates the use of two methods of the exception object. The
first one is straightforward, getMessage(). It retrieves the message of the exception that
was thrown. The message is set when the exception is instantiated and then thrown in
UserNameValidationBean.

The second method, printStackTrace(), is somewhat trickier. It prints the trace of the
classes and methods through which the exception propagates in Java. This is useful information for developers since it helps to track down the root of the problem. It is less interesting to users since the stack trace tends to be very blunt and unfriendly. There are several
versions of the printStackTrace() method that accept different parameters depending on
where the printout should be directed. The print output could go to standard out, which is
the console, or a buffered character stream. Buffered streams allow developers to progressively add bits and pieces of data as a computation is in progress. The JSP implicit object
out is such an object. The problem is that the out object is of type JspWriter and none of
the printStackTrace() methods take as an argument a JspWriter object. Fortunately
there is a printStackTrace() method that will take a PrintWriter object, which is a close
relative to JspWriter. PrintWriter and JspWriter are derived from a common abstract
class, Writer. This allows PrintWriter objects to be created from a reference to the
JspWriter (out) object using the constructor method of PrintWriter. Once an instance
of PrintWriter is created with a reference to out the instance can be passed to the
printStackTrace() method, which will print to the out object and be rendered in the
browser.

Listing 14.11 will help you understand how the exception object and its methods are used.

14

LISTING 14.11 Referencing the exception Object from an Error Page
(badLoginWithExceptionObject.jsp)

```
1: <HTML><HEAD><TITLE></TITLE></HEAD><BODY>
2: <%@ page isErrorPage = "true"%>
3: <P>Error = <%= exception.getMessage()%>
4: <% PrintWriter writer = new PrintWriter(out); %>
5: <P>Stack = <% exception.printStackTrace(writer); %>
6: <P><A HREF=login.jsp>Try again</A>
7: </BODY></HTML>
```

ANALYSIS   Line 2 declares the JSP as an error page. Line 3 uses the exception object to get the message of the error. The message is set when it is thrown from the JavaBean UserNameValidationBean. Line 4 creates an instance of class PrintWriter and initializes it with a reference to the JSP implicit object out. Line 5 calls method printStackTrace() with the PrintWriter instance, which has a reference to the out object. Line 6 gives the user another chance to log in.

Figure 14.5 shows the output of the JSP when the user uses a username that has less than 4 characters. Note that the error message thrown from the JavaBean is accessed through the exception object and printed in the page. The stack trace is listed showing the propagation of the exception through several methods and classes before being caught.

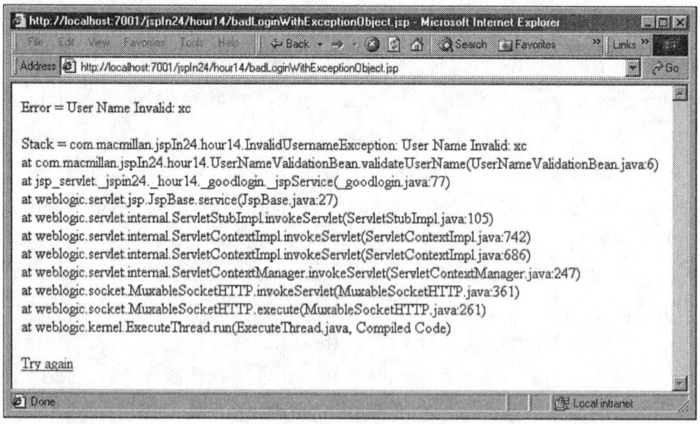

FIGURE 14.5

An error page can access the exception *object to show detailed information about the exception thrown.*

Summary

This hour presented mechanisms for managing errors that occur when an application is executing. Java exceptions were introduced as the means to encapsulate and propagate errors. You first learned how Java raises exceptions when errors are detected by the JVM.

Several examples showed you how to create and raise custom exceptions. The examples covered several combinations of throwing and raising exceptions in JavaBeans and JSPs.

Q&A

Q **Would exceptions be useful in validating parameters from a form? How would that be done?**

A Exceptions would certainly be useful in validating parameters submitted with forms. To process the parameters you would need to enumerate the fields of the form and the ranges or policies of each field. If the values of the submitted fields don't match the ranges or policies for the fields, an exception would be raised. The exception could contain an enumeration of the fields that had trouble and a message that politely asks the user to complete the highlighted fields appropriately. The enumeration of the troubled fields would be used to highlight the fields by either bolding them or setting their color to red.

Q **The examples in this hour showed exceptions being instantiated with a string message. Is this the only thing that an exception has to inform the user of the problem?**

A Custom exceptions can have constructors with as many extra parameters as you see necessary. In any case the first thing any constructor should do is invoke `super()` to set the error message. After that you can set the extra data from the arguments to the constructor.

Workshop

The quiz questions and activities are provided for your further understanding. See Appendix A, "Answers," for the answers to the quiz.

Quiz

1. What is the stack trace?
2. How is a page declared to be an error page?

Activity

Create a JSP that displays three fields in a form. If any field is empty when the form is submitted, raise an exception that will cause the form to be redisplayed with an asterisk next to the empty field.

14

HOUR 15

Inserting Applets into Your JSPs

The argument for inserting small programs into your HTML documents was made in Hour 1, "Introduction to Web Applications." The evolution of the Web was discussed in that hour and you were introduced to the Plug-In Web. The goal of the Plug-In architecture is to have more of the processing power on the client side, thereby taking some of the workload off of the server, which can then service more client requests. The small programs that were embedded into the HTML documents came in two flavors, Java applets and ActiveX controls. Sun Microsystems is responsible for the specification of Java applets.

As you discovered in Hour 6, "Understanding the Layout of a JSP," JSPs offer six preset action tags that can be used to replace large sections of code with simple tags. One of these is called the `plugin` action tag. It allows you to insert a Java applet or a JavaBean component into your JSP. JavaBean components can be used to create a graphical user interface (GUI) on the client side. The `plugin` action tag is converted to the appropriate `object` tag or `embed` tag in your HTML documents. You can use `object` tags, `embed` tags, or `applet` tags in your HTML documents to insert Java applets.

This hour focuses on the `plugin` action tag. You will learn

- The general syntax of a JSP action tag
- How to use the `plugin` action tag to insert a Java applet into your JSP
- How to pass parameters to the Java applet

The General Syntax of a JSP Action Tag

The JSP action tags perform common tasks such as accessing a server-side JavaBean object, including the output of other JSPs, and forwarding the request to another JSP.

Some action tags take bodies and they can be used for initialization, making available special variables, and using other action tags to further define what is happening. For example, the `include` action tag can tag a body made up of `setProperty` actions that initialize the JavaBean object when it is created.

The general syntax of an action tag that does not contain a body is

```
<jsp:action action_parameters />
```

The general syntax of an action tag that does contain a body is

```
<jsp:action action_parameters>
  //body
</jsp:action>

  action::= plugin | useBean | setProperty |
           getProperty | include | forward
  action_parameters::= dependent_on_the_type_of_action
```

 Having preset action tags is convenient, but what if you perform a block of code frequently that is not encompassed in one of the standard action tags? You can extend the functionality of your JSPs by importing a tag library. Tag libraries define new action tags that can be used in your JSPs. Hour 19, "Extending JSP Functionality with Tag Libraries," will discuss defining new actions and importing them into your JSP by importing a tag library.

Using the `plugin` Action to Insert an Applet

The stage is set for you to learn the particulars of inserting Java applets into your JSPs using the `plugin` action tag. You understand why you want to insert an applet into your JSP and you know that JSPs provide an action tag to accomplish it. Take a look at the syntax of the `plugin` action tag:

15

```
<jsp:plugin type="bean | applet"
            code="objectCode"
            codebase="objectCodeBase"
            { align="alignment" }
            { archive="archiveList" }
            { height="height" }
            { hspace="hspace" }
            { jreversion="jreversion" }
            { name="componentName" }
            { vspace="vspace" }
            { width="width" }
            { nspluginurl="url" }
            { iepluginurl="url" }>
    <params>
      <param name="name" value="paramValue" >
    </params>
    <fallback>text</fallback>
</jsp:plugin>
```

Table 15.1 discusses each of the attributes of the plugin action tag and also says where it is defined, the HTML specification or the JSP 1.1 specification.

TABLE 15.1 The Attributes of the plugin Action Tag

Attribute	Description	Specification
type	The type of component being inserted into the JSP.	JSP 1.1
code	The applet class file.	HTML
codebase	Optional base URI for applet class file.	HTML
align	Vertical or horizontal alignment.	HTML
archive	Comma-separated archive list.	HTML
height	Initial height in pixels.	HTML
hspace	Horizontal gutter. The amount of white space to the top and bottom of the applet.	HTML
jreversion	The specification version of the required version of the Java Runtime Environment(JRE) for the component. The default is 1.1.	JSP 1.1
name	Allows applets to find each other.	HTML
vspace	Vertical gutter. The amount of white space to the left and right of the applet.	HTML
width	Initial width in pixels.	HTML
nspluginurl	The URL of where the JRE version can be downloaded for Netscape Navigator. The default is implementation defined.	JSP 1.1

TABLE 15.1   continued

Attribute	Description	Specification
iepluginurl	The URL of where the JRE version can be downloaded for Internet Explorer. The default is implementation defined.	JSP 1.1

The parameters passed to the applet are specified using param tags passing the name of the parameter and the value. A params tag is used to group the param tags since there could be more than one.

The fallback tag is used to display text in case the user's browser is not Java enabled. If the user cannot view the applet, the text in the fallback tag will be displayed.

Let's examine a very simple JSP that inserts an applet using the plugin action. The applet was downloaded from http://www.javafile.com, which has a wealth of free applets for people to download and use. The site simply asks that you put a URL to its site from your page. Of course, it is always good to look at each of the applets you are downloading to see if there are any further restrictions.

Listing 15.1 shows the code for the simple JSP that inserts an applet, AdderApplet.class. The applet is an interactive calculator allowing you to do the basic types of arithmetic. Before you type in the code in this listing, copy the AdderApplet.class file to your working directory for this hour, c:\weblogic\myserver\public_html\hour15.

LISTING 15.1   A Simple JSP that Uses the plugin Action Tag to Insert a Basic Applet into the JSP (SimpleApplet.jsp)

```
 1: <HTML>
 2: <HEAD><TITLE>Inserting a Simple Applet</TITLE></HEAD>
 3:
 4: <BODY LINK="blue" VLINK="purple" ALINK="silver">
 5:
 6: <CENTER>
 7:
 8:   <FONT FACE="Trebuchet" SIZE="7" COLOR="navy">
 9:     Interactive Calculator
10:   </FONT>
11:
12:   <BR><BR>
13:
14:   <jsp:plugin code="AdderApplet.class"
15:               width="200"
16:               height="250">
17:   </jsp:plugin>
18:
19:   <BR><BR>
```

LISTING 15.1   continued

```
20:
21:   <A HREF="http://www.javafile.com">
22:      Download free Applets at www.javafile.com
23:   </A>
24:
25: </CENTER>
26:
27: </BODY>
28: </HTML>
```

ANALYSIS   Line 14 begins the plugin action tag. Notice the open angle bracket, the keyword jsp, the colon, and then the name of the action, plugin. The code for this applet is the AdderApplet.class file, which is specified with the code attribute in line 14. The AdderApplet.class file should be in the same directory as your JSP.

Line 15 specifies the width of the applet to be 200 pixels, and line 16 specifies the height of the applet to be 250 pixels. This applet does not take any parameters so there was no need to use the params and param tags.

Notice there is no fallback tag. This is not a required tag, but if the user does not have Java enabled, he will only get a blank page—he will not know that an applet was supposed to be there.

The plugin action tag will be converted to the appropriate embed or object tag in the resulting HTML document. Listing 15.2 shows the resulting HTML document from the SimpleApplet.jsp.

LISTING 15.2   Resulting HTML Document from Executing SimpleApplet.jsp

```
 1: <HTML>
 2: <HEAD><TITLE>Inserting a Simple Applet</TITLE></HEAD>
 3:
 4: <BODY LINK="blue" VLINK="purple" ALINK="silver">
 5:
 6: <CENTER>
 7:
 8:   <FONT FACE="Trebuchet" SIZE="7" COLOR="navy">
 9:     Interactive Calculator
10:   </FONT>
11:
12:   <BR><BR>
13:
14:   <EMBED type="application/x-java-applet"
15:   code="AdderApplet.class"  width="200"  height="250">
16:
17:
```

Listing 15.2   continued

```
18:  </EMBED>
19:
20:
21:   <BR><BR>
22:
23:   <A HREF="http://www.javafile.com">
24:     Download free Applets at www.javafile.com
25:   </A>
26:
27: </CENTER>
28:
29: </BODY>
30: </HTML>
```

Analysis   Notice the `plugin` action tag was replaced in the HTML document with an `embed`
tag. The type of object being embedded is specified in line 14 as `application/`
`x-java-applet`. The `embed` tag is given the same attributes you provided for the `plugin`
action; they are in line 15. The output from running this JSP is shown in Figure 15.1.

Figure 15.1

*The simple JSP with a
Java applet is viewed
in a browser.*

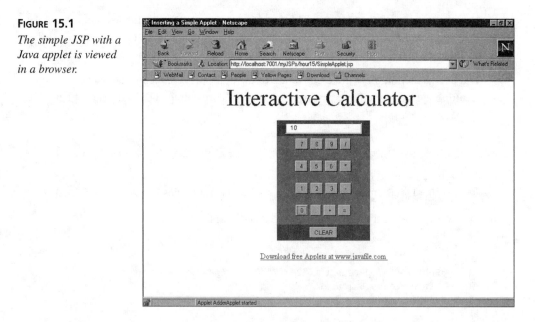

Play with the applet and have some fun. It is an interactive calculator that allows you to
do all the basic arithmetic operations.

Defining Initial Parameters for the Applet with the `param` Tags

15

The Java applet is a Java class, and it can take parameters that are specified in the HTML document. The parameters are passed into the applet using `param` tags. Since there can be more than one parameter passed to the applet, all the `param` tags are grouped together with a `params` tag. When you receive an applet (for example, if you download it from the Web) the parameters that it takes are specified in the documentation. The general syntax of the `params` tag and the `param` tag are

```
<params>
  <param name="parameterName" value="parameterValue">
  ...
</params>
```

where *parameterName* is the name of the attribute defined by the applet and *parameterValue* is a valid value for that particular parameter.

Make sure to use double quotes around your parameter name and the parameter value or the JSP compiler won't understand the tags. What the compiler doesn't understand, it doesn't process, and all your work will be ignored by the browser.

Listing 15.3 is a simple example of an applet using the `param` tags. The applet takes as parameters two images, which need to be of the same size. When the user's mouse moves over the image, the picture toggles between the two images you specified. This applet was downloaded from `http://www.javafile.com`. The applet can also take a URL as a parameter so that images can act as hyperlinks.

Before you type in this JSP, you need to set up the working environment by copying the files `fraid1.gif`, `fraid2.gif`, and `rollOver.class` to your working directory for this hour, `c:\weblogic\myserver\public_html\myJSPs\hour15`. Once you have done that, type in the code in Listing 15.3, which is the `ImageRoll.jsp`.

LISTING 15.3 Adding an Applet that Takes Parameters to a JSP (`ImageRoll.jsp`)

```
 1: <HTML>
 2: <HEAD><TITLE>Inserting a Simple Applet</TITLE></HEAD>
 3:
 4: <BODY>
 5:
 6: <CENTER>
 7:
 8:    <FONT FACE="Trebuchet" SIZE="7" COLOR="navy">
 9:       Rolling Images
10:    </FONT>
11:
```

LISTING 15.3   continued

```
12:    <BR><BR>
13:
14:    <FONT SIZE="5" COLOR="purple">
15:      Move your mouse on and off the image to see
16:      it change
17:    </FONT>
18:
19:    <BR><BR>
20:
21:    <jsp:plugin code="rollOver.class"
22:                width="33"
23:                height="37">
24:       <params>
25:         <param name="imgOff" value="fraid2.gif">
26:         <param name="imgOn" value="fraid1.gif">
27:         <param name="HLink" value="http://www.javafile.com">
28:       </params>
29:    </jsp:plugin>
30:
31: </CENTER>
32:
33: </BODY>
34: </HTML>
```

ANALYSIS   Line 21 starts the plugin action tag. It defines the Java class that defines the applet, rollOver.class. This file needs to be in the same directory as the JSP. Lines 22 and 23 specify the width and height of the applet in pixels. The width and height specified should be the same size as the images so the images only toggle when the mouse is over the image.

Since you are passing parameters to this applet you use the params tag to surround the param tags. Line 24 starts the params tag and it is closed on line 28.

Line 25 specifies the image to show when the mouse is off the image. The parameter name is imgOff and it is specified as the image fraid2.gif.

The image to show when the mouse is over the image is specified in line 26. The parameter name is imgOn and it is specified as the image fraid1.gif.

The third parameter that this applet can take is a URL so that the images can act as a hyperlink. Line 27 specifies this parameter, named HLink, and it has a value of http://www.javafile.com.

As in the first example, this JSP did not specify a fallback tag, since it is an optional tag. This means, however, if the user does not have Java enabled in her browser, she will see only a blank page and not be aware that there was supposed to be a Java applet there. Figure 15.2 shows the output of running this JSP with the mouse off the image.

FIGURE 15.2

ImageRoll.jsp *with a Java applet that takes parameters is viewed in a browser. With the mouse off the image, the viewer sees* fraid2.gif.

Figure 15.3 shows a screen shot with the mouse over the image.

FIGURE 15.3

With the mouse over the image, the view sees fraid1.gif.

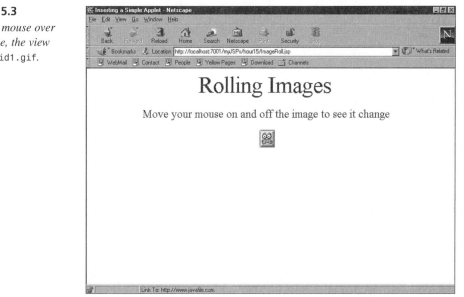

As you can see from the two screen shots, the image changes depending on whether you have the mouse on or off the image. Listing 15.4 shows the HTML document that was generated from running this JSP.

LISTING 15.4   HTML Document Resulting from Running ImageRoll.jsp

```
 1: <HTML>
 2: <HEAD><TITLE>Inserting a Simple Applet</TITLE></HEAD>
 3:
 4: <BODY>
 5:
 6: <CENTER>
 7:
 8:    <FONT FACE="Trebuchet" SIZE="7" COLOR="navy">
 9:      Rolling Images
10:    </FONT>
11:
12:    <BR><BR>
13:
14:    <FONT SIZE="5" COLOR="purple">
15:      Move your mouse on and off the image to see
16:      it change
17:    </FONT>
18:
19:    <BR><BR>
20:
21:    <EMBED type="application/x-java-applet"
22:           code="rollOver.class"
23:           width="33"
24:           height="37"
25:           imgOff="fraid2.gif"
26:           HLink="http://www.javafile.com"
27:           imgOn="fraid1.gif">
28:
29:    </EMBED>
30:
31:
32: </CENTER>
33:
34: </BODY>
35: </HTML>
```

ANALYSIS   As you can see, the plugin action tag was replaced with an embed tag in line 21. The attributes you specified for the plugin action are attributes of the embed tag (lines 21–24). However, also note on lines 25–27 that the parameters you specified with the param tags are now attributes of the embed tag.

Utilizing All Parts of the plugin Action

You have seen a simple example of an applet that does not take any parameters, and an applet that takes three parameters. Take a look at another one, which utilizes all the parts of the plugin action, the fallback tag included. This applet places text in orbit around an image, both the image and the text being totally configurable. You can also specify the angle of the tilt of the text orbiting the image, the background of the image, and the color of the text. This applet also was downloaded from http://www.javafile.com. You are going to write a JSP that utilizes this applet in this section.

Before you begin, set up your environment and copy the appropriate files into your working directory:

1. Place the image files background.gif and JFLogo.gif into your working directory for this hour, c:\weblogic\myserver\public_html\hour15.

2. Create a new subdirectory off of hour15 called orbiterClasses: c:\weblogic\ myserver\public_html\hour15\orbiterClasses.

3. Copy the following .class files into the orbiterClasses directory: Orbiter. class, tdFace.class, tdFont.class, tdMatrix.class, tdModel.class, tdObject.class, tdPolygon.class, tdVector.class, and tdViewpoint.class.

Since the .class files are located in another directory from the JSP you are going to need to use the codebase attribute to specify the location of the .class files.

Once you have the files in your working directory, you can write a JSP that utilizes this Java applet. Listing 15.5 shows the code for TextInOrbit.jsp that utilizes the Java applet, which puts text in orbit around an image.

LISTING 15.5 A JSP that Uses the plugin Action to Embed an Applet into the JSP (TextInOrbit.jsp)

```
 1: <HTML>
 2: <HEAD><TITLE>Orbiting Text</TITLE></HEAD>
 3:
 4: <BODY>
 5: <CENTER>
 6:
 7: <FONT SIZE="5" COLOR="navy">
 8:    Download
 9: </FONT>
10:
11: <FONT SIZE="7" color="red">
12:    FREE
13: </FONT>
14:
15: <FONT SIZE="5" COLOR="navy">
16:    Java Applets
17: </FONT>
18:
19: <BR><BR>
20:
21: This is one of the applets that can be downloaded. You
```

LISTING 15.5   continued

```
22: can change the background image and the text.
23:
24: <BR><BR>
25:
26: <jsp:plugin type="applet"
27:             code="Orbiter.class"
28:             codebase="http://localhost:7001/myJSPs/hour15/orbiterClasses"
29:             width="348"
30:             height="245">
31:     <params>
32:       <param name="tilt" value="35">
33:       <param name="string" value="The JavaFILE!      free java applets">
34:       <param name="planet" value="JFlogo.gif">
35:       <param name="url" value="http://www.javafile.com">
36:       <param name="background" value="background.gif">
37:       <param name="text_color_front" value="0000FF">
38:     </params>
39:
40:     <fallback>
41:       <FONT SIZE="5" COLOR="purple">
42:         There is a really cool Applet that is supposed to
43:         be running here. Too bad you have Java turned off
44:       </FONT>
45:     </fallback>
46:
47: </jsp:plugin>
48:
49: </CENTER>
50:
51: </BODY>
52: </HTML>
```

ANALYSIS   Line 26 begins the `plugin` action and defines the type of component to place in the resulting HTML document; the attribute type is specified as `applet`.

The code for the applet is defined in line 27 as `Orbiter.class`. However, this `.class` file is not located in the same directory as the JSP file, so you need to specify where it is located. This is done in line 28 with the `codebase` attribute, which takes a URI to the location of the `.class` files. Since you placed the `.class` files in the directory `orbiterClasses` off the `hour15` directory, the URI to these files is `http://localhost:7001/myJSPs/hour15/orbiterClasses`.

Lines 29 and 30 use the `width` and `height` attributes to specify the width and height of the applet in units of pixels. Therefore the applet will be 348 pixels wide and 245 pixels tall.

Line 31 begins the `params` tag and it is closed on line 38. The `params` tag surrounds all the param tags.

Lines 32–37 are the param tags to pass in parameters to the applet. Line 32 is for the parameter tilt, which specifies the angle to orbit the text around the image. This parameter is set to 35 degrees.

The text that orbits the image is specified in line 33 with the attribute string. The value for the text is set to "The JavaFILE!   free java applets".

Line 34 specifies the image the text is going to orbit around. The name of this attribute is planet and the image is JFLogo.gif.

The image can be used as a hyperlink and so there is a parameter, url, that can be set to link to another Web site. This parameter and its value (http://www.javafile.com) are set in line 35.

Another parameter this applet takes is the background for the image, which is specified in line 36. If you do not specify the background, it will be black. The parameter name for this is background and its value in this example is background.gif, which is just a white background.

The last parameter you can set is the color of the text that orbits the image. The parameter, text color front, and its value, 0000FF (navy), are set in line 37.

The fallback tag (lines 40–45) specifies text that will appear if the user does not have Java enabled in his browser.

Figure 15.4 shows a JSP with the applet running.

FIGURE 15.4

The example JSP uses an applet that sends text orbiting around an image.

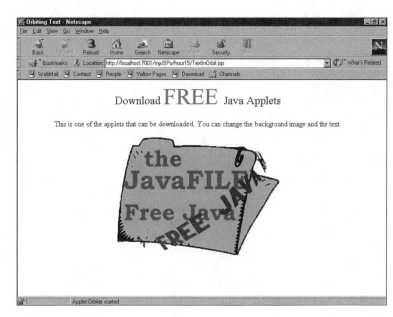

As you can see, this JSP loaded and executed the applet. However, what happens if the browser does not have Java enabled? Figure 15.5 shows the JSP's output if the user does not have Java enabled.

FIGURE 15.5

A user who does not have Java enabled in his browser will see this text instead.

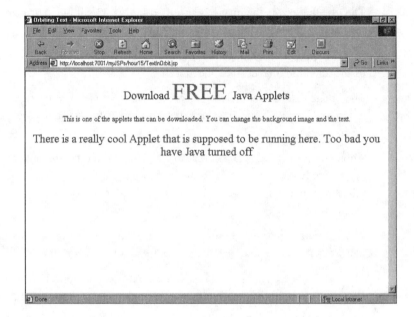

As the figure shows, the text specified in the `fallback` tag is displayed to the screen. Take a look at Listing 15.6, which shows the HTML code that is generated when this JSP is executed.

LISTING 15.6   HTML Code Generated by Executing `TextInOrbit.jsp`

```
 1: <HTML>
 2: <HEAD><TITLE>Orbiting Text</TITLE></HEAD>
 3:
 4: <BODY>
 5: <CENTER>
 6:
 7: <FONT SIZE="5" COLOR="navy">
 8:    Download
 9: </FONT>
10:
11: <FONT SIZE="7" color="red">
12:    FREE
13: </FONT>
14:
15: <FONT SIZE="5" COLOR="navy">
16:    Java Applets
```

LISTING 15.6   continued

15

```
17: </FONT>
18:
19: <BR><BR>
20:
21: This is one of the Applets that can be downloaded. You
22: can change the background image and the text.
23:
24: <BR><BR>
25:
26: <EMBED type="application/x-java-applet"
27:        code="Orbiter.class"
28:        width="348"
29:        codebase="http://localhost:7001/myJSPs/hour15/orbiterClasses"
30:        height="245"
31:        text_color_front="0000FF"
32:        tilt="35"
33:        string="The JavaFILE!    free java applets"
34:        background="background.gif"
35:        planet="JFlogo.gif"
36:        url="http://www.javafile.com">
37:
38:    <NOEMBED>
39:
40:       <FONT SIZE="5" COLOR="purple">
41:         There is a really cool Applet that is supposed to
42:         be running here. Too bad you have Java turned off
43:       </FONT>
44:
45:    </NOEMBED>
46: </EMBED>
47:
48:
49: </CENTER>
50:
51: </BODY>
52: </HTML>
```

ANALYSIS The plugin action tag is converted to the embed tag (line 26). All the attributes of the plugin action are transferred to be attributes of the embed tag, and the parameters that were specified become attributes of the embed tag (lines 26–36).

A new tag, the noembed tag, opens in line 38 and closes in line 45. It surrounds the text specified in the fallback tag. If Java is not enabled on the user's browser, this text will appear onscreen. If Java is enable, this text won't appear because the applet will load and execute.

Summary

The `plugin` action tag allows you to insert Java applets into your JSPs. Parameters can be passed into the applet by using `param` tags and passing the name and value of the parameter with the `name` and `value` attributes. Remember to place the values for the name and value attributes in double quotes since JSPs ignore any unknown tags.

Q&A

Q What should I do if the applet does not load and execute?

A The first thing you can do is look at the code of the HTML file. One way to do this is to right-click in the browser and select View Source.

If the `plugin` action tag is still there, then it is not being interpreted by the JSP compiler. If this is the case, make sure that the parameter values have double quotes around them, that the tags are nested properly, and that there is a close tag for each of your open tags.

If the embed tag is there and the fallback text is showing, make sure you have Java enabled in your browser.

Workshop

The quiz questions and activities are provided for your further understanding. See Appendix A, "Answers," for the answers to the quiz.

Quiz

1. What tag is used to pass a parameter to an applet, and what are its attributes?

2. What does the `codebase` attribute specify?

3. Why do you want to use the `fallback` tag?

Activity

Modify the parameters for each of the applets that take parameters, and view them in the browser. The parameters allow you to configure the applet to your liking, so change the images that are shown, the text that appears, and background and text colors.

HOUR 16

Using JavaBeans in a JSP

Web applications are often divided into two parts: the presentation and the business logic. The presentation piece encompasses all of what the user sees on a browser and is usually the product of the execution of some JSP. The business part consists of several Java classes that work together to model and execute the regulations, procedures, and workflow of the business.

JavaBeans is a standard for writing Java classes. The JavaBeans specification make Java classes convenient to use in many different applications including JSPs. This hour explains what JavaBeans are and how to use them in JSPs.

The following topics are covered in this hour:

- Instantiating and using JavaBeans in JSPs
- JavaBean scope
- Setting and getting JavaBean properties
- Using forms with JSPs

Understanding JavaBeans

Web applications are often divided into a *presentation layer* and a *business logic layer*. The presentation layer is what the user sees and interacts with in a browser. The business layer consists of several Java classes that work together to model and execute the workflow of a business, including business policies, rules, and procedures for handling business transactions.

JSPs fall in the category of presentation layer and JavaBeans in the category of business logic layer. JSPs are meant to be used for generating dynamic Web pages. Embedded java code in JSP scriptlets should be used to programmatically decide the layout and content of the page. For any serious computation tasks, you should consider creating specialized Java code like JavaBeans. Scriptlets can create instances of Java classes and use them as objects.

To illustrate how the different parts of a Web application can be classified as either in the presentation layer or the business logic layer, consider a Web site that sells several hundreds of items on the Web. The Web site might consist of the following Web pages: a welcome page, a catalog page, a shopping cart page, and a billing and shipping information page. These Web pages make up the presentation layer of the Web application and may be implemented by JSPs such as home.jsp, catalog.jsp, shoppingcart.jsp, billing.jsp, shipping.jsp, and any other supporting JSPs. Users interact with the Web pages by clicking hyperlinks and buttons to transition between the pages.

To illustrate the business logic layer, consider the scenario of the user browsing through the catalog, finding an item he wants, and adding it to the shopping cart. A reasonable interaction in the presentation layer would be that when the user clicks a hyperlink called "Add to shopping cart" on the catalog.jsp page, he is presented with the content of the shopping cart by transitioning to shoppingcart.jsp. (Remember in Hour 12, "Keeping Track of the User Session," you learned how to use the session object to keep track of items.) Another way of creating a shopping cart is to have a JavaBean implement the shopping cart in Java code and use it from the presentation layer. The JavaBean would be written in Java. The source of the class could be called something like ShoppingCart.java and have methods to compute everything you could expect to know from a shopping cart, such as what items are in the shopping cart, the total cost of the items in the shopping cart, how many of some items are in the cart, shipping information about a given item, and so on. The shopping cart could be written or persisted to a database for customers who intend to purchase the items in the near future. The shopping cart JavaBean could interact with other JavaBeans to update inventory, compute taxes for the items, determine credit card authorization, and so forth. In other words, JavaBeans could do a lot of the behind-the-scenes grunt work that is part of the details of running a particular business. These mechanisms comprise the business logic.

JavaBeans are particularly convenient because they lend themselves to be represented or referenced with special JSP tags. For a Java class to comply with the JavaBean specification, it must have a constructor with no arguments and getXxx() and setXxx() methods for each xxx class variable. Complying with JavaBeans specification is not a requirement, and any Java class can be used as a JavaBean from within a JSP.

16

The following sections will show several examples of JavaBeans. The first example introduces you to simple JavaBeans that model generic employees and a payroll. A JSP uses the beans to generate a dynamic payroll Web page. Then the lifecycle of JavaBeans is introduced and you learn how to control the lifecycle with the scope of the JavaBean. The use of scope is illustrated with an example JavaBean that implements an online shopping cart. Special JSP tags are then introduced to access and alter the attributes of a JavaBean. Finally, the special tags are used in conjunction with HTML forms to initialize JavaBeans in an efficient way.

Employee JavaBean: A Simple Example

This section introduces you to the Employee JavaBean that will be used throughout the rest of this hour. The JavaBean can be used to model employees and associated data like names, Social Security numbers, and salaries. The JavaBean complies with JavaBean specifications by declaring a constructor with no arguments and set and get methods for each of the variables in the class.

The Employee JavaBean is declared in Listing 16.1. The attributes of the bean will be populated with random values created by the utility JavaBean declared in Listing 16.2, RandomPeopleGenerator.java.

The example JSP of listing 16.3, randomPayRoll.jsp, illustrates how the JavaBean is instantiated and used to create a listing of random employees. The random data is created by using a second JavaBean that can generate random names, integers, and Social Security numbers.

The JavaBeans are compiled using the javac compiler that comes with any JDK or any other development environment you might be using. The JavaBeans (found on this book's CD-ROM) need to be compiled to a directory where your application server can find them. If you are using WebLogic Server and a JDK from Sun, you can use the following javac command to compile your JavaBeans from a DOS shell prompt:

```
javac -d d:\WLS51\classes *.java
```

This command assumes that you have WLS installed in your d: directory and that you are located in the same directory as the file Employee.java. The classes directory under the installation directory of WLS is where WLS keeps most of its classes and archives.

The compiler will create a directory structure (if it's not there already) beneath the d:\ WLS51\classes directory according to the package name of the Employee JavaBean. So for the package name jspin24hrs.hour16, the directory jspin24hrs.hour16 will be created and an Employee.class file will be put there.

When the application server accesses the JSP, the page will create an Employee instance in memory. If you change and recompile the code of a JavaBean after the application server has already instantiated the JavaBean, the new class will not be accessed because an old copy already exists in memory. As of WLS version 5.1, the only way for changes to take effect is to reboot the server.

Check out the next few listings and the analysis that follows for more details.

LISTING 16.1   A JavaBean that Models an Employee (Employee.java)

```
 1: package jspin24hrs.hour16;
 2: public class Employee {
 3:    String firstName, lastName, name;
 4:    String address, city, state, country;
 5:    int zip, salary, ssn;
 6:    public Employee(){}
 7:    public void setFirstName(String fn){firstName = fn;}
 8:    public String getFirstName(){return firstName;}
 9:    public void setLastName(String ln){lastName = ln;}
10:    public String getLastName(){return lastName;}
11:    public void setName(String n){name = n;}
12:    public String getName(){return name;}
13:    public void setAddress(String a){address = a;}
14:    public String getAddress(){return address;}
15:    public void setCity(String c){city = c;}
16:    public String getCity(){return city;}
17:    public void setState(String s){state = s;}
18:    public String getState(){return state;}
19:    public void setZip(int z){zip = z;}
20:    public int getZip(){return zip;}
21:    public void setCountry(String c){country = c;}
22:    public String getCountry(){return country;}
23:    public void setSalary(int s){salary = s;}
24:    public int getSalary(){return salary;}
25:    public void setSsn(int s){ssn = s;}
26:  public int getSsn(){return ssn;}
27: }
```

LISTING 16.2 A Utility JavaBean for Generating Random Data for Random Employees (RandomPeopleGenerator.java)

```
 1: package jspin24hrs.hour16;
 2: public class RandomPeopleGenerator {
 3:   String[] names = {"Katerina","Rafael","Alexandra","Cristina","Emilia",
 4:                     "Victoria","Giuseppe","Marco", "Simona", "Dante"};
 5:   public String getRandomName(){
 6:     int nameIndex = (int)(names.length*Math.random());
 7:     return names[nameIndex];
 8:   }
 9:   public int getRandomSSN(){
10:     String randomSSN="0";
11:     for(int j=0; j<8; j++)
12:       randomSSN = randomSSN + ((int)(9 * Math.random()));
13:     return Integer.parseInt(randomSSN);
14:   }
15:   public int getRandomInt(int maxInt){
16:   return (int)(maxInt * Math.random());
17:   }
18: }
```

LISTING 16.3 A JSP that Uses JavaBeans to Generate a Random Payroll with Random Names, Social Security Numbers, and Salaries (randomPayroll.jsp)

```
 1: <HTML><HEAD><TITLE>A Random Payroll</TITLE></HEAD><BODY>
 2: <jsp:useBean id="employee" class=" jspin24hrs.hour16.Employee"/>
 3: <jsp:useBean id="randomNames"
 4:              class=" jspin24hrs.hour16.  RandomPeopleGenerator"/>
 5: <%@ page import=" jspin24hrs.hour16.*"%>
 6: <TABLE WIDTH=100%>
 7:    <TR><TD BGCOLOR=AAAAAA ALIGN=CENTER>Names  </TD>
 8:       <TD BGCOLOR=AAAAAA ALIGN=CENTER>SSN    </TD>
 9:       <TD BGCOLOR=AAAAAA ALIGN=CENTER>Salary </TD>
10:    </TR>
11: <%  for(int j=0; j<10; j++){
12:       employee.setFirstName(randomNames.getRandomName());
13:       employee.setSsn(randomNames.getRandomSSN());
14:       employee.setSalary(randomNames.getRandomInt(90)*1000); %>
15:       <TR><TD BGCOLOR=DDDDDD> <%= employee.getFirstName() %></TD>
16:          <TD BGCOLOR=DDDDDD ALIGN=RIGHT>
17:                            <%= employee.getSsn()  %></TD>
18:          <TD BGCOLOR=DDDDDD ALIGN=RIGHT>
19:                            $<%= employee.getSalary()%></TD>
20:       </TR>
21: <%  }%>
22: </TABLE>
23: </BODY></HTML>
```

ANALYSIS Listing 16.1 declares a JavaBean called `Employee`. Lines 3–5 add some typical data associated with employees such as name, Social Security number, and salary. To comply with JavaBean specifications, line 6 declares a constructor with no arguments, and `set` and `get` methods for each of the class variables from line 7 on. The example consists of creating an instance of the `Employee` JavaBean, initializing it with random data, and then printing out the data in a table.

To generate the random data, Listing 16.2 declares the `RandomPeopleGenerator` class. This is not technically a JavaBean but it can be used just like any other Java class. The class will be used to generate random names from an array of names, generate random Social Security numbers, and generate random integers for the salary.

The `randomPayRoll.jsp` of Listing 16.3 creates an `Employee` instance in line 2 and a `RandomPeopleGenerator` instance in line 3. Lines 6–10 create a table and some titles. Next the JSP creates 10 rows using the `for` loop in line 11. Inside the loop the code sets some attributes of the `Employee` instance with the `set` methods in lines 12–14, and then a row is created using the `get` methods in lines 15–20.

Figure 16.1 shows a sample output of `randomPayroll.jsp`.

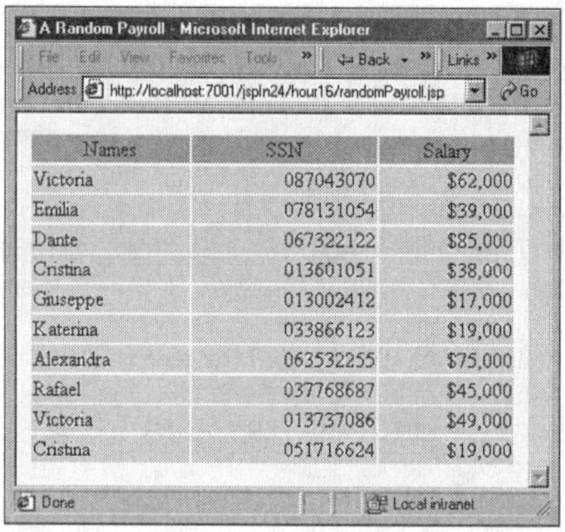
A Random Payroll - Microsoft Internet Explorer
File Edit View Favorites Tools Back Links
Address http://localhost:7001/jspIn24/hour16/randomPayroll.jsp Go
Names SSN Salary
Victoria 087043070 $62,000
Emilia 078131054 $39,000
Dante 067322122 $85,000
Cristina 013601051 $38,000
Giuseppe 013002412 $17,000
Katerina 033866123 $19,000
Alexandra 063532255 $75,000
Rafael 037768687 $45,000
Victoria 013737086 $49,000
Cristina 051716624 $19,000
Done
Local intranet

FIGURE 16.1
`randomPayroll.jsp` *generates a random list of employees, Social Security numbers, and salaries.*

Understanding JavaBean Scope

The scope of a JavaBean refers to the lifespan of a JavaBean after it has been instantiated. The scope of a JavaBean ranges from the lifetime of the page to the lifetime of the executing application server. The scope is set using the `scope` parameter of the `<jsp:useBean>` tag with the syntax:

```
<jsp:useBean id="beanName" class="beanClass" scope="beanScope">
```

`beanScope` can take one of these four values: `page`, `request`, `session`, or `application`.

The default value of the scope is page. This causes the instance of the JavaBean to be stored in the javax.servlet.jsp.PageContext of the current page. The instance is only available from the latest invocation of the JSP. The instance is not available to JSPs that might be included, and it is discarded at the end of the page request.

> The PageContext object provides methods to explicitly get objects that are implicitly available in JSPs like request, response, and session. The PageContext object is responsible for giving access to the objects available to all JSPs and servlets. Additionally, the PageContext object allows you to store and retrieve attributes across several JSPs as well as forward or redirect requests to other JSPs.

If the scope is set to request, the JavaBean instance is stored in the ServletRequest object (the request object was covered in Hour 10, "Processing Requests from the User"). In this case the instance is available to included JSPs that share the same request object. The instance is still discarded at the end of the request.

If the scope is set to session, the JavaBean instance is stored in the HttpSession object, and can be used across HTTP requests.

If the scope is set to application, the JavaBean instance is stored in the ServletContext object. This means that the JavaBean instance is available to any object (JSPs and Servlets, for instance) running in the same application server for the lifespan of the application server.

The following section uses the session scope to keep track of a shopping cart JavaBean across several shopping pages.

Implementing a Shopping Cart with JavaBeans

Hour 12 covered techniques for keeping track of user information across several JSPs using the HttpSession object. An example of a shopping cart was used to illustrate how several JSPs could share information through attributes in the session object. A better way of accomplishing the same task is to use JavaBeans to represent the items and the shopping cart and to use specialized methods of the JavaBeans to initialize and update instances of these objects. The state of the objects can be kept automatically in the HttpSession or the ServletContext by setting the scope of the JavaBeans to session or application, respectively. This way the JavaBeans can be shared across several JSPs.

Listing 16.4 declares a JavaBean called Item that can model a simple generic item in a shopping cart. Listing 16.5 declares a JavaBean called ShoppingCart that can model a shopping cart for keeping track of the items that a user is purchasing. The content of the shopping cart is kept in a vector and its content is administered through the methods of the ShoppingCart class. There are methods for adding an Item object to the vector, deleting an Item from the vector, emptying the whole cart, retrieving all of the items as an enumeration, and iterating through all of the items and computing the total cost of the shopping cart. Listing 16.6 declares the cds.jsp page that uses the JavaBeans to create a single ShoppingCart instance to which several Item instances can be added.

You should try the example with several settings for the scope parameter. You will find that the JSPs only work as intended if the scope is set to either session or application. In all other settings the shopping cart never has more items than the last item added.

LISTING 16.4 A JavaBean that Represents Items in the Shopping Cart (Item.java)

```
 1: package jspin24hrs.hour16;
 2: public class Item {
 3:    String SKU, name, description;
 4:    double price;
 5:    public Item(){}
 6:    public Item(String s, String n, String d, double p){
 7:      SKU= s;
 8:      name = n;
 9:      description = d;
10:      price = p;
11:    }
12:    public String getName(){return name;}
13:    public String getSku(){return SKU;}
14:    public String getDescription(){return description;}
15:  public double getPrice(){return price;}
16: }
```

LISTING 16.5 A JavaBean that Models a Shopping Cart (ShoppingCart.java)

```
 1: package jspin24hrs.hour16;
 2: import java.util.*;
 3: public class ShoppingCart {
 4:    Vector items = new Vector(10);
 5:    public void addItem(Item i){items.addElement(i);}
 6:    public void deleteItem(String sku){
 7:      Enumeration itemEnum = getItems();
 8:      while(itemEnum.hasMoreElements()){
 9:        Item item = (Item)itemEnum.nextElement();
10:        if(item.getSku().equals(sku)){
11:          items.removeElement(item);
12:          break;
13:    }}}
```

LISTING 16.5   continued

```
14:    public void emptyCart(){ items = new Vector(10); }
15:    public Enumeration getItems(){ return items.elements(); }
16:    public double computeTotal(){
17:      Enumeration itemEnum = getItems();
18:      double total = 0;
19:      while(itemEnum.hasMoreElements()){
20:        Item item = (Item)itemEnum.nextElement();
21:        total = total + item.getPrice();
22:      }
23:  return total;
24: }}
```

16

LISTING 16.6   The CDs and Shopping Cart Content (cds.jsp)

```
1: <HTML><HEAD><TITLE>Example of Using Session Scope</TITLE></HEAD><BODY>
2: <jsp:useBean id="shoppingCart"
3:       class=" jspin24hrs.hour16.ShoppingCart" scope="session"/>
4: <%@ page import=" jspin24hrs.hour16.Item" %>
5: [ Shop for CDs ] <A HREF="toys.jsp">Shop for Toys</A>
6: <H1> Online CD Catalog </H1>
7: <TABLE>
8: <TR><TD BGCOLOR=AAAAAA ALIGN=CENTER>Name</TD><TD BGCOLOR=AAAAAA>SKU</TD>
9:     <TD BGCOLOR=AAAAAA>Decription</TD><TD BGCOLOR=AAAAAA>Price</TD>
10:     <TD BGCOLOR=AAAAAA> </TD></TR>
11: <% String[] names= {"Tchaikovsky","Mendelssohn","Haydn","Schumann","Bach"};
12:     String[] SKUs = {"A111","2B22","33C3","444D","E555"};
13:     double[] prices = {12.00, 23.50, 34.00, 45.50, 56.00};
14:     for(int j=0; j<names.length; j++){ %>
15:       <TR><TD BGCOLOR=DDDDDD><%=names[j]%>   </TD>
16:         <TD BGCOLOR=DDDDDD><%=SKUs[j]%>    </TD>
17:         <TD BGCOLOR=DDDDDD>Music CD        </TD>
18:         <TD BGCOLOR=DDDDDD><%=prices[j]%>0</TD>
19:         <TD BGCOLOR=DDDDDD>
20: <A HREF="cds.jsp?name=<%=names[j]%>&sku=<%=SKUs[j]%>&price=<%=prices[j]%>">
21:             Add</A></TD></TR>
22: <% } %>
23: </TABLE>
24: <A HREF=cds.jsp?name=emptyCart>Empty Shopping Cart</A>
25: <HR>
26: <H1> Content of Shopping Cart </H1>
27: <% String name = request.getParameter("name");
28:    if(name!=null){
29:      if(name.equals("emptyCart")){
30:        shoppingCart.emptyCart();
31:      } else if(name.equals("deleteItem")) {
32:        String sku = request.getParameter("sku");
33:        shoppingCart.deleteItem(sku);
```

LISTING 16.6 continued

```
34:      } else {
35:        String sku = request.getParameter("sku");
36:        double price = Double.parseDouble(request.getParameter("price"));
37:        Item newItem = new Item(sku, name, "Music CD", price);
38:        shoppingCart.addItem(newItem);
39:    }} %>
40: <TABLE>
41: <TR><TD BGCOLOR=AAAAAA ALIGN=CENTER>Name</TD><TD BGCOLOR=AAAAAA>SKU</TD>
42:    <TD BGCOLOR=AAAAAA>Decription</TD>
43:    <TD BGCOLOR=AAAAAA>Price</TD><TD BGCOLOR=AAAAAA> </TD>
44:    </TR>
45: <% Enumeration items = shoppingCart.getItems();
46:    while(items.hasMoreElements()){
47:      Item item = (Item)items.nextElement(); %>
48:      <TR><TD BGCOLOR=DDDDDD><%=item.getName()%>          </TD>
49:          <TD BGCOLOR=DDDDDD><%=item.getSku()%>          </TD>
50:          <TD BGCOLOR=DDDDDD><%=item.getDescription()%>        </TD>
51:          <TD BGCOLOR=DDDDDD ALIGN=RIGHT><%=item.getrice()%>0</TD>
52:          <TD BGCOLOR=DDDDDD>
53:             <A HREF="cds.jsp?name=deleteItem&sku=<%=item.getSku()%>">
54:             Remove</A></TD>
55: <% } %>
56:      <TR><TD> </TD><TD> </TD><TD BGCOLOR="DDDDDD">Total</TD>
57:      <TD BGCOLOR=DDDDDD ALIGN=RIGHT><%=shoppingCart.computeTotal()%>0
58:      </TD></TR>
59:  </TABLE></BODY></HTML>
```

ANALYSIS Listing 16.4 declares a JavaBean called Item that is used to represent items in a shopping cart. The data of the item consists of a unique SKU, a name, a description, and a unit price declared in lines 3 and 4. Lines 5 and 6 declare two constructors. The latter one takes arguments to initialize the class data from lines 6–10. Lines 12–15 declare get methods for each of the class data members.

Listing 16.5 declares the ShoppingCart JavaBean. This class keeps track of items of type Item in a vector called items declared in line 4. The items vector is administered through method addItem() in line 5, method deleteItem() in line 6, and method emptyCart() in line 14. The names of the methods pretty much describe what the methods accomplish. Method getItems() in line 15 is used to get the items as an Enumeration. Method computeTotal() in line 16 goes through the items and accumulates the individual prices to compute the total value of the items in the shopping cart.

Listing 16.6 lists the implementation of the cds.jsp page. Line 2 instantiates the ShoppingCart JavaBean, and line 3 sets the scope to session. Line 4 imports the Item class. Line 5 defines a simple navigation bar to jump between shopping for CDs and shopping for toys. Lines 6–27 create the catalog of the CDs that are for sale, links to add CDs to the shopping cart, and a link to empty the whole shopping cart. The catalog is created using the table declared in line 7. The first row in line 8 defines titles for the columns: Names, SKU, Description, and Price. Lines 11–13 declare several arrays with hard-coded data for the CDs: names, SKUs, and prices. These would be read from a database in a real-world implementation. The for loop in line 14 iterates through the elements in the arrays and creates a row for each element in lines 15–21. Lines 20 and 21 create a hyperlink called Add with its reference pointing to the JSP itself. The query string contains the Items information to be added to the shopping cart. Line 24 declares a hyperlink at the end of the table for deleting all items from the shopping cart.

Lines 26 handles requests to the JSP and prints out the content of the shopping cart. Line 27 gets the request parameter called name. If it exists, the value is checked to see if it's a plain item (line 34), a command to empty the cart (line 29), or a command to delete an item (line 31). If it's a command to empty the cart, line 30 calls method emptyCart() on the shoppingCart JavaBean. If it's the command to delete an item, line 32 gets the sku parameter of the item to be deleted and then line 33 calls method deleteItem() on the shoppingCart JavaBean. If it's none of the commands then it must be an item to be added to the shopping cart. The parameters of the item are extracted from the request object and a new instance of Item is created with the parameters in line 37 and added to the shopping cart in line 38. After the request is handled, the JSP lists the current content of the shopping cart in the table declared in line 40. The first row is titles, as always. Line 45 gets all of the items from the shopping cart as an enumeration. Line 46 iterates through all the items one at a time with a while loop. The current item is extracted from the enumeration in line 47, and the attributes of the item are retrieved in lines 48–51 to create a row of the table. In the last column of each row a hyperlink is added to remove the item of that row. In line 57, the computeTotal() method of the ShoppingCart JavaBean puts the total value of the shopping cart into the last row of the table.

The code of toys.jsp is almost identical. The only changes are in the names of the items, prices, SKUs, and descriptions, as well as the URLs that refer to the toys.jsp instead of cds.jsp. You can find the listings of both JSPs on the CD-ROM. Figure 16.2 shows the result of having added several CDs and toys to the shopping cart.

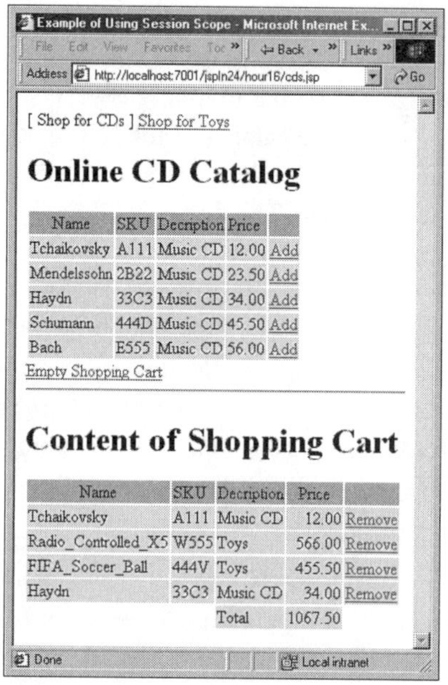

FIGURE 16.2

JavaBeans are used to add items to the shopping cart and to provide the total price.

Setting and Getting JavaBean Properties

JSPs provide two tags for setting and getting values of variables in a JavaBean. From a JSP variables are referred to as *properties* of the JavaBean. Hence the names of the tags are setProperty and getProperty. Their syntax is as follows:

```
<jsp:setProperty name="someName" property="someProperty" value="someValue"/>
<jsp:getProperty name="someName" property="someProperty"/>
```

These tags expect set and get methods declared in the JavaBean for each of the properties you want to set or get with these tags. So the syntax lines expect a property called *someProperty* to exist in the JavaBean as well as methods setSomeProperty() and getSomeProperty().

Use the setProperty tag within the useBean tags to initialize the JavaBean. Here's an example:

```
<jsp:useBean id="someBean" class="jspin24hrs.hour16.SomeClass">
  <jsp:setProperty name="someBean"
                   property="someProperty"
                   value="someValue">
  <jsp:setProperty name="someBean"
                   property="someOtherProperty"
                   value="someOtherValue">
</jsp:useBean>
```

After the bean has been declared and optionally initialized, you can keep using the setProperty and getProperty tags to set and get values for the JavaBean properties.

The JSP in Listing 16.7 uses the Employee JavaBean declared earlier. The JavaBean has quite a few properties with corresponding set and get methods. The JavaBean is instantiated and then used in a for loop that sets and gets its attribute with random values and creates a table with the results.

16

LISTING 16.7 Accessing the JavaBean Attributes Using JSP Set and Get Property Tags (setAndGetProperties.jsp)

```
 1: <HTML><HEAD><TITLE>A Random Payroll</TITLE></HEAD><BODY>
 2: <%@ page import=" jspin24hrs.hour16.*"%>
 3: <jsp:useBean id="employee"
 4:              scope="page"
 5:              class=" jspin24hrs.hour16.Employee"/>
 6: <jsp:useBean id="randomPeople"
 7:              class=" jspin24hrs.hour16.RandomPeopleGenerator"/>
 8: <TABLE WIDTH=100%>
 9:     <TR><TD BGCOLOR=AAAAAA ALIGN=CENTER>Names   </TD>
10:         <TD BGCOLOR=AAAAAA ALIGN=CENTER>SSN     </TD>
11:         <TD BGCOLOR=AAAAAA ALIGN=CENTER>Salary </TD>
12:     </TR>
13: <%  for(int j=0; j<10; j++){
14:         String firstName = randomPeople.getRandomName();
15:         int ssn = randomPeople.getRandomSSN();
16:         int salary = randomPeople.getRandomInt(90)*1000; %>
17:     <jsp:setProperty name="employee" property="firstName"
18:                       value="<%=firstName%>"/>
19:     <jsp:setProperty name="employee" property="ssn"
20:                       value="<%=ssn%>"/>
21:     <jsp:setProperty name="employee" property="salary"
22:                       value="<%=salary%>"/>
23:     <TR><TD BGCOLOR=DDDDDD>
24:         <jsp:getProperty name="employee" property="firstName"/></TD>
25:        <TD BGCOLOR=DDDDDD ALIGN=RIGHT>
26:         <jsp:getProperty name="employee" property="ssn"/></TD>
27:        <TD BGCOLOR=DDDDDD ALIGN=RIGHT>
28:         $<jsp:getProperty name="employee" property="salary"/></TD>
29:     </TR>
30: <%  }%>
31: </TABLE>
32: </BODY></HTML>
```

Listing 16.7 is very similar to Listing 16.3, but it uses setProperty and getProperty tags instead of the set and get methods of the JavaBean.

Using Forms with JavaBeans

HTML forms are used to gather information from users, and that information is, in general, delivered to JSPs in the form of name/value pairs in the request object. For instance, a form may be gathering information about a user, such as his name, address, and salary. The form sends this information to a JSP as several unrelated name/value pairs in the request object.

JavaBeans can be used to group the disparate values of the request parameters into a cohesive and logical unit. This can be accomplished by extracting the values of the parameters in the request object sent by the form and setting the properties of an appropriate JavaBean.

To set the properties of a JavaBean with the parameter values in a request object, you normally would have to extract every single parameter value and use the following tag for each of the properties of the JavaBean that you want to set:

```
<jsp:setProperty name="beanName"
                 property="parameter1"
                 value="<%=request.getParameter("parameterA")%>" />
```

The strings *parameter1* and *parameterA* are not necessarily the same. If there are a lot of properties to be set, this can get quickly out of hand.

The <jsp:setProperty> tag provides a special syntax that can be used to set the properties of a JavaBean with the field values of the HTML form all at once. The syntax is as follows:

```
<jsp:setProperty name="beanName" property="*" />
```

Note the asterisk (*) as the property. This syntax means that all the properties of the JavaBean *beanName* whose names match the parameter names in the request object should be set to the values of the parameters in the request object.

This means that instead of going through each of the properties of the JavaBean, a single tag can set all of the properties. This only works if the name of the parameter and the name of the properties are the same. For example, if a form declares two fields as follows:

```
<FORM>
  <INPUT NAME=field1 ... >
  <INPUT NAME=field2 ... >
</FORM>
```

and the JavaBean complies with JavaBean specification as follows:

```
public class SomeJavaBean {
  String field1, field2;
  public SomeJavaBean(){}
```

```
  public void setField1(String f) { field1 = f; }
  public String getField1() { return field1; }
  public void setField2(String f) { field2 = f; }
  public String getField2() { return field2; }
}
```

then the asterisk in the properties field of the `setProperty` tag automatically sets the values of variables `field1` and `field2` when the form is submitted. If for some reason the name of the parameter in the form cannot be the same as the property name of the variable in the JavaBean, then you have to set it explicitly.

The JSP in Listing 16.8 uses the `Employee` JavaBean declared earlier and declares an HTML form to set its properties.

LISTING 16.8   A JSP that Uses a Form and a JavaBean (forms.jsp)

```
 1: <HTML><HEAD><TITLE>JavaBeans and Forms</TITLE></HEAD><BODY>
 2: <jsp:useBean id="formBean" class=" jspin24hrs.hour16.Employee"/>
 3: <jsp:setProperty name="formBean" property="*" />
 4: <TABLE><TR>
 5: <TD VALIGN=TOP>
 6: <H3>Input</H3>
 7: <FORM ACTION=forms.jsp METHOD=POST><TABLE>
 8:    <TR><TD>First Name:</TD>
 9:       <TD><INPUT TYPE=TEXT NAME=firstName VALUE="Cristoforo"></TD></TR>
10:    <TR><TD>Last Name:</TD>
11:       <TD><INPUT TYPE=TEXT NAME=lastName VALUE="Colombo"></TD></TR>
12:    <TR><TD><INPUT TYPE=SUBMIT NAME=Submit VALUE="Submit"></TD>
13:       <TD></TD></TR>
14: </TABLE></FORM>
15: </TD>
16: <TD VALIGN=TOP>
17: <H3>Output</H3>
18: <TABLE>
19:    <TR><TD>First Name:</TD>
20:       <TD><jsp:getProperty name="formBean" property="firstName"/></TD></TR>
21:    <TR><TD>Last Name:</TD>
22:       <TD><jsp:getProperty name="formBean" property="lastName" /></TD></TR>
23:    <TR><TD> </TD></TR><TR><TD> </TD></TR><TR><TD> </TD></TR>
24: </TABLE>
25: </TD></TR></TABLE>
26: </BODY></HTML>
```

ANALYSIS   In line 2, Listing 16.8 instantiates an `Employee` JavaBean and refers to it as `formBean`. Line 3 sets up the bean to set all its attributes from the request generated by the form declared in line 7. The form is declared in the left cell of a two-cell table declared in line 4. In lines 9–11, the form declares several text input fields to get

16

some of the properties from the user. The names of the fields are the same as the properties declared in the JavaBean, including case. When the user submits the form, the properties of the JavaBean are set. The result of the submission is shown in the right cell of the two-cell table (line 16). The output consists of getting the properties that were set by the form using <jsp:getProperty> tag (lines 20–22).

Figure 16.3 shows the resulting Web page after the form has been submitted.

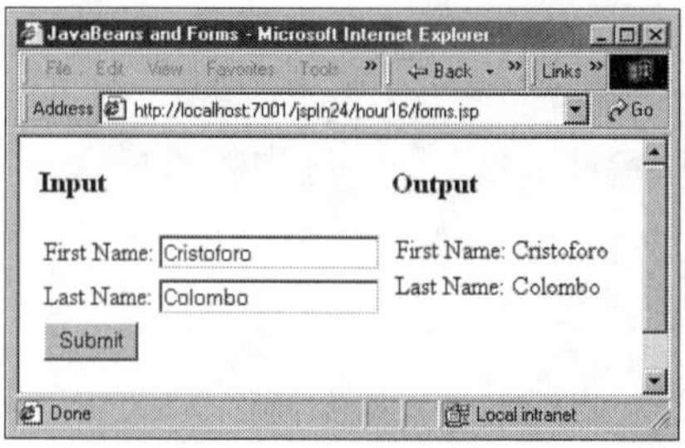

FIGURE 16.3

JavaBeans setProperty *and* getProperty *tags can be used with HTML forms.*

Summary

In this hour you were introduced to JavaBeans and how they can be created and used from JSPs. Then the scope of a JavaBean was used to configure its lifespan, and a shopping cart example illustrated the relevance of the scope. Finally, the use of forms and JavaBeans was demonstrated.

Q&A

Q **Variables in a JavaBean can be set or read using the method calls or the** setProperty **and** getProperty **tags. Why the redundancy?**

A Variables in a JavaBean are accessible to a JSP in three ways. You can access a variable directly from a scriptlet by referencing its name as in *myBean.myVariable*. You can also use the appropriate set or get method to set or access the variable's value. Finally you can use the JSP tags setProperty and getProperty. Referencing the variables or using the methods give you the most flexibility, allowing you to combine the variables' value in expressions, statements, and method calls. The tags give you simplicity and allow tools to easily manipulate JavaBeans. Tags in general, HTML, XML, or JSP, make it easier to create development tools to manipulate documents and source code.

Q **In a previous hour, the** session **object was used to implement a shopping cart. This time a JavaBean was used. Which one is better and why?**

A The purpose of Hour 12 was to teach you how to maintain stateful information across several requests to JSPs. This was accomplished through several mechanisms: cookies, a `session` object, and URL encoding. The implementation of the shopping cart with the `session` object provided an opportunity to illustrate the use of the `session` object, as well as to be able to contrast how the same functionality could be accomplished with a JavaBean. In a real-life implementation of a shopping cart, the JavaBean implementation presented in this hour is better than the one shown in Hour 12 only because of good programming practices. Remember, JSPs are best suited to manage the logic of dynamically laying out a page, creating dynamic content, and directly interacting with the user (the presentation layer). Any heavy computation like a real shopping cart might need to connect to a database or connect to several catalogs. A JavaBean is better suited to handle these tasks.

16

Workshop

The quiz questions and activities are provided for your further understanding. See Appendix A, "Answers," for the answers to the quiz.

Quiz

1. Describe each of the four JavaBean scope settings. What is each best suited for?
2. How can JavaBeans be used with HTML forms?

Activity

Write a JavaBean that can model an online catalog. Name the source file `Catalog.java`. The catalog should provide hierarchies of categories and subcategories. An example of categories and subcategories is the category vehicle. A subcategory of vehicle is automobile. A subcategory of automobile is a particular brand that has specific items. The JavaBean should provide methods that would allow a JSP to browse the hierarchies of categories and items associated to categories. You should implement the following methods of the class `Catalog` to provide the browsing functionality:

`String[] getCategories(String parentCategory)`   Gets the names of the categories under the `parentCategory`

`String[] getItems(String parentCategory)`   Gets the names of the items under the `parentCategory`

`String getParentCategory(String subCategory)`   Gets the parent category of the `subCategory`

The Catalog class should use the following arrays of CategoryNames and SubCategories to define the hierarchy of categories. The CategoryNames array defines the names of the categories. The SubCategories array is a two dimensional array that defines the subcategories of the nth category in the CategoryNames array. Here is an example of the CategoryName array that defines several categories and subcategories:

Index	CategoryName
0	Toys
1	Music
2	Construction
3	Educational
4	Preschool
5	Classical
6	Rock
7	Country

The relationship of what category is a subcategory of which is defined by the SubCategories array. For any given index of the array, the array should contain the subcategories of the category in CategoryNames with the same index. For instance, the example SubCategories array below defines that for index 0 (category Toys) there are 3 subcategories: category 2 (Construction), category 3 (Educational), and category 4 (Preschool). Also for index 1 (category Music) there are 3 subcategories: category 5 (Classical), category 6 (Rock), category 7 (Country).

Index	Subcategory 1	Subcategory 2	Subcategory 3
0	3	4	5
1	6	7	8

To simplify things, allow a category to have just three subcategories. Also, the SubCategories array may allow subcategories to have subcategories themselves. To allocate the SubCategories array, use the following syntax:

```
int[][] SubCategories = new int[2][N];
```

where N is the number of categories.

Create a JSP called catalog.jsp that uses the Catalog JavaBean to create a listing of the categories as hyperlinks pointing to catalog.jsp. The hyperlinks should have enough information in their query string for the JSP to determine which category was clicked. The JSP should refresh the catalog listing to reflect the content of the new category.

Hour 17

Accessing a Database from a JSP

In this hour, you will learn how to connect to a database from a JSP. Java-based applications generally use JDBC (Java Database Connectivity) to access a database. Although there are entire books on JDBC and SQL, this hour will cover the basics that you need in order to use JSPs to interact with databases.

I first give an overview of the basics of JDBC and SQL to create and connect to a database. I then explain how to use JDBC within a JSP to update and query a database. To illustrate the use of JSPs to access databases I provide an example of a database for tracking contact information. As a more advanced example, you will create a small online catalog that users can browse and search.

The main topics covered in this hour are

- Creating a database
- Understanding Java Database Connectivity (JDBC)
- Connecting to a database
- Querying a database

- Updating a database

- Creating a JSP for tracking your contacts in a database

Creating a Database

To understand how JSPs access a database, you first need to create a database to connect to. For the examples in this hour, I will use a simple database manager called Cloudscape that comes with the WebLogic Server 5.1 download. Cloudscape is also available as a free download at www.cloudscape.com. Cloudscape is an all-Java database available in the WLS installation directory. If WLS version 5.1 has been installed (from this book's CD-ROM) in D:\wls51 then Cloudscape can be found in D:\wls51\eval\cloudscape.

Version 2.0 of Cloudscape is implemented by three jar files located under the Cloudscape lib directory, D:\wls51\eval\cloudscape\lib. These are cloudscape.jar, client.jar, and tools.jar. These jar files need to be in your system CLASSPATH environment variable.

New Term: CLASSPATH Environment Variable

The CLASSPATH, like PATH, is an environment variable that contains a list of paths or directories separated by semicolons. The CLASSPATH is used by the JVM to search for classes. When you execute a Java class using the java command the JVM will search for the Java class in the directories listed in the CLASSPATH. If the class is not found then the JVM will raise an exception informing you that it was unable to find the class.

There is a newer version of Cloudscape, version 3.0, but this version does not come free with WLS. If you get an evaluation copy or purchase it, read its documentation on how to install and use it.

Using Cloudscape's Cloudview

First, create a directory in which to put all your work. Create a directory for this hour under the JSP directory you have been using for all the exercises and activities—for example, d:\wls51\myserver\public_html\myJSPs\hour17\.

Start Cloudscape using the following command line at a DOS prompt:

```
java COM.cloudscape.tools.cview
```

This will start a Java application called Cloudview shown in Figure 17.1.

FIGURE **17.1**

The Cloudview graphic user interface.

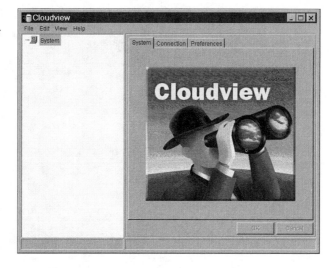

To create the database, follow these steps:

1. From the File menu, select New, Database. The New Database window appears.

2. Choose the working directory by clicking the Directory button and navigating to the d:\wls51\myserver\public_html\myJSPs\hour17\ directory. This will fill the Name field with the name of the directory.

3. Append to this name a name for your database. You will build a database that holds the names and phone numbers of some of your acquaintances so choose an appropriate name like Phonebook.

4. Click OK when you're finished. Cloudscape will create a directory called phonebook under the hour17 directory.

> The phonebook directory and its contents are managed by Cloudscape and you should not make any changes to it other than with Cloudview. Otherwise you might corrupt the database and Cloudscape won't be able to recognize it as a valid database.

After you have created the database, Cloudview should look like Figure 17.2.

Creating Tables

Data in a database is contained in tables. Tables organize data in a set of rows or records. There can be any number of rows in a table. Every row has a set of fields that make up the columns of the table. You enter data into the database by creating tables and then filling the fields in the rows with data.

FIGURE 17.2

Creating the
Phonebook *database*
with Cloudview.

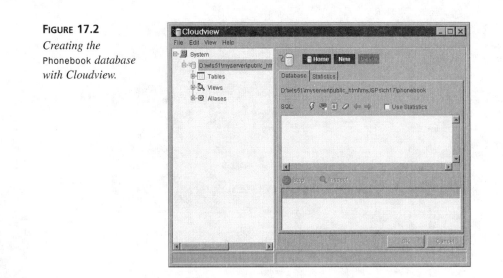

To create a table in Cloudview click Tables on the left-side tree and then click New on the right side. Change the name of the table by typing **CONTACTTABLE** in the Name field. Add three columns to the table by clicking twice on the plus sign (+) next to the Columns label.

Edit the names of the columns by selecting each column name under the Name column and typing the following names: **LAST**, **FIRST**, **PHONE**. Set the type of each of the columns to be of CHAR type (a single character) by clicking the types under the Type column. Set the length of each of the fields by selecting the lengths under the Length column and typing the value **20** for all the fields (strings of 20 characters). When you're finished, click the OK button. See Figure 17.3.

FIGURE 17.3

The CONTACTTABLE *table*
has three columns:
LAST, FIRST, *and* PHONE.

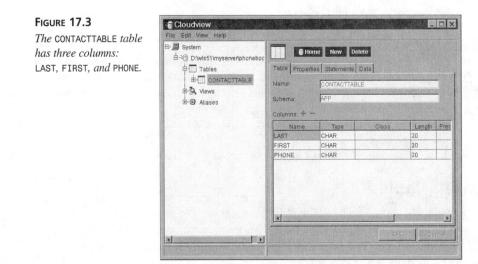

Creating Records

Now that you have created a table, you want to populate it with data from some of your colleagues. To enter data into the database, click the Data tab. Cloudview will show the CONTACTTABLE table with the three columns you just created.

Create a row of data by clicking the plus sign (+) above the table and filling out each of the fields under each of the columns. Click the plus sign again and fill in the data for another of your colleagues. Repeat these steps until you have the data for about five people in the database. When you've finished entering data in the database, click the Save button to the left of the plus sign. Cloudview should look similar to the one in Figure 17.4 when you're finished.

FIGURE 17.4

The Phonebook *database stores contact information of acquaintances in the* CONTACTTABLE *table.*

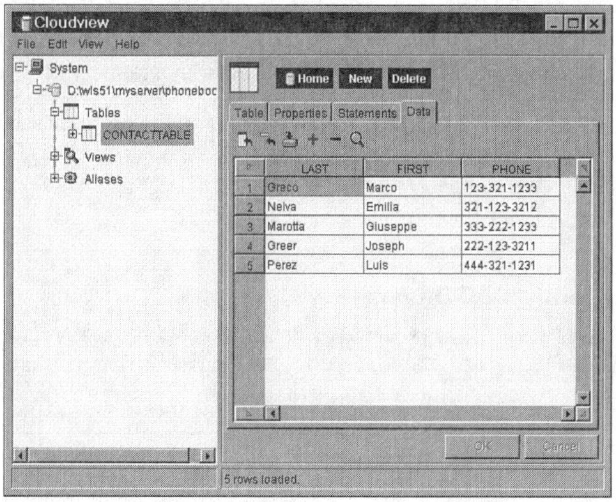

If you do not save your data before leaving this screen, it will be lost.

To make sure that the database was saved properly, exit from Cloudview by choosing Exit under the File menu. Start Cloudscape and open up the database again. Your database should be listed as a shortcut under the File menu so that by selecting it you open the database directly without having to browse for it. Alternatively, select File, Open to navigate to where you saved the database and open it to check that your data was actually saved. Double-click the Tables item in the tree on the left side and choose the CONTACTTABLE table. Then on the right side, choose the Data tab to verify your data. When you're finished, you can close Cloudview.

You now have a small database that we can use to show how a JSP can connect and interact with a database.

Java Database Connectivity (JDBC)

Although there are entire books that deal with Java Database Connectivity (JDBC), I will cover the basic parts to give you a sense of how JSPs can interact with databases. In the next section, you will create several JSPs that illustrate each one of the concepts I discuss. For full coverage of JDBC, I recommend *Database Programming with JDBC and Java* from O'Reilly and Associates.

JDBC is an Application Programming Interface (API) that allows Java programs to connect to and interact with databases. The API is a set of classes and interfaces packaged under the Java packages `java.sql` and `javax.sql`. The goal of the JDBC API is to provide a consistent and standard way of accessing databases from a number of diverse vendors.

The JDBC API strives to shield developers from having to deal with the details of which database vendor is being used. This is achieved by using drivers provided by the database vendors.

> **New Term: JDBC Drivers**
>
> JDBC drivers are classes provided by database vendors. Java programs, including JavaServer Pages, use JDBC drivers to obtain a connection to a database and then use the connection to query and update the database.

Figure 17.5 shows the process of a JSP accessing a database through JDBC. When the JSP is invoked, it uses the JDBC API to access the database through queries and updates. JDBC interacts with the underlying database in terms of SQL. If a SQL statement causes resulting rows from the database, these are packaged by JDBC in a `ResultSet` object. The JSP processes the rows and dynamically generates HTML for the browser. Finally, the browser renders the page for the user.

There are, in simple terms, five JDBC classes and interfaces of which you must be aware: the driver class for your database, the `DriverManager` class, the `Connection` interface, the `Statement` interface, and the `ResultSet` interface. These are used to connect to and interact with the database in the following way:

1. The JSP code instantiates, loads, and registers the driver with the `DriverManager` by passing the name of the driver class to `Class.forName()`.

2. The `DriverManager` is used in the JSP code to obtain a `Connection` object with the `DriverManager.getConnection()` method.

3. A `Statement` object is created with the `Connection.createStatement()` method.

4. The JSP code interacts with the database by executing queries or updates with the `Statement.executeQuery()` method or `Statement.executeUpdate()` method.

5. If a query is executed, the JSP code processes the `ResultSet` object returned by the `Statement.executeQuery()` method.

The next few sections cover these steps in more detail.

FIGURE 17.5
The process involved in a JSP using JDBC to access a database.

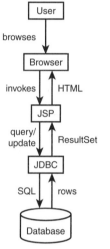

JDBC Drivers

JDBC Drivers are classes provided by database vendors that implement the interfaces that a programmer uses to interact with the database. When you purchase a database compatible with JDBC, you also receive a JDBC driver or pointers to where you can download one. The driver's job is to communicate SQL queries and updates at the JDBC level down to the SQL interpretation level of the database and to package and communicate any results back to the JDBC layer.

Vendors often create JDBC drivers that are optimized to work with a particular application server. Table 17.1 shows some of the drivers that are available for use with WebLogic Server 5.1 or better.

TABLE 17.1 JDBC Drivers

Vendor/Database	Type	Class Name and URL
Oracle	2	weblogic.jdbc.oci.Driver
		jdbc:weblogic:oracle

TABLE 17.1   continued

Vendor/Database	Type	Class Name and URL
	2	`weblogic.jdbc20.oci.Driver` `jdbc20:weblogic:oracle`
Sybase	2	`weblogic.jdbc.dblib.Driver` `jdbc:weblogic:Sybase`
Microsoft SQL Server	2	`weblogic.jdbc.dblib.Driver` `jdbc:weblogic:mssqlserver`
Microsoft SQL Server 4	4	`weblogic.jdbc.mssqlserver4.Driver` `jdbc:weblogic:mssqlserver4`
Informix	4	`weblogic.jdbc.Informix.Driver` `jdbc:weblogic:informix4`
Cloudscape	4	`COM.cloudscape.core.JDBCDriver` `jdbc:cloudscape`

The driver you are going to use for the Cloudscape database comes with WebLogic Server, although it has not been optimized in any particular way to work with that server. We will come back to the URL shortly in the section "Getting a `Connection` to the Database."

There are four types of JDBC drivers, and the Type column of Table 17.1 shows the type of each of the drivers listed there. The type of a driver refers to whether it is an all-Java implementation (Type 4) or not (Type 1 and 2) and whether it is meant to be used in a multitier architecture (Type 3). The tradeoffs of whether a database is an all-Java implementation are that if it is (Type 4), it can run on any machine that has a Java Virtual Machine, it can be downloaded from the server so that the user always has the latest version of the application, and there is little to no administration at the local machine. On the other hand, native drivers (Type 2) tend to be faster because they are optimized for the underlying machine architecture, but suffer from having to be configured for each individual machine; the maintenance and upgrades are more difficult, too. In a multitier architecture, a JDBC driver can be used by middleware software to optimize performance of the lifecycle management of connections (Type 3). Creating and managing connections is expensive in terms of the resources involved—that is, time and memory. Middleware software can create connections when an application is first started so that the cost is incurred only once and connections can be reused and shared among a set of users. These are advanced topics that are better covered in an enterprise book that deals with the issues of designing and creating very large applications.

To use a driver you need to instantiate it from your JSP code, configure it, and obtain a Connection object. To instantiate the Cloudscape JDBC driver, use the method Class.forName(*String className*), which instantiates the named class:

```
Class.forName("COM.cloudscape.core.JDBCDriver");
```

The argument to the forName() method is a fully qualified class name that can be found in the system CLASSPATH. For Cloudscape, the COM.cloudscape.core.JDBCDriver class is located in cloudscape.jar, which should be in your system CLASSPATH. The virtual machine will look for the class and instantiate it. When the JDBC driver is instantiated, it registers itself with the class DriverManager.

Getting a Connection to the Database

After the JDBC driver has registered with the driver manager, you can use the DriverManager.getConnection(*String*) method to obtain a Connection object from the DriverManager object. Here is an example of getting a connection to the Phonebook database from the DriverManager:

```
Connection con = DriverManager.getConnection("jdbc:cloudscape:Phonebook");
```

The argument to the getConnection() method consists of a URL with a syntax that depends on the database vendor. To make correct use of the URL you need to read the documentation of your database provider. For Cloudscape, the URL syntax is

```
jdbc:cloudscape:databaseName
```

The first portion of the URL, jdbc, identifies the communication protocol being used. The second part, cloudscape, identifies the vendor-specific protocol. Subsequent portions of the URL depend on the particular database vendor you choose. For Cloudscape it identifies the path and database name. If the database is located in the same directory as the JSP, it suffices to use the name of the database.

The Connection object returned by DriverManager provides methods to manage the life-cycle of a connection to a database as well as methods to create different types of SQL statement objects. For the purpose of this hour, the focus is on one particularly useful method for creating Statement objects, Connection.createStatement().

```
Statement sqlStatement = con.createStatement();
```

The Statement object represents an SQL statement used to directly interact with the underlying database. Database interactions consist of querying and updating the database.

Interacting with the Database with the `Statement` Object

The `Statement` object provides methods to update and query the database. Two of the more important methods are

```
ResultSet Statement.executeQuery(String)
void Statement.executeUpdate(String)
```

You use the `executeQuery()` method when you want to query the database with an SQL query criterion and expect a set of rows that match the criterion. You use the `executeUpdate()` method when you want to update or change the database content and don't expect any results back. Here's an example of performing a query:

```
String sql = "SELECT FROM TOYTABLE (TOYBRAND=LEGO, PRICE<10)";
ResultSet columns = sqlStatement.executeQuery(sql);
```

These two lines create a `String` object that contains a legal SQL statement. The statement says that you want to select from the table called `TOYTABLE` those rows that match certain criteria: The column `TOYBRAND` is equal to `LEGO`, and the `PRICE` column is less than $10. In other words, you want all the LEGO toys that cost less than $10. This assumes that there is such a table called `TOYTABLE` that at least has columns `TOYBRAND` and `PRICE`. Those columns that match the criteria will be packaged into a `ResultSet` object and returned by the `Statement` object.

Navigating Query Results with the `ResultSet` Object

The `ResultSet` object represents a set of rows created by the database as a result of having performed a query. The `ResultSet` object is similar to an `Enumeration` object. To inspect each row in the `ResultSet` object, use the method `ResultSet.next()`. The `ResultSet` object keeps track of the current row position. The current row position is often referred to as a cursor. Initially the cursor does not point to any row. The `next()` method causes the cursor to advance to the next row, starting with the first, and to scroll through the `ResultSet` every time the `next()` method is invoked. If there are still rows to scroll through, it returns `true`; otherwise, if there are no more rows, `next()` returns `false`. Typically you use a `while` loop that tests the result of the `next()` method to scroll through all the columns in the `ResultSet` object.

When the cursor points to a particular row, you can use several of the `ResultSet` get methods to get the data in each of the columns of the current row. The get methods allow you to get a column content by its ordered index in the row or by the name of the column. Here are some of the more common get methods:

get-by-column name methods	get-by-index methods
getInt(String *colName*)	getInt(int *index*)
getFloat(String *colName*)	getFloat(int *index*)

get-by-column name methods	get-by-index methods
getDouble(String *colName*)	getDouble(int *index*)
getLong(String *colName*)	getLong(int *index*)
getString(String *colName*)	getString(int *index*)

Here's an example of using the `ResultSet` object to browse through all the rows of a ResultSet:

```
while(columns.next()) {
  String last = columns.getString("LastNameCol");
  String first = columns.getString("FirstNameCol");
  int phone = columns.getInt(3);
  ...do something with the variables last, first, and phone...
}
```

It is essential that the `next()` method be invoked before any get method is used because the cursor does not refer to any column until the very first `next()` method call is invoked.

A JSP that Interacts with a Database

To illustrate the concepts covered in the previous section, you will create several small JSPs that implement a simple feature of interacting with a database. You will then create a larger JSP in the following section.

You'll create a JSP that interacts with the `Phonebook` database you built earlier in this hour. First, you'll create a JSP that prints the content of the database and then you'll build a JSP that allows you to update the content of the database.

Printing the Contents of a Database with a JSP

Now that I have covered JDBC in general and shown you how to create a database, you are going to create a JSP that connects to the `Phonebook` database and prints out its content.

Figure 17.6 shows the output of the JSP that you are going to create. Your JSP output will be different because you have your own set of contacts in your `Phonebook` database. Listing 17.1 shows the JSP code.

LISTING 17.1 A JSP that Prints the Content of the `Phonebook` Database (`phonebook.jsp`)

```
1: <HTML>
2: <HEAD> <TITLE>Listing the content of a Database</TITLE> </HEAD>
3: <BODY>
4: <P> Content of the Phonebook database:
5: <TABLE BORDER=1 CELLPADDING=0 CELLSPACING=0>
6: <TR> <TD> Last  </TD>
```

17

LISTING 17.1 continued

```
 7:        <TD> First </TD>
 8:        <TD> Phone </TD>
 9: </TR>
10: <%
11:   Class.forName("COM.cloudscape.core.JDBCDriver");
12:   java.sql.Connection connection = java.sql.DriverManager.getConnection(
13:   "jdbc:cloudscape:D:/wls51/myserver/public_html/myJSPs/hour17/phonebook");
14:   java.sql.Statement statement = connection.createStatement();
15:   java.sql.ResultSet columns = statement.executeQuery(
16:   "SELECT * FROM CONTACTTABLE");
17:   while(columns.next()) {
18:     String last  = columns.getString("LAST");
19:     String first = columns.getString("FIRST");
20:     String phone = columns.getString("PHONE");     %>
21:       <TR>  <TD> <%= last  %> </TD>
22:             <TD> <%= first %> </TD>
23:             <TD> <%= phone %> </TD>
24:       </TR>
25: <% } %>
26: </TABLE>
27: </BODY>
28: </HTML>
```

FIGURE 17.6

JSP prints out all the contacts in the Phonebook *database.*

ANALYSIS Lines 5–9 create a table with three columns with the headers Last, First, and Phone. Line 11 loads and registers the Cloudscape JDBC driver with the DriverManager. Line 12 gets a Connection object from the DriverManager that connects to the Phonebook database. Note the full path to the database. Line 14 creates a Statement object from the Connection object. Line 15 queries the database for all the rows in the table CONTACTTABLE. The resulting rows are packaged into the columns of the ResultSet object. Line 17 enters a while loop that initially places the cursor on the first row. Lines 18–20 retrieve the values under the columns named LAST, FIRST, and PHONE of the current row and copy their content to local variables last, first, and phone. Lines 21–23 add a row with three columns containing the last, first, and phone of one of your contacts. Note that one row is added for each of the rows in the columns of the ResultSet object.

Updating a Database with a JSP

The previous example showed you how to view the content of a database. Now you will enhance that example with the capability of adding a new contact using an HTML form. The HTML form will acquire a new contact from the user and post it to the same JSP for processing. The JSP will process the form and update the database. Lines 4–11 and 23–31 of Listing 17.2 were added to the previous example. Figure 17.7 shows the JSP and Listing 17.2 lists the corresponding JSP code.

FIGURE 17.7

The JSP for adding contacts to the Phonebook database.

17

LISTING 17.2   JSP Code for Adding Contacts to the Phonebook Database
(updatePhonebook.jsp)

```
 1 <HTML>
 2 <HEAD> <TITLE>Listing the content of a Database</TITLE> </HEAD>
 3 <BODY>
 4 <P> Update Database Content
 5 <FORM ACTION="updatePhonebook.jsp" METHOD="POST">
 6   Last Name:    <INPUT TYPE=TEXT NAME=lastParam> <BR>
 7   First Name:   <INPUT TYPE=TEXT NAME=firstParam><BR>
 8   Phone Number: <INPUT TYPE=TEXT NAME=phoneParam><BR>
 9   <INPUT TYPE=Submit VALUE="Add to Database">
10 </FORM>
11 <HR>
12 <P> Content of the Phonebook database:
13 <TABLE BORDER=1 CELLPADDING=0 CELLSPACING=0>
14 <TR> <TD> Last  </TD>
15       <TD> First </TD>
16       <TD> Phone </TD>
17 </TR>
18 <%
19   Class.forName("COM.cloudscape.core.JDBCDriver");
20   java.sql.Connection connection = java.sql.DriverManager.getConnection("
```

LISTING 17.2   continued

```
21    jdbc:cloudscape:D:/wls51/myserver/public_html/myJSPs/hour17/phonebook");
22    java.sql.Statement statement = connection.createStatement();
23    Enumeration parameters = request.getParameterNames();
24    if(parameters.hasMoreElements()) {
25      String lastValue  = request.getParameter("lastParam");
26      String firstValue = request.getParameter("firstParam");
27      String phoneValue = request.getParameter("phoneParam");
28      statement.executeUpdate(
29        "INSERT INTO CONTACTTABLE (\"LAST\", \"FIRST\", \"PHONE\") VALUES
30        ('"+lastValue+"','"+firstValue+"','"+phoneValue+"')");
31    }
32    java.sql.ResultSet columns = statement.executeQuery(
33                "SELECT * FROM CONTACTTABLE");
34    while(columns.next()) {
35      String last  = columns.getString("LAST");
36      String first = columns.getString("FIRST");
37      String phone = columns.getString("PHONE");       %>
38        <TR>  <TD> <%= last  %> </TD>
39              <TD> <%= first %> </TD>
40              <TD> <%= phone %> </TD>
41        </TR>
42 <% } %>
43 </TABLE>
44 </BODY>
45 </HTML>
```

ANALYSIS   Lines 4–11 declare an HTML form that has three text fields. The form gathers the last name, first name, and phone number for a new contact, packages it in an `HttpServletRequest` object, and `POST`s it to the `updatePhonebook` JSP.

Lines 23–31 extract the parameters from the `request` object and insert them in the database. Line 23 gets all the parameters (if any). Line 24 tests to see if any parameters were submitted. Lines 23 and 24 are necessary because the form is being submitted to itself and the first time the page comes up, the parameters will be empty. If indeed parameters were submitted, lines 25–27 copy the values of the parameters into local string variables `lastValue`, `firstValue`, and `phoneValue`. The values are used in lines 28–30 to construct an SQL `INSERT` command. The `INSERT` command inserts the values into table `CONTACTTABLE` under the columns `LAST`, `FIRST`, and `PHONE`.

Lines 32–45 are the same as lines 15–28 in the previous example. The content of the database is printed out, including any contacts that were added.

Summary

This hour showed you how to create JavaServer Pages that connect to a database. First, you created a database called `Phonebook` and populated it with contact information from your acquaintances. You also were introduced to the notion of tables, rows, records, columns, and fields.

Java Database Connectivity is an API that allows Java programs to connect to databases. I briefly covered JDBC drivers and some of the more useful JDBC classes and interfaces such as `DriverManager`, `Connection`, `Statement`, and `ResultSet`.

To help you understand the concepts, you created a JSP that connected to the `Phonebook` database and dynamically generated an HTML page with the database content.

Finally, you enhanced your JSP to allow contacts to be dynamically added to the database.

Q&A

Q How do I connect to my Access database?

A To connect to an Access database you can use the Type 1 driver by Sun Microsystems. The driver class name is `com.sun.jdbc.odbc.Driver` and its URL is `jdbc:odbc:DSNEntry`. The driver class is in the `jdbc.sql` package. The `DSNEntry` is a virtual name that refers to a real database through ODBC. In Windows 2000 you can use the ODBC Data Source Administrator to create these entries. To do this, assume you have an Access database called `c:\myDB.mdb`. From the Start menu, select Settings, Control Panel, Administrative Tools, Data Sources. Once in the ODBC Data Source Administrator window (see Figure 17.8), select the User DSN tab, MS Access Database, and then click the Add button.

FIGURE 17.8
ODBC Data Source Administrator window.

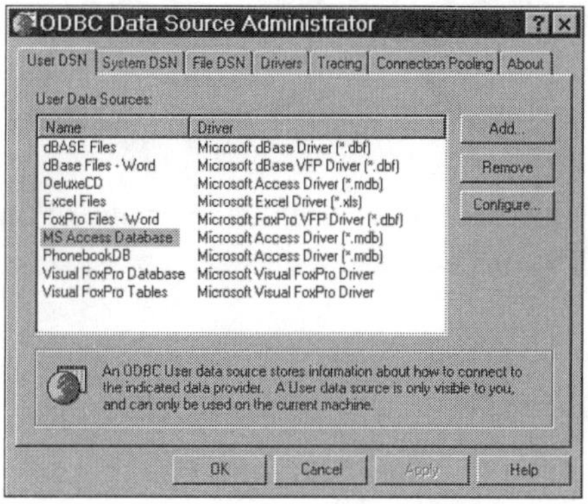

The Add button takes you to the Create New Data Source window where you to choose the driver (see Figure 17.9)—Microsoft Access Driver—and then click Finish.

FIGURE **17.9**

Choosing the driver.

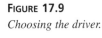

After you have chosen the driver, the ODBC Microsoft Access Setup window allows you configure the data source (see Figure 17.10). Choose a name for the database in the Data Source Name field. This field must match the DNS entry parameter in the JDBC URL. Then select the database by clicking the Select button. Browse until you find c:\myDB.mdb. Click OK until you are done.

FIGURE **17.10**

Configuring the data source.

Workshop

The quiz questions and activities are provided for your further understanding. See Appendix A, "Answers," for the answers to the quiz.

Quiz

1. What are the classes and interfaces that are usually involved when using JDBC to connect to a database?

2. Name three get functions from the ResultSet object that allow you to access data from fields in a record.

Activity

Create a JSP that accepts the name of a Cloudscape database and prints out the content of the database without knowing the names of the columns or the number of fields per row.

HOUR 18

Substituting Text in a JSP

Sometimes you want to include data, such as a copyright, a company logo, or a menu bar, in each of your JavaServer Pages. If you typed the copyright into each of your JSPs and then your copyright changed, you would have to go into each JSP to modify it. Well, there is a better way: Instead of typing the text into each JSP, write a file and then bring that file into your JSP. When you separate the data from the JSP, you only need to update one file with changes—any JSP using that file automatically receives the update.

The JSP specification allows data to be inserted into a JSP in one of two ways, the include directive and the include action. The include directive treats the included file as a static document and inserts that file's code into the JSP. The include action treats the included file as a dynamic object and inserts the output of the included file. Hour 20, "Using Multiple JSPs to Handle the Request," discusses the include action in detail.

In this hour you will

- Learn how the data is inserted into the JSP using the include directive
- Follow examples of using the include directive

Understanding the `include` Directive

The `include` directive sees the included file as a static object and therefore inserts that file's code into the JSP. The inclusion of the code happens at translation time, so the code of the included HTML or JSP is inserted into the JSP, translated into the Servlet code, compiled, and then executed. (The translation phase of a JSP was discussed in Hour 3, "Introduction to Servlets.") As you will see in the examples, the point where the `include` directive is located in the JSP is where the HTML document you're including will be placed.

You can have more than one `include` directive in your JSP. This allows you to include, for example, your company banner at the top and a copyright at the bottom of your page.

> There are many reasons to use the `include` directive, inserting the company banner and copyright are just two reasons. An HTML document that creates a menu bar, could be included in each of your JSPs using the `include` directive. The `include` directive is an easy way to give your JSPs the same look and feel.

Using the `include` Directive

Using the `include` directive makes it easy for you to update text without needing to modify the code for all your JSPs.

Before taking a look at the general syntax of the `include` directive, it would be beneficial examine the general syntax of a JSP directive:

```
<%@ directive_type directive_attributes %>
```

The `directive_type` is one of the JSP directives, `page`, `include`, and `taglib`. The `page` directive was covered in Hour 14, "Creating Error Pages," and the `taglib` directive is discussed in Hour 19, "Extending JSP Functionality with Tag Libraries."

The `directive_attributes` depend on which directive you are using. Each of the three types of directives takes different attributes. Hour 14 showed how to use the attributes of the `page` directive to create error pages and use error pages. The attributes of the taglib directive are discussed in detail in Hour 19. The `include` directive takes one attribute, the file to be included.

Now that you have seen the general syntax of the JSP directives, it is time to focus on the `include` directive. The general syntax of the `include` directive is as follows.

```
<%@ include file="Relative_URL_and_Filename" %>
```

You can see that the `directive_type` is `include` and the `directive_attributes` is `file`.

The value for the file attribute is a relative path and is the name of the file that should be included into your JSP. It is the responsibility of the server to resolve the address to the included file. If your JSP is in the c:\weblogic\myserver\myJSPs\hour18 folder, and you want to include a file called copyright.html located in the folder c:\weblogic\myserver\myJSPS\hour18\includedFiles, then your include directive would look like:

```
<%@ include file="includedFiles\copyright.html" %>
```

What happens if the included file contents change? It would be helpful if there was a way for the JSP container to be notified of changes in included files, however the JSP 1.1 specification does not describe or require that the JSP container be notified when included files are modified.

Examples of the `include` Directive

This section contains several examples using the include directive. The first example includes a company banner at the top of the JSP, the second example includes a JSP, and the third shows what happens when the included file cannot be found.

Including a Text Document

In this example the JSP is going to include a text document, formatted using HTML tags, that contains a company banner. The banner is to be included at the top of all of the company's JSPs; putting it into a separate file allows the company to modify its banner once and propagate the changes to all its JSPs. Listing 18.1 shows the HTML file to be included in the JSP.

LISTING 18.1   An HTML File that Contains a Company Banner (companyBanner.html)

```
1: <TABLE WIDTH="100%" BGCOLOR="teal">
2:   <TR><TD ALIGN="center">
3:      <FONT SIZE=7 COLOR="black">Huskies R Us</FONT>
4:    </TD>
5:   </TR>
6: </TABLE>
```

The companyBanner.html file creates a table with one row and one column that contains the text "Huskies R Us."

This table is very simple. It contains one cell that has the text "Huskies R Us" within it. Of course, some formatting was done; the text is centered in the cell, the font is black and the background color of the table is teal.

Listing 18.2 shows the JSP that includes the text from the companyBanner.html file.

LISTING 18.2   A JSP that Includes the Text from Another File
(IncludeTextExample.jsp)

```
 1: <HTML>
 2: <HEAD><TITLE>Including Text From Another File</TITLE></HEAD>
 3: <BODY>
 4: <%@ include file="includedFiles\companyBanner.html" %>
 5: <CENTER>
 6:    <IMG SRC="images\spaceShip.gif" />
 7:    <H1>
 8:      UNDER CONSTRUCTION
 9:      <BR>
10:      Please Come Again
11:    </H1>
12: </CENTER>
13: </BODY>
14: </HTML>
```

ANALYSIS To fully understand what is happening, take a walk through the code in Listing 18.2. Lines 1–3 begin the HTML page, and line 4 is the include directive. The other lines explain the HTML tags that are used.

Line 4 is the new tag you are learning: the include directive tag.

```
4: <%@ include file="includedFiles\companyBanner.html" %>
```

The directive tags use the characters <%@ to begin a directive and %> to end the directive tag. include specifies it to be the include directive, and it takes one parameter, the file attribute. The file attribute is a relative path to the file that will be included. In this example, the companyBanner.html file will be included and it is located in a subdirectory named includedFiles.

Lines 5–10 define the layout of the rest of the page, including the CENTER tag and the IMAGE tag for the spaceship graphic.

Lines 11–14 close open tags in the appropriate order—the level 1 heading tag, the CENTER tag, the BODY tag, and the HTML tag.

Figure 18.1 shows the output of the JSP with the HTML document included.

When you view an HTML document in a browser you can look at the HTML code by viewing the source. Listing 18.3 shows the HTML of the page that was generated from IncludeTextExample.jsp, including the companyBanner.html code.

FIGURE 18.1

*The banner in is the text
of an HTML document
included in the JSP.*

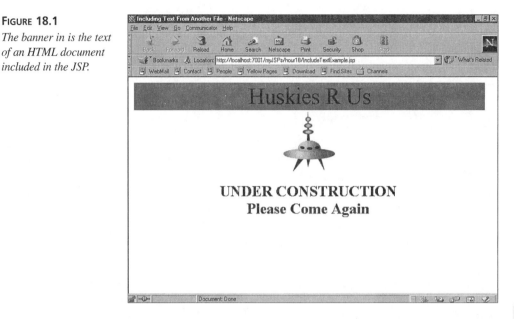

FIGURE 18.1

*The banner in is the text
of an HTML document
included in the JSP.*

LISTING 18.3   The Final HTML Generated from the `IncludeTextExample.jsp` File

18

```
 1: <HTML>
 2: <HEAD><TITLE>Including Text From Another File</TITLE></HEAD>
 3: <BODY>
 4: <TABLE WIDTH="100%" BGCOLOR="teal">
 5:   <TR><TD ALIGN="center">
 6:         <FONT SIZE=7 COLOR="black">Huskies R Us</FONT>
 7:      </TD>
 8:   </TR>
 9: </TABLE>
10: <CENTER>
11:   <IMG SRC="images\spaceShip.gif" />
12:   <H1>
13:     UNDER CONSTRUCTION
14:     <BR>
15:     Please Come Again
16:   </H1>
17: </BODY>
18: </HTML>
```

Compare the code in Listings 18.3 and 18.2. The difference is that where Listing 18.2
had the `include` directive (line 4), Listing 18.3 actually contains the code from the
`companyBanner.html` document (lines 4–9).

Including Another JSP

Now take a look at how JSP code is inserted into another JSP. The code of the included JSP is inserted into your JSP and then your JSP is translated into the Servlet and executed. In this situation only one JSP is being translated and executed, but it contains the code of two. Listing 18.4 is a JSP that calculates the fibonacci numbers of 0-19 and will be included into another JSP.

Listing 18.4   The JSP Whose Code Will Be Inserted into Another JSP (FibonacciComputation.jsp)

```
 1: <HTML>
 2: <HEAD><TITLE>Calculating the Fibonacci Numbers</TITLE></HEAD>
 3: <BODY BGCOLOR="navy" TEXT="yellow">
 4: <%! int [] fib; %>
 5: <CENTER>
 6: <H1>Calculating the Fibonacci Numbers of 0-19</H1>
 7: <br>
 8: The fibonacci number of 0 is 0
 9: <BR>
10: The fibonacci number of 1 is 1
11:
12: <BR>
13: <% fib = new int[20];
14:     fib[0] = 0;
15:     fib[1] = 1;
16:     for (int i=2; i<20; i++) {
17: %>
18: The fibonacci number of <%= i%> is <% fib[i] = fib[i-1] + fib[i-2]; %>
19: <%= fib[i] %>
20: <br>
21: <% }%>
22: </CENTER>
23: </BODY>
24: </HTML>
```

The FibonacciComputation.jsp calculates the fibonacci numbers for 0 to 19.

ANALYSIS   Line 4 uses declaration tags (<%! and %>) to declare a variable, fib, as an array of integers. (In Hour 7, "Declaring Variables and Methods in a JSP," you learned to use those tags.)

Lines 13–17 are Java code inserted into the JSP using scriptlets. Hour 9, "Controlling JSPs with Java Scriptlets," showed you the special tags (<% and %>) that allow Java code to be inserted into a JSP. The code within these tags is translated into the service(...) method of the Servlet code.

Line 18 inserts the value of i using the expression tags. (In Hour 8, "Inserting Java Expressions in a JSP," you learned to insert Java expressions by using the special tags <%= and %>). These tags are a shorthand notation for out.print(expression) within scriptlet tags.

Listing 18.5 is the JSP that includes code from the FibonacciComputation.jsp.

LISTING 18.5 A JSP that Includes the Code from Another JSP
(IncludeJSPExample.jsp)

```
1: <HTML>
2: <HEAD><TITLE>Including Text From Another File</TITLE></HEAD>
3: <BODY>
4: <%@ include file="includedFiles\FibonacciComputation.jsp" %>
5: </BODY>
6: </HTML>
```

Line 4 in Listing 18.5 does the work of including FibonacciComputation.jsp into IncludeJSPExample.jsp. It uses the include directive, and the file is located in subdirectory, relative to IncludeJSPExample.jsp, called includedFiles.

The output of IncludeJSPExample.jsp is shown in Figure 18.2.

FIGURE 18.2

The contents of FibonacciComputation .jsp *show up in the output of* IncludeJSPExample. jsp.

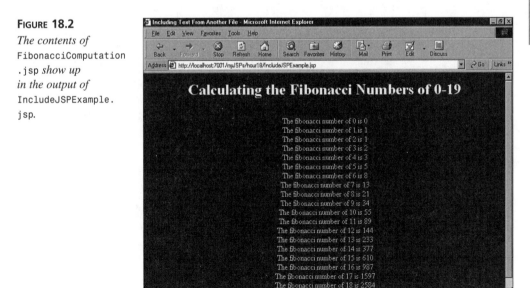

The `include` directive treats the included file as a static document. Since the JSPs are not static documents, you generally will not use the `include` directive to include their code. This example illustrates what happens if you do find yourself using the `include` directive with a JSP. Hour 20 will show how to include the output of a JSP by using the `include` action.

File to Include Is Missing

You have now seen how to include an HTML document and a JavaServer Page in a JSP, but what happens when the included file cannot be found? Listing 18.6 shows a JSP including a copyright HTML document that does not exist.

LISTING 18.6   A JSP that tries to include a file that is non-existent.
(`MissingIncludeFile.jsp`)

```
 1: <HTML>
 2: <HEAD><TITLE>Including a non-existent HTML document</TITLE></HEAD>
 3: <BODY>
 4: <%@ include file="copyright.html" %>
 5: <TABLE WIDTH="100%">
 6:   <TR><TD WIDTH="40%" ALIGN="center">
 7:         <IMG SRC="images\crayon.gif" /></TD>
 8:     <TD WIDTH="60%">
 9:         This document is trying to include a file that does not exist.
10:         <BR>
11:         By running this program you can see how different servers will
12:         <BR>
13:         handle this situation.
14:         <P>
15:         BEA's WebLogic Server creates a comment in the generated HTML
16:         <BR>
17:         document so it does not interrupt the page.
18:         <P>
19:         Tomcat creates an error message and displays that to the screen.
20:     </TD>
21:   </TR>
22: </TABLE>
23: </BODY>
24: </HTML>
```

The `include` directive in line 4 is including a file called `copyright.html`. However, this file does not exist. What do you think will happen when JSP is run? Well, what happens really depends on which server you are using. For example, BEA's WebLogic Server (WLS) creates a message in the generated HTML code as a comment, so it does not appear in the Web page, while Tomcat puts out an error message to the Web page. Figure 18.3 shows the output of `MissingIncludeFile.jsp` running on WLS, and Figure 18.4 shows the same file running on Tomcat.

FIGURE 18.3

WebLogic Server does not post an error message to your Web page when your JSP cannot locate the file that is being included.

FIGURE 18.4

Tomcat puts out an error message on your Web page alerting the user to the fact the included file could not be found.

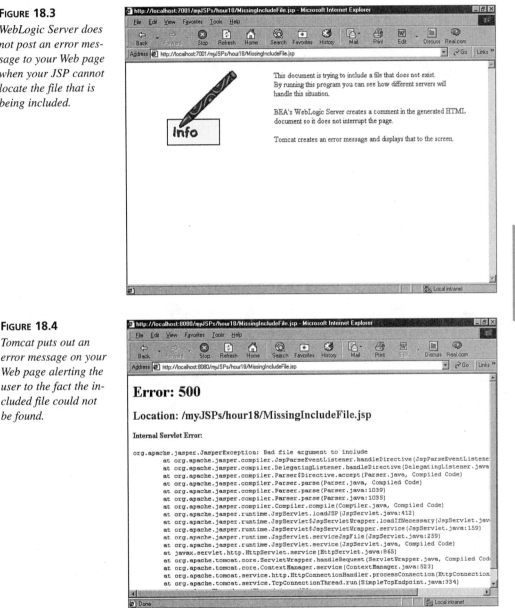

18

While WLS outputs the file without an error message, the HTML code for this JSP contains an HTML comment that says the included file could not be located. The generated HTML for this file, with the comment is shown in Listing 18.7.

LISTING 18.7 The Generated HTML Document from the `MissingIncludeFile.jsp` Running on WLS

```
 1: <HTML>
 2: <HEAD><TITLE>Including a non-existent HTML document</TITLE></HEAD>
 3: <BODY>
 4: <!-- cannot include file 'copyright.html', resource not found -->
 5:
 6: <TABLE WIDTH="100%">
 7:   <TR><TD WIDTH="40%" ALIGN="center">
 8:        <IMG SRC="images\crayon.gif" /></TD>
 9:     <TD WIDTH="60%">
10:        This document is trying to include a file that does not exist.
11:        <BR>
12:        By running this program you can see how different servers will
13:        <BR>
14:        handle this situation.
15:        <P>
16:        BEA's WebLogic Server creates a comment in the generated HTML
17:        <BR>
18:        document so it does not interrupt the page.
19:        <P>
20:        Tomcat creates an error message and displays that to the screen.
21:     </TD>
22:   </TR>
23: </BODY>
24: </HTML>
```

Take a moment to examine the HTML code in Listing 18.7. As you can see, an HTML comment was inserted on line 4, the same place where the `include` directive was in the JSP. This comment explains that the resource is missing, so it could not be included into the document.

Remember the difference between Tomcat and WLS, Tomcat does not make any changes to the JSP as WLS does.

Summary

JSPs allow you to enter data by two methods, the `include` directive and the `include` action. This hour explained how the `include` directive works, the syntax of using it, and the result of this type of `include`. The `include` directive has the general syntax of

```
<%@ include file="Relative_URL_and_Filename" %>
```

The `include` directive has one attribute, the file to include in the JSP, and it is a relative path to the file. The code from that file is inserted into your JSP, translated to the Servlet code, and then compiled and executed. Hour 20 will discuss the other method of including data, the `include` action.

Q&A

Q What is the difference between the `include` directive and the `include` action?

A The `include` directive allows you to insert pre-parsed text into your JSPs, while the `include` action inserts the output of other JSPs. The `include` directive looks at the included file as a static object; the `include` action sees the included file as a dynamic object that takes a request. You will examine the `include` action in Hour 20.

Q When is the code from the included file inserted into the JSP?

A The code is inserted into the JSP at translation time. The `include` directive treats the included file as a static document and inserts the file's code at the location of the `include` directive in the JSP.

Workshop

18

The quiz questions and activities are provided for your further understanding. See Appendix A, "Answers," for the answers to the quiz.

Quiz

1. What is the general syntax of the `include` directive?

2. When using the `include` directive, how is the text of the file included?

3. How do you specify the filename and location for the included file?

Activity

Write a JSP that includes a company banner at the top of the page and a copyright at the bottom. Be as creative as you can with your Web page. The copyright at the bottom could be separated from the rest of the page with a horizontal line.

HOUR 19

Extending JSP Functionality with Tag Libraries

All of the action tags you have learned thus far have been predefined. In Hour 15, "Inserting Applets into Your JSPs," you saw how to use the plugin action to insert Java applets and JavaBean components into your JSPs. The useBean, setProperty, and getProperty actions were covered in Hour 16, "Using JavaBeans in a JSP." Hour 20, "Using Multiple JSPs to Handle the Request," will discuss the include and forward actions.

All of these actions allow you to perform standard tasks, but what if you often use a block of code that is not encompassed in one of these actions? What if you frequently do queries on a database from within your JSPs? You would want to define your own action tags so you could employ those tags in your JSPs instead of using the code to access that database.

A benefit of using custom tags over JavaBeans or other server-side utility classes is that tags can contain bodies where a JSP element of template data can be used.

Extending the functionality of JSPs with custom tags is where tag libraries come into play. Tag libraries allow you to create your own action tags.

The JSP 1.1 specification allows you to create your own action tags, however it does not support the creation of custom directives.

In this hour you will learn

- What a tag library is
- How to use a tag library

Understanding a Tag Library

A *tag library* is a collection of user-defined action tags. New custom actions are defined using tag handlers. A tag library description (TLD) is used to describe the composition of the tag library.

Tag handlers are server-side objects that are used at runtime to evaluate custom actions in a JSP. There are two interfaces that the tag handlers can implement, Tag and BodyTag. The Tag interface is used when the custom action does not use its body, if it even has one. If the custom action wants to manipulate its body content, the tag handler implements the BodyTag interface. The tag handlers can also use the TagSupport and the BodyTagSupport classes as base classes.

The focus of this hour will be how to use available tag libraries and not on writing your own tag handler classes. There are several examples that come with BEA's WebLogic Server 5.1. You will be using their tag libraries to add more functionality to your JSPs in this hour.

A tag library description (TLD) is used to describe the tag library in general, each of its individual tags, version information on the JSP container and the tag library, and information on each action defined. The TLD is written in XML and has a .tld extension.

The `taglib` Directive

The `taglib` directive is used to import a tag library into your JSP. It locates the tag library and assigns it a unique handle, a reference to that particular tag library. Therefore, when you want to use a custom action from that tag library, you specify the unique reference to the tag library and the name of the action you want to invoke. The general syntax of the `taglib` directive is

```
<%@ taglib uri="TagLibraryURI" prefix="tagPrefix" %>
```

The `uri` attribute takes a Uniform Resource Identifier that specifies the location of the tag library descriptor. This can be a relative URI or an absolute URI.

The prefix is a unique way to identify the custom tags that are part of the tag library. Up to this point in this book all the actions you have used had a prefix of `jsp`. Now you will uniquely identify the contents of this JSP with the `prefix` attribute.

An example of the `taglib` directive is

```
<%@ taglib uri="META-INF/taglib.tld" prefix="example" %>
```

The TLD `taglib.tld` will be looked for in a directory named `META-INF` off the root of the Web Application.

> A *Web Application* is a new concept in the Servlet 2.2 specification. It is a grouping of server-side resources such as JSPs, HTML documents, and Servlets. In WebLogic Server, if you do not explicitly define a Web Application, your JSPs will be implicitly placed in one with the root of the Web Application as the `public_html` directory. Hour 24, "Packaging and Deploying an Enterprise Application," you will create a Web Application and deploy it.

19

The `prefix` is `example`, so if the tag library provided a custom tag called `increment` that did not have a body, the actions would look like

```
<example:increment />
```

Another example of a `taglib` directive is

```
<%@ taglib uri="weblogic/taglib/session" prefix="session" %>
```

The URI is an alias that resolves to a directory in a Web Application. Web applications use a `web.xml` file to describe the server-side resources, such as Servlets, JSPs, and HTML documents that comprise the Web Application, and the mapping is done in that file. The prefix in the example `taglib` is `session`, which uniquely identifies the tag library. An example of using that tag library would be

```
<session:list />
```

Of course, this example assumes there is a custom action called list that does not take any body.

Examples of Using Tag Libraries

BEA's WebLogic Server comes with several examples of tag libraries, and you are going to write some JSPs that use them. The first example uses a tag library that provides custom actions to keep track of page hits. The next example provides a custom action that lists the elements in the session object. The last example uses a tag library that provides a custom action to color the code of an included file according to the attributes passed into the custom action tag.

> When you write your own custom tags they can be used on any JSP 1.1 compliant server.

Using a Custom Action to Track Page Hits

The first example involves keeping track of page hits. Of course, you want to have some fun with it, so each hit on the page will be a goal for the Boston Bruins hockey team. Before you can start writing your JSP and working with the tag library, though, you need to set up your environment. To do so, follow these steps.

1. Compile the tag handlers for the example and place them in a directory where WebLogic Server will be able to find them.

> WebLogic Server can locate Java files located off the c:\weblogic\myserver\serverclasses directory when you start WLS through the START menu. The Java .class files will be located in their package structure off this directory.

Open a DOS prompt and set up your system PATH to point to your JDK:

`c:\>set PATH=c:\jdk1.2.2\bin`

This tells DOS where to find the java, javac, and other JDK commands, and ensures that your Java commands are found. If your JDK is in another directory, point to that directory.

2. Compile the Java classes for this tag library. The files for this example are found in the directory c:\weblogic\examples\jsp\tagext\counter, so change to that directory.

3. Once you are in the `counter` directory, you can compile the Java source code files and place them in their package structure off the `c:\weblogic\myserver\serverclasses` directory.

`counter>`**`javac -d c:\weblogic\myserver\serverclasses *.java`**

These Java source code files are the tag handlers for this tag library. WLS will be able to find the files in the `serverclasses` directory.

> The `-d` option specifies the root directory to place the generated `.class` files into. The `.class` files are placed in their package structure off this root directory.

4. Create the subdirectory for this hour: `c:\weblogic\myserver\myJSPs\hour19`. Your JSPs will be in this directory.

5. Copy the tag library description `counter.tld` from the `c:\weblogic\examples\jsp\tagext\counter` directory to the `META-INF` directory off the `public_html` directory.

`counter>copy counter.tld \weblogic\myserver\public_html\META-INF`

Now that the files are compiled and WLS can find them, and the TLD is in the proper spot, it is time to write a JSP that uses the tag library. The tag library provides two custom actions that keep track of page hits. To have some fun with it, every time you refresh the page, the Boston Bruins will score a goal. The first custom action this tag library provides displays the current page hit count, and the second custom action increments the page hit count. Listing 19.1 shows the code for the JSP, `HelpTheBruins.jsp`.

LISTING 19.1   JSP that Uses Custom Tags to Keep Track of Page Hits (HelpTheBruins.jsp)

```
 1: <HTML>
 2: <HEAD><TITLE>Keeping Track Of Page Hits</TITLE></HEAD>
 3: <BODY BGCOLOR="yellow" LINK="navy" ALINK="silver" VLINK="navy">
 4:
 5: <%@ taglib uri="META-INF/counter.tld" prefix="pageCount" %>
 6:
 7: <pageCount:increment />
 8:
 9: <CENTER>
10:   <H1>Help The Boston Bruins Score Goals</H1>
11:
12:   <H2>
13:     Do you bleed black and gold?
14:     <BR><BR>
```

19

LISTING **19.1** continued

```
15:     Do you want to help the Boston Bruins Score Goals?
16:     </H2>
17:
18: </CENTER>
19:
20: <BR>
21:
22: <H2>
23:     If you answered 'YES', this is your chance. Keep refreshing
24:     this page and you will see their goal count increase.
25:
26:     <BR><BR>
27:
28:     Either refresh the page through the browser's refresh button,
29:     or click on the following URL,
30:
31:     <A HREF="http://localhost:7001/myJSPs/hour19/helpTheBruins.jsp">
32:     Help The Bruins
33:     </A>
34:
35: </H2>
36:
37: <BR>
38:
39: <CENTER>
40:     <H1>Bruins Have <pageCount:display /> Goals</H1>
41:     <H2>Keep Up Your Efforts</H2>
42: </CENTER>
43:
44: </BODY>
45: </HTML>
```

ANALYSIS Line 5 imports the tag library into the JSP. The uri points to the tag library descriptor, counter.tld, that you placed in the META-INF directory. The prefix assigns a name of pageCount to uniquely identify the actions defined in this tag library. The library defines a custom action called increment, which increments the page hit count, and another called display, which displays the page count.

Line 7 uses the increment action. Notice it uses the prefix you assigned in the taglib directive to refer back to that tag library. Line 40 uses the display action to present the current page count as the number of goals that the Bruins have scored. Both of these are empty tags—that is, tags that do not need a body—so remember to use the forward slash before ending them.

Figure 19.1 shows the output of executing this JSP.

FIGURE 19.1

The JSP uses custom tags to keep track of page hits.

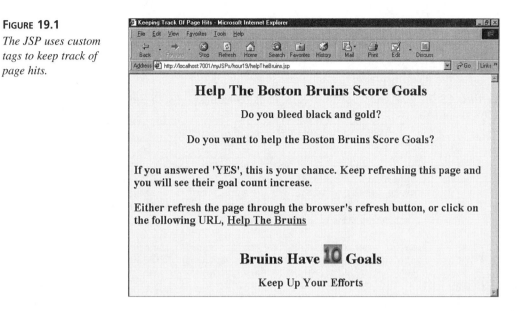

Keep refreshing the page and you will see the goal count for the Bruins increasing. You have now written a JSP that used a tag library to increase its functionality. In the next example you will see a custom action that uses its body.

Listing Elements of a `session` Object

Now take a look at a tag library that provides one action tag that lists the elements of a `session` object. This custom tag will use its body. Before you start using the tag library you need to set up the environment, compiling the programs you are going to use and placing them in a directory in which WLS will be able to locate them. Here are the steps:

1. Just as you did in the first example, set your system PATH so your Java commands can be located:

   ```
   c:\>set PATH=c:\jdk1.2.2\bin
   ```

2. Change directories to the directory that contains the tag handler `.java` source code files, `c:\weblogic\examples\jsp\tagext\session`.

3. Compile the tag handler classes, placing them in their appropriate package structure off the `c:\weblogic\myserver\serverclasses` directory:

   ```
   session>javac -d c:\weblogic\myserver\serverclasses *.java
   ```

4. Copy the TLD to the `META-INF` directory off your `public_html` directory:

   ```
   session\WEB-INF>copy session.tld \weblogic\myserver\public_html\META-INF
   ```

19

Now it is time to program the JSP. Write a JSP that allows the user to input items into a "shopping cart," which is actually just a `session` object that uses a custom action tag to display the items in the cart. Listing 19.2 shows the code for this JSP.

LISTING 19.2   JSP that Uses Custom Tags to Keep Track of Session Data (SessionData.jsp)

```
 1: <%@ taglib uri="META-INF/session.tld" prefix="sessionData" %>
 2:
 3: <% String action = request.getParameter("action");
 4:    if ((action != null) && (action.equals("Add Item"))){
 5:      String itemName = request.getParameter("txtItem");
 6:      String itemAmount = request.getParameter("txtAmount");
 7:      session.setAttribute(itemName, itemAmount);
 8:    }
 9:    else if ((action != null) && (action.equals("delete"))) {
10:      String deletedItem = request.getParameter("deletedItem");
11:      session.removeAttribute(deletedItem);
12:    }
13: %>
14:
15:
16:
17: <HTML>
18: <HEAD><TITLE>Shopping Cart</TITLE></HEAD>
19: <BODY TEXT="navy">
20: <CENTER>
21: <FONT FACE="Trebuchet" SIZE="7">
22:    Shopping Cart
23: </FONT>
24: </CENTER>
25:
26: <BR><BR>
27:
28: This site will allow you to enter item into your shopping
29: cart. Simply enter the item name and the value. This will
30: be stored in an HTTPSession object. You can add to your
31: shopping cart and remove items from your shopping cart.
32: The JSP is employing special tags to accomplish the manipulation
33: of your shopping cart.
34:
35: <BR><BR>
36:
37: <CENTER>
38: <FONT SIZE="5">
39:    Shopping Cart Items
40: </FONT>
41: </CENTER>
42:
43: <TABLE WIDTH="100%" BGCOLOR="silver">
```

LISTING 19.2   continued

```
44: <sessionData:list>
45:   <TR><TD ALIGN="center" WIDTH="33%"><%= name %></TD>
46:       <TD ALIGN="center" WIDTH="33%"><%= value %></TD>
47:       <TD ALIGN="center" WIDTH="34%">
48: <%
49:    String partLink="http://localhost:7001/myJSPs/hour19/SessionData.jsp";
50:    String deleteLink=partLink + "?action=delete&deletedItem=" + name;
51: %>
52:           <A HREF="<%=deleteLink%>">delete</A></TD></TR>
53: </sessionData:list>
54: </TABLE>
55:
56: <BR>
57:
58: <CENTER>
59: <FONT SIZE="5">
60:   Enter New Item
61: </FONT>
62: </CENTER>
63:
64: <FORM NAME="ShoppingForm"
65:  ACTION="http://localhost:7001/myJSPs/hour19/SessionData.jsp"
66:  METHOD="POST">
67:
68:   <TABLE WIDTH="100%" BGCOLOR="yellow">
69:     <TR><TD ALIGN="right" WIDTH="50%">Enter Item Name</TD>
70:         <TD WIDTH="50%"><INPUT TYPE="text" NAME="txtItem" VALUE="" /></TD>
71:     </TR>
72:
73:     <TR><TD ALIGN="right">Enter Item Amount</TD>
74:         <TD><INPUT TYPE="text" NAME="txtAmount" VALUE="" /></TD>
75:     </TR>
76:
77:     <TR><TD ALIGN="center" COLSPAN="2">
78:          <INPUT TYPE="submit" NAME="action" VALUE="Add Item" />
79:         </TD>
80:     </TR>
81:   </TABLE>
82:
83: </FORM>
84:
85: </BODY>
86: </HTML>
```

19

ANALYSIS   There are a few things to note about this example. First, you can place large pieces of code before your first HTML tag. That keeps the document easy to read. In this example, line 1 declares the tag library that the JSP is using. Notice the uri points to a TLD named `session.tld` in the `META-INF` directory (you have already copied that file into the `META-INF` directory off the `c:\weblogic\myserver\public_html` directory). The prefix assigns the name `sessionData` to uniquely define this tag library.

Lines 44–53 use the one action tag this tag library defines. The tag name is `list`, and it uses a body. There are two variables, `name` and `value`, available in the body of the `list` action tag. Within the body of that tag you have available two variables, `name` and `value`, to get the name and value of the `session` object. This JSP formats those values into a table to output to the user. This table also provides a hyperlink that will delete the particular element from the `session` object. Figure 19.2 shows the output of this JSP.

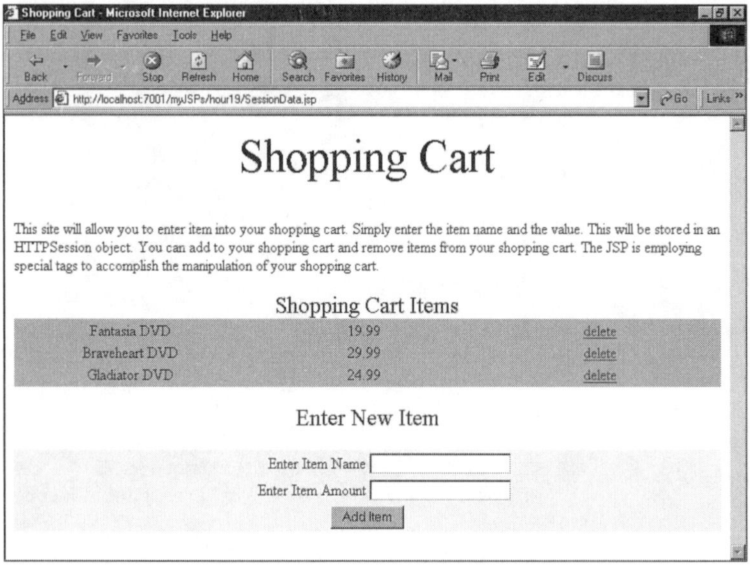

FIGURE 19.2

The JSP listing the elements from a session *object.*

As the figure shows, the output of the `session` object is formatted in a table with a hyperlink to the far right that allows the user to delete the item.

Using a Custom Action Tag with Attributes

In the first example a tag library provided custom actions that did not contain a body or attributes. The second example utilized a tag library that defined one custom action that took a body. This example utilizes a tag library that provides a custom action that accepts attributes. The custom action takes attributes that are used to color the text of an included file. You can specify the color of comments, quoted text, and the general color and style of the font. The JSP you are going to write allows the user to input the colors for these parts of the included files. However, before you jump into coding the JSP, you need to do the setup.

1. Just as in the previous examples, set your system PATH in a DOS prompt.

2. Compile your Java classes for this example. They are located in c:\weblogic\ examples\jsp\tagext\quote. Therefore, change directories to this one (if you have not done so already)and compile the Java source code files and place them in the serverclasses directory.

    quote>**javac -d c:\weblogic\myserver\serverclasses *.java**

3. Copy the TLD over to the META-INF directory off the public_html directory.

    quote\WEB-INF>**copy quote.tld c:\weblogic\myserver\public_html\META-INF**

4. Copy over the Java source code file for including into the JSP.

    quote>**copy CodeTag.java c:\weblogic\myserver\public_html\myJSPs\hour19**

The stage is all set for you to write a JSP that uses this tag library. Listing 19.3 shows the code for the JSP.

LISTING 19.3 A JSP that Uses a Custom Action that Takes Attributes and Colors Code Accordingly (ColorCode.jsp)

```
 1: <%@ taglib uri="META-INF/quote.tld" prefix="quote" %>
 2:
 3: <% String changes = request.getParameter("sbtChangeColors");
 4:
 5:    //set default values for the color scheme
 6:    String quoteColor = "blue";
 7:    String commentColor= "purple";
 8:    String fontColor = "navy";
 9:    String fontStyle = "Trebuchet";
10:    String font = "face="+fontStyle+ " color="+fontColor;
11:
12:    //the user has submitted choices for the colors
13:    if (changes != null) {
14:      quoteColor = request.getParameter("txtQuoteColor");
15:      commentColor = request.getParameter("txtCommentColor");
16:      fontColor = request.getParameter("txtFontColor");
17:      fontStyle = request.getParameter("sltFontStyle");
18:      font = "face=" + fontStyle + " color=" + fontColor;
19:    }
20: %>
21:
22: <HTML>
23: <HEAD><TITLE>Highlighting Code</TITLE></HEAD>
24: <BODY>
25:
26: <CENTER>
27:   <H1><FONT COLOR="red">Having Fun With Colors</FONT></H1>
28: </CENTER>
29:
```

19

LISTING 19.3 continued

```
30: <TABLE WIDTH="100%" BGCOLOR="yellow">
31: <FORM NAME="fontColors"
32:       ACTION="http://localhost:7001/myJSPs/hour19/colorCode.jsp"
33:       METHOD="POST">
34:
35:   <TR><TD ALIGN="right">Enter the color for quotes: </TD>
36:       <TD><INPUT TYPE="text" NAME="txtQuoteColor" VALUE="" /></TD>
37:   </TR>
38:
39:   <TR><TD ALIGN="right">Enter the color for comments: </TD>
40:       <TD><INPUT TYPE="text" NAME="txtCommentColor" VALUE="" /></TD>
41:   </TR>
42:
43:   <TR><TD ALIGN="right">Enter the color for font: </TD>
44:       <TD><INPUT TYPE="text" NAME="txtFontColor" VALUE="" /></TD>
45:   </TR>
46:
47:   <TR><TD ALIGN="right">Select the font style: </TD>
48:       <TD><SELECT NAME="sltFontStyle">
49:             <OPTION>Trebuchet</OPTION>
50:             <OPTION>Courier New</OPTION>
51:          </SELECT>
52:       </TD>
53:   </TR>
54:   <TR><TD COLSPAN="2" ALIGN="center">
55:       <INPUT TYPE="submit" NAME="sbtChangeColors" VALUE="Submit Changes" />
56:       </TD>
57:   </TR>
58:
59: </FORM>
60: </TABLE>
61:
62:
63: <quote:code quoteColor="<%=quoteColor%>"
64:             commentColor="<%=commentColor%>"
65:             defaultFont="<%=font%>">
66:
67:    <%@ include file="CodeTag.java" %>
68:
69: </quote:code>
70:
71: <TABLE WIDTH="100%" BGCOLOR="silver">
72:   <TR><TH COLSPAN="2" ALIGN="center">Color Scheme</TH></TR>
73:
74:   <TR><TD ALIGN="center" WIDTH="50%">Quote</TD>
75:       <TD ALIGN="center" WIDTH="50%"><%= quoteColor %></TD>
76:   </TR>
77:
78:   <TR><TD ALIGN="center">Comment</TD>
79:       <TD ALIGN="center"><%= commentColor %></TD>
```

LISTING 19.3 continued

```
80:    </TR>
81:
82:    <TR><TD ALIGN="center">Font Color</TD>
83:        <TD ALIGN="center"><%= fontColor %></TD>
84:    </TR>
85:
86:    <TR><TD ALIGN="center">Font Style</TD>
87:        <TD ALIGN="center"><%= fontStyle %></TD>
88:    </TR>
89: </TABLE>
90:
91: </BODY>
92: </HTML>
```

ANALYSIS Line 1 imports the tag library into the JSP and gives it a unique reference name, quote. This tag library provides one custom action that prints out an included file and changes its color depending on the attributes in the custom tag.

Line 63 starts using this tag, by specifying quote and then the name of the tag, code. This tag takes a few attributes: quoteColor, commentColor, and defaultFont. Since this JSP strives to be dynamic in that the client should be able to specify the colors, the values of these attributes are taken from the HTML form elements. Therefore, the client inputs the colors for the various parts of the code, and this tag takes those colors for its attributes.

FIGURE 19.3

This JSP uses a tag library that uses attributes in the tag.

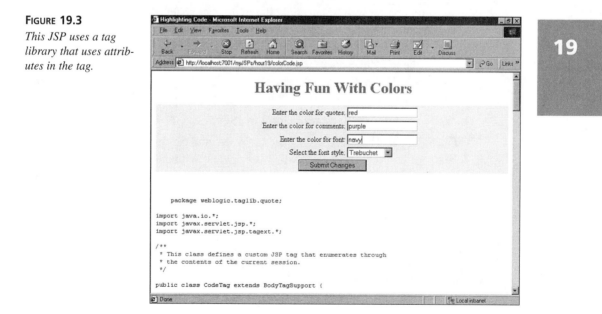

19

Enter some new colors into the HTML form and click the Submit button. You will see the colors of the code elements change according to your specification.

Summary

JSPs provide six predefined action tags that you can use in place of a chunk of code. Actions that you use frequently can be replaced with a custom tag that you define in a tag library. A tag library is a collection of tag handlers, the actual coding of what the action does, and a tag library description (TLD) that describes what tags are part of this tag library.

The `taglib` directive is used to import a tag library into a JSP. The location of the tag library and a unique reference name assigned to the tag library are included in the `taglib` directive. After specifying the tag library with the `taglib` directive, you are free to use the custom tags defined in the tag library.

Q&A

Q Why are the tag library descriptors in the `META-INF` directory off of `c:\weblogic\ myserver\public_html` and not `c:\weblogic\myserver\public_html\myJSPs\ hour19`?

A When the JSP container is trying to resolve the location of the tag library, it looks in the root of the Web Application. If you do not explicitly place your JSPs in a Web Application, they are implicitly placed in one with the root being the `c:\ weblogic\myserver\public_html` directory. Therefore, when the JSP specifies the TLD to be in a directory `META-INF`, the JSP container is going to search the root of the Web Application, `c:\weblogic\myserver\public_html`, to find it. Again, you will be going in much more detail about Web Applications in Hour 24.

Q Why are custom action tags helpful in JSPs?

A One of the goals of JavaServer Pages is to separate the responsibilities and to allow beginner Java programmers to write these pages. With the custom tags, non-Java programmers can create dynamic content on the Web by writing JSPs with custom action tags instead of needing to write the code.

Workshop

The quiz questions and activities are provided for your further understanding. See Appendix A, "Answers," for the answers to the quiz.

Quiz

1. What is a tag handler?

2. What language is the tag library descriptor written in?

3. When you are using custom actions in a JSP, how does it know which tag library your custom action is defined within?

Activity

Write a JSP that utilizes all the tag libraries discussed in this hour. One of the tag libraries keeps track of page hits so you can capture the page hits and display them as the number of jellybeans in a jar, or something else that has a continuously growing number. The session tracker can keep track of the colors of jellybeans in a jar or what you are counting. Finally, with the quote tag library you can bring in another `.class` file playing with the output colors. Have some fun with it.

19

Hour **20**

Using Multiple JSPs to Handle the Request

Many times you want to spread the work of your application among multiple JSPs. Perhaps you would have one JSP accept the request, parse through the request, and save the data to a JavaBean. The JSP would then forward the request to another JSP that takes the data out of the JavaBean and formats it in an easy-to-read fashion. Then again, maybe you want one JSP to look over the work of the other JSPs, so your primary JSP includes the output of other JSPs. You saw these scenarios in Hour 5, "Understanding the JSP Application Models," but this hour is going to go into much more detail about these scenarios.

In this hour you will learn

- How to use the `include` action
- How to use the `forward` action

Reviewing the Including Requests Application Model

The JSP specification describes many models of how JSPs can interact with each other. Hour 5 discussed many of the application models, such as the Simple Model and the N-Tier Model. Recall from that discussion there is an application model called the Including Requests Model, which is shown in Figure 20.1.

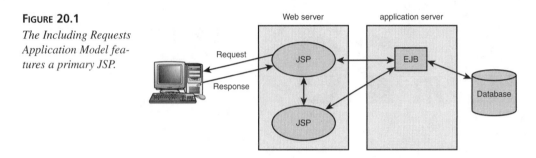

In the Including Requests Application Model, a primary JavaServer Page oversees the work of other JSPs. It is the responsibility of the primary JSP to accept the request from the user and generate a response to the user. The response could include the output of other JavaServer Pages, though. This model is accomplished by using the `include` action.

A Review of JSP Actions

Before looking at the `include` action, it is helpful to discuss the general syntax of a JSP action. The `include` action is just one of the six JSP actions. In Hour 15, "Inserting Applets into Your JSPs," you saw the `applet` action that allowed you to insert Java applets into your JSPs. Hour 16, "Using JavaBeans in a JSP," introduced you to the `useBean` action that allows you to use a JavaBean, and also showed you the `getProperty` and `setProperty` actions. So from your experience, recall that the general syntax of a JSP action is

```
<jsp:action_Name action_parameters />
```

Many of the actions are empty tags, so don't forget to put the forward slash before you close the tag. The `action_Name` is the name of the action you want to perform. For the include action the `action_Name` is `include`. This hour also discusses the `forward` action whose `action_Name` is `forward`. In Hour 15, you saw that the `action_Name` to insert an applet was `applet`, and Hour 16 talked about the `getProperty`, `setProperty`, and `useBean` actions.

The *action_parameters* are dependent on the action you are performing. Each of the actions takes various properties. The include and forward actions take the name of another JSP as the *action_parameter*.

Using the include Action

The general syntax of the include action is

```
<jsp:include page"="RelativeURL_to_JSP""/>
```

Comparing the include action to the general syntax of a JSP action, the *action_Name* is include, and the *action_parameter* is page, which is a relative URL to the JSP you want included.

Understanding the Difference Between the include Action and the include Directive

The difference between the include action and the include directive is how the included file is treated. The include directive treats the included file as a static document and simply inserts the file's code into the generated Servlet code. The include action treats the included file as a dynamic document and therefore includes the output of the included file. The generated Servlet code makes a call to include the output of the file instead of including the code.

> Remember, if you are including static documents such as HTML documents or images, you will use the include directive. Inserting dynamic pages such as JSPs would require the include action.

Implementing the include Action

Now it is time to look at an example that uses the include action. This example includes an HTML document, a JSP that displays golfer statistics, a JSP that displays course information, and a JSP that inserts the other JSPs based on the input from the HTML form. The entry point into the application is an HTML document that lets users decide if they want to view golfer statistics and course statistics. Listing 20.1 shows the code for the HTML document.

20

LISTING 20.1 An HTML Document that Asks Users What Data They Want to View (DataSelection.html)

```
1: <HTML>
2: <HEAD><TITLE>Select Your Data</TITLE></HEAD>
```

LISTING 20.1   continued

```
 3: <BODY BGCOLOR="cyan">
 4:   <CENTER>
 5:     <FONT SIZE="5" COLOR="navy">Select The Data You Want To View</FONT>
 6:   </CENTER>
 7:
 8:   <FORM NAME="DataSelection"
 9:         ACTION="http://localhost:7001/myJSPs/hour20/DataPresentation.jsp"
10:         METHOD="POST">
11:   <TABLE WIDTH="100%" ALIGN="center">
12:     <TR ALIGN="center">
13:       <TD><INPUT TYPE="checkbox" NAME="stats" VALUE="golferStats" CHECKED>
14:           All Golfer Statistics
15:       </TD>
16:     </TR>
17:     <TR><TD> </TD></TR>
18:     <TR ALIGN="center">
19:       <TD><INPUT TYPE="checkbox" NAME="course" VALUE="courseStats" CHECKED>
20:           All Course Statistics
21:       </TD>
22:     </TR>
23:     <TR><TD> </TD></TR>
24:     <TR ALIGN="center">
25:       <TD><INPUT TYPE="submit" NAME="btnSubmit" VALUE="View Data"></TD>
26:     </TR>
27:   </TABLE>
28:   </FORM>
29: </BODY>
30: </HTML>
```

ANALYSIS   Lines 8–10 define an HTML form with a name of DataSelection, an action of a JSP called DataPresentation.jsp, and a method of POST. Therefore, when the user clicks View Data, the submit button, the data of the form is packaged and sent to the server to trigger the DataPresentation.jsp file.

This form is comprised of two checkboxes: one to select golfer statistics and one to select course statistics. The checkbox for the golfer statistics has a value of golferStats (defined on line 13) and the checkbox for the course statistics has a value of courseStats (defined on line 19).

Users can select what data they want to view and then click the submit button. When the submit button is clicked, the data is sent to the server and the JavaServer Page DataPresentation.jsp is triggered. DataPresentation.jsp determines what the user selected (what data the user wants to view), and then includes the appropriate JSPs. Listing 20.2 is the code for the DataPresentation.jsp file.

LISTING 20.2   A JSP that Parses the Input from an HTML Form and Includes the
Appropriate JSP to Service the User's Request (DataPresentation.jsp)

```
 1: <HTML>
 2: <HEAD><TITLE>Including the Output of Other JSPs</TITLE></HEAD>
 3: <BODY>
 4: <% Enumeration enum = request.getParameterNames();
 5:    while (enum.hasMoreElements()) {
 6:       String inputName = (String)enum.nextElement();
 7:       String inputValue = request.getParameter(inputName);
 8:       if (inputValue.equals("golferStats")) {
 9: %>
10:          <jsp:include page="ShowGolferStats.jsp" />
11: <%
12:       } else if (inputValue.equals("courseStats")){
13: %>
14:          <jsp:include page="ShowCourseStats.jsp" />
15:
16: <%    } //end else clause
17:    } //end while loop
18: %>
19: </BODY>
20: </HTML>
```

ANALYSIS   Line 4 parses the request and gets an enumeration of the names of the HTML
form elements that were submitted by the user. Only the names of the selected
elements will be sent to the server.

Line 5 starts the while loop that will loop through the elements of the enumeration,
which contains only the names of the HTML form elements sent to the server. The
while loop is concluded on line 17. Within the while loop the values for each of the
HTML form elements are determined. If the value of the form element is golferStats,
ShowGolferStats.jsp will be included in the JSP. The code for ShowGolferStats.jsp
is shown in Listing 20.3. If the user selected to view the course statistics then one of the
values of the HTML form elements is courseStats and that JSP will include the file
ShowCourseStats.jsp. The code for ShowCourseStats.jsp is shown in Listing 20.4.

Take a moment to examine the include action tags on lines 10 and 14. The include
actions are empty tags, so there is a forward slash before the closing tag. Also note that
there is no path specified for the JSP being included. Since there is no path specified,
these files are located in the same directory as the DataPresentation.jsp file.

Now take some time to study the files that are included. Both included files are going to
access a database to retrieve their respective data. The ShowGolferStats.jsp file will
retrieve a golfer name, the course name, and the number of shots for the 18 holes. Listing
20.3 shows the code for the ShowGolferStats.jsp file.

20

LISTING 20.3 A JSP that Retrieves Golfer Information from a Database
(ShowGolferStats.jsp)

```
 1: <HTML>
 2: <HEAD><TITLE>Golfer Statistics</TITLE></HEAD>
 3: <BODY>
 4: <%@ page import="java.sql.*;" %>
 5: <H1 ALIGN="center">Golfer Statistics</H1>
 6: <TABLE BORDER="2" WIDTH="100%" BGCOLOR="pink">
 7:   <%
 8:     Class.forName("COM.cloudscape.core.JDBCDriver").newInstance();
 9:     Connection conn =
10:       DriverManager.getConnection("jdbc:cloudscape:c:\\GolfDB");
11:     Statement statement = conn.createStatement();
12:     String sql = "SELECT * FROM GOLFDATA";
13:     ResultSet rs = statement.executeQuery(sql);
14:     while (rs.next()) {
15:   %>
16:   <TR><TD COLSPAN="10">
17:       Name: <%= rs.getString("NAME") %>
18:     </TD>
19:   </TR>
20:   <TR><TD COLSPAN="10">
21:       Course: <%= rs.getString("COURSE") %>
22:     </TD>
23:   </TR>
24:   <TR ALIGN="center"><TD>Front Nine</TD>
25:     <TD>Hole 1: <BR><%= rs.getString("Hole1") %></TD>
26:     <TD>Hole 2: <BR><%= rs.getString("Hole2") %></TD>
27:     <TD>Hole 3: <BR><%= rs.getString("Hole3") %></TD>
28:     <TD>Hole 4: <BR><%= rs.getString("Hole4") %></TD>
29:     <TD>Hole 5: <BR><%= rs.getString("Hole5") %></TD>
30:     <TD>Hole 6: <BR><%= rs.getString("Hole6") %></TD>
31:     <TD>Hole 7: <BR><%= rs.getString("Hole7") %></TD>
32:     <TD>Hole 8: <BR><%= rs.getString("Hole8") %></TD>
33:     <TD>Hole 9: <BR><%= rs.getString("Hole9") %></TD>
34:   </TR>
35:   <TR ALIGN="center"><TD>Back Nine</TD>
36:     <TD>Hole 10: <BR><%= rs.getString("Hole10") %></TD>
37:     <TD>Hole 11: <BR><%= rs.getString("Hole11") %></TD>
38:     <TD>Hole 12: <BR><%= rs.getString("Hole12") %></TD>
39:     <TD>Hole 13: <BR><%= rs.getString("Hole13") %></TD>
40:     <TD>Hole 14: <BR><%= rs.getString("Hole14") %></TD>
41:     <TD>Hole 15: <BR><%= rs.getString("Hole15") %></TD>
42:     <TD>Hole 16: <BR><%= rs.getString("Hole16") %></TD>
43:     <TD>Hole 17: <BR><%= rs.getString("Hole17") %></TD>
44:     <TD>Hole 18: <BR><%= rs.getString("Hole18") %></TD>
45:   </TR>
46: <% } //end while loop
47:
48:   if (statement != null)
49:     statement.close();
```

LISTING 20.3   continued

```
50:    if (conn != null)
51:      conn.close();
52: %>
53: </TABLE>
54: </BODY>
55: </HTML>
```

ANALYSIS Although this code does not contain any `include` actions, it reviews accessing a database from a JSP, a topic from Hour 17.

Since this JSP is going to be using a database, the package `java.sql.*` is imported using the `page` directive in line 4.

Lines 8–10 set up the database driver, `COM.cloudscape.core.JDBCDriver`, for the `cloudscape` database that comes with BEA WebLogic Server. A connection is established using the `DriverManager` class and specifying the appropriate driver URL. As you can see from line 10, the database is called `GolfDB` and is located on the `C:\` drive.

Line 11 uses the connection to this database to create a statement. Line 12 creates an SQL string that selects all the data from the table `GOLFDATA`. This table contains a golfer's name, the course she played, and the number of strokes for each hole.

The SQL statement is executed in line 13 and the `ResultSet` that is returned is captured in the variable `rs`. Line 14 starts a `while` loop that will loop through all the elements in the `ResultSet`, which means it will loop through each row in the database. This `while` loop is ended on line 46.

During the `while` loop, table rows are created. One row contains the golfer's name, which is done in line 17. Notice that the values for the table cells can be Java expressions using the expression JSP tags. The `ResultSet` class has methods that can be used to retrieve data from particular columns in the database. Another row in the table is the course name, which is retrieved in line 21. The front nine holes are formatted in lines 24–34, and the back nine holes are formatted in lines 35–45.

A JSP to show the course statistics was included in this example, and its code is shown in Listing 20.4.

20

LISTING 20.4   A JSP that Retrieves Golf Course Information from a Database (`ShowCourseStats.jsp`)

```
1: <HTML>
2: <HEAD><TITLE>Course Statistics</TITLE></HEAD>
3: <BODY>
4: <%@ page import="java.sql.*;" %>
```

LISTING 20.4   continued

```
 5: <H1 ALIGN="center">Course Statistics</H1>
 6: <TABLE BORDER="2" WIDTH="100%" BGCOLOR="pink">
 7:   <%
 8:     Class.forName("COM.cloudscape.core.JDBCDriver").newInstance();
 9:     Connection conn =
10:       DriverManager.getConnection("jdbc:cloudscape:c:\\GolfDB");
11:     Statement statement = conn.createStatement();
12:     String sql = "SELECT * FROM COURSEDATA";
13:     ResultSet rs = statement.executeQuery(sql);
14:     while (rs.next()) {
15:   %>
16:   <TR><TD COLSPAN="10">
17:       Course: <%= rs.getString("COURSE") %>
18:     </TD>
19:   </TR>
20:   <TR ALIGN="center"><TD>Front Nine</TD>
21:     <TD>Hole 1: <BR><%= rs.getString("Hole1") %></TD>
22:     <TD>Hole 2: <BR><%= rs.getString("Hole2") %></TD>
23:     <TD>Hole 3: <BR><%= rs.getString("Hole3") %></TD>
24:     <TD>Hole 4: <BR><%= rs.getString("Hole4") %></TD>
25:     <TD>Hole 5: <BR><%= rs.getString("Hole5") %></TD>
26:     <TD>Hole 6: <BR><%= rs.getString("Hole6") %></TD>
27:     <TD>Hole 7: <BR><%= rs.getString("Hole7") %></TD>
28:     <TD>Hole 8: <BR><%= rs.getString("Hole8") %></TD>
29:     <TD>Hole 9: <BR><%= rs.getString("Hole9") %></TD>
30:   </TR>
31:   <TR ALIGN="center"><TD>Back Nine</TD>
32:     <TD>Hole 10: <BR><%= rs.getString("Hole10") %></TD>
33:     <TD>Hole 11: <BR><%= rs.getString("Hole11") %></TD>
34:     <TD>Hole 12: <BR><%= rs.getString("Hole12") %></TD>
35:     <TD>Hole 13: <BR><%= rs.getString("Hole13") %></TD>
36:     <TD>Hole 14: <BR><%= rs.getString("Hole14") %></TD>
37:     <TD>Hole 15: <BR><%= rs.getString("Hole15") %></TD>
38:     <TD>Hole 16: <BR><%= rs.getString("Hole16") %></TD>
39:     <TD>Hole 17: <BR><%= rs.getString("Hole17") %></TD>
40:     <TD>Hole 18: <BR><%= rs.getString("Hole18") %></TD>
41:   </TR>
42:   <% } //end while loop
43:
44:   if (statement != null)
45:     statement.close();
46:   if (conn != null)
47:     conn.close();
48:   %>
49: </TABLE>
50: </BODY>
51: </HTML>
```

ANALYSIS This code is very similar to the code for the ShowGolferStats.jsp file. The main difference is that it gets its information from COURSEDATA table in the GolfDB database. Take a moment to study lines 44–47. It is always a good idea to close your statements and connections to databases when you are done using them. That way you don't leave unused resources open.

What does it look like to put all these files together? Well, the user first requests the HTML document. Figure 20.2 shows the DataSelection.html file.

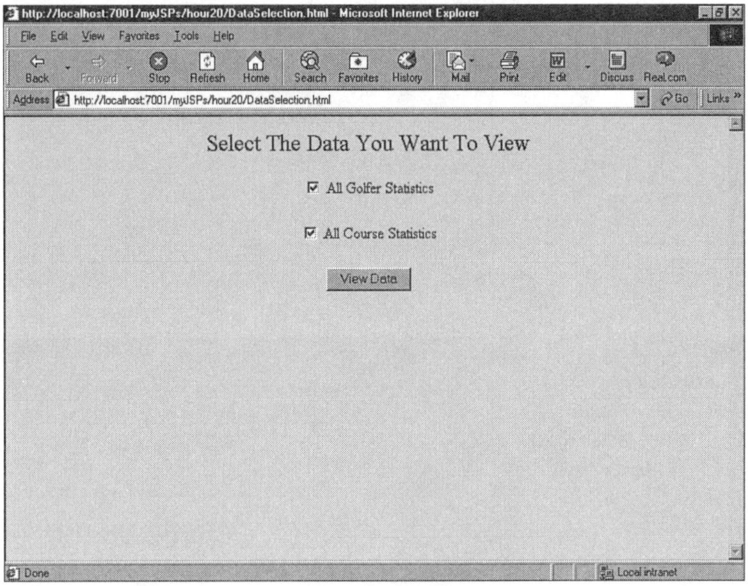

FIGURE 20.2

The HTML document allows the user to select the data he wants to view.

The user selects to view the golfer statistics or the course information, and then clicks View Data, the submit button. Remember from the code that the HTML document will send the data to the server and trigger the DataPresentation.jsp. The output depends on the input, of course. If the user selected to view both, he will see golfer statistics and course information in one document. Figure 20.3 shows the golfer statistics output, and Figure 20.4 shows the rest of the document that contains the course statistics.

Scroll down to see the course information (see Figure 20.4) below the golfer statistics.

The include action allows developers to take advantage of other JSPs to do the work. One JSP, the DataPresentation.jsp in the previous example, parsed the user's request and included the JSP files that would satisfy that request.

20

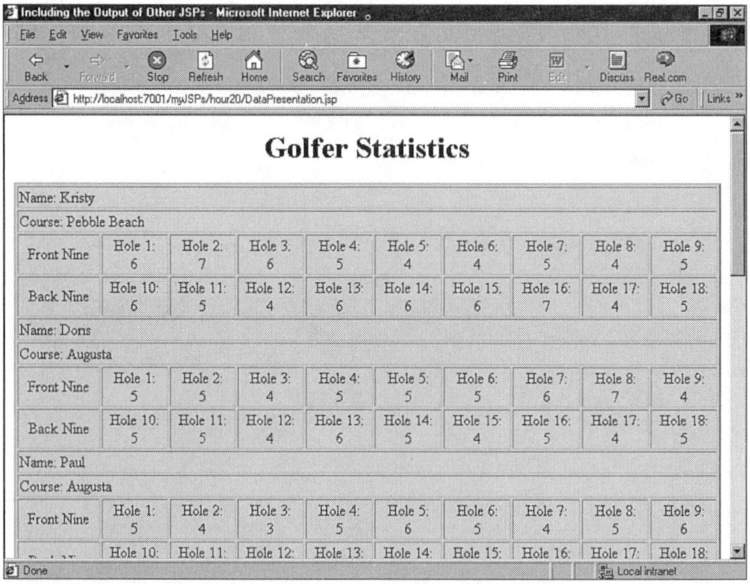

Including the Output of Other JSPs - Microsoft Internet Explorer

http://localhost:7001/myJSPs/hour20/DataPresentation.jsp

Golfer Statistics

Name: Kristy									
Course: Pebble Beach									
Front Nine	Hole 1: 6	Hole 2: 7	Hole 3: 6	Hole 4: 5	Hole 5: 4	Hole 6: 4	Hole 7: 5	Hole 8: 4	Hole 9: 5
Back Nine	Hole 10: 6	Hole 11: 5	Hole 12: 4	Hole 13: 6	Hole 14: 6	Hole 15: 6	Hole 16: 7	Hole 17: 4	Hole 18: 5
Name: Doris									
Course: Augusta									
Front Nine	Hole 1: 5	Hole 2: 5	Hole 3: 4	Hole 4: 5	Hole 5: 5	Hole 6: 5	Hole 7: 6	Hole 8: 7	Hole 9: 4
Back Nine	Hole 10: 5	Hole 11: 5	Hole 12: 4	Hole 13: 6	Hole 14: 5	Hole 15: 4	Hole 16: 5	Hole 17: 4	Hole 18: 5
Name: Paul									
Course: Augusta									
Front Nine	Hole 1: 5	Hole 2: 4	Hole 3: 3	Hole 4: 5	Hole 5: 6	Hole 6: 5	Hole 7: 4	Hole 8: 5	Hole 9: 6
	Hole 10:	Hole 11:	Hole 12:	Hole 13:	Hole 14:	Hole 15:	Hole 16:	Hole 17:	Hole 18:

FIGURE 20.3
The top of a JSP that includes other JSPs shows the golfer statistics that were included.

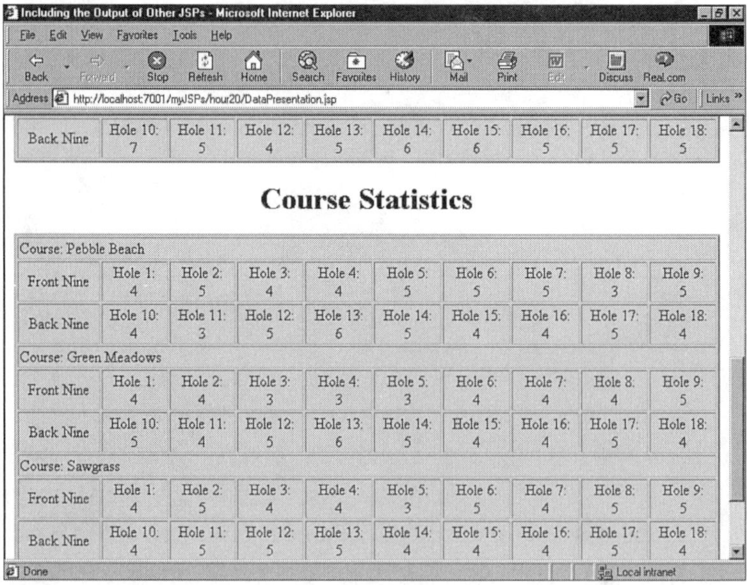

Including the Output of Other JSPs - Microsoft Internet Explorer

http://localhost:7001/myJSPs/hour20/DataPresentation.jsp

Back Nine	Hole 10: 7	Hole 11: 5	Hole 12: 4	Hole 13: 5	Hole 14: 6	Hole 15: 6	Hole 16: 5	Hole 17: 5	Hole 18: 5

Course Statistics

Course: Pebble Beach									
Front Nine	Hole 1: 4	Hole 2: 5	Hole 3: 4	Hole 4: 4	Hole 5: 5	Hole 6: 5	Hole 7: 5	Hole 8: 3	Hole 9: 5
Back Nine	Hole 10: 4	Hole 11: 3	Hole 12: 5	Hole 13: 6	Hole 14: 5	Hole 15: 4	Hole 16: 4	Hole 17: 5	Hole 18: 4
Course: Green Meadows									
Front Nine	Hole 1: 4	Hole 2: 4	Hole 3: 3	Hole 4: 3	Hole 5: 3	Hole 6: 4	Hole 7: 4	Hole 8: 4	Hole 9: 5
Back Nine	Hole 10: 5	Hole 11: 4	Hole 12: 5	Hole 13: 6	Hole 14: 5	Hole 15: 4	Hole 16: 4	Hole 17: 5	Hole 18: 4
Course: Sawgrass									
Front Nine	Hole 1: 4	Hole 2: 5	Hole 3: 4	Hole 4: 4	Hole 5: 3	Hole 6: 5	Hole 7: 4	Hole 8: 5	Hole 9: 5
Back Nine	Hole 10: 4	Hole 11: 5	Hole 12: 5	Hole 13: 5	Hole 14: 4	Hole 15: 4	Hole 16: 4	Hole 17: 5	Hole 18: 4

FIGURE 20.4
The bottom of a JSP that includes other JSPs shows the course information that was included.

Just to emphasize what is happening during the `include` action, the included JSPs are translated into their Servlet code, compiled, and then executed. It is the output of that execution that is inserted into the primary JSP. Next you are going to see how to forward a user's request to another JSP.

Reviewing the Forwarding Requests Application Model

Recall from the discussion in Hour 5 that one of the JSP application models is the Forwarding Requests Model (shown in Figure 20.5).

FIGURE 20.5

JSPs are "chained" in the Forwarding Requests Application Model.

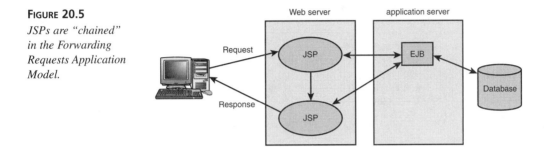

In the Forwarding Requests Application Model one JSP accepts the request from the user, possibly stores data in a JavaBean, and then forwards the request to another JSP. This is also known as *JSP chaining*, since you are in essence chaining some JavaServer Pages together. Therefore, in this scenario, one JSP accepts the request but another JSP is responsible for sending the response back to the user.

Using the `forward` Action

The general syntax of the `forward` action is:

```
<jsp:forward page="RelativeURL_to_JSP"/>
```

Notice that the `forward` action is much like the `include` action: they both take a `page` attribute that is a relative path to the file to that which is being included or forwarded. Also note that this is an empty tag so there is a forward slash before the closing >.

Implementing the `forward` Action

Now it is time to look at the `forward` action in an example. This example is going to insert golfer statistics into the database. The user enters the application from an HTML document that requests his name, course name, and then his stroke count for each hole. Listing 20.5 shows the code for the HTML document.

20

LISTING 20.5   An HTML Document that Allows the User to Input Information about a Round of Golf (InputGolferStats.jsp)

```
 1: <HTML>
 2: <HEAD><TITLE>Form to Input Golfer Statistics</TITLE></HEAD>
 3: <BODY>
 4: <CENTER>
 5:   <FONT COLOR="navy" SIZE="6">
 6:     Input Golfer Statistics
 7:   </FONT>
 8: </CENTER>
 9: <FORM NAME="STATS"
10:       ACTION="http://localhost:7001/myJSPs/hour20/AddGolferStats.jsp"
11:       METHOD="POST">
12:   <TABLE BORDER="2" WIDTH="100%" BGCOLOR="yellow">
13:     <TR><TD COLSPAN="10">
14:         Golfer Name:
15:         <INPUT TYPE="text" NAME="name" VALUE="Minnie" SIZE="30">
16:       </TD>
17:     </TR>
18:     <TR><TD COLSPAN="10">
19:         Course Name:
20:         <INPUT TYPE="text" NAME="course" VALUE="Pebble Beach" SIZE="30">
21:       </TD>
22:     </TR>
23:     <TR ALIGN="center">
24:       <TD>Front Nine</TD>
25:       <TD>Hole 1: <INPUT TYPE="text" NAME="hole1" VALUE="4" SIZE="5"></TD>
26:       <TD>Hole 2: <INPUT TYPE="text" NAME="hole2" VALUE="3" SIZE="5"></TD>
27:       <TD>Hole 3: <INPUT TYPE="text" NAME="hole3" VALUE="4" SIZE="5"></TD>
28:       <TD>Hole 4: <INPUT TYPE="text" NAME="hole4" VALUE="4" SIZE="5"></TD>
29:       <TD>Hole 5: <INPUT TYPE="text" NAME="hole5" VALUE="5" SIZE="5"></TD>
30:       <TD>Hole 6: <INPUT TYPE="text" NAME="hole6" VALUE="4" SIZE="5"></TD>
31:       <TD>Hole 7: <INPUT TYPE="text" NAME="hole7" VALUE="5" SIZE="5"></TD>
32:       <TD>Hole 8: <INPUT TYPE="text" NAME="hole8" VALUE="4" SIZE="5"></TD>
33:       <TD>Hole 9: <INPUT TYPE="text" NAME="hole9" VALUE="4" SIZE="5"></TD>
34:     </TR>
35:     <TR ALIGN="center">
36:       <TD>Back Nine</TD>
37:       <TD>Hole 10: <INPUT TYPE="text" NAME="hole10" VALUE="5" SIZE="5"></TD>
38:       <TD>Hole 11: <INPUT TYPE="text" NAME="hole11" VALUE="6" SIZE="5"></TD>
39:       <TD>Hole 12: <INPUT TYPE="text" NAME="hole12" VALUE="4" SIZE="5"></TD>
40:       <TD>Hole 13: <INPUT TYPE="text" NAME="hole13" VALUE="3" SIZE="5"></TD>
41:       <TD>Hole 14: <INPUT TYPE="text" NAME="hole14" VALUE="3" SIZE="5"></TD>
42:       <TD>Hole 15: <INPUT TYPE="text" NAME="hole15" VALUE="5" SIZE="5"></TD>
43:       <TD>Hole 16: <INPUT TYPE="text" NAME="hole16" VALUE="4" SIZE="5"></TD>
44:       <TD>Hole 17: <INPUT TYPE="text" NAME="hole17" VALUE="5" SIZE="5"></TD>
45:       <TD>Hole 18: <INPUT TYPE="text" NAME="hole18" VALUE="3" SIZE="5"></TD>
46:     </TR>
47:     <TR><TD ALIGN="center" COLSPAN="10">
48:         <INPUT TYPE="submit" NAME="btnSubmit" Value="Submit Scores">
49:       </TD>
```

LISTING 20.5   continued

```
50:     </TR>
51:    </TABLE>
52:  </FORM>
53:  </BODY>
54:  </HTML>
```

ANALYSIS   On line 10, this form specifies the JSP that is executed on the server to be
AddGolferStats.jsp. The form is full of text fields, one for the user's name, one
for the course name, and one for each of the 18 holes on the golf course. When the user
clicks the submit button, the name/value pairs of each of the form elements will be sent
to the server for the AddGolferStats.jsp to parse through. Listing 20.6 shows the code
for the JSP on the server.

LISTING 20.6   A JSP that Parses the Information from the Web Client, Stores it in
a JavaBean, and Updates a Database with the Information (AddGolferStats.jsp)

```
 1: <HTML>
 2: <HEAD><TITLE>Add Golfer Statistics</TITLE></HEAD>
 3: <BODY>
 4: <jsp:useBean id="stats"
 5:            class="jspin24hrs.hour20.GolfStatsBean"
 6:            scope="request" />
 7: <jsp:setProperty name="stats" property="*"/>
 8: <BR>
 9: <% stats.updateDatabase(); %>
10: <jsp:forward page="StatsPresentation.jsp" />
11: </BODY>
12: </HTML>
```

The JavaBean needs to be compiled and placed in a directory so it can be
found by your JSPs (see Hour 16, "Using JavaBeans In a JSP"). If you are following the suggested directory structure for this book place it in the directory c:\weblogic\myserver\classfiles\jspin24hours\hour20 and your JSPs
will be able to use it.

20

ANALYSIS   There is not much to this JSP, so it is a wise idea to step through the code. This JSP
is going to parse the request from the Web client and store it in a JavaBean. It is
also going to use the JavaBean to update the database with the data from the user. Lines
4–6 are the useBean tag setting up the JavaBean. The JavaBean is going to be referenced
by stats as declared in line 4. The JavaBean class is GolfStatsBean and is part of the
jspin24hrs.hour20 package. This class will be found in

c:\weblogic\myserver\serverclasses\jspin24hrs\hour20. The code for the JavaBean can be seen in Listing 20.7. The bean will be visible throughout the lifetime of the user's request; this means that the JSP that is forwarded to will also be able to use this JavaBean. The scope of the bean was set in line 6.

Line 7 is a rather magical line. With this one line quite a bit of work is done. It will parse the request and store the values of the form elements into the attributes of the JavaBean. The form element names need to match the attributes of the JavaBean, but once that is done all the attributes will be set automatically. Now all the user information is stored in the JavaBean for other JSPs to use.

Line 9 uses a method of the JavaBean to update the database with the information passed from the HTML form.

Finally, you see the forward action on line 10. As you can tell from this line, the request is going to be sent to a JSP called StatsPresentation.jsp. This JSP is going to retrieve the client's data from the JavaBean and format it nicely for the user so he can see what was inserted into the database. Listing 20.8 shows the code for the StatsPresentation.jsp.

Before looking at the code of the final JSP, which is responsible for sending the response to the user, take a moment to examine the JavaBean code shown in Listing 20.7.

LISTING 20.7 A JavaBean that Stores Golfer Information and Updates the Database (GolfStatsBean.java)

```
 1: package jspin24hrs.hour20;
 2:
 3: import java.sql.*;
 4:
 5: public class GolfStatsBean{
 6:   String name, course;
 7:   int hole1, hole2, hole3, hole4, hole5, hole6, hole7, hole8, hole9;
 8:   int hole10, hole11, hole12, hole13, hole14, hole15, hole16;
 9:   int hole17, hole18;
10:
11:   public void setName(String inputName){
12:     name = inputName;
13:   }
14:   public String getName(){
15:     return name;
16:   }
17:   public void setCourse(String inputCourse){
18:     course = inputCourse;
19:   }
20:   public String getCourse(){
21:     return course;
22:   }
23:   public void setHole1(int strokes){
```

LISTING 20.7   continued

```
24:     hole1 = strokes;
25:   }
26:   public int getHole1(){
27:     return hole1;
28:   }
29:   public void setHole2(int strokes){
30:     hole2 = strokes;
31:   }
32:   public int getHole2(){
33:     return hole2;
34:   }
35:   public void setHole3(int strokes){
36:     hole3 = strokes;
37:   }
38:   public int getHole3(){
39:     return hole3;
40:   }
41:   public void setHole4(int strokes){
42:     hole4 = strokes;
43:   }
44:   public int getHole4(){
45:     return hole4;
46:   }
47:   public void setHole5(int strokes){
48:     hole5 = strokes;
49:   }
50:   public int getHole5(){
51:     return hole5;
52:   }
53:   public void setHole6(int strokes){
54:     hole6 = strokes;
55:   }
56:   public int getHole6(){
57:     return hole6;
58:   }
59:   public void setHole7(int strokes){
60:     hole7 = strokes;
61:   }
62:   public int getHole7(){
63:     return hole7;
64:   }
65:   public void setHole8(int strokes){
66:     hole8 = strokes;
67:   }
68:   public int getHole8(){
69:     return hole8;
70:   }
71:   public void setHole9(int strokes){
72:     hole9 = strokes;
73:   }
74:   public int getHole9(){
```

20

LISTING 20.7   continued

```
 75:    return hole9;
 76:  }
 77:  public void setHole10(int strokes){
 78:    hole10 = strokes;
 79:  }
 80:  public int getHole10(){
 81:    return hole10;
 82:  }
 83:  public void setHole11(int strokes){
 84:    hole11 = strokes;
 85:  }
 86:  public int getHole11(){
 87:    return hole11;
 88:  }
 89:  public void setHole12(int strokes){
 90:    hole12 = strokes;
 91:  }
 92:  public int getHole12(){
 93:    return hole12;
 94:  }
 95:  public void setHole13(int strokes){
 96:    hole13 = strokes;
 97:  }
 98:  public int getHole13(){
 99:    return hole13;
100:  }
101:  public void setHole14(int strokes){
102:    hole14 = strokes;
103:  }
104:  public int getHole14(){
105:    return hole14;
106:  }
107:  public void setHole15(int strokes){
108:    hole15 = strokes;
109:  }
110:  public int getHole15(){
111:    return hole15;
112:  }
113:  public void setHole16(int strokes){
114:    hole16 = strokes;
115:  }
116:  public int getHole16(){
117:    return hole16;
118:  }
119:  public void setHole17(int strokes){
120:    hole17 = strokes;
121:  }
122:  public int getHole17(){
123:    return hole17;
```

LISTING 20.7   continued

```
124:    }
125:    public void setHole18(int strokes){
126:      hole18 = strokes;
127:    }
128:    public int getHole18(){
129:      return hole18;
130:    }
131:    public void updateDatabase(){
132:      try{
133:        Class.forName("COM.cloudscape.core.JDBCDriver").newInstance();
134:        Connection conn =
135:          DriverManager.getConnection("jdbc:cloudscape:c:\\GolfDB");
136:
137:        String sql = "INSERT INTO GOLFDATA
138:                      VALUES(?, ?, ?, ?, ?, ?, ?, ?, ?, ?, ?, ?,
139:                             ?, ?, ?, ?, ?, ?, ?, ?)";
140:        PreparedStatement statement = conn.prepareStatement(sql);
141:        statement.setString(1, name);
142:        statement.setString(2, course);
143:        statement.setInt(3, hole1);
144:        statement.setInt(4, hole2);
145:        statement.setInt(5, hole3);
146:        statement.setInt(6, hole4);
147:        statement.setInt(7, hole5);
148:        statement.setInt(8, hole6);
149:        statement.setInt(9, hole7);
150:        statement.setInt(10, hole8);
151:        statement.setInt(11, hole9);
152:        statement.setInt(12, hole10);
153:        statement.setInt(13, hole11);
154:        statement.setInt(14, hole12);
155:        statement.setInt(15, hole13);
156:        statement.setInt(16, hole14);
157:        statement.setInt(17, hole15);
158:        statement.setInt(18, hole16);
159:        statement.setInt(19, hole17);
160:        statement.setInt(20, hole18);
161:
162:        statement.executeQuery();
163:
164:        if (statement != null)
165:          statement.close();
166:        if (conn != null)
167:          conn.close();
168:      }
169:      catch(Exception e)  { System.out.println("My error: " + e);}
170:    }
171: }
```

20

ANALYSIS Lines 6–9 specify the attributes of the JavaBean. Notice that the attribute names match the names of the HTML form elements. That way you can use the setProperty action to set all properties with one statement.

Lines 11–130 contain all the accessor methods for the JavaBean. You need a get*AttributeName*() method for each attribute of the JavaBean and you have a set*AttributeName*(...) method for each attribute.

Lines 131–170 define a method called updateDatabase() that does what it says—it updates the database with the values from the HTML form. This method was called in the AddGolferStats.jsp to insert the user's information into the database.

After the user fills in the HTML form and clicks the submit button, his information is sent to the AddGolferStats.jsp. That JSP uses one setProperty action to set all the attributes of the JavaBean with the data sent from the HTML form. The JSP also updates the database. Then it forwards the request to another JSP, StatsPresentation.jsp, to format the response back to the user. The code for the StatsPresentation.jsp is shown in Listing 20.8.

LISTING 20.8   A JSP that Formats the Response to the User
(StatsPresentation.jsp)

```
 1: <HTML>
 2: <HEAD><TITLE>Golf Statistics - Presented</TITLE></HEAD>
 3: <BODY>
 4: <CENTER>
 5: <FONT SIZE="7" COLOR="green">Golf Statistics</FONT>
 6: </CENTER>
 7: <jsp:useBean id="stats"
 8:             class="jspin24hrs.hour20.GolfStatsBean"
 9:             scope="request"/>
10:
11: <TABLE BORDER="1" WIDTH="100%" BGCOLOR="silver">
12:    <TR><TD COLSPAN="10">Name: <%= stats.getName() %> </TD></TR>
13:    <TR><TD COLSPAN="10">Course: <%= stats.getCourse() %> </TD></TR>
14:    <TR ALIGN="center"><TD>Front Nine:</TD>
15:        <TD>Hole 1: <BR><%= stats.getHole1() %> </TD>
16:        <TD>Hole 2: <BR><%= stats.getHole2() %> </TD>
17:        <TD>Hole 3: <BR><%= stats.getHole3() %> </TD>
18:        <TD>Hole 4: <BR><%= stats.getHole4() %> </TD>
19:        <TD>Hole 5: <BR><%= stats.getHole5() %> </TD>
20:        <TD>Hole 6: <BR><%= stats.getHole6() %> </TD>
21:        <TD>Hole 7: <BR><%= stats.getHole7() %> </TD>
22:        <TD>Hole 8: <BR><%= stats.getHole8() %> </TD>
23:        <TD>Hole 9: <BR><%= stats.getHole9() %> </TD>
24:    </TR>
25:    <TR ALIGN="center"><TD>Back Nine:</TD>
26:        <TD>Hole 10: <BR><%= stats.getHole10() %> </TD>
27:        <TD>Hole 11: <BR><%= stats.getHole11() %> </TD>
28:        <TD>Hole 12: <BR><%= stats.getHole12() %> </TD>
```

LISTING 20.8   continued

```
29:        <TD>Hole 13: <BR><%= stats.getHole13() %> </TD>
30:        <TD>Hole 14: <BR><%= stats.getHole14() %> </TD>
31:        <TD>Hole 15: <BR><%= stats.getHole15() %> </TD>
32:        <TD>Hole 16: <BR><%= stats.getHole16() %> </TD>
33:        <TD>Hole 17: <BR><%= stats.getHole17() %> </TD>
34:        <TD>Hole 18: <BR><%= stats.getHole18() %> </TD>
35:   </TR>
36: </TABLE>
37: <BR>
38: <BR>
39: <BR>
40: <A HREF="http://localhost:7001/myJSPs/hour20/InputGolferStats.html">
41: Add More Statistics
42: </A>
43: </BODY>
44: </HTML>
```

This JSP uses the same JavaBean that was set in the AddGolferStats.jsp. That way this JSP can use the accessor methods of the JavaBean to retrieve the values of the data sent from the client. This JSP just needs to use expression tags to insert values from the JavaBean. Therefore, it formats the output back to the client and it also has a hyperlink back to the HTML document that allows the client to add more data.

Take a moment to step through the flow of this application. The user enters his data into the HTML form, which is shown in Figure 20.6.

FIGURE 20.6

The HTML form allows the user to input golf statistics.

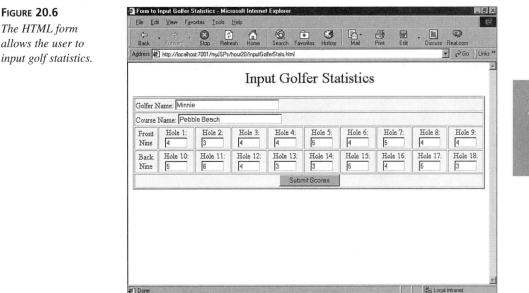

20

When the user clicks the submit button, his request goes to the AddGolferStats.jsp.
The JSP parses the request, and stores the golf data into a JavaBean, and updates a database with the data. It then forwards the request to the StatsPresentation.jsp, which
forms the response (shown in Figure 20.7) back to the client.

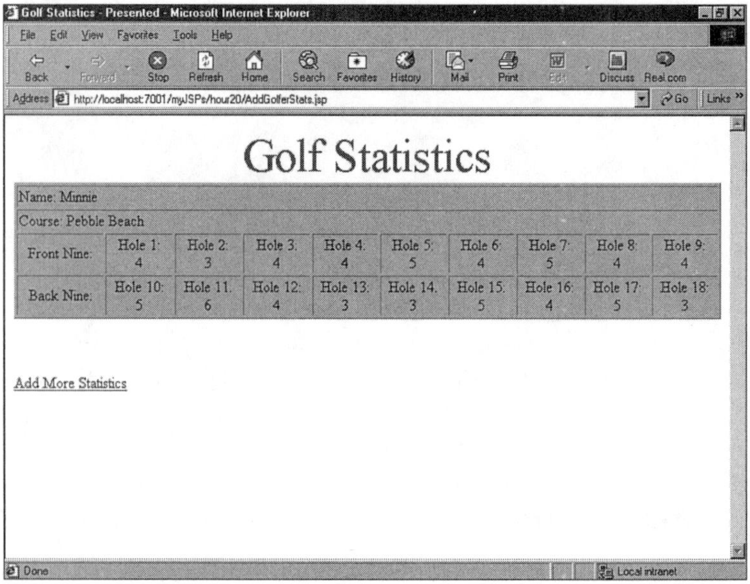

FIGURE 20.7

StatsPresentation.jsp
formats the response
back to the user.

The StatsPresentation.jsp just outputs the user's information in a table to show the
user exactly what was inserted into the database.

Summary

Spreading the work of your application among multiple JSPs is often desirable. There are
many ways to separate the work among the JSPs, and this hour discussed two models.
The Including Request Model has a primary JavaServer Page that looks over the work of
other JSPs, and includes the output of those files into its page. This model is accomplished using the include action tag:

```
<jsp:include page="RelativeURLtoIncludedFile"/>
```

The Forwarding Requests Model was another way of separating work with one JSP
accepting the request from the user and forwarding the request to another JSP that is
responsible for sending the response back to the user. This type of application model is
also called JSP chaining, where the chain of JSPs could be any number. This model is
accomplished with the forward action tag:

```
<jsp:forward page="RelativeURLtoForwardedFile"/>
```

Keep in mind that both these actions are empty tags so don't forget the forward slash at the end.

Q&A

Q What are the pros and cons of using the two models discussed in this hour?

A The advantage of using both models is that you are separating the work of your application among multiple JSPs, thereby making your application more scalable. An advantage of the Including Requests Model is that one JSP is responsible for the request and generating the response, but it is able to take advantage of other JSPs to do the work. A disadvantage to the Forwarding Requests Model is that one JSP is responsible for the request and another takes care of the response, thereby the workflow could get complicated in your application.

Q How many JSPs can be used in the application models discussed in this hour?

A Both application models allow for many JSPs to be used. There is no limit to the number of JSPs that can be used, which means that these application models allow for easy scalability to your applications. When you want to offer a new service, you just add another JSP.

Workshop

The quiz questions and activities are provided for your further understanding. See Appendix A, "Answers," for the answers to the quiz.

Quiz

1. What is the attribute that both the `include` and `forward` actions take?
2. What is the difference between the `include` action and the `include` directive?
3. What would the `forward` action tag look like if you wanted to forward to a JSP called `ForwardToMe.jsp` that was two subdirectories below your JSP, `forwardedFiles/anotherSubdirectory`?

Activity

Write an application that asks the user for a name and then returns all of the user's statistics from the database. The HTML document has the user input a name; one JSP takes that information, retrieves the statistics from the database, and forwards the information to another JSP to format back to the user.

20

PART IV

Creating an Enterprise Application

Hour

HOUR 21

Designing an Enterprise Application

You have learned the nuts and bolts of writing JavaServer Pages, now it is time to put it all together. Over the remaining hours of this book, you are going to write a Web application that uses JavaServer Pages, JavaBeans, and a database. The application is going to be a human resources Web site that allows employees to view their benefits, change their names, addresses, and phone numbers, and view company policies. There will also be the capability to add new employees. Typically, only managers will be able to add new employees, but you are just writing the pages to implement this capability. Usually, the server in which you deploy the application, will handle the security issues. This is a very common part of a company's intranet.

Writing this application allows you to put almost all that you have learned into a practical example. You will use the `include` directive, the `include` action, the `forward` action, scriptlets, expressions, the `page` directive, and much more. Take your time with this exercise and embellish where you see fit. Work hard and have fun.

In this hour you learn:

- The requirements of the Husky World Human Resources site
- The resources needed for the Husky World Human Resources site

Gathering Design Requirements

The application you are going to write and deploy is a human resources Web site for a company called Husky World. You will use the `include` directive to include a company banner that says "Husky World" in yellow letters with a navy background. This Web site will allow employees to

- View the company policies.
- View the insurance benefits the company offers.
- View their personal insurance benefits.
- Change their personal profiles, their names, addresses, and phone numbers.
- View their current time-off information.
- Add new employees.

There should be a welcome page into the human resources Web site that gives the user choices as to what he or she wants to do. The choices could be just a group of hyperlinks that take the users to the parts of the site where they want to go. Figure 21.1 shows a use case diagram that graphically displays what users on the Web site will be able to do.

A use case diagram models the capabilities of your Web site. It models the users of your system and anything that can trigger an activity in your application. The person or thing that can trigger an activity in your application is called an *Actor*. Use case diagrams are one way to graphically display what your application does. Throughout the planning of your application, your use case diagrams change and evolve as more requirements are received from your users. It is very important to have a use case diagram, because you can ensure that your system provides all the capabilities required.

After taking a look at what the user can do on the Web site, it is necessary to look at scenarios of the user's actions on the Web site.

One scenario is that the employee wants to view the company policies. The employee could start at the home page and then follow a link to the appropriate page, which will be `PresentCompanyPolicies.jsp`. Figure 21.2 shows this flow in a graphical format.

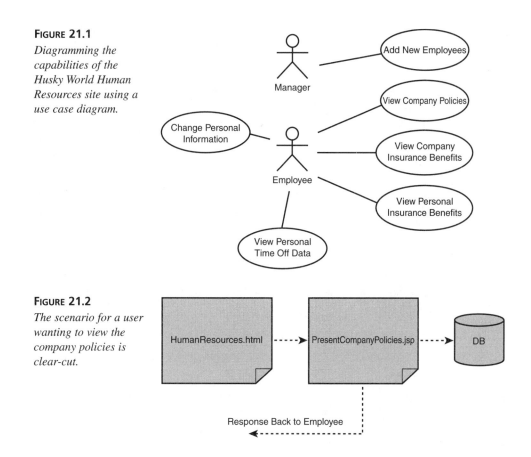

FIGURE 21.1
Diagramming the capabilities of the Husky World Human Resources site using a use case diagram.

FIGURE 21.2
The scenario for a user wanting to view the company policies is clear-cut.

This is a straightforward scenario. The user will click a hyperlink to the `PresentCompanyPolicies.jsp`, which outputs the company policy and retrieves data about insurance benefits that are offered by the company.

Maybe the employee is interested in changing his name, phone number and/or address. The employee will go to the home page and follow the appropriate link to `InputEmployeeInfo.html`. Figure 21.3 graphically displays this scenario.

This scenario is more involved than the first one. The employee clicks a hyperlink on the home page and goes to an HTML document that has the employee fill in his ID number and the changes he needs to make in his name, address, and phone number. When the employee submits the form, it goes to the server and the JSP `UpdateEmployeeInfo.jsp` parses the data, stores it in a JavaBean, and forwards the request to a JSP that handles the presentation back to the employee, `PresentChangeOfEmployeeData.jsp`. `PresentChangeOfEmployeeData.jsp` retrieves the employee ID from the JavaBean and the rest of the employee information from the database.

21

FIGURE 21.3
*This is the scenario for
a user wanting to
change his name,
phone number and
address.*

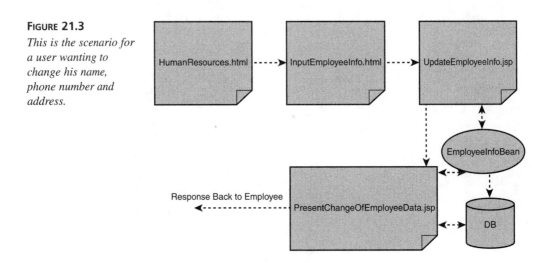

The following list shows the order in which the HTML and JSP files are executed, and a description of each file:

1. `HumanResources.html` — home page.

2. `InputEmployeeInfo.html` — HTML document that allows the employee to input his information.

3. `UpdateEmployeeInfo.jsp` — A JSP that parses the request, stores the user's information in a JavaBean, and then forwards the request to another JSP. .

4. `PresentChangeOfEmployeeData.jsp` — A JSP that presents the changes to the employee's information.

Have you started formulating in your mind how these scenarios could be implemented? While reading these scenarios start contemplating what JSP tags you have seen that will help accomplish these tasks.

What if the employee wants to look at his personal benefits? The employee should be able to view his days off and personal insurance information. Figure 21.4 shows this scenario graphically.

This scenario is much more involved than the others are. Of course the user enters the Web site through the home page, clicks a hyperlink, and goes to an HTML document that provides the user with a choice: what personal benefit he wants to view. Once the employee makes his selection, his request is sent to the JSP `PersonalInfo.jsp`. The JSP parses the request and includes the appropriate JavaServer Pages to service the request. For example, if the user wants to view his time-off data, then `PresentTimeOffData.jsp` is included. On the other hand, if the employee wants to view his insurance benefits, then `PresentPersonalHealthCareInfo.jsp` is included.

FIGURE 21.4

What if an employee wants to view his benefits? This scenario is followed.

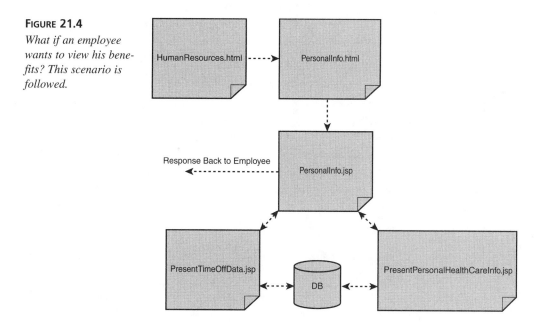

The employee also may just want to view the insurance benefits the company offers. This is another straightforward scenario, graphically displayed in Figure 21.5.

FIGURE 21.5

This is the scenario for an employee wanting to view the company's insurance benefits.

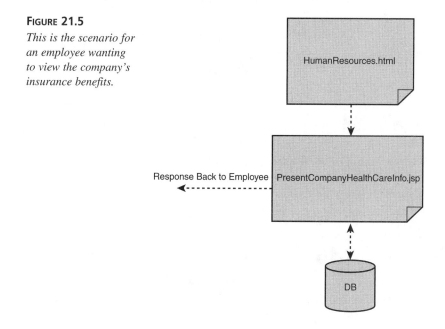

21

The employee starts at the home page, the same as the other scenarios, and clicks a hyperlink to go to a JSP that retrieves the company benefits from the database.

The last scenario to consider is when a new employee comes to work for Husky World. His information will have to be added to the database. Instead of going directly to the database, a nice graphical user interface will be provided, which makes it simpler to add the data. Therefore, the Husky World Human Resources site will offer the capability of adding new employees. Of course, in the real world the new employee would probably be added by a manager. Security for your Web sites is configured in the server in which your application is deployed. The focus of this example is on writing the capability. Figure 21.6 shows this scenario graphically.

FIGURE 21.6

This scenario is used when a new employee needs to be added to the database.

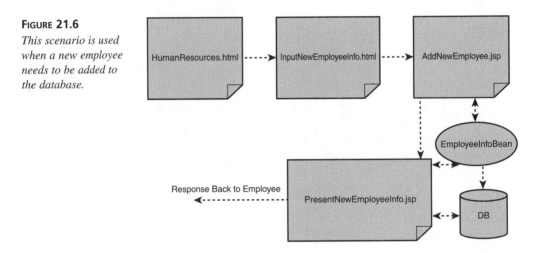

Again the user is going to start at the home page and select a hyperlink to the appropriate page. The appropriate page is an HTML document that allows the user to insert the new employee's information, `InputNewEmployeeInfo.html`. Once the information has been entered and the submit button has been clicked, the information is sent back to the server the JSP `AddNewEmployee.jsp` accepts the request. This JSP parses the request, stores the values in a JavaBean, updates the database, and then forwards the request to another JSP to present the data, `PresentNewEmployeeInfo.jsp`.

Designing the Application

Now it is time to list the resources needed for building this application. Table 21.1 shows the HTML and JSP documents that will be used, and a description of each.

TABLE 21.1   HTML and JSP Documents for the Husky World Human Resources site Application

Document	Description
HumanResources.html	Welcome Page into the Web site
CompanyBanner.html	Used to insert the company name on each page
SiteNavigator.html	Used to insert a table of hyperlinks for other pages
InputEmployeeInfo.html	Allows user to change name, address, and phone number
InputNewEmployeeInfo.html	Allows user to add information for a new employee
PersonalInfo.html	Allows user to decide what personal information to view
AddNewEmployee.jsp	Parses the input from the InputNewEmployeeInfo.html form, puts the form data into a JavaBean, updates the database, and forwards the request on
PresentNewEmployeeInfo.jsp	Takes information out of a JavaBean and formats it
PersonalInfo.jsp	Determines what personal information the user wants to view and includes the appropriate files
PresentPersonalHealthCareInfo.jsp	Takes the employee ID from the request object and retrieves the employee's information from the database
PresentTimeOffData.jsp	Takes an employee's ID from the request object and retrieves the employee's data from the database
PresentChangeOfEmployeeData.jsp	Takes the employee ID from a JavaBean and gets the employee's data from the database to show the changes
PresentCompanyHealthCareInfo.jsp	Accesses the database and retrieves the insurance benefits the company offers
PresentCompanyPolicies.jsp	Displays the company policy; also shows the insurance benefits the company offers
UpdateEmployeeInfo.jsp	Inserts information into a JavaBean and then updates the database
EmployeeInfoBean.java	In package jspin24hrs.project; used to change employee's data
NewEmployeeBean.java	In package jspin24hrs.project; used to insert a new employee's data

21

A database is needed for this application, you will use a database called HumanResourcesDB in the root C:\ directory. Table 21.2 shows the columns, their type of data, and the table they are in.

TABLE 21.2   Database Setup

Column	Data Type
Table: EMPLOYEEINFO	
ID	int
NAME	varchar(100)
ADDRESS	varchar(100)
PHONE	varchar(12)
WORKSTATUS	varchar(50)
TOTALSICKDAYS	int
TAKENSICKDAYS	int
TOTALPERSONALTIME	int
TAKENPERSONALTIME	int
HEALTHCAREPLAN	varchar(100)
DENTALPLAN	varchar(100)
VISIONPLAN	varchar(100)
Table: BENEFITINFO	
PLANNAME	varchar(100)
DEDUCTIBLE	int
DOCTORSINPLANCOVERAGE	int
DOCTORSOUTOFPLANCOVERAGE	int

Once all the pages have been written, you will bundle them up in a Web archive. The concept of the Web archive is new in the Servlet2.2 specification. A Web archive is much like a zip file, in that it bundles together all the files and you can deploy just one package. Hours 22, "Creating a Presentation Layer," and 23, "Programming the Business Logic," will have you implement all these scenarios. Hour 24, "Packaging and Deploying an Enterprise Application," will go into detail about Web archive packages.

Summary

In this hour you began the process of building an application. You looked at the requirements of an application by examining various scenarios and figuring out how to implement them. You also learned what resources you will need for the application. In the next hour you will begin building this application.

Q&A

Q Why is a use case diagram helpful?

A Use case diagrams are used to graphically display the entities that can invoke an activity in the application, and also what those entities can do.

Q What database is this application using?

A BEA WebLogic Server comes with an evaluation copy of Informix Cloudscape. This application is going to use that database for all its needs.

Workshop

The quiz questions and activities are provided for your further understanding. See Appendix A, "Answers," for the answers to the quiz.

Quiz

1. What are the two ways to access a database with a JSP?

2. What are the two ways to send data from an HTML form to the server?

3. Where would an application like this human resources Web site be found?

4. Why do you model your application before beginning to code?

Activity

Review the requirements for this application. Can you think of other services this application could provide? How would you implement those new services? What resources do you need for the new services?

21

HOUR 22

Creating a Presentation Layer

Now it is time to begin writing the Husky World Human Resources application that you designed in Hour 21. In this hour you are going to write the company banner HTML document, the site navigator, the welcome page, and the JSPs responsible for displaying the company's health care information and policies.

In this hour you will

- Write parts of the Husky World Human Resources site
- Review using the include directive to include static documents in your JSPs
- Review accessing a database directly from your JSPs

Building the Application

In this hour you are going to provide implementation for the scenarios of viewing personal information, company policies, and company benefits. You will also write the home page of the site, the company banner, and a site navigator. The files that will be written in this hour are listed and described in Table 22.1.

TABLE 22.1   The HTML and JSPs that Will Be Written in this Hour

Document	Description
HumanResources.html	Welcome Page into the Web Site
CompanyBanner.html	Used to insert the company name on each page
SiteNavigator.html	Used to insert a table of hyperlinks for other pages
PersonalInfo.html	Allows user to decide what personal information he wants to view
PersonalInfo.jsp	Determines what personal information the user wants to view and includes the appropriate files
PresentPersonalHealthCareInfo.jsp	This JSP takes the employee ID from the request object and retrieves the employee's information from the database
PresentTimeOffData.jsp	This JSP takes an employee's ID from the request object and retrieves the employee's data from the database
PresentCompanyHealthCareInfo.jsp	This JSP takes the employee ID from the request object and retrieves the employee's information from the database
PresentCompanyPolicies.jsp	This JSP displays the company policy and it also shows the insurance benefits the company offers

In the previous hours your JSPs were located in a directory myJSPs/hour*XX*, where the *XX* corresponded to the hour you were working in. Since you are working on the same application in Hour 22, "Creating a Presentation Layer," and Hour 23, "Programming the Business Logic," it's recommended that you place all JSPs and HTML files in a directory named myJSPs/project.

Writing `CompanyBanner.html`

It is much easier to write an HTML document that contains the company banner than to put the HTML code in each of the JavaServer Pages. If your company banner changes then you only need to make the changes in one place, rather than in all of your JavaServer Pages. Listing 22.1 shows the code for the CompanyBanner.html document.

LISTING 22.1   An HTML Document that Contains a One-Cell Table that Holds the Company Name (CompanyBanner.html)

```
1: <TABLE WIDTH="100%" BORDER="0" BGCOLOR="navy">
2:   <TR ALIGN="center">
3:     <TD><FONT SIZE="7" COLOR="yellow">Husky World</FONT></TD>
4:   </TR>
5: </TABLE>
```

22

A very common formatting technique used in HTML documents is the table format technique. There are no tags in HTML that allow you to indent your image or text to a certain location on the page. That is where tables come into play. You do not need to show the borders of the table; therefore, it provides a wonderful way of arranging your text and images on your HTML page.

The code in the `CompanyBanner.html` file is straightforward. There is a table with one row and one column—in other words, one cell. The table will be as wide as the browser; therefore, the text will be centered on the page. The background of the table is navy and the text, "Husky World," is yellow.

FIGURE 22.1

The company banner for Husky World is created in a single file.

Husky World

The banner is going to be included into almost all of the JSP files. You will have to insert the code into the other HTML files since they cannot insert other files dynamically.

Writing `SiteNavigator.html`

It is very important for users of the Web site to find their way around effortlessly. A site navigator—a set of hyperlinks that jump to the main pages—on each page allows users to surf through the site with ease. Listing 22.2 shows the code for the `SiteNavigator.html` document.

LISTING 22.2   An HTML Document that Allows Easy Navigation Through the Web Site (SiteNavigator.html)

```
 1: <BODY ALINK="yellow" VLINK="yellow" LINK="yellow">
 2: <TABLE WIDTH="100%" BORDER="0" BGCOLOR="navy">
 3: <TR ALIGN="center">
 4:   <TD COLSPAN=2><FONT SIZE="4" COLOR="yellow">Site Navigator</FONT></TD>
 5: </TR>
 6: <TR ALIGN="center">
 7:   <TD><A HREF=
 8:       "http://localhost:7001/myJSPs/project/PresentCompanyPolicies.jsp">
 9:       Look at Company Policies</A>
10:   </TD>
11:   <TD><A HREF="http://localhost:7001/myJSPs/project/PersonalInfo.html">
12:       Look At Personal Information</A>
13:   </TD>
14: </TR>
15: <TR ALIGN="center">
16:   <TD><A HREF=
```

LISTING 22.2   continued

```
17:           "http://localhost:7001/myJSPs/project/InputEmployeeInfo.html">
18:         Change Employee Information</FONT>
19:    </TD>
20:    <TD><A HREF=
21: "http://localhost:7001/myJSPs/project/PresentCompanyHealthCareInfo.jsp">
22:         Look At Health Care Options</A>
23:    </TD>
24: </TR>
25: <TR ALIGN="center">
26:    <TD COLSPAN="2"><A HREF=
27:                "http://localhost:7001/myJSPs/project/HumanResources.html">
28:             Home Page</A>
29:    </TD>
30: </TR>
31: </TABLE>
32: </BODY>
```

ANALYSIS The SiteNavigator.html file is a table that contains five hyperlinks to the main pages of the Web site. Line 1 is used to specify the color of the hyperlinks. The ALINK attribute specifies the color of the active links, the VLINK specifies the color of the visited link, and the LINK attribute specifies the color of unvisited hyperlinks. Notice the colors for all three are the same, just for aesthetic purposes.

Lines 7–10 create a hyperlink to PresentCompanyPolicies.jsp. This JSP will present the company policies and the insurance benefits they offer.

Lines 11–13 create a hyperlink to PersonalInfo.html. This HTML document is going to ask users what personal information they want to view: their insurance benefits, their current time off status, or both.

Lines 16–19 create a hyperlink to InputEmployeeInfo.html. This HTML document allows users to input their names, addresses, and phone numbers. Therefore, employees can modify these attributes of their profile.

Lines 20–23 create a hyperlink to the JSP PresentCompanyHealthCareInfo.jsp, which presents the insurance benefits that Husky World provides.

Lines 26–29 create a hyperlink to the home page, HumanResources.html. This allows users to return to the home page from any place in the Web site.

Figure 22.2 shows the SiteNavigator.html document.

Figure 22.2
The site navigator helps users navigate the Web site.

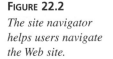

This document will be inserted into most of the JSPs, but like `CompanyBanner.html`, you will have to insert the code into the other HTML files since they cannot insert other files dynamically.

Writing the Home Page

Now it is time to write the home page, `HumanResources.html`. This page is going to contain five hyperlinks so users can decide what they want to do. Each hyperlink allows users to do one of the scenarios discussed in Hour 21:

- View the company policies.
- View the insurance benefits the company offers.
- View their personal insurance benefits.
- Change their personal profiles, their names, addresses, and phone numbers.
- View their current time-off information.
- Add new employees to the database.

Listing 22.3 is the code for the `HumanResources.html` file.

LISTING 22.3　The Home Page for the Human Resources Web Site
(`HumanResources.html`)

```
 1: <HTML>
 2: <HEAD><TITLE></TITLE></HEAD>
 3: <BODY LINK="navy" ALINK="navy" VLINK="navy">
 4:
 5:
 6: <!-- inserts the company banner -->
 7: <TABLE WIDTH="100%" BORDER="0" BGCOLOR="navy">
 8:   <TR ALIGN="center">
 9:     <TD><FONT SIZE="7" COLOR="yellow">Husky World</FONT></TD>
10:   </TR>
11: </TABLE>
12:
13: <!-- the heading for the page -->
14: <CENTER>
15:   <FONT SIZE="5" COLOR="navy">
16:     Welcome To Your Human Resources Department Online<P>
17:   </FONT>
18:   <FONT SIZE="4" COLOR="navy">
19:       Select Where You Would Like To Go<P>
```

LISTING 22.3   continued

```
20:    </FONT>
21:
22: <!-- hyperlinks to the various scenarios of the Website -->
23: <A HREF=
24:    "http://localhost:7001/myJSPs/project/PresentCompanyPolicies.jsp">
25:    Take a Look At the Company Policies
26: </A>
27: <P>
28: <A HREF=
29:    "http://localhost:7001/myJSPs/project/PresentCompanyHealthCareInfo.jsp">
30:    Take a Look At Health Care Plan Options
31: </A>
32: <P>
33: <A HREF=
34:    "http://localhost:7001/myJSPs/project/PersonalInfo.html">
35:    Take a Look At Personal Information: time off, health care information
36: </A>
37: <P>
38: <A HREF=
39:    "http://localhost:7001/myJSPs/project/InputEmployeeInfo.html">
40:    Change Your Employee Information
41: </A><P>
42: <A HREF=
43:    "http://localhost:7001/myJSPs/project/InputNewEmployeeInfo.html">
44:    Add New Employee
45: </A>
46:
47: </CENTER>
48: </BODY>
49: </HTML>
```

ANALYSIS   Since the home page is an HTML document, you have to insert the code for the company banner, as previously mentioned. Lines 7–11 are the code for the company banner.

Lines 15–20 are the heading for the page. It welcomes employees to the Web site and tells them to select what they want to do. Each of the following hyperlinks represents one of the scenarios for the Web site.

Lines 23–26 create the hyperlink to PresentCompanyPolicies.jsp. This is the scenario when the employee wants to view the company policies.

Lines 28–31 create a hyperlink to PresentCompanyHealthCareInfo.jsp, which pulls the insurance benefits the company offers from a database.

Lines 33–36 create a hyperlink to the HTML document PersonalInfo.html. This hyperlink represents the scenario of employees wanting to view their personal information. The PersonalInfo.html file contains a checklist that allows users to choose what to view.

Lines 38–41 create a hyperlink to `InputEmployeeInfo.html`. This HTML file allows the users to change their names, addresses, and phone numbers.

Lines 42–45 create a hyperlink to `InputNewEmployeeInfo.html`. This HTML document is a form that allows the user to input all the new employee's information.

Figure 22.3 is a snapshot of the `HumanResources.html` document.

FIGURE 22.3

The home page welcomes Husky World employees.

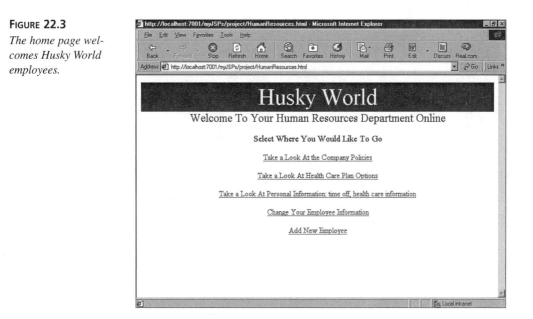

Writing `PresentCompanyHealthCareInfo.jsp`

At this point you have written the home page for your application and other miscellaneous files that you will use. The home page has a hyperlink to `PresentCompanyHealthCareInfo.jsp`, which retrieves the company's insurance benefits from the database. Listing 22.4 shows the code for this JSP.

LISTING 22.4 The JSP that Retrieves Company Insurance Benefits from a Database (`PresentCompanyHealthCareInfo.jsp`)

```
1: <HTML>
2: <HEAD><TITLE>Health Plan Information</TITLE></HEAD>
3: <BODY>
4:
5: <%@ include file="CompanyBanner.html" %>
6: <%@ page import="java.sql.*" %>
7:
8: <CENTER>
```

LISTING 22.4 continued

```
 9:    <FONT SIZE="5" COLOR="navy">
10:      Health, Vision, And Dental Plans
11:    </FONT>
12: </CENTER>
13:
14: <TABLE WIDTH="100%" BORDER="1">
15:    <TH WIDTH="40%">Plan Name</TH>
16:    <TH WIDTH="20%">Deductible</TH>
17:    <TH WIDTH="20%">Coverage for Doctors in Plan</TH>
18:    <TH WIDTH="20%">Coverage for Doctors out of Plan</TH>
19: <%
20:    Class.forName("COM.cloudscape.core.JDBCDriver").newInstance();
21:    Connection conn =
22:      DriverManager.getConnection("jdbc:cloudscape:c:\\HumanResourcesDB");
23:    Statement statement = conn.createStatement();
24:    String sql = "SELECT * FROM BENEFITINFO";
25:    ResultSet rs = statement.executeQuery(sql);
26:    while (rs.next()) {
27: %>
28:  <TR><TD><%= rs.getString("PLANNAME") %></TD>
29:      <TD ALIGN="center"><%= rs.getString("DEDUCTIBLE") %></TD>
30:      <TD ALIGN="center"><%= rs.getString("DOCTORSINPLANCOVERAGE")%></TD>
31:      <TD ALIGN="center"><%= rs.getString("DOCTORSOUTOFPLANCOVERAGE")%></TD>
32:  </TR>
33: <% } //end while loop
34:    if (statement != null)
35:      statement.close();
36:    if (conn != null)
37:      conn.close();
38: %>
39: </TABLE>
40: <BR>
41: <%@ include file="SiteNavigator.html" %>
42: </BODY>
43: </HTML>
```

ANALYSIS This JSP is going to retrieve company-offered insurance benefits from the database. Many of the JSP-creation techniques learned throughout this book are covered in this single JSP.

Line 5 uses the include directive to include the CompanyBanner.html file. Recall that the include directive sees the included file as a static document and inserts the code of the included file into the JSP. A major benefit of using the include directive is that you can keep a company banner, a copyright, and a menu bar in separate files so if there are changes that need to be made you only need to make the changes once.

22

Line 6 uses the `page` directive to import a Java package into your code. Java places similar classes into packages as a way of keeping similar classes together. Since this JSP is going to be doing database access, you need to import the appropriate files from the `java.sql` package; therefore it is much simpler to just import all the classes from that file.

Lines 8–12 write the heading for the page—the purpose of the page—so users know what they are looking at. This page is going to output the benefits the company offers. Therefore, the heading is Health, Vision, and Dental Plans.

Line 14 begins a table that formats the output of the insurance benefits.

Lines 15–18 are the headings for the columns in the table. The information from the database will be the plan's name, the deductible, and the percentage of coverage for doctors in the plan and doctors out of the plan.

It is time to create a connection to the database, and the first step is to declare what driver you are going to use. Since this application is using a `cloudscape` database the driver is `COM.cloudscape.core.JDBCDriver`. Line 20 declares this driver as the driver to use.

Once the driver for the database is declared, you need to get a connection to the appropriate database. Lines 21–22 retrieve a connection to a database called `HumanResourcesDB` that is located in the root `c:\` directory. To get a connection to a database you use the `DriverManager` class, found in the `java.sql` package, and its method `getConnection(...)`. A parameter to the `getConnection(...)` method is a URL to the database. For this database it is `jdbc:cloudscape:c:\\HumanResourcesDB`.

Line 23 creates a statement that you can use to execute SQL statements on your database. Line 24 creates a SQL string, a simple `SELECT` statement that selects all elements out of the table `BENEFITINFO`.

Line 25 executes the query and captures the result in a `ResultSet` object. This object can then be looped through to get all the information from the database. A `while` loop is used to go through the elements in the `ResultSet` object. Lines 26–33 are the `while` loop. While there are more elements in the `ResultSet` object you are going to create a new row in the table and output the plan name, deductible, and the percentage covered for doctors in the plan and doctors out of the plan. Lines 28–31 are the lines that get the information out of the `ResultSet` object. JSP expression tags can be used to insert the values from the `ResultSet` into the HTML table.

Lines 34–37 test if the statement and connection are open and close them if they are open. Remember it is always good practice to close your statements and connections.

Line 41 includes the `SiteNavigator.html` file at the bottom of the JSP. Figure 22.4 shows the output of the `PresentCompanyHealthCareInfo.jsp` file.

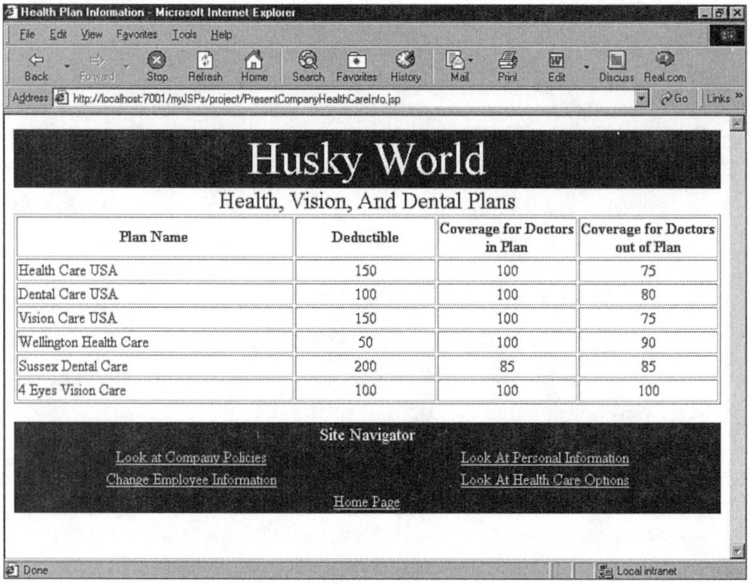

FIGURE 22.4

PresentCompanyHealth
CareInfo.jsp *outputs
the company's health
care information.*

The PresentCompanyHealthCareInfo.jsp outputs the information in the table BENEFIT-
INFO in the HumanResourcesDB database.

Writing the JSP to Present the Company's Policies

The JSP that outputs the company's policies is also going to output the benefits the company offers. Recall that the employee will get to this page from a hyperlink on the home
page or the site navigator. Listing 22.5 is the code for this file.

LISTING 22.5 JSP that Presents Company Policies and Benefits Offered
(PresentCompanyPolicies.jsp)

```
 1: <HTML>
 2: <HEAD><TITLE>Company Policies</TITLE></HEAD>
 3: <BODY>
 4:
 5: <%@ include file="CompanyBanner.html" %>
 6: <%@ page import="java.sql.*" %>
 7:
 8: <CENTER>
 9:   <FONT SIZE="5" COLOR="navy">
10:     Company Policies
11:   </FONT>
12: </CENTER>
13:
```

LISTING 22.5   continued

```
14: <!-- Company policy -->
15: <FONT SIZE="4">
16:   Our number one company policy at Husky World is to
17:   be nice to your fellow co-workers. And always be nice
18:   to doggies.
19: </FONT>
20:
21: <BR>
22:
23: <CENTER>
24:   <FONT SIZE="5" COLOR="navy">
25:     Health, Vision, And Dental Plans
26:   </FONT>
27: </CENTER>
28:
29: <TABLE WIDTH="100%">
30:   <TH WIDTH="40%">Plan Name</TH>
31:   <TH WIDTH="20%">Deductible</TH>
32:   <TH WIDTH="20%">Coverage for Doctors in Plan</TH>
33:   <TH WIDTH="20%">Coverage for Doctors out of Plan</TH>
34: <%
35:   Class.forName("COM.cloudscape.core.JDBCDriver").newInstance();
36:   Connection conn =
37:     DriverManager.getConnection("jdbc:cloudscape:c:\\HumanResourcesDB");
38:   Statement statement = conn.createStatement();
39:   String sql = "SELECT * FROM BENEFITINFO";
40:   ResultSet rs = statement.executeQuery(sql);
41:   while (rs.next()) {
42: %>
43:   <TR><TD><%= rs.getString("PLANNAME") %></TD>
44:     <TD><%= rs.getString("DEDUCTIBLE") %></TD>
45:     <TD><%= rs.getString("DOCTORSINPLANCOVERAGE") %></TD>
46:     <TD><%= rs.getString("DOCTORSOUTOFPLANCOVERAGE") %></TD>
47:   </TR>
48: <% } //end while loop
49:   if (statement != null)
50:     statement.close();
51:   if (conn != null)
52:     conn.close();
53: %>
54: </TABLE>
55:
56: <BR>
57:
58: <%@ include file="SiteNavigator.html" %>
59: </BODY>
60: </HTML>
```

ANALYSIS The first step in the JSP is to include the `CompanyBanner.html` file, which is done in line 5. The `include` directive inserts the code from the HTML file into the JSP.

Line 6 is the `page` directive and is importing the classes from the `java.sql` package. These classes are necessary for accessing a database from within the JSP.

The heading on the page is done in lines 8–12, letting users know what the page allows them to do.

The company policy is in lines 15–19 and is just text formatted with a font tag. The company policy is very simple and just tells the employees to be nice to one another.

Lines 23–27 are the heading for the insurance information. The information is formatted in a table that is started in line 29. Lines 30–33 are the column headers for the table, describing the data in each column.

This JSP is going to access the database directly, so line 35 specifies the driver for the database. Since this application uses the Cloudscape database, the driver is `COM.cloudscape.core.JDBCDriver`. After specifying the driver, you get a connection using the `DriverManager` class in the `java.sql` package and specify the database URL. The connection to the database is made in lines 36–37. The URL for the database is `jdbc:cloudscape:c:\\HumanResources`.

Now that the connection has been established, it can be used to create a statement. The statement is created in line 38, and a SQL string is defined in line 39. The SQL string is a simple `SELECT` statement that retrieves all information from the table `BENEFITINFO`. The SQL statement is executed in line 40 and saves the result in a `ResultSet` object referenced by the variable `rs`.

Lines 41–48 are the `while` loop that cycles through all the elements in the `ResultSet` object. Lines 43–46 are the JSP expression tags inserting the column values into the output table.

Lines 49–52 close the statement and connection objects if they are still open.

The last point you should notice is the `include` directive found in line 58. It inserts the code from the `SiteNavigator.html` file into the JSP. Figure 22.5 shows the output of this JSP.

This page can be reached from a hyperlink on the home page or a hyperlink on the site navigator. Employees like being kept up to date on happenings and this page could be a place to do that.

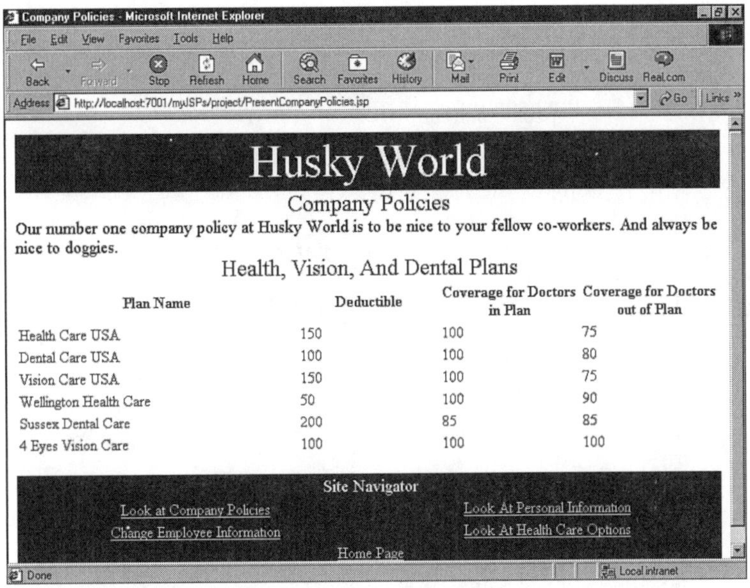

FIGURE 22.5

A snapshot of the JSP that outputs the company's policies and benefits.

This application is very similar to one found on a company's intranet. Of course, before this goes into production, you would have to set up some security. Only employees should have access to this site, and you could design it so only managers could add new employees. The security would be configured on the server in which you are deploying your application.

Allowing Employees to View Personal Benefits

Many human resource sites permit users to view their personal benefits, such as the time off they have accrued, the amount of time they have taken off, and their insurance benefits. The user starts at an HTML form that has check boxes that allows users to select what personal information they want to view. This HTML file, PersonalInfo.html, is shown in Listing 22.6.

LISTING 22.6   HTML Form that Allows Users to Choose What Personal
Information to View (PersonalInfo.html)

```
1: <HTML>
2: <HEAD><TITLE>Retrieve Personal Information</TITLE></HEAD>
3: <BODY ALINK="yellow" VLINK="yellow" LINK="yellow">
4:
```

LISTING 22.6   continued

```
 5: <!-- insert the company banner -->
 6: <TABLE WIDTH="100%" BORDER="0" BGCOLOR="navy">
 7:   <TR ALIGN="center">
 8:     <TD><FONT SIZE="7" COLOR="yellow">Husky World</FONT></TD>
 9:   </TR>
10: </TABLE>
11:
12: <!-- tells the user what to input -->
13: <CENTER>
14:   <FONT SIZE="5" COLOR="navy">
15:     Enter Your Employee ID And Select Info To View<P>
16:   </FONT>
17: </CENTER>
18:
19: <!-- the user inserts their id and selects what to view -->
20: <TABLE WIDTH="100%">
21: <FORM NAME="EmployeeID"
22:       ACTION="http://localhost:7001/myJSPs/project/PersonalInfo.jsp"
23:       METHOD="POST">
24:   <TR ALIGN="center">
25:     <TD>Employee ID:
26:         <INPUT TYPE="text" NAME="id" VALUE="1" SIZE="10">
27:     </TD>
28:   </TR>
29:   <TR><TD> </TD></TR> <!-- blank row -->
30:   <TR ALIGN="center">
31:     <TD><INPUT TYPE="checkbox" NAME="timeOff"
32:                VALUE="getTimeOff" CHECKED>
33:         Get Personal Time Off Information
34:     </TD>
35:   </TR>
36:   <TR><TD> </TD></TR> <!-- blank row -->
37:   <TR ALIGN="center">
38:     <TD><INPUT TYPE="checkbox" NAME="healthCare"
39:                VALUE="getHealthCare" CHECKED>
40:         Get Personal Health Care Information
41:     </TD>
42:   </TR>
43:   <TR><TD> </TD></TR> <!-- blank row -->
44:   <TR ALIGN="center">
45:     <TD><INPUT TYPE="submit" NAME="btnSubmit"
46:                VALUE="Get Personal Information"></TD>
47:   </TR>
48: </FORM>
49: </TABLE>
50:
51: <BR><BR>
52:
53: <!-- insert the site navigator -->
```

22

LISTING 22.6   continued

```
54: <TABLE WIDTH="100%" BORDER="0" BGCOLOR="navy">
55: <TR ALIGN="center">
56:   <TD COLSPAN=2><FONT SIZE="4" COLOR="yellow">Site Navigator</FONT></TD>
57: </TR>
58: <TR ALIGN="center">
59:   <TD><A HREF=
60:       "http://localhost:7001/myJSPs/project/PresentCompanyPolicies.jsp">
61:       Look at Company Policies</A>
62:   </TD>
63:   <TD><A HREF=
64:       "http://localhost:7001/myJSPs/project/PersonalInfo.html">
65:       Look At Personal Information</A>
66:   </TD>
67: </TR>
68: <TR ALIGN="center">
69:   <TD><A HREF=
70:       "http://localhost:7001/myJSPs/project/InputEmployeeInfo.html">
71:       Change Employee Information</A>
72:   </TD>
73:   <TD><A HREF=
74:     "http://localhost:7001/myJSPs/project/PresentCompanyHealthCareInfo.jsp">
75:     Look At Health Care Options</A>
76:   </TD>
77: </TR>
78: <TR ALIGN="center">
79:   <TD COLSPAN="2">
80:     <A HREF="http://localhost:7001/myJSPs/project/HumanResources.html">
81:       Home Page</A>
82:   </TD>
83: </TR>
84: </TABLE>
85: </BODY>
86: </HTML>
```

ANALYSIS   Lines 6–10 contain the code for the company banner. (Remember, since this is an HTML document you have to insert the code yourself.)

This HTML document creates a form that contains a text box for the user to enter his ID (lines 25–27), and two checkboxes that allow the user a choice. One checkbox is given the name `timeOff` and its value is `getTimeOff`. The other checkbox is given the name `healthCare` and the value is `getHealthCare`. The names of the checkboxes will be used on the server side in a JSP to determine what personal information to display. Lines 31–32 declare the checkbox for time off and lines 45–46 declare the checkbox for health care information. Notice that both have the attribute CHECKED in their tags so they will be checked when the page loads.

When the user clicks Get Personal Information—the submit button—the data will be bundled up and sent to the server for PersonalInfo.jsp to parse. This is declared in line 22, the action attribute of the form tag. Figure 22.6 shows the output of this HTML document.

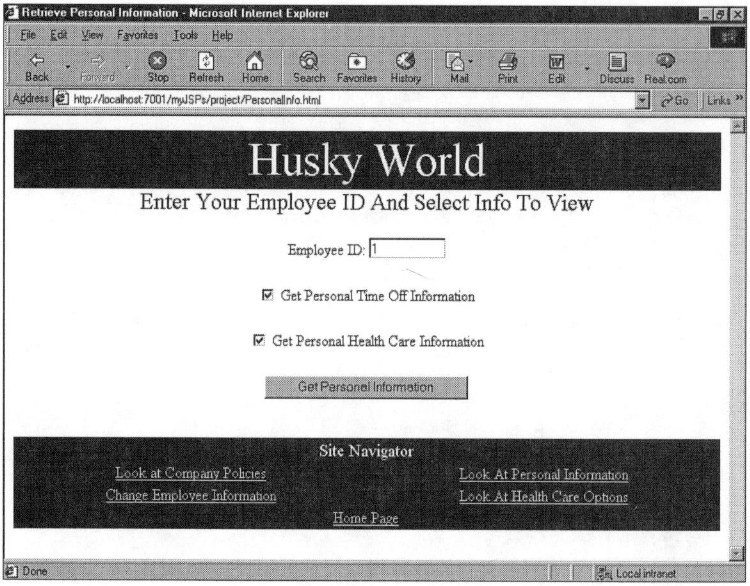

FIGURE 22.6

PersonalInfo.html *allows employees to check on their available days off, among other things.*

PersonalInfo.jsp determines what information the user wants to view and includes the appropriate JSP to display the data. Listing 22.7 shows the code for the PersonalInfo.jsp file.

LISTING 22.7   JSP that Parses User's Input and Includes the Appropriate JSP(s) to Service the Request (PersonalInfo.jsp)

```
 1: <HTML>
 2: <HEAD><TITLE></TITLE></HEAD>
 3: <BODY>
 4:
 5: <%@ include file="CompanyBanner.html" %>
 6:
 7: <%
 8:     Enumeration input = request.getParameterNames();
 9:     while(input.hasMoreElements()) {
10:       String name = (String) input.nextElement();
11:       String value = request.getParameter(name);
12:       if (value.equals("getTimeOff")) {
13: %>
14:         <jsp:include page="PresentTimeOffData.jsp" />
15:
```

22

LISTING 22.7 continued

```
16: <%    } else if (value.equals("getHealthCare")) {  %>
17:
18:        <jsp:include page="PresentPersonalHealthCareInfo.jsp" />
19:
20: <%
21:        } //end else
22:    } // end while loop
23: %>
24:
25: <%@ include file="SiteNavigator.html" %>
26:
27: </BODY>
28: </HTML>
```

ANALYSIS Just like the other JSPs seen so far, the `include` directive is used twice: Once in line 5 to include the company banner, and once in line 25 to include the site navigator.

This JSP is responsible for parsing the request from the user and determining what JSPs to include, via the `include` action. Line 8 gets the input from the user and puts it in an enumeration. The `while` loop that starts on line 9 goes through the enumeration, first getting the name of the object (line 10), and then using that name in line 11 to get the value. If the value of the input element is `getTimeOff`, this JSP will include `PresentTimeOffData.jsp`. If the input element's value is `getHealthCare`, then `PresentPersonalHealthCareInfo.jsp` will be included.

The JSP `PresentTimeOffData.jsp` is responsible for retrieving the employee's time off information from the database. This code is shown in Listing 22.8. This JSP is expecting to receive some parameters and hence is not a standalone JSP.

LISTING 22.8 JSP that Presents an Employee's Time-Off Status
(`PresentTimeOffData.jsp`)

```
1: <HTML>
2: <HEAD><TITLE>Your Time Off Data</TITLE></HEAD>
3: <BODY>
4:
5: <%@ page import="java.sql.*" %>
6: <%! int employeeID; %>
7:
8: <H1 ALIGN="center">Your Current Time Off Status</H1>
9:
10: <TABLE WIDTH="100%">
11: <%
12:    employeeID = Integer.valueOf(request.getParameter("id")).intValue();
13:    Class.forName("COM.cloudscape.core.JDBCDriver").newInstance();
```

LISTING 22.8   continued

```
14:     Connection conn =
15:        DriverManager.getConnection("jdbc:cloudscape:c:\\HumanResourcesDB");
16:     Statement statement = conn.createStatement();
17:     String sql = "SELECT * FROM EMPLOYEEINFO WHERE ID = " + employeeID;
18:     ResultSet rs = statement.executeQuery(sql);
19:     rs.next();
20: %>
21:     <TR><TD ALIGN="right" WIDTH="50%">Employee Name:</TD>
22:        <TD WIDTH="50%"><%= rs.getString("NAME") %></TD>
23:     </TR>
24:     <TR><TD ALIGN="right">Total Sick Days:</TD>
25:        <TD> <%= rs.getString("TOTALSICKDAYS") %></TD>
26:     </TR>
27:     <TR><TD ALIGN="right">Taken Sick Days: </TD>
28:        <TD><%= rs.getString("TAKENSICKDAYS") %></TD>
29:     </TR>
30:     <TR><TD ALIGN="right">Total Personal Time (in hours): </TD>
31:        <TD><%= rs.getString("TOTALPERSONALTIME") %></TD>
32:     </TR>
33:     <TR><TD ALIGN="right">Taken Personal Time (in hours): </TD>
34:        <TD><%= rs.getString("TAKENPERSONALTIME") %></TD>
35:     </TR>
36: </TABLE>
37: <BR>
38: </BODY>
39: </HTML>
```

ANALYSIS   This page does not include the company banner or the site navigator since it is inserted into another JSP that handles inserting those files. This file accesses a database directly, so the class files in the java.sql package need to be imported; this is accomplished in line 5. The page directive is used to import the java.sql package.

Line 6 uses a JSP declaration tag to declare a variable called employeeID that is of type int. This variable will contain the employee ID that the user inserted into the HTML form. The ID will be used to get the employee's information from the database.

The other JSP that can be used to display personal information about the employee is PresentPersonalHealthCareInfo.jsp. It is responsible for displaying the insurance benefits an employee has. The code for this JSP is shown in Listing 22.9.

LISTING 22.9   JSP that Presents an Employee's Personal Information
(PresentPersonalHealthCareInfo.jsp)

22

```
 1: <HTML>
 2: <HEAD><TITLE>Your Health Care Information</TITLE></HEAD>
 3: <BODY>
 4:
 5: <%@ page import="java.sql.*" %>
 6: <%! int employeeID; %>
 7:
 8: <H1 ALIGN="center">Your Health Care Plans</H1>
 9:
10: <TABLE WIDTH="100%">
11: <% employeeID = Integer.valueOf(request.getParameter("id")).intValue();
12:    Class.forName("COM.cloudscape.core.JDBCDriver").newInstance();
13:    Connection conn =
14:       DriverManager.getConnection("jdbc:cloudscape:c:\\HumanResourcesDB");
15:    Statement statement = conn.createStatement();
16:    String sql = "SELECT * FROM EMPLOYEEINFO WHERE ID = " + employeeID;
17:    ResultSet rs = statement.executeQuery(sql);
18:    rs.next();
19: %>
20:
21:    <TR><TD ALIGN="right" WIDTH="50%">Employee Name:</TD>
22:       <TD WIDTH="50%"><%= rs.getString("NAME") %></TD>
23:    </TR>
24:    <TR><TD ALIGN="right" WIDTH="50%">Health Care Plan:</TD>
25:       <TD WIDTH="50%"><%= rs.getString("HEALTHCAREPLAN") %></TD>
26:    </TR>
27:    <TR><TD ALIGN="right" WIDTH="50%">Dental Plan:</TD>
28:       <TD WIDTH="50%"><%= rs.getString("DENTALPLAN") %></TD>
29:    </TR>
30:    <TR><TD ALIGN="right" WIDTH="50%">Vision Plan:</TD>
31:       <TD WIDTH="50%"><%= rs.getString("VISIONPLAN") %></TD>
32:    </TR>
33: </TABLE>
34:
35: <BR>
36:
37: </BODY>
38: </HTML>
```

This JSP is very much like the PresentTimeOffData.jsp in that it takes the employee's
ID number from the HTML form and retrieves the employee's information from the
database. Figure 22.7 shows the output of the PresentInfo.jsp if the user wants to view
his time-off status.

FIGURE 22.7

PersonalInfo.jsp
*outputs an employee's
time-off status in
response to the
employee's request.*

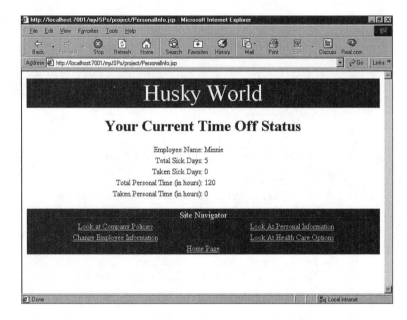

Figure 22.8 shows the output if the user wants to view her insurance benefits.

FIGURE 22.8

PersonalInfo.jsp
*provides a view of
insurance benefits in
response to a user
request.*

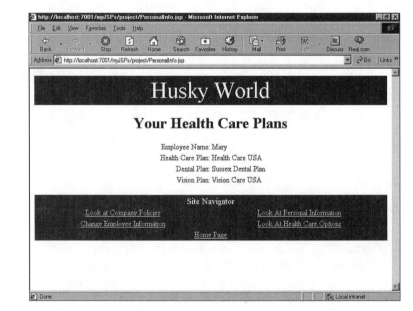

22

Of course, it is possible to view all your personal information; you simply select both checkboxes on the HTML form, PersonalInfo.html.

Now you have written the part of the application for users to view their benefits. In the next hour you will finish creating the parts of the application. Good work to this point— and enjoy the rest.

Summary

In this hour you began to put what you've learned about JSPs to a practical purpose. You created part of a Web site that provides employees with information from their human resources department. This is a very common application for a company's intranet. The technologies used so far have been JSPs and a database. In the next hour you are going to start using JavaBeans to access the database. Remember to feel free to embellish these pages you are creating. Use other techniques you learned throughout the book in this application.

Q&A

Q What server should I use for this application?

A BEA WebLogic Server would be a good for this application because you will this as a real-world example. In Hour 24 you are going to bundle it and deploy it on WLS as a Webarchive file, and set up security on it. Tomcat is not a production environment as WLS is.

Workshop

The quiz questions and activities are provided for your further understanding. See Appendix A, "Answers," for the answers to the quiz.

Quiz

1. What two directives were used in the PresentCompanyPolicies.jsp file?

2. What is a benefit of including a file into a JSP, via the include directive?

3. What action is used in the PersonalInfo.jsp file? How does this JSP action work?

4. Many times a Servlet parses the user's request and uses a JSP to present the response. If you were to apply this philosophy to the Husky World Human Resources site, what JSP(s) would be replaced with Servlets?

Activity

Design the scenarios you have coded in this hour in another way. The JSPs in this hour accessed the database directly; what is another way to handle database access? What else could the company policy JSP produce for the employee?

Hour 23

Programming the Business Logic

In the last hour you began creating the Husky World Human Resources Web site. There's still a lot of work to do, but you'll finish the project in this hour. The capabilities for adding new employees and changing existing employees' information need to be written. The user is going to input information, whether it is a new employee's information or a change of information, into an HTML document. The HTML document will send the data to a JSP on the server. This JSP will parse the request, place the data into a JavaBean, use the JavaBean to update the database, and then forward the request to another JSP to present the information back to the user. Since the first JSP placed the data in the JavaBean, when the request is forwarded to the presentation JSP, it simply needs to grab the presentation data from the JavaBean.

In this hour you will put to practical use:

- The forward action
- The useBean action
- The setProperty action
- Database access

Overview

You need to contemplate what parts of the application still need to be written. In Hour 21, "Designing an Enterprise Application," the functionality of the Husky World Human Resources Web site was laid out. The user would be able to

- View the company policies.
- View the insurance benefits the company offers.
- View his personal insurance benefits.
- Change his personal profile, name, addresses, and phone numbers.
- View his current time-off information.
- Add new employees.

The only thing left is to provide the capability of adding a new user and allowing a user to change his profile. This uses an HTML document for the user to fill in, whether it is a new employee's data or a change in his profile, a JavaBean to store the data and help with database access, and then another JSP to present the data to the user.

Adding New Employees Through the Husky World Human Resources Web Site

New employees come to a company all the time. There should be a nice, easy way to add employee information without needing to go directly to the database. Therefore, you are going to add a capability within the Husky World Human Resources Web site to add new employee information.

The user will insert the new employee's information—name, address, phone number, and benefit information—into an HTML document. Listing 23.1 shows the code for this HTML document, InputNewEmployeeInfo.html.

LISTING 23.1   An HTML Document that Allows the User to Input New Employee Information (InputNewEmployeeInfo.html)

```
1: <HTML>
2: <HEAD><TITLE>New Employee Information</TITLE></HEAD>
3: <BODY>
4:
5: <!-- insert the company banner -->
6: <TABLE WIDTH="100%" BORDER="0" BGCOLOR="navy">
7:   <TR ALIGN="center">
8:     <TD><FONT SIZE="7" COLOR="yellow">Husky World</FONT></TD>
9:   </TR>
```

LISTING 23.1   continued

```
10: </TABLE>
11:
12: <CENTER>
13:   <FONT SIZE="5" COLOR="navy">
14:     Enter The New Employee's Information
15:   </FONT>
16: </CENTER>
17:
18: <TABLE WIDTH="100%">
19: <FORM NAME="newEmployee"
20:       ACTION="http://localhost:7001/myJSPs/project/AddNewEmployee.jsp"
21:       METHOD="POST">
22:
23:   <TR><TD WIDTH="50%" ALIGN="right">Employee ID: </TD>
24:       <TD WIDTH="50%">
25:         <INPUT TYPE="text" NAME="id" VALUE="">
26:       </TD>
27:   </TR>
28:   <TR><TD WIDTH="50%" ALIGN="right">Name: </TD>
29:       <TD WIDTH="50%">
30:         <INPUT TYPE="text" NAME="name" VALUE="Peggy">
31:       </TD>
32:    </TR>
33:   <TR><TD WIDTH="50%" ALIGN="right">Address: </TD>
34:       <TD WIDTH="50%">
35:         <INPUT TYPE="text" NAME="address" VALUE="Maynard, MA">
36:       </TD>
37:   </TR>
38:   <TR><TD WIDTH="50%" ALIGN="right">Phone Number: </TD>
39:       <TD WIDTH="50%">
40:         <INPUT TYPE="text" NAME="phone" VALUE="555-555-7845">
41:       </TD>
42:   </TR>
43:   <TR><TD WIDTH="50%" ALIGN="right">Work Status: </TD>
44:       <TD WIDTH="50%">
45:         <INPUT TYPE="text" NAME="workstatus" VALUE="full-time">
46:       </TD>
47:   </TR>
48:   <TR><TD WIDTH="50%" ALIGN="right">Total Sick Days: </TD>
49:       <TD WIDTH="50%">
50:         <INPUT TYPE="text" NAME="totalSickDays" VALUE="5">
51:       </TD>
52:   </TR>
53:   <TR><TD WIDTH="50%" ALIGN="right">Taken Sick Days: </TD>
54:       <TD WIDTH="50%">
55:         <INPUT TYPE="text" NAME="takenSickDays" VALUE="0">
56:       </TD>
57:   </TR>
58:   <TR><TD WIDTH="50%" ALIGN="right">Total Personal Time(in hours): </TD>
59:       <TD WIDTH="50%">
```

23

LISTING 23.1   continued

```
60:             <INPUT TYPE="text" NAME="totalPersonalTime" VALUE="120">
61:         </TD>
62:     </TR>
63:     <TR><TD WIDTH="50%" ALIGN="right">Taken Personal Time(in hours):</TD>
64:         <TD WIDTH="50%">
65:             <INPUT TYPE="text" NAME="takenPersonalTime" VALUE="0">
66:         </TD>
67:     </TR>
68:     <TR><TD WIDTH="50%" ALIGN="right">Health Care Plan: </TD>
69:         <TD WIDTH="50%">
70:             <INPUT TYPE="text" NAME="healthCarePlan" VALUE="Health Care USA">
71:         </TD>
72:     </TR>
73:     <TR><TD WIDTH="50%" ALIGN="right">Dental Plan: </TD>
74:         <TD WIDTH="50%">
75:             <INPUT TYPE="text" NAME="dentalPlan" VALUE="Dental USA">
76:         </TD>
77:     </TR>
78:     <TR><TD WIDTH="50%" ALIGN="right">Vision Plan: </TD>
79:         <TD WIDTH="50%">
80:             <INPUT TYPE="text" NAME="visionPlan" VALUE="Vision USA">
81:         </TD>
82:     </TR>
83:     <TR><TD COLSPAN="2" ALIGN="center">
84:         <INPUT TYPE="submit" NAME="btnSubmit" VALUE="Add New Employee"></TD>
85:     </TR>
86: </FORM>
87: </TABLE>
88: </BODY>
89: </HTML>
```

ANALYSIS Remember that since this is an HTML file, you cannot use an `include`; you must insert the code for the company banner into the page. Lines 6–10 are the code for the company banner, which we are using to provide a common look to all the pages in the Web site.

Lines 12–16 set the heading (Enter The New Employee's Information) for the page. Headings let users know the purpose of the page.

Lines 19–21 are the open tag for the FORM element. Line 19 starts the tag and defines the name of the form, newEmployee. Line 20 is the ACTION attribute of the FORM tag and specifies the JSP that will be run when the user clicks the submit button, `http://localhost:7001/myJSPs/project/AddNewEmployee.jsp`. The METHOD attribute is specified in line 21 to be POST, which means the data in the form will be sent to the server in a packet.

There are many text fields in this form. It is important to note the names of these elements in the form because the JavaBean is going to need the same names as attributes so the JSP can use the setProperty action to set all values automatically. Table 23.1 shows each text field from Listing 23.1, including the number of the code line where it is defined, a description of the field, and the name of the field.

TABLE 23.1 Form Elements for Adding a New Employee

Line Number	Description	Name
25	Employee ID	id
30	Employee name	name
35	Employee address	address
40	Employee phone number	phone
45	Employee's work status: full-time or part-time	workstatus
50	Total number of sick days for the employee	totalSickDays
55	Number of sick days the employee has taken	takenSickDays
60	Total number of hours of personal time	totalPersonalTime
65	Number of hours of personal time the employee has taken	takenPersonalTime
70	Employee's health care plan name	healthCarePlan
75	Employee's dental plan name	dentalPlan
80	Employee's vision plan name	visionPlan
84	The submit button	btnSubmit

23

Figure 23.1 shows the output of this HTML file in a browser.

Once the user has filled in the employee information, he clicks the submit button and the data in the form is packaged and sent to the server. At the server, the JSP AddNewEmployee.jsp is executed. This JSP will parse through the request storing the data in a JavaBean (NewEmployeeBean). After the data is stored in the JavaBean, it calls the method updateDatabase() in the JavaBean to update the database with the new employee's information. The JSP invokes this method, but the logic of storing the information into the database is located in the JavaBean. Once the database is updated, the AddNewEmployee.jsp forwards the user's request to another JSP (PresentNewEmployeeInfo.jsp), to present the new employee's information. The code for AddNewEmployee.jsp is shown in Listing 23.2.

LISTING 23.2 JSP that Uses a JavaBean to Insert Data into a Database and then Forwards the Request to Another JSP (AddNewEmployee.jsp)

```
1: <HTML>
2: <HEAD>
3:   <TITLE>Update DB With New Employee Information</TITLE>
```

LISTING 23.2   continued

```
 4: </HEAD>
 5: <BODY>
 6: <jsp:useBean id="newEmployee"
 7:              class="jspin24hrs.project.NewEmployeeBean"
 8:              scope="request"/>
 9: <jsp:setProperty name="newEmployee" property="*"/>
10: <% newEmployee.updateDatabase(); %>
11: <jsp:forward page="PresentNewEmployeeInfo.jsp"/>
12: </BODY>
13: </HTML>
```

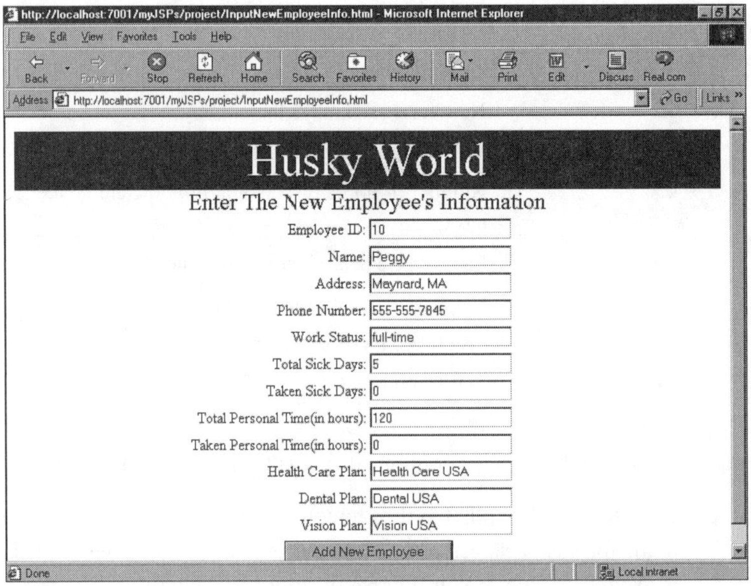

FIGURE 23.1

An HTML document generates a form that allows users to input the new employee's information.

The code for the AddNewEmployee.jsp is relatively short, but it does quite a bit. This JSP is going to use a JavaBean to pass information to another JSP, and it uses this JavaBean to update the database. The JavaBean is initialized in lines 6–8. Line 6 starts the useBean action and assigns the id attribute to newEmployee. That way, the JavaBean will be accessed using that id. The class for the JavaBean is specified in line 7 to be jspin24hrs.project.NewEmployeeBean and the scope of the bean is request. That way any JSP during the processing of the user's request can use this bean.

Line 9 is a short line but it does a lot of work. The setProperty action is used to set the properties of the bean. If the property attribute of this action tag is assigned the asterisk, *, then all properties in the request get mapped into the corresponding names in the bean. That is why it was important to know the names of the elements in the HTML form, because you are going to want the same names in the JavaBean.

Line 10 is using the updateDatabase() method of the JavaBean to update the database. Then the request is forwarded to another JSP to present the information to the user, which is done using the forward action in line 11.

The JavaBean that is used has the same attributes as the HTML form, the accessor methods for these elements, and a method to update the database. The code for the JavaBean is shown in Listing 23.3.

23

LISTING 23.3 Maintains Information About a New Employee and Helps in Updating the Database (NewEmployeeBean.java)

```
 1: package jspin24hrs.project;
 2:
 3: import java.sql.*;
 4:
 5: public class NewEmployeeBean {
 6:    private String name, address, phone, workstatus;
 7:    private String healthCarePlan, dentalPlan, visionPlan;
 8:    private int id, totalSickDays, takenSickDays;
 9:    private int totalPersonalTime, takenPersonalTime;
10:
11:    public void setName(String input){
12:       name = input;
13:    }
14:    public String getName(){
15:      return name;
16:    }
17:    public void setAddress(String input){
18:      address = input;
19:    }
20:    public String getAddress(){
21:      return address;
22:    }
23:    public void setPhone(String input){
24:      phone = input;
25:    }
26:    public String getPhone(){
27:      return phone;
28:    }
29:    public void setWorkstatus(String input){
30:      workstatus = input;
31:    }
32:    public String getWorkstatus(){
33:        return workstatus;
34:    }
35:    public void setHealthCarePlan(String input){
36:      healthCarePlan = input;
37:    }
38:    public String getHealthCarePlan(){
39:        return healthCarePlan;
```

LISTING 23.3   continued

```
40:    }
41:    public void setDentalPlan(String input){
42:      dentalPlan = input;
43:    }
44:    public String getDentalPlan(){
45:      return dentalPlan;
46:    }
47:    public void setVisionPlan(String input){
48:      visionPlan = input;
49:    }
50:    public String getVisionPlan(){
51:      return visionPlan;
52:    }
53:    public void setId(int input){
54:        id = input;
55:    }
56:    public int getId(){
57:      return id;
58:    }
59:    public void setTotalSickDays(int input){
60:      totalSickDays = input;
61:    }
62:    public int getTotalSickDays(){
63:      return totalSickDays;
64:    }
65:    public void setTakenSickDays(int input){
66:      takenSickDays = input;
67:    }
68:    public int getTakenSickDays(){
69:      return takenSickDays;
70:    }
71:    public void setTotalPersonalTime(int input){
72:      totalPersonalTime = input;
73:    }
74:    public int getTotalPersonalTime(){
75:      return totalPersonalTime;
76:    }
77:    public void setTakenPersonalTime(int input){
78:      takenPersonalTime = input;
79:    }
80:    public int getTakenPersonalTime(){
81:        return takenPersonalTime;
82:    }
83:    public void updateDatabase() {
84:      try{
85:        Class.forName("COM.cloudscape.core.JDBCDriver").newInstance();
86:        Connection conn =
87:          DriverManager.getConnection("jdbc:cloudscape:c:\\HumanResourcesDB");
88:        String sql = "INSERT INTO EMPLOYEEINFO VALUES " +
```

LISTING 23.3   continued

```
 89:                    "(?, ?, ?, ?, ?, ?, ?, ?, ?, ?, ?, ?)";
 90:        PreparedStatement statement = conn.prepareStatement(sql);
 91:        statement.setInt(1, id);
 92:        statement.setString(2, name);
 93:        statement.setString(3, address);
 94:        statement.setString(4, phone);
 95:        statement.setString(5, workstatus);
 96:        statement.setInt(6, totalSickDays);
 97:        statement.setInt(7, takenSickDays);
 98:        statement.setInt(8, totalPersonalTime);
 99:        statement.setInt(9, takenPersonalTime);
100:        statement.setString(10, healthCarePlan);
101:        statement.setString(11, dentalPlan);
102:        statement.setString(12, visionPlan);
103:        statement.executeQuery();
104:    }
105: catch (Exception e) {}
106:    }
107: }
```

ANALYSIS   The package of this class is defined in line 1 to be `jspin24hrs.project`. Since this class is going to be doing database access, the classes in the `java.sql` package need to be imported, which is done in line 3. The class is started in line 5 and the attributes are defined in lines 6–9. Notice that the names of the attributes match the names of the elements in the HTML form from `InputNewEmployeeInfo.html` (Listing 23.1).

Accessor methods are created in lines 11–81. These methods either return the attributes' values or they set the attributes' values.

This JavaBean's `updateDatabase()` method, defined in lines 83–106, updates the database with the values stored in its attributes. It is beneficial to take a good look at this code. Take a good look at this code; it is enclosed in a `try` block since the database access could raise exceptions. The first statement, line 85, sets the driver for the database this method is using. This application is using the `cloudscape` database, so the driver is `COM.cloudscape.core.JDBCDriver`. After the driver type is set, a connection to the database needs to be created.

After using the bean the `AddNewEmployee.jsp` forwards the request to `PresentNewEmployeeInfo.jsp`, shown in Listing 23.4.

LISTING 23.4   JSP that Presents the Information Stored in the JavaBean
(`PresentNewEmployeeInfo.jsp`)

```
1: <HTML>
2: <HEAD><TITLE>Present New Employee Information</TITLE></HEAD>
3: <BODY>
```

LISTING 23.4 continued

```
 4: <%@ include file-"CompanyBanner.html" %>
 6: <jsp:useBean id="newEmployee"
 7:             class="jspin24hrs.project.NewEmployeeBean"
 8:             scope="request"/>
 9: <CENTER>
10:   <FONT SIZE="5" COLOR="navy">
11:     New Employee Has Been Entered Into The Database
12:   </FONT>
13: </CENTER>
14: <TABLE WIDTH="100%" BORDER="1">
15:   <TR><TD ALIGN="right" WIDTH="50%">Name:</TD>
16:       <TD WIDTH="50%"><%= newEmployee.getName() %></TD>
17:   </TR>
18:   <TR><TD ALIGN="right" WIDTH="50%">Address:</TD>
19:       <TD WIDTH="50%"><%= newEmployee.getAddress() %></TD>
20:   </TR>
21:   <TR><TD ALIGN="right" WIDTH="50%">Phone Number:</TD>
22:       <TD WIDTH="50%"><%= newEmployee.getPhone() %></TD>
23:   </TR>
24:   <TR><TD ALIGN="right" WIDTH="50%">Work Status:</TD>
25:       <TD WIDTH="50%"><%= newEmployee.getWorkstatus() %></TD>
26:   </TR>
27:   <TR><TD ALIGN="right" WIDTH="50%">Total Sick Days:</TD>
28:       <TD> <%= newEmployee.getTotalSickDays() %></TD>
29:   </TR>
30:   <TR><TD ALIGN="right" WIDTH="50%">Taken Sick Days: </TD>
31:       <TD><%= newEmployee.getTakenSickDays() %></TD>
32:   </TR>
33:   <TR><TD ALIGN="right" WIDTH="50%">Total Personal Time (in hours): </TD>
34:       <TD><%= newEmployee.getTotalPersonalTime() %></TD>
35:   </TR>
36:   <TR><TD ALIGN="right" WIDTH="50%">Taken Personal Time (in hours): </TD>
37:       <TD><%= newEmployee.getTakenPersonalTime() %></TD>
38:   </TR>
39:   <TR><TD ALIGN="right" WIDTH="50%">Health Care Plan:</TD>
40:       <TD WIDTH="50%"><%= newEmployee.getHealthCarePlan() %></TD>
41:   </TR>
42:   <TR><TD ALIGN="right" WIDTH="50%">Dental Plan:</TD>
43:       <TD WIDTH="50%"><%= newEmployee.getDentalPlan() %></TD>
44:   </TR>
45:   <TR><TD ALIGN="right" WIDTH="50%">Vision Plan:</TD>
46:       <TD WIDTH="50%"><%= newEmployee.getVisionPlan() %></TD>
47:   </TR>
48: </TABLE>
49: <%@ include file="SiteNavigator.html" %>
50: </BODY>
51: </HTML>
```

ANALYSIS   Line 4 is the `include` directive that is including the code of the static document, `CompanyBanner.html`, into the JSP.

Recall the scenario: the user entered his information into an HTML form, the data was sent to the server, and the JSP AddNewEmployee.jsp handled the request. This JSP parsed the input, updated the attributes of a NewEmployeeBean JavaBean with the values from the form, and then updated the database. Since the JavaBean has all the values from the form, and its scope was request, then the JSP PresentNewEmployeeInfo.jsp only needs to get the attributes from the NewEmployeeBean JavaBean and format them for the response back to the user.

Lines 6–8 get a handle to the JavaBean that contains the user information. The useBean action is used and the id given to the bean is newEmployee. This JavaBean is in the package jspin24hrs.project and the class name is NewEmployeeBean. The code for this class was shown in Listing 23.3. Since the information is already stored in the JavaBean, this JSP just needs to extract the data and display it.

Lines 14–48 create an HTML table to display the information and use expression tags to insert the attributes of the JavaBean. For example, line 16 uses the accessor method getName() to retrieve the new employee's name. There was an accessor method for each attribute so these methods can be used to retrieve the new employee's information.

Figure 23.2 shows the output of this JSP.

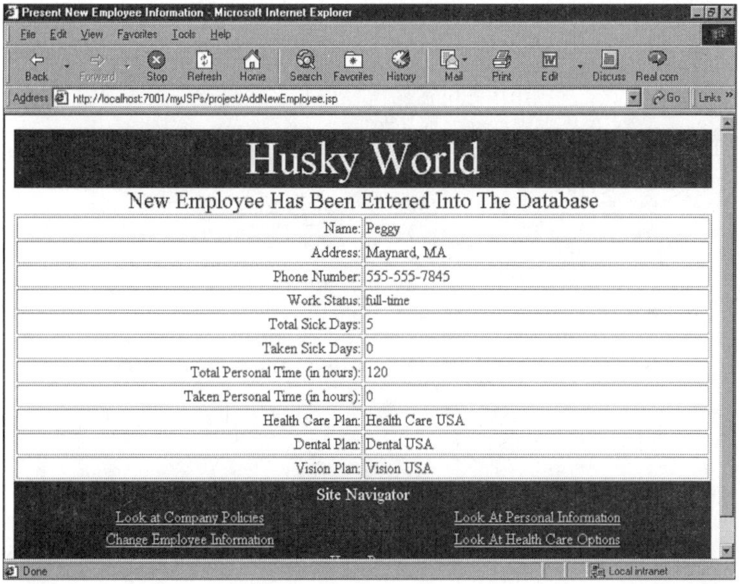

FIGURE 23.2

You can view the output of adding a new user.

Now you have given users the capability to add new employees' information to the Web site.

Writing Capabilities to Change Employee's Information

The only piece of the Web site left to write is the one to allow current employees to change their information, such as their names, phone numbers, and addresses. In this scenario, the current employee will enter his employee ID and his new information into an HTML form. Listing 23.5 shows the code for InputEmployeeInfo.html.

LISTING 23.5   An HTML Document that Allows Users to Change Their Information (InputEmployeeInfo.html)

```
 1: <HTML>
 2: <HEAD><TITLE>Change of Information</TITLE></HEAD>
 3: <BODY>
 4: <TABLE WIDTH="100%" BORDER="0" BGCOLOR="navy">
 5:   <TR ALIGN="center">
 6:     <TD><FONT SIZE="7" COLOR="yellow">Husky World</FONT></TD>
 7:   </TR>
 8: </TABLE>
 9: <CENTER>
10:   <FONT SIZE="5" COLOR="navy">
11:     Please Enter Your Information<BR>
12:     Fill in all fields
13:   </FONT>
14: </CENTER>
15: <TABLE WIDTH="100%">
16: <FORM NAME="updateInfo"
17:     ACTION="http://localhost:7001/myJSPs/project/UpdateEmployeeInfo.jsp"
18:     METHOD="POST">
19:   <TR><TD WIDTH="40%" ALIGN="right">Current ID: </TD>
20:       <TD WIDTH="60%"><INPUT TYPE="text" NAME="id"></TD>
21:   </TR>
22:   <TR><TD WIDTH="40%" ALIGN="right">New Name: </TD>
23:       <TD WIDTH="60%"><INPUT TYPE="text" NAME="name" VALUE="Mickey"></TD>
24:   </TR>
25:   <TR><TD WIDTH="40%" ALIGN="right">New Address: </TD>
26:       <TD WIDTH="60%">
27:         <INPUT TYPE="text" NAME="address" VALUE="St. Louis, MO">
28:       </TD>
29:   </TR>
30:   <TR><TD WIDTH="40%" ALIGN="right">New Phone: </TD>
31:       <TD WIDTH="60%">
32:         <INPUT TYPE="text" NAME="phone" VALUE="555-555-1234">
33:       </TD>
34:   </TR>
35:   <TR><TD COLSPAN="2" ALIGN="center">
36:       <INPUT TYPE="submit" NAME="btnSubmit" VALUE="Update Profile"></TD>
37:   </TR>
```

LISTING 23.5   continued

```
38: </TABLE>
39: </FORM>
40: </BODY>
41: </HTML>
```

ANALYSIS   Lines 4–8 contain the code for the company banner since HTML documents cannot dynamically include other documents.

The HTML form is started with the FORM tag on lines 16–18. The name of the form is updateInfo and the data of the form is sent to the server in a packet, as defined by using the POST method. When the data is sent to the server, the JSP UpdateEmployeeInfo.jsp, which you will see later in this hour, is executed to accept the request.

Remember, it is important to note the names of the form elements since they need to match the attributes of the JavaBean. If they match, you can use the setProperty attribute to automatically update all the values. Table 23.2 shows the form elements from Listing 23.5, including the number of the code line where each is defined, and the description and the name of each element.

TABLE 23.2   HTML Form Elements for Updating a Current Employee's Information

Line Number	Description	Name
20	Employee's ID	id
23	Employee's name	name
27	Employee's address	address
32	Employee's phone number	phone

The output of this HTML document is shown in Figure 23.3.

Once the employee is finished entering his information, the data is sent to the server, and the JSP UpdateEmployeeInfo.jsp is executed. The code for this JSP is shown in Listing 23.6.

LISTING 23.6   JSP that Adds Data to a JavaBean and then Forwards the Request to Another JSP (UpdateEmployeeInfo.jsp)

```
1: <HTML>
2: <HEAD><TITLE>Updating Employee Information</TITLE></HEAD>
3: <BODY>
4: <jsp:useBean id="empInfo"
5:             class="jspin24hrs.project.EmployeeInfoBean"
6:             scope="request"/>
```

23

LISTING 23.6 continued

```
 7:
 8: <jsp:setProperty name="empInfo" property="*" />
 9:
10: <% empInfo.updateDatabase(); %>
11:
12: <jsp:forward page="PresentChangeOfEmployeeData.jsp" />
13: </BODY>
14: </HTML>
```

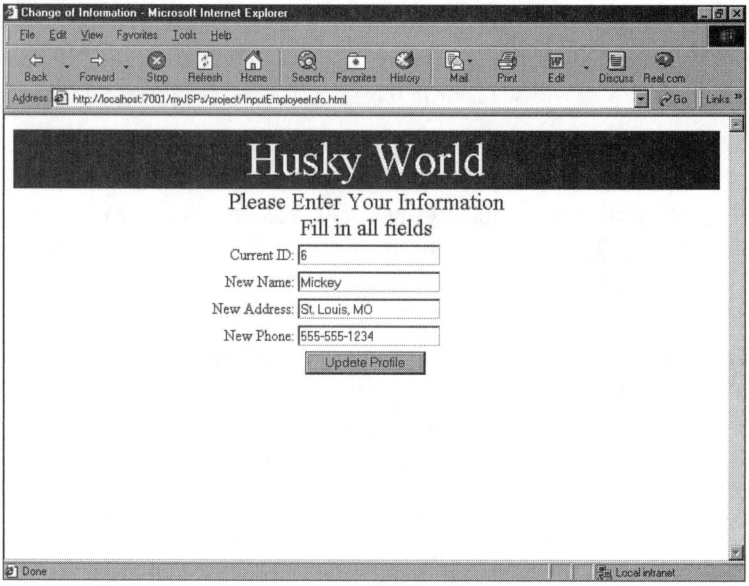

FIGURE 23.3

An HTML document allows users to change their personal profiles.

The code for this JSP is very short because it takes advantage of JSP tags to do the work. Lines 4–6 set up the JavaBean EmployeeInfoBean in package jspin24hrs.project to have the id of empInfo and a scope of request. Therefore, another JSP will be able to retrieve information from this bean while the request is alive.

Line 8 is a rather magical line, in the respect that it does so much work for one line of code. This setProperty tag takes all the elements from the HTML form and updates the matching attributes in the JavaBean with the values.

Line 10 calls a method updateDatabase() on the JavaBean that updates the database with the user's new information. After this JSP updates the database, it forwards the user's request to another JSP to present the change of information, PresentChangeOfEmployeeData.jsp, which you will see a little later in this hour.

The JavaBean code for EmployeeInfoBean is shown in Listing 23.7.

LISTING 23.7   Code for the JavaBean Used in the Change-of-Employee-Information
Scenario (EmployeeInfoBean.java)

```
 1: package jspin24hrs.project;
 2:
 3: import java.sql.*;
 4:
 5: public class EmployeeInfoBean {
 6:   private String name, address, phone;
 7:   private int id;
 8:
 9:   public void setName(String input){
10:     name = input;
11:   }
12:   public String getName(){
13:     return name;
14:   }
15:   public void setAddress(String input){
16:     address = input;
17:   }
18:   public String getAddress(){
19:     return address;
20:   }
21:   public void setPhone(String input){
22:     phone = input;
23:   }
24:   public String getPhone(){
25:     return phone;
26:   }
27:   public void setId(int input){
28:     id = input;
29:   }
30:   public int getId(){
31:     return id;
32:   }
33:   public void updateDatabase(){
34:     try{
35:       Class.forName("COM.cloudscape.core.JDBCDriver").newInstance();
36:       Connection conn =
37:        DriverManager.getConnection("jdbc:cloudscape:c:\\HumanResourcesDB");
38:       String sql = "UPDATE EMPLOYEEINFO SET " +
39:                    "NAME=?, ADDRESS=?, PHONE=? WHERE ID=?";
40:       PreparedStatement statement = conn.prepareStatement(sql);
41:       statement.setString(1, name);
42:       statement.setString(2, address);
43:       statement.setString(3, phone);
44:       statement.setInt(4, id);
45:       statement.executeQuery();
46:     }
47:     catch (Exception e) {}
48:   }
49: }
```

23

ANALYSIS   Line 1 specifies this class to be in the package jspin24hrs.project. Java uses
           packages to group classes of similar functionality. This file should be located in
the directory c:\weblogic\myserver\serverclasses\jspin24hrs\project. This will
allow WLS to find this class when it is needed.

Line 3 imports all the classes in the package java.sql because this JavaBean does database access.

The attributes of this class—name, address, phone, and id—are declared in lines 6 and 7. Notice they match the names of the form elements declared in the HTML form. After the attributes are declared, the accessor methods are written to set and get these attributes.

Lines 33–48 define a method called updateDatabase(), in the EmployeeInfoBean JavaBean, that will update the user's information in the database. It uses the employee ID to find the correct user and then updates the information.

Once the database information is updated, the user's request is forwarded to the PresentChangeOfEmployeeData.jsp to create the response to the user. This JSP will grab the employee's ID from the EmployeeInfoBean JavaBean and then retrieve his information from the database. Listing 23.8 shows the code for that JSP.

LISTING 23.8   The JSP to Present the Employee's New Information
(PresentChangeOfEmployeeData.jsp)

```
 1: <HTML>
 2: <HEAD><TITLE></TITLE></HEAD>
 3: <BODY>
 4: <%@ include file="CompanyBanner.html" %>
 5: <%@ page import="java.sql.*" %>
 6: <jsp:useBean id="empInfo"
 7:             class="jspin24hrs.project.EmployeeInfoBean"
 8:             scope="request"/>
 9: <CENTER>
10:   <FONT SIZE="5" COLOR="navy">
11:     Your New Information
12:   </FONT>
13: </CENTER>
14: <TABLE WIDTH="100%" BORDER="1">
15: <%
16:     int employeeID = empInfo.getId();
        try {
17:     Class.forName("COM.cloudscape.core.JDBCDriver").newInstance();
18:     Connection conn =
19:       DriverManager.getConnection("jdbc:cloudscape:c:\\HumanResourcesDB");
20:     Statement statement = conn.createStatement();
21:     String sql = "SELECT * FROM EMPLOYEEINFO WHERE ID = " + employeeID;
```

LISTING 23.8   continued

```
22:     ResultSet rs = statement.executeQuery(sql);
23:     while(rs.next()){
24: %>
25:         <TR><TD ALIGN="right" WIDTH="50%">Name:</TD>
26:             <TD WIDTH="50%"><%= rs.getString("NAME") %></TD>
27:         </TR>
28:         <TR><TD ALIGN="right" WIDTH="50%">Address:</TD>
29:             <TD WIDTH="50%"><%= rs.getString("ADDRESS") %></TD>
30:         </TR>
31:         <TR><TD ALIGN="right" WIDTH="50%">Phone Number:</TD>
32:             <TD WIDTH="50%"><%= rs.getString("PHONE") %></TD>
33:         </TR>
34:         <TR><TD ALIGN="right" WIDTH="50%">Work Status:</TD>
35:             <TD WIDTH="50%"><%= rs.getString("WORKSTATUS") %></TD>
36:         </TR>
37:         <TR><TD ALIGN="right" WIDTH="50%">Total Sick Days:</TD>
38:             <TD> <%= rs.getString("TOTALSICKDAYS") %></TD>
39:         </TR>
40:         <TR><TD ALIGN="right" WIDTH="50%">Taken Sick Days: </TD>
41:             <TD><%= rs.getString("TAKENSICKDAYS") %></TD>
42:         </TR>
43:         <TR><TD ALIGN="right" WIDTH="50%">Total Personal Time(in hours): </TD>
44:             <TD><%= rs.getString("TOTALPERSONALTIME") %></TD>
45:         </TR>
46:         <TR><TD ALIGN="right" WIDTH="50%">Taken Personal Time(in hours): </TD>
47:             <TD><%= rs.getString("TAKENPERSONALTIME") %></TD>
48:         </TR>
49:         <TR><TD ALIGN="right" WIDTH="50%">Health Care Plan:</TD>
50:             <TD WIDTH="50%"><%= rs.getString("HEALTHCAREPLAN") %></TD>
51:         </TR>
52:         <TR><TD ALIGN="right" WIDTH="50%">Dental Plan:</TD>
53:             <TD WIDTH="50%"><%= rs.getString("DENTALPLAN") %></TD>
54:         </TR>
55:         <TR><TD ALIGN="right" WIDTH="50%">Vision Plan:</TD>
56:             <TD WIDTH="50%"><%= rs.getString("VISIONPLAN") %></TD>
57:         </TR>
58: <% }//end while loop
       } //end try block
       catch (Exception e) {}%>
59: </TABLE>
60: <%@ include file="SiteNavigator.html" %>
61: </BODY>
62: </HTML>
```

ANALYSIS   Since the JavaBean did not contain all the user's information, this JSP uses the employee's ID to retrieve his updated information from the database and present it.

23

Line 4 uses the `include` directive to include the code from the `CompanyBanner.html` file. Line 5 uses the page directive to import the `java.sql` package because this JSP (like some of the others) is going to do some database access. Lines 6–8 set up the JavaBean to retrieve the employee ID: the `id` is `empInfo`, the `scope` is `request` and the class is `EmployeeInfoBean`.

Line 15 starts a JSP scriptlet tag so Java code can be inserted into the JSP. Line 16 gets the employee ID out of the JavaBean by using an accessor method, and stores it in a variable called `employeeID`.

New Term: Accessor Methods

Accessor methods provide access to attributes of a JavaBean. They have the syntax of `getXXX()` and `setXXX(...)` where *XXX* is the name of the attribute. This gives users controlled access to the attributes.

The driver for the database is defined in line 17. (Since the database is a `cloudscape` database, its driver is `COM.cloudscape.core.JDBCDriver`.) A connection to the database is created in lines 18 and 19 with the `DriverManager` class from the `java.sql` package. Once a connection to the database is created, that connection can be used to create a `statement`, as is done in line 20. This JSP is selecting all of the columns in the database where the column ID matches the employee's ID, so line 21 defines the SQL statement to select this information.

Once you have a statement and an SQL string, you can execute that query and retrieve the information in a `ResultSet` object. Line 22 executes the query and stores the information in a `ResultSet` object.

Lines 23–58 make up a `while` loop that cycles through the information in the `ResultSet` and outputs the employee's information (see Figure 23.4).

Now you have finished your human resources Web site. You have provided your employees with numerous benefits through this site and allowed them to do minor maintenance on their personal profiles.

The next step is going to be bundling the application into a Web archive, a new concept in the Servlet 2.2 specification. A Web archive is much like a zip file on the Windows platform; it simply allows you to neatly bundle your application. In the next hour you will learn how to package these files into a Web archive and deploy them on WebLogic Server.

FIGURE 23.4

An HTML document allows users to change their personal information.

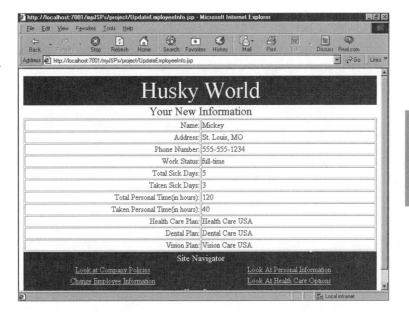

FIGURE 23.4

An HTML document allows users to change their personal information.

Summary

Throughout the book you have been learning the pieces of building JSPs, and now you have applied your knowledge to a real-life example. You have created a human resources Web site using JSPs and a couple JavaBeans. In Hour 22 you built JSPs that displayed company policies and benefits and personal benefits. This hour, you created the capabilities for the user to add a new employee and to change a current employee's information. You have seen two ways to access a database—from the JSP directly to the database, and with the JSP using a JavaBean to manage the connection to the database.

Q&A

Q Could some of these scenarios be implemented differently?

A Absolutely. Many of these scenarios could be implemented several different ways. Wherever there was database access directly from the JSP, that could have been accomplished through a server-side resource such as a JavaBean. Maybe your HTML forms would have been set up differently so that users could enter more information to change in their profiles.

Workshop

The quiz questions and activities are provided for your further understanding. See Appendix A, "Answers," for the answers to the quiz.

Quiz

1. What directive imported the appropriate files for doing database access?

2. What is a benefit of using the `include` directive?

3. When you execute an SQL statement on a database, what type of object is your data stored in?

Activity

You have created the capability of adding new employees, but what about removing employees? Map out how you would implement the capability of removing employees and then write the page(s) to do it.

HOUR 24

Packaging and Deploying an Enterprise Application

Your journey of JSP enlightenment has almost come to an end. However, there is one last part of the Husky World Human Resources Application project to complete. In Hour 21 you designed this human resources Web site to allow employees to change their current profiles, look at company policies, and look at their personal benefits. In Hours 22 and 23 you worked through the different scenarios of the Web site and you implemented the application with HTML documents, JSPs, and a couple of JavaBeans.

Now it is time to take that application and bundle it into a Web archive file. A Web archive file is a new concept defined in the Servlet 2.2 specification that describes how to bundle together a Web application into a single file that has a .war extension. The Web archive helps to organize your Web applications and to increase its portability.

In this hour you will learn

- What a Web Archive is
- The directory structure of a Web archive

- How to create a Web archive
- How to set up security on the project
- How to deploy the Web archive

What Is a Web Archive File?

A Web archive file is made up of server-side resources that comprise a Web application. The resources that compose this application can include

1. Servlets
2. JavaServer Pages
3. Static HTML documents
4. Server-side classes
5. Other resources specific to the application

The Servlet 2.2 specification describes the directory structure for this application and how to bundle the files in the portable Web archive (.war) file. The .war file is portable because it can be deployed on any Servlet 2.2 compliant server, whether it is a Web server or an application server.

Each Web archive file has a deployment descriptor that describes the resources that make up the Web application and how this application should be deployed on the server. It can describe welcome files, the JSPs and Servlets that are part of the application, and security constraints.

New Term: Welcome File

Welcome files are to greet users at a particular area on your Web site. This is the equivalent to the index.html file, in fact that is often the name of the file. If they don't ask for a particular document, you want to send them a file to help them navigate their way through your application. For example, if you request www.amazon.com, you are not requesting a particular file, but you get its home page. That is because Amazon has that file listed to be its welcome page.

You can think of a Web archive as similar to a WinZip file. It is used to bundle together, or package, files.

Setting Up the Directory Structure for the Web Archive

There is a specific directory structure defined for Web archive files. All of the resources that make up the Web application are categorized in this directory structure. The root of the archive is the root of the Web application. All files in the root of the Web application are considered public and can be served to clients. Two directories are located off the root directory: META-INF and WEB-INF. Files located under these two directories are considered private files and cannot be served to your clients.

Deployment descriptors are used to describe your Web application and the resources that it contains. You always have one deployment descriptor, web.xml, and you may have a second deployment descriptor, weblogic.xml, if you are deploying in BEA's WebLogic Server. The web.xml file describes the resources in the Web application, the welcome files, error pages, and security constraints. The weblogic.xml file handles mapping of external resources, such as EJBs. All deployment descriptors are located under the WEB-INF directory. You will be writing the web.xml file for the Husky World Human Resource Web site later this hour. Since that application does not access any EJBs, the second .xml file is not necessary.

Under the WEB-INF directory is a subdirectory named classes. This directory contains server-side classes such as Servlets, JavaBeans, and utility classes.

Another subdirectory of the WEB-INF directory is lib, which contains any jar files used be the application.

New Term: Jar File

A jar file is a way to bundle Java classes together. This is much like a Windows zip file. The jar utility is a utility that bundles the files. The jar utility is part of the Sun JDK. This is the same utility that you are going to use to create the .war files.

Now it is time to create the appropriate directory structure for the Husky World Human Resources Web site. For this Web application, create a directory called myWebApp under your c:\ directory. Within the c:\myWebApp directory, copy all the HTML and JSP files from the human resources project. The files should be located in c:\weblogic\myserver\ myJSPs\project. The files that should be copied into the myWebApp directory are

    AddNewEmployee.jsp

    CompanyBanner.html

    HumanResources.html

24

```
InputEmployeeInfo.html

InputNewEmployeeInfo.html

PersonalInfo.html

PersonalInfo.jsp

PresentChangeOfEmployeeData.jsp

PresentCompanyHealthCareInfo.jsp

PresentCompanyPolicies.jsp

PresentNewEmployeeInfo.jsp

PresentPersonalHealthCareInfo.jsp

PresentTimeOffData.jsp

SiteNavigator.hmtl

UpdateEmployeeInfo.jsp
```

Take a moment to think about some of these files. Are there any that should not be served to the client? Well, two files that should not be served to the client are `CompanyBanner.html` and `SiteNavigator.html`. These files are simply used in the JSP files and should not be sent individually to the client. Since these files should be private, place them in the `META-INF` directory. You are going to deploy your Web application into a server, and the server is going to look in the `META-INF` directory for the deployment descriptor(s).

Making Appropriate Changes to Your HTML and JSP Files

Now that the location of the files has changed, all of the HTML documents and JSPs need to be tweaked to reflect their new location. Instead of using direct URLs in the HTML files, you use relative paths for more flexibility.

There are a few files that do not need any modifications. They do not contain any hyperlinks or references to other documents in the Web application. The files that do not need any modifications are

```
CompanyBanner.html

PresentPersonalHealthCareInfo.jsp

PresentTimeOffData.jsp
```

One example of a file that needs changing is shown in Listing 24.1, the `SiteNavigator.html` file.

LISTING 24.1   HTML Document that Allows Easy Navigation Through the Web
Application (SiteNavigator.html)

```
 1: <BODY ALINK="yellow" VLINK="yellow" LINK="yellow">
 2: <TABLE WIDTH="100%" BORDER="0" BGCOLOR="navy">
 3:   <TR ALIGN="center">
 4:     <TD COLSPAN=2><FONT SIZE="4" COLOR="yellow">Site Navigator</FONT></TD>
 5:   </TR>
 6:   <TR ALIGN="center">
 7:     <TD><A HREF="./PresentCompanyPolicies.jsp"> <!--change in code-->
 8:         Look at Company Policies
 9:         </A>
10:     </TD>
11:     <TD><A HREF="./PersonalInfo.html"> <!--change in code-->
12:         Look At Personal Information
13:         </A>
14:     </TD>
15:   </TR>
16:   <TR ALIGN="center">
17:     <TD><A HREF="./InputEmployeeInfo.html"> <!--change in code-->
18:         Change Employee Information
19:         </A>
20:     </TD>
21:     <TD><A HREF="./PresentCompanyHealthCareInfo.jsp"> <!--change in code-->
22:         Look At Health Care Options
23:         </A>
24:     </TD>
25:   </TR>
26:   <TR ALIGN="center">
27:     <TD COLSPAN="2"><A HREF="./HumanResources.html"> <!--change in code-->
28:                     Home Page
29:                     </A>
30:     </TD>
31:   </TR>
32: </TABLE>
33: </BODY>
```

24

ANALYSIS   The hyperlinks to the other files need to be relative to the HTML page,
SiteNavigator.html. Line 7 is the first occurrence of a necessary change. The
hyperlink needs to be relative to the Web archive root instead of giving it the full URL to
the page. Therefore the . (dot) notation is used to specify the path of the current page,
which is the root of the current Web archive, and then the path and name of the appropriate file. So, line 7 specifies the hyperlink to go to the root of the Web archive and
serve the file PresentCompanyPolicies.jsp.

Other modifications include the following:

The hyperlink in Line 11 now requests the document in the root of the Web archive
named PersonalInfo.html.

Line 17 changes the hyperlink located in the anchor tag. The new hyperlink requests the document in the root of the Web archive named InputEmployeeInfo.html.

The hyperlink in Line 21 now specifies the file the JSP, PresentCompanyHealthCareInfo.jsp, in the root directory of the Web archive file.

The last modification to SiteNavigator.html is in line 27, where the hyperlink now specifies the file HumanResources.html in the root of the Web archive.

Now it is just a matter of going through each of the HTML and JSP files of the Husky World Human Resources Web application and updating the hyperlinks and references to other resources in the Web archive. Remember, the goal is to have relative paths instead of hard-coded paths so that the flexibility of moving the Web archive is increased.

Listing 24.2 is the code for the AddNewEmployee.jsp file. There is a comment in the code to show where the modification was made.

LISTING 24.2 The JSP to Add New Employees (AddNewEmployee.jsp)

```
1: <HTML>
2: <HEAD><TITLE>Update DB With New Employee Information</TITLE></HEAD>
3: <BODY>
4: <jsp:useBean id="newEmployee"
5:              class="jspin24hrs.project.NewEmployeeBean"
6:              scope="request"/>
7: <jsp:setProperty name="newEmployee" property="*"/>
8: <% newEmployee.updateDatabase(); %>
9: <jsp:forward page="/PresentNewEmployeeInfo.jsp" /> <!--change in code-->
10:
11: </BODY>
12: </HTML>
```

ANALYSIS Line 9 contains the hyperlink to PresentNewEmployeeInfo.jsp, which needed some tweaking. Listing 24.3 is the code for the HumanResources.html file. Again there are comments in the code pointing out the changes that were made.

LISTING 24.3 Home Page (HumanResources.html)

```
1: <HTML>
2: <HEAD><TITLE></TITLE></HEAD>
3: <BODY LINK="navy" ALINK="navy" VLINK="navy">
4:
5:
6: <!-- inserts the company banner -->
7: <TABLE WIDTH="100%" BORDER="0" BGCOLOR="navy">
8:   <TR ALIGN="center">
9:     <TD><FONT SIZE="7" COLOR="yellow">Husky World</FONT></TD>
```

LISTING 24.3   continued

```
10:    </TR>
11: </TABLE>
12:
13: <!-- the heading for the page -->
14: <CENTER>
15:    <FONT SIZE="5" COLOR="navy">
16:      Welcome To Your Human Resources Department Online<P>
17:    </FONT>
18:    <FONT SIZE="4" COLOR="navy">
19:        Select Where You Would Like To Go<P>
20:    </FONT>
21:
22: <!-- hyperlinks to the various scenarios of the web site -->
23: <A HREF="./PresentCompanyPolicies.jsp"> <!--change in code-->
24:    Take a Look At the Company Policies
25: </A>
26: <P>
27: <A HREF="./PresentCompanyHealthCareInfo.jsp"> <!--change in code-->
28:    Take a Look At Health Care Plan Options
29: </A>
30: <P>
31: <A HREF="./PersonalInfo.html"> <!--change in code-->
32:    Take a Look At Personal Information: time off, health care information
33: </A>
34: <P>
35: <A HREF="./InputEmployeeInfo.html"> <!--change in code-->
36:   Change Your Employee Information
37: </A><P>
38: <A HREF="./InputNewEmployeeInfo.html"> <!--change in code-->
39:    Add New Employee
40: </A>
41:
42: </CENTER>
43: </BODY>
44: </HTML>
```

ANALYSIS   Lines 23, 27, 31, 35, and 38 contain hyperlinks that needed to be modified. Listing 24.4 shows the code for InputEmployeeInfo.html with comments to point out the necessary changes.

LISTING 24.4   Changing Employee Information (InputEmployeeInfo.html)

```
1: <HTML>
2: <HEAD><TITLE>Change of Information</TITLE></HEAD>
3: <BODY>
4: <TABLE WIDTH="100%" BORDER="0" BGCOLOR="navy">
5:    <TR ALIGN="center">
```

24

LISTING 24.4   continued

```
 6:      <TD><FONT SIZE="7" COLOR="yellow">Husky World</FONT></TD>
 7:    </TR>
 8:  </TABLE>
 9:  <CENTER>
10:    <FONT SIZE="5" COLOR="navy">
11:      Please Enter Your Information<BR>
12:      Fill in all fields
13:    </FONT>
14:  </CENTER>
15:  <TABLE WIDTH="100%">
16:  <!--change the ACTION attribute in the FORM tag-->
17:  <FORM NAME="updateInfo"
18:        ACTION="./UpdateEmployeeInfo.jsp"
19:        METHOD="POST">
20:    <TR><TD WIDTH="40%" ALIGN="right">Current ID: </TD>
21:        <TD WIDTH="60%"><INPUT TYPE="text" NAME="id"></TD>
22:    </TR>
23:    <TR><TD WIDTH="40%" ALIGN="right">New Name: </TD>
24:        <TD WIDTH="60%"><INPUT TYPE="text" NAME="name" VALUE="Mickey"></TD>
25:    </TR>
26:    <TR><TD WIDTH="40%" ALIGN="right">New Address: </TD>
27:        <TD WIDTH="60%">
28:          <INPUT TYPE="text" NAME="address" VALUE="St. Louis, MO">
29:        </TD>
30:    </TR>
31:    <TR><TD WIDTH="40%" ALIGN="right">New Phone: </TD>
32:        <TD WIDTH="60%">
33:          <INPUT TYPE="text" NAME="phone" VALUE="555-555-1234">
34:        </TD>
35:    </TR>
36:    <TR><TD COLSPAN="2" ALIGN="center">
37:          <INPUT TYPE="submit" NAME="btnSubmit" VALUE="Update Profile"></TD>
38:    </TR>
39:  </TABLE>
40:  </FORM>
41:  </BODY>
42:  </HTML>
```

The only change that was required was the ACTION attribute in line 18. Listing 24.5 is the code for InputNewEmployeeInfo.html; as with the other files the change is commented.

LISTING 24.5   Adding New Employee Information (InputNewEmployeeInfo.html)

```
1: <HTML>
2: <HEAD><TITLE>New Employee Information</TITLE></HEAD>
3: <BODY>
4:
```

LISTING 24.5 continued

```
 5: <!-- insert the company banner -->
 6: <TABLE WIDTH="100%" BORDER="0" BGCOLOR="navy">
 7:   <TR ALIGN="center">
 8:     <TD><FONT SIZE="7" COLOR="yellow">Husky World</FONT></TD>
 9:   </TR>
10: </TABLE>
11:
12: <CENTER>
13:   <FONT SIZE="5" COLOR="navy">
14:     Enter The New Employee's Information
15:   </FONT>
16: </CENTER>
17:
18: <TABLE WIDTH="100%">
19: <!--change the ACTION attribute of the FORM tag -->
20: <FORM NAME="newEmployee"
21:       ACTION="./AddNewEmployee.jsp"
22:       METHOD="POST">
23:
24:   <TR><TD WIDTH="50%" ALIGN="right">Employee ID: </TD>
25:       <TD WIDTH="50%">
26:         <INPUT TYPE="text" NAME="id" VALUE="">
27:       </TD>
28:   </TR>
29:   <TR><TD WIDTH="50%" ALIGN="right">Name: </TD>
30:       <TD WIDTH="50%">
31:         <INPUT TYPE="text" NAME="name" VALUE="Peggy">
32:       </TD>
33:   </TR>
34:   <TR><TD WIDTH="50%" ALIGN="right">Address: </TD>
35:       <TD WIDTH="50%">
36:         <INPUT TYPE="text" NAME="address" VALUE="Maynard, MA">
37:       </TD>
38:   </TR>
39:   <TR><TD WIDTH="50%" ALIGN="right">Phone Number: </TD>
40:       <TD WIDTH="50%">
41:         <INPUT TYPE="text" NAME="phone" VALUE="555-555-7845">
42:       </TD>
43:   </TR>
44:   <TR><TD WIDTH="50%" ALIGN="right">Work Status: </TD>
45:       <TD WIDTH="50%">
46:         <INPUT TYPE="text" NAME="workstatus" VALUE="full-time">
47:       </TD>
48:   </TR>
49:   <TR><TD WIDTH="50%" ALIGN="right">Total Sick Days: </TD>
50:       <TD WIDTH="50%">
51:         <INPUT TYPE="text" NAME="totalSickDays" VALUE="5">
52:       </TD>
53:   </TR>
54:   <TR><TD WIDTH="50%" ALIGN="right">Taken Sick Days: </TD>
```

24

LISTING 24.5   continued

```
55:        <TD WIDTH="50%">
56:          <INPUT TYPE="text" NAME="takenSickDays" VALUE="0">
57:        </TD>
58:    </TR>
59:    <TR><TD WIDTH="50%" ALIGN="right">Total Personal Time(in hours): </TD>
60:        <TD WIDTH="50%">
61:          <INPUT TYPE="text" NAME="totalPersonalTime" VALUE="120">
62:        </TD>
63:    </TR>
64:    <TR><TD WIDTH="50%" ALIGN="right">Taken Personal Time(in hours):</TD>
65:        <TD WIDTH="50%">
66:          <INPUT TYPE="text" NAME="takenPersonalTime" VALUE="0">
67:        </TD>
68:    </TR>
69:    <TR><TD WIDTH="50%" ALIGN="right">Health Care Plan: </TD>
70:        <TD WIDTH="50%">
71:          <INPUT TYPE="text" NAME="healthCarePlan" VALUE="Health Care USA">
72:        </TD>
73:    </TR>
74:    <TR><TD WIDTH="50%" ALIGN="right">Dental Plan: </TD>
75:        <TD WIDTH="50%">
76:          <INPUT TYPE="text" NAME="dentalPlan" VALUE="Dental USA">
77:        </TD>
78:    </TR>
79:    <TR><TD WIDTH="50%" ALIGN="right">Vision Plan: </TD>
80:        <TD WIDTH="50%">
81:          <INPUT TYPE="text" NAME="visionPlan" VALUE="Vision USA">
82:        </TD>
83:    </TR>
84:    <TR><TD COLSPAN="2" ALIGN="center">
85:          <INPUT TYPE="submit" NAME="btnSubmit" VALUE="Add New Employee"></TD>
86:    </TR>
87: </FORM>
88: </TABLE>
89: </BODY>
90: </HTML>
```

Line 21 contains the ACTION attribute of the FORM tag, which is the only change necessary for this JSP. Listing 24.6 is the code for the HTML page, PersonalInfo.html.

LISTING 24.6   Retrieving Personal Information (PersonalInfo.html)

```
1: <HTML>
2: <HEAD><TITLE>Retrieve Personal Information</TITLE></HEAD>
3: <BODY ALINK="yellow" VLINK="yellow" LINK="yellow">
4:
5: <!-- insert the company banner -->
```

LISTING 24.6   continued

```
 6: <TABLE WIDTH="100%" BORDER="0" BGCOLOR="navy">
 7:   <TR ALIGN="center">
 8:      <TD><FONT SIZE="7" COLOR="yellow">Husky World</FONT></TD>
 9:   </TR>
10: </TABLE>
11:
12: <!-- tells the user what to input -->
13: <CENTER>
14:   <FONT SIZE="5" COLOR="navy">
15:     Enter Your Employee ID And Select Info To View<P>
16:   </FONT>
17: </CENTER>
18:
19: <!-- the user inserts their id and selects what to view -->
20: <TABLE WIDTH="100%">
21: <FORM NAME="EmployeeID"
22:     ACTION="./PersonalInfo.jsp"
23:     METHOD="POST">
24: <TR ALIGN="center">
25:   <TD>Employee ID:
26:      <INPUT TYPE="text" NAME="id" VALUE="1" SIZE="10">
27:   </TD>
28: </TR>
29: <TR><TD> </TD></TR> <!-- blank row -->
30: <TR ALIGN="center">
31:   <TD><INPUT TYPE="checkbox" NAME="timeOff" VALUE="getTimeOff" CHECKED>
32:       Get Personal Time Off Information
33:   </TD>
34: </TR>
35: <TR><TD> </TD></TR> <!-- blank row -->
36: <TR ALIGN="center">
37:   <TD><INPUT TYPE="checkbox" NAME="healthCare" VALUE="getHealthCare"
     CHECKED>
38:       Get Personal Health Care Information
39:   </TD>
40: </TR>
41: <TR><TD> </TD></TR> <!-- blank row -->
42: <TR ALIGN="center">
43:   <TD><INPUT TYPE="submit"
44:             NAME="btnSubmit"
45:             VALUE="Get Personal Information">
46:   </TD>
47: </TR>
48: </FORM>
49: </TABLE>
50:
51: <BR><BR>
52:
53: <!-- insert the site navigator -->
54: <BODY ALINK="yellow" VLINK="yellow" LINK="yellow">
```

24

LISTING 24.6　continued

```
55: <TABLE WIDTH="100%" BORDER="0" BGCOLOR="navy">
56:   <TR ALIGN="center">
57:     <TD COLSPAN=2><FONT SIZE="4" COLOR="yellow">Site Navigator</FONT></TD>
58:   </TR>
59:   <TR ALIGN="center">
60:     <TD><A HREF="./PresentCompanyPolicies.jsp"> <!--change in code-->
61:          Look at Company Policies
62:          </A>
63:     </TD>
64:     <TD><A HREF="./PersonalInfo.html"> <!--change in code-->
65:          Look At Personal Information
66:          </A>
67:     </TD>
68:   </TR>
69:   <TR ALIGN="center">
70:     <TD><A HREF="./InputEmployeeInfo.html"> <!--change in code-->
71:          Change Employee Information
72:          </A>
73:     </TD>
74:     <TD><A HREF="./PresentCompanyHealthCareInfo.jsp"> <!--change in code-->
75:          Look At Health Care Options
76:          </A>
77:     </TD>
78:   </TR>
79:   <TR ALIGN="center">
80:     <TD COLSPAN="2"><A HREF="./HumanResources.html"> <!--change in code-->
81:                     Home Page
82:                     </A>
83:     </TD>
84:   </TR>
85: </TABLE>
86: </BODY>
87: </HTML>
```

Keep in mind that some of the .jsp files have a little more work involved when changing the paths to relative paths. For example, Listing 24.7 shows the code for the JSP PresentChangeOfEmployeeInfo.jsp.

LISTING 24.7　Presenting the Change of Employee Information (PresentChangeOfEmployeeInfo.jsp)

```
1: <HTML>
2: <HEAD><TITLE></TITLE></HEAD>
3: <BODY>
4: <%@ include file="WEB-INF/CompanyBanner.html" %> <!--change in code-->
5: <%@ page import="java.sql.*" %>
6: <jsp:useBean id="empInfo"
7:          class="jspin24hrs.project.EmployeeInfoBean"
```

LISTING 24.7 continued

```
 8:              scope="request"/>
 9: <CENTER>
10:   <FONT SIZE="5" COLOR="navy">
11:     Your New Information
12:   </FONT>
13: </CENTER>
14: <TABLE WIDTH="100%" BORDER="1">
15: <%
16:     int employeeID = empInfo.getId();
17:     try {
18:     Class.forName("COM.cloudscape.core.JDBCDriver").newInstance();
19:     Connection conn =
20:       DriverManager.getConnection("jdbc:cloudscape:c:\\HumanResourcesDB");
21:     Statement statement = conn.createStatement();
22:     String sql = "SELECT * FROM EMPLOYEEINFO WHERE ID = " + employeeID;
23:     ResultSet rs = statement.executeQuery(sql);
24:     while(rs.next()){
25: %>
26:       <TR><TD ALIGN="right" WIDTH="50%">Name:</TD>
27:         <TD WIDTH="50%"><%= rs.getString("NAME") %></TD>
28:       </TR>
29:       <TR><TD ALIGN="right" WIDTH="50%">Address:</TD>
30:         <TD WIDTH="50%"><%= rs.getString("ADDRESS") %></TD>
31:       </TR>
32:       <TR><TD ALIGN="right" WIDTH="50%">Phone Number:</TD>
33:         <TD WIDTH="50%"><%= rs.getString("PHONE") %></TD>
34:       </TR>
35:       <TR><TD ALIGN="right" WIDTH="50%">Work Status:</TD>
36:         <TD WIDTH="50%"><%= rs.getString("WORKSTATUS") %></TD>
37:       </TR>
38:       <TR><TD ALIGN="right" WIDTH="50%">Total Sick Days:</TD>
39:         <TD> <%= rs.getString("TOTALSICKDAYS") %></TD>
40:       </TR>
41:       <TR><TD ALIGN="right" WIDTH="50%">Taken Sick Days: </TD>
42:         <TD><%= rs.getString("TAKENSICKDAYS") %></TD>
43:       </TR>
44:       <TR><TD ALIGN="right" WIDTH="50%">Total Personal Time(in hours): </TD>
45:         <TD><%= rs.getString("TOTALPERSONALTIME") %></TD>
46:       </TR>
47:       <TR><TD ALIGN="right" WIDTH="50%">Taken Personal Time(in hours): </TD>
48:         <TD><%= rs.getString("TAKENPERSONALTIME") %></TD>
49:       </TR>
50:       <TR><TD ALIGN="right" WIDTH="50%">Health Care Plan:</TD>
51:         <TD WIDTH="50%"><%= rs.getString("HEALTHCAREPLAN") %></TD>
52:       </TR>
53:       <TR><TD ALIGN="right" WIDTH="50%">Dental Plan:</TD>
54:         <TD WIDTH="50%"><%= rs.getString("DENTALPLAN") %></TD>
55:       </TR>
56:       <TR><TD ALIGN="right" WIDTH="50%">Vision Plan:</TD>
57:         <TD WIDTH="50%"><%= rs.getString("VISIONPLAN") %></TD>
```

24

LISTING 24.7   continued

```
58:      </TR>
59: <% }//end while loop
60:    } // end try block
61:    catch (Exception e) {};
62: %>
63: </TABLE>
64: <%@ include file="WEB-INF/SiteNavigator.html" %> <!--change in code-->
65: </BODY>
66: </HTML>
```

This JSP uses the include directive to dynamically include the code from two HTML files, CompanyBanner.html and SiteNavigator.html. Well, those two HTML documents were moved to the WEB-INF directory in the Web archive so they would be private and not served to clients. Therefore, references to these files need to reflect the change of location.

Line 4 is the include directive for the HTML file CompanyBanner.html. Notice the file attribute now specifies the location of the file to be in the WEB-INF directory.

Line 64 is the include directive for the HTML document SiteNavigator.html. Again, this file attribute reflects the change in location of SiteNavigator.html to the WEB-INF directory.

Listing 24.8 shows the code for PresentCompanyHealthCareInfo.jsp and comments indicate the necessary changes.

LISTING 24.8   Presenting the Company Health Care Benefits
(PresentCompanyHealthCareInfo.jsp)

```
 1: <HTML>
 2: <HEAD><TITLE>Health Plan Information</TITLE></HEAD>
 3: <BODY>
 4:
 5: <%@ include file="WEB-INF/CompanyBanner.html" %> <!--change in code-->
 6: <%@ page import="java.sql.*" %>
 7:
 8: <CENTER>
 9:    <FONT SIZE="5" COLOR="navy">
10:      Health, Vision, And Dental Plans
11:    </FONT>
12: </CENTER>
13:
14: <TABLE WIDTH="100%" BORDER="1">
15:    <TH WIDTH="40%">Plan Name</TH>
16:    <TH WIDTH="20%">Deductible</TH>
17:    <TH WIDTH="20%">Coverage for Doctors in Plan</TH>
18:    <TH WIDTH="20%">Coverage for Doctors out of Plan</TH>
19: <%
```

LISTING 24.8 continued

```
20:    Class.forName("COM.cloudscape.core.JDBCDriver").newInstance();
21:    Connection conn =
22:      DriverManager.getConnection("jdbc:cloudscape:c:\\HumanResourcesDB");
23:    Statement statement = conn.createStatement();
24:    String sql = "SELECT * FROM BENEFITINFO";
25:    ResultSet rs = statement.executeQuery(sql);
26:    while (rs.next()) {
27: %>
28:    <TR><TD><%= rs.getString("PLANNAME") %></TD>
29:      <TD ALIGN="center"><%= rs.getString("DEDUCTIBLE") %></TD>
30:      <TD ALIGN="center"><%= rs.getString("DOCTORSINPLANCOVERAGE") %></TD>
31:      <TD ALIGN="center"><%= rs.getString("DOCTORSOUTOFPLANCOVERAGE") %></TD>
32:    </TR>
33: <% } //end while loop
34:    if (statement != null)
35:      statement.close();
36:    if (conn != null)
37:      conn.close();
38: %>
39: </TABLE>
40: <BR>
41: <%@ include file="WEB-INF/SiteNavigator.html" %> <!--change in code-->
42: </BODY>
43: </HTML>
```

Listing 24.9, the code for `PresentCompanyPolicies.jsp`, needs similar changes to the include directives.

LISTING 24.9 Presenting the Company Policies (`PresentCompanyPolicies.jsp`)

```
1: <HTML>
2: <HEAD><TITLE>Company Policies</TITLE></HEAD>
3: <BODY>
4:
5: <%@ include file="WEB-INF/CompanyBanner.html" %> <!--change in code-->
6: <%@ page import="java.sql.*" %>
7:
8: <CENTER>
9:   <FONT SIZE="5" COLOR="navy">
10:     Company Policies
11:   </FONT>
12: </CENTER>
13:
14: <!-- Company policy -->
15: <FONT SIZE="4">
16:   Our number one company policy at Husky World is to
17:   be nice to your fellow co-workers. And always be nice
18:   to doggies.
```

LISTING 24.9   continued

```
19: </FONT>
20:
21: <BR>
22:
23: <CENTER>
24:   <FONT SIZE="5" COLOR="navy">
25:     Health, Vision, And Dental Plans
26:   </FONT>
27: </CENTER>
28:
29: <TABLE WIDTH="100%">
30:   <TH WIDTH="40%">Plan Name</TH>
31:   <TH WIDTH="20%">Deductible</TH>
32:   <TH WIDTH="20%">Coverage for Doctors in Plan</TH>
33:   <TH WIDTH="20%">Coverage for Doctors out of Plan</TH>
34: <%
35:   Class.forName("COM.cloudscape.core.JDBCDriver").newInstance();
36:   Connection conn =
37:     DriverManager.getConnection("jdbc:cloudscape:c:\\HumanResourcesDB");
38:   Statement statement = conn.createStatement();
39:   String sql = "SELECT * FROM BENEFITINFO";
40:   ResultSet rs = statement.executeQuery(sql);
41:   while (rs.next()) {
42: %>
43:   <TR><TD><%= rs.getString("PLANNAME") %></TD>
44:       <TD><%= rs.getString("DEDUCTIBLE") %></TD>
45:       <TD><%= rs.getString("DOCTORSINPLANCOVERAGE") %></TD>
46:       <TD><%= rs.getString("DOCTORSOUTOFPLANCOVERAGE") %></TD>
47:   </TR>
48: <% } //end while loop
49:   if (statement != null)
50:     statement.close();
51:   if (conn != null)
52:     conn.close();
53: %>
54: </TABLE>
55:
56: <BR>
57:
58: <%@ include file="WEB-INF/SiteNavigator.html" %> <!--change in code-->
59: </BODY>
60: </HTML>
```

Another JSP, `PresentNewEmployeeInfo.jsp`, and another two changes are necessary. Listing 24.10 shows the code for `PresentNewEmployeeInfo.jsp` and comments point out the modifications.

LISTING 24.10 Presenting New Employee Information (`PresentNewEmployeeInfo.jsp`)

```
 1: <HTML>
 2: <HEAD><TITLE>Present New Employee Information</TITLE></HEAD>
 3: <BODY>
 4: <%@ include file="WEB-INF/CompanyBanner.html" %> <!--change in code-->
 5: <jsp:useBean id="newEmployee"
 6:              class="jspin24hrs.project.NewEmployeeBean"
 7:              scope="request"/>
 8: <CENTER>
 9:   <FONT SIZE="5" COLOR="navy">
10:     New Employee Has Been Entered Into The Database
11:   </FONT>
12: </CENTER>
13: <TABLE WIDTH="100%" BORDER="1">
14:   <TR><TD ALIGN="right" WIDTH="50%">Name:</TD>
15:       <TD WIDTH="50%"><%= newEmployee.getName() %></TD>
16:   </TR>
17:   <TR><TD ALIGN="right" WIDTH="50%">Address:</TD>
18:       <TD WIDTH="50%"><%= newEmployee.getAddress() %></TD>
19:   </TR>
20:   <TR><TD ALIGN="right" WIDTH="50%">Phone Number:</TD>
21:       <TD WIDTH="50%"><%= newEmployee.getPhone() %></TD>
22:   </TR>
23:   <TR><TD ALIGN="right" WIDTH="50%">Work Status:</TD>
24:       <TD WIDTH="50%"><%= newEmployee.getWorkstatus() %></TD>
25:   </TR>
26:   <TR><TD ALIGN="right" WIDTH="50%">Total Sick Days:</TD>
27:       <TD> <%= newEmployee.getTotalSickDays() %></TD>
28:   </TR>
29:   <TR><TD ALIGN="right" WIDTH="50%">Taken Sick Days: </TD>
30:       <TD><%= newEmployee.getTakenSickDays() %></TD>
31:   </TR>
32:   <TR><TD ALIGN="right" WIDTH="50%">Total Personal Time (in hours): </TD>
33:       <TD><%= newEmployee.getTotalPersonalTime() %></TD>
34:   </TR>
35:   <TR><TD ALIGN="right" WIDTH="50%">Taken Personal Time  (in hours): </TD>
36:       <TD><%= newEmployee.getTakenPersonalTime() %></TD>
37:   </TR>
38:   <TR><TD ALIGN="right" WIDTH="50%">Health Care Plan:</TD>
39:       <TD WIDTH="50%"><%= newEmployee.getHealthCarePlan() %></TD>
40:   </TR>
41:   <TR><TD ALIGN="right" WIDTH="50%">Dental Plan:</TD>
42:       <TD WIDTH="50%"><%= newEmployee.getDentalPlan() %></TD>
43:   </TR>
44:   <TR><TD ALIGN="right" WIDTH="50%">Vision Plan:</TD>
45:       <TD WIDTH="50%"><%= newEmployee.getVisionPlan() %></TD>
46:   </TR>
47: </TABLE>
48: <%@ include file="WEB-INF/SiteNavigator.html" %> <!--change in code-->
49: </BODY>
50: </HTML>
```

24

Once all the files are up to date, you can write the deployment descriptor that describes your resources in the Web application.

Creating the Deployment Descriptor

Web archive files contain one, possibly two, deployment descriptors, which are used to describe the resources in the Web application, any security constraints, and references to external resources. XML is used to write these deployment descriptors. The one deployment descriptor you will always have is named web.xml. An optional second descriptor file is named weblogic.xml, if you are deploying on BEA's WebLogic Server. The web.xml file describes the resources of the Web application, welcome files, error pages, and security constraints. The weblogic.xml file describes mappings to external resources such as EJBs. Both .xml files are located in the WEB-INF directory.

Are you ready to write the deployment descriptor for the human resources Web application? Since this application did not use any external resources, the weblogic.xml file is not needed. You only need to write the web.xml deployment descriptor. Listing 24.11 shows the code for the web.xml file for the application.

The Extensible Markup Language (XML) is used throughout the J2EE platform to describe applications. Since XML is a meta-language, it describes other tag languages, and it is a great way to describe you own documents and the elements of those documents.

LISTING 24.11   Deployment Descriptor for the Human Resources Web Application (web.xml)

```
 1: <?xml version="1.0"?>
 2: <!DOCTYPE web-app PUBLIC
 3:    "-//Sun Microsystems, Inc.//DTD Web Application 1.2//EN"
 4:    "http://java.sun.com/j2ee/dtds/web-app_2_2.dtd">
 5:
 6: <web-app>
 7:    <context-param>
 8:       <param-name>weblogic.jsp.compileCommand</param-name>
 9:       <param-value>d:/jdk1.2.2/bin/javac.exe</param-value>
10:    </context-param>
11:    <context-param>
12:       <param-name>weblogic.jsp.pageCheckSeconds</param-name>
13:       <param-value>1</param-value>
14:    </context-param>
15:    <servlet>
```

LISTING 24.11   continued

```
16:            <servlet-name>AddNewEmployee</servlet-name>
17:            <jsp-file>AddNewEmployee.jsp</jsp-file>
18:        </servlet>
19:        <servlet>
20:          <servlet-name>PersonalInformation</servlet-name>
21:          <jsp-file>PersonalInfo.jsp</jsp-file>
22:        </servlet>
23:        <servlet>
24:            <servlet-name>PresentChangeofEmployeeData</servlet-name>
25:            <jsp-file>PresentChangeOfEmployeeData.jsp</jsp-file>
26:        </servlet>
27:        <servlet>
28:            <servlet-name>PresentCompanyHealthCareInfo</servlet-name>
29:            <jsp-file>PresentCompanyHealthCareInfo.jsp</jsp-file>
30:        </servlet>
31:        <servlet>
32:            <servlet-name>PresentCompanyPolicies</servlet-name>
33:            <jsp-file>PresentCompanyPolicies.jsp</jsp-file>
34:        </servlet>
35:        <servlet>
36:            <servlet-name>PresentNewEmployeeInfo</servlet-name>
37:            <jsp-file>PresentNewEmployeeInfo.jsp</jsp-file>
38:        </servlet>
39:        <servlet>
40:            <servlet-name>PresentPersonalHealthCareInfo</servlet-name>
41:            <jsp-file>PresentPersonalHealthCareInfo.jsp</jsp-file>
42:        </servlet>
43:        <servlet>
44:            <servlet-name>PresentTimeOffData</servlet-name>
45:            <jsp-file>PresentTimeOffData.jsp</jsp-file>
46:        </servlet>
47:        <servlet>
48:            <servlet-name>UpdateEmployeeInfo</servlet-name>
49:            <jsp-file>UpdateEmployeeInfo.jsp</jsp-file>
50:        </servlet>
51:        <welcome-file-list>
52:          <welcome-file>HumanResources.html</welcome-file>
53:        </welcome-file-list>
54:        <login-config>
55:          <auth-method>BASIC</auth-method>
56:        </login-config>
57:    </web-app>
```

24

ANALYSIS   The first line in the code is located at the top of all XML files. It simply states that this document is an XML document version 1.0.

The content of the web.xml file is surrounded with a <web-app> tag. The tag starts on line 6 and closes on line 57. Within the <web-app> tag is where the real content of the document lies, specifying your Servlets and JSPs, welcome files, and security on the Web application.

Recall from Hour 4, "Configuring Application Servers," that you set up a Servlet named JSPServlet in the weblogic.properties file to handle all requests with the .jsp extension. After you registered the JSPServlet, you set up initial arguments such as the compileCommand that pointed to your JDK compiler. Well, the JSPServlet is automatically registered for your Web archive files. However, you need to specify the initial arguments still in the web.xml file. You use the <context-param> tag to surround the initial argument name and value you are specifying. Lines 7–10 use the <context-param> tag to specify the JDK compiler to use. Line 8 has the name of the parameter, <param-name>, specified to weblogic.jsp.compileCommand. Line 9 sets the value, <param-value>, of the compileCommand attribute to be d:/jdk1.2.2/bin/javac.exe. Again, this is the compiler you want to use to compile the Java in the JSPs.

In this file you need to declare the Servlet and/or JSPs in your Web application. The human resources Web application does not contain any Servlets, but it does contain many JSPs. The <servlet> tag is used to declare Servlets and JSPs. The <servlet> tag contains other tags—<servlet-name> and <jsp-file> —if you are declaring JSPs. Take a look at lines 15–18 for a moment. In this example, a JSP AddNewEmployee.jsp is declared as part of the Web application and assigned the name AddNewEmployee. This set of tags is repeated for each of the JSPs in the Web application.

In the web.xml file, you can specify files to be welcome files. That way if the client does not request a particular file but has a more generic request, such as http://www.amazon.com, a document will be sent instead of showing a directory structure of amazon.com. Line 51 is the <welcome-file-list> that starts a list of <welcome-file> tags specifying your welcome files. Line 52 states that HumanResources.html is a welcome page for this Web application.

Security on your Web application can be specified in the web.xml file. For a human resources Web application it makes sense that only employees should have access to the application. Therefore, you use the <login-config> tag to specify that a login to the system is required. Lines 54–56 use this `<login-config>` and line 55 specifies the authentication method to be BASIC. This means users will be sent a dialog box asking for them to insert their usernames and passwords.

If security is set up on the human resources Web application, you are going to need to set up usernames and passwords. Usernames and passwords can be configured in your `weblogic.properties` file. The general syntax of specifying a username and password is

```
weblogic.password.UserName=Password
```

You need to specify a username and password for each employee. The following lines can be added to your `weblogic.properties` file to add some users.

```
weblogic.password.Mickey=IloveMyMommy
weblogic.password.Minnie=IloveMyDaddy
weblogic.password.Todd=ChicagoIL
weblogic.password.Stacie=StLouisMO
weblogic.password.Mary=BostonMA
```

Once you place these lines in the `weblogic.properties` file and then restart WLS, you will have five users: Mickey, Minnie, Todd, Stacie, and Mary. These people will be able to sign in to your Web application by providing their usernames and passwords.

Generating the `.war` File

The Web archive file is created using the `jar` utility, which packages Java classes much like a WinZip program. The following instructions explain how to create a `.war` file:

1. Begin a DOS prompt and make sure that your JDK is in your system path. This allows you to use the JDK commands such as `java`, `javac`, and `jar`. You can set the environment variable in the DOS prompt by stating:

   ```
   set PATH=Path_To_Your_JDK_Bin_Directory
   ```

   such as:

   ```
   set PATH=c:\jdk1.2.2\bin
   ```

2. Go to the root directory of your Web application; for this example, it is myWebApp.

3. Now that you are in the root directory of your Web application, the `jar` utility can be used to generate the `.war` file. The command to generate the Web archive is

   ```
   c:\myWebApp>jar cf HumanResources.war *
   ```

   The option `cf` specifies to create a new file and specify the filename. The filename of the Web archive will be HumanResources.war and the asterisk specifies to add all files and subdirectories to the Web archive.

24

Congratulations on creating your first Web archive file. Since your application is in the .war file it is much more portable on your system. This .war file can be taken and deployed from anywhere on your system.

Deploying the .war File

Now that you have generated your Web archive file, it is time to deploy it on WebLogic Server. Deployment involves mapping the Web archive name to a context. This context is how the user is going to request documents from his browser. All you have to do to deploy the .war is add one line to the weblogic.properties file:

```
weblogic.httpd.webApp.humanResources=c:\\myWebApp\\HumanResources.war
```

This gives the application the context name of humanResources and it points to the .war file you created.

Making Requests to Your Application

You have created the Web archive file and deployed it on WebLogic Server. Now it is time to make requests on the Web application. Open your browser of choice, whether that is Internet Explorer or Netscape Navigator. For the URL you state the name of your server, the listen port, and then the context name you assigned to your Web archive file. For example, **http://localhost:7001/humanResources**. Since you are not requesting a particular file, you are served the welcome file, the HTML document HumanResources. html. Figure 24.1 is a snapshot of the welcome page, HumanResources.html.

FIGURE 24.1

Viewing the welcome page of the Husky World Human Resources Web site from the Web archive file.

Navigate through the Web application and notice the URL of the pages. You will see that all the pages are being requested through the context you specified, humanResources.

Summary

Web applications can be bundled into Web archive files to make for easy portability. The Web archive files are deployed on a server. For BEA WebLogic server you just needed to add one line to the weblogic.properties file and, when the server starts, your Web application is deployed.

Congratulations on all your work so far. The wondrous journey of JSP enlightenment has come to an end for now, but never stop learning and always work hard and have fun.

Q&A

Q Now that I have learned JSPs, where do I go from here?

A If you want to learn the Java Enterprise Platform (JEP), the next step could be learning Servlet programming. You should brush up on your Java skills before tackling this, however. After brushing up on your Java skills, you can move into technologies such as RMI and EJBs. Just do one technology at a time and you will be fine. Just remember, never stop learning.

Workshop

The quiz questions and activities are provided for your further understanding. See Appendix A, "Answers," for the answers to the quiz.

Quiz

1. What is a benefit of a Web archive file?

2. What specification describes Web archive files?

3. What XML file is used to describe the Web application, and where is this file located?

Activity

CompanyBanner.html and SiteNavigator.html are probably not the only files that should not be served to the client. What other files should not be served to the client? Modify the Web archive structure and then the HTML and JSP files to reflect these changes.

APPENDIX A

Answers

Answers for Hour 1, "Introduction to Web Applications"

Quiz

1. What are the four types of Web structures?

   The Static Web, the Plug-In Web, the Dynamic Web, and the N-tier Web.

2. Why are there so many parts to the N-tier Web?

   So that each part can concentrate on its responsibilities and optimize them as much as possible. It follows the philosophy: Do one thing and do it well.

3. What are the two types of client-side scripting languages, and what can they do?

   JavaScript and VBScript are the two types of client-side scripting languages. They allow small business applications, such as form validation, to run on the client.

Answers for Hour 2, "Building Your First JSP"

Quiz

1. What is a CGI program?

   A CGI program is a server-side program that generates dynamic content to a Web client. They can be written in C, C++, Perl, and Java.

2. What are the similarities between ASPs and JSPs? What are some of the benefits of JSPs?

   ASPs and JSPs are both CGI programs that deliver dynamic content with HTML documents. Because they both reside on the server, they have access to server-side resources. Another similarity is their syntax. The tags they use to embed VBScript and Java are very similar.

   Some benefits of JSPs are the portability of JSPs and JSPs use the powerful programming language of Java.

3. What extension do you save JSPs with and how do you specify it when saving in a text editor?

   Save JSPs with a `.jsp` extension. Remember when saving using Notepad to save it as a text document and surround the name of the file with double quotations. This will prevent Notepad from adding the `.txt` extension.

Answers for Hour 3, "Introduction to Servlets"

Quiz

1. What method, in the lifecycle of a JSP/Servlet, is used for initialization?

   The `init(...)` method is used to initialize a JSP/Servlet. An object that implements the `ServletConfig` interface is passed in as one of the arguments and this makes it possible to retrieve initialization parameters.

2. What kind of Servlet accepts HTTP requests and generates HTTP responses?

   An `HttpServlet` accepts HTTP requests and generates HTTP responses. This is the type of Servlet that is used on the Web.

3. Describe the `doXXX(...)` methods.

   The `doXXX(...)` methods are used to process form requests depending on the type of method used by the form. If the form sent the data by the GET method, the `doGet(...)` method is used. If the form used the POST method, the `doPost(...)` method is used.

Answers for Hour 4, "Configuring Application Servers"

Quiz

1. What happens if you set the initial argument property `pageCheckSecs` equal to `0`?

   If the `pageCheckSecs` is equal to `0`, WLS will always check to see if the JSP has been modified since the last request. If it has, WLS will translate it into the Servlet code and then compile it to the bytecode before executing.

2. Where do you place you JSP files for this book? How does that correlate to the URL you use to request them?

   The JSP files are located under `myserver/public_html/myJSPs/hourX`, where X stands for the hour you are working in. This means when you make a request to a JSP, you need to provide the path to it, such as `http://localhost:7001/myJSPs/hour4`.

Answers for Hour 5, "Understanding the JSP Application Models"

Quiz

1. What application model describes using server-side resources such as EJBs to manage your backend resources?

   The N-tier Model describes JSPs using EJBs to manage resources to backend systems such as databases and legacy systems.

2. What actions are used in the Including Requests Model and the Forwarding Requests Model, respectively?

   The `include` action is used for the Including Requests Model and the `forward` action is used for the Forwarding Requests Model.

3. If your application follows the Loosely Coupled Model and one JSP changes, does it affect the other JSP application?

   In the Loosely Coupled Model one JSP application does not need to change if the other one has.

A

Answers for Hour 6, "Understanding the Layout of a JSP"

Quiz

1. What are four of the implicit or built-in objects available to a JSP?

   The implicit objects available to a JSP are `request`, `response`, `session`, `out`, `config`, `pageContext`, `application`, and `page`.

2. What is the JSP declaration tag used for?

   The JSP declaration tag is used to declare variables and methods. These can then be referenced by their declared name or identifier throughout the rest of the JSP source code.

Answers for Hour 7, "Declaring Variables and Methods in a JSP"

Quiz

1. What is method overloading?

   Method overloading consists of declaring several methods with the same name but different signature. A method signature consists of the combination of the return type, method name, and argument list. Method overloading is used to provide a functionality without limiting the type of the input data needed to provide the functionality.

2. What is a data type?

   A data type is a classification of the format of data and its characteristics. The characteristics of a data type consists of the format for representing the data in memory, the value of the data and the operations that can operate on the data.

3. How are `Enumerations` and `Vectors` related to one another?

   `Enumerations` and `Vectors` are both collections of objects. They are available in the standard Java package `java.util` as `java.util.Enumeration` and `java.util.Vector`. You can get an enumeration of the elements in a `Vector` as an `Enumeration` by using the method `Vector.elements()`.

Answers for Hour 8, "Inserting Java Expressions in a JSP"

Quiz

1. What happens when a JSP evaluates a JavaBean instance?

   The toString() method of the JavaBean is called to get the string representation of the object. If the method is not defined, the JSP searches up the inheritance tree of the object until it finds a toString() method. If none can be found, the JSP uses the toString() method for the Object class since all classes inherit from the Object class.

Answers for Hour 9, "Controlling JSPs with Java Scriplets"

Quiz

1. What are the differences and similarities of the break and continue statements?

   Both the break and continue statements are used to interrupt the normal flow of execution. They are both meant to be used within a Java code block nested within another Java code block. The break statement in the inner Java code block causes execution to halt and continue in the outer code block. The continue statement is intended to be used in an iterative control structure. A continue statement will cause execution to halt and continue with the next iteration.

2. How would you implement a for loop using a while loop?

   Consider the syntax of the for loop:

   ```
   for(initStatement; conditionalExpression; updateStatement){
       ...
       javaStatements
       ...
   }
   ```

   The initStatement is executed once and is usually used to initialize an iteration variable. The iteration variable is tested in the conditionalStatement every time the loop is executed to see if the loop should continue. The conditionalExpression usually consists of comparing the iteration variable to some boundary value. Every time around the loop the for loop executes the updateStatement, which usually increments or decrements the iteration variable toward its boundary value. The javaStatements are executed once every iteration.

A

To implement the `for` loop using a `while`, all the actions taken by the `for` loop must be implemented. The initialization of the `iteration` variable can easily be accomplished right before the beginning of the `while` loop. The updating of the iteration variable can be done at the very end of the loop. The `conditionalExpression` can be implemented in the `while`'s `conditionalExpression`. The following is a generic `while` statement that implements a generic `for` loop:

```
initStatement;
while(conditionalExpression){
    ...
    javaStatements
    ...
    updateStatement
}
```

So the following for loop:

```
for(int i=0; i<=10; i++){
    out.println("JSPs are great");
}
```

has the following implementation with a while statement:

```
int i=0;
while(i<=10){
    out.println("JSPs are great");
    i++;
}
```

Answers for Hour 10, "Processing Requests from the User"

Quiz

1. What are the methods used to process parameters in a query string?

   The methods used to process parameters in query string are

   - `String getParameter(String paramName)`
   - `Enumeration getParameterNames()`
   - `String[] getParameterValues(String paramName)`

2. What are the different parts of a URL?

   The different parts of a URL are the protocol, the server machine, the port, the virtual path, and the query string.

3. When is a request generated and how can the JSP process it?

A request is generated by the browser when the user either clicks a hyperlink or submits an HTML form. The request can be processed by the JSP using the API of the request object.

Answer for Hour 11, "Generating a Dynamic Response for the User"

Quiz

1. The JSP listed below wants to create a contact list from the data stored in the string and integer arrays. Find what is wrong with the source code and fix it.

The question says that the data is stored in string and integer arrays, but these are not declared as such in lines 2 and 4. Also, the variable's names and numbers must be referenced as arrays, and not as single variables in line 8. Finally, the number of numbers must match the number of names in line 4.

```
 1: <HTML><HEAD><TITLE></TITLE></HEAD><BODY>
 2: <%  String[] names = {"Katerina Lozada", "Rafael Greco", "Pasquale
    Marotta",
 3:                          "Alexander Zahringer"};
 4:     int[] numbers = {1233212, 2344323, 3455434, 4566545, 5677656};
 5:     <TABLE>
 6:     <TR><TD>Names</TD><TD>Numbers</TD></TR>
 7:     for(int j=0; j<names.length(); j++){ %>
 8:        <TR> <TD>names[j]</TD><TD>numbers[j]</TD> </TR>
 9: <%  }  %>
10:     </TABLE>
11: %>
12: </BODY></HTML>
```

Answers for Hour 12, "Keeping Track of the User Session"

Quiz

1. When would you use URL encoding?

Always, because users might have their cookies disabled on their browsers and URL encoding is smart enough to figure out if cookies are enabled or not, to encode the URL if necessary.

A

2. How would you create a Cookie called `FavoriteColor` with a value of `Blue`?

Create an instance of the `Cookie` class with the constructor `Cookie()` and use as arguments "`FavoriteColor`", and "`Blue`". Then add the cookie to the `response` object using its `addCookie()` method. Use the line below:

```
response.addCookie(new Cookie("FavoriteColor", "Blue"));
```

Answers for Hour 13, "Configuring and Initializing JSPs"

Quiz

1. How would you change the package name of a Servlet that is compiled from a JSP?

You would use the `-package` option of the `weblogic.jspc` compiler.

2. From within a JSP how would you find out the name by which the corresponding Servlet is registered in the configuration file?

The method `config.getServletName()` returns the name under which the Servlet is registered with the application server.

3. How would you list all the names of the initialization parameters from within a JSP?

You would use the method `config.getInitParameterNames()` to get an `Enumeration` that contains all the names of the initialization parameters. You would then iterate through the enumeration and print each element individually.

Answers for Hour 14, "Creating Error Pages"

Quiz

1. What is the stack trace?

The stack trace is a list of all the methods in a chain of nested method calls from where the first method called occurred all the way up to where an exception is thrown.

2. How is a page declared to be an error page?

A page is declared to be an error page by setting the `isErrorPage` attribute of the page directive to `true` using the following syntax:

```
<%@ page isErrorPage=true %>
```

Answers for Hour 15, "Inserting Applets into Your JSPs"

Quiz

1. What tag is used to pass a parameter to an applet and what are its attributes?

   The param tag is used to pass a parameter to an applet. It takes two attributes, name and value. The attributes are the name of the parameter, as specified by the applet class, and the value you are assigning it.

2. What does the codebase attribute specify?

   The codebase attribute is a URI that points to the location of the .class files for the applet.

3. Why do you want to use the fallback tag?

   The fallback tag is used to specify text that will appear if the user does not have Java enabled on his browser. This is helpful for letting the user know what the page is supposed to contain.

Answers for Hour 16, "Using JavaBeans in a JSP"

Quiz

1. Describe each of the four JavaBean scope settings. What is each best suited for?

   The four javabean scope settings are:

   Page—JavaBeans of page scope are stored in the PageContext object and are only available to the current page. Page scope variables are useful for short-term information that isn't passed between JSPs.

   Request—JavaBeans of request scope are stored in the ServletRequest object and available to the called JSP and all its included JSPs. Request scope objects are useful for short term information.

   Session—JavaBeans of session scope are stored into the HttpSession object and can be used by all JSPs and servlets in the current request. Session scope objects are excellent for passing information between pages, JSPs, and other servlets.

   Application—Application scope objects are stored in the ServletContext object and are useful for storing global information, such as how often a given page has been referenced. Note that you cannot be 100% accurate when using application scope objects for such information when you have different instances of application servers running on the same machine, because they will NOT share application scope objects!

2. How can JavaBeans be used with HTML forms?

The JSP `setProperty` tag has a special syntax that allows you to initialize JavaBeans with parameter values in an HTML form. The syntax of the `setProperty` tag for HTML forms is

```
<jsp:setProperty name="theJavaBean" property="*">
```

The tag automatically extracts the parameter values from an HTML form and initializes the variables of *theJavaBean*. For this to work, the names of the variables and the names of the form input fields must be the same.

Answers for Hour 17, "Accessing a Database from a JSP"

Quiz

1. What are the classes and interfaces that are usually involved when using JDBC to connect to a database?

   `DriverManager`, `Connection`, `Statement`, and `ResultSet`

2. Name three get functions from the `ResultSet` object that allow you to access data from fields in a record.

   `ResultSet.getString()`, `ResultSet.getInt()`, and `ResultSet.getBoolean()`.

Answers for Hour 18, "Substituting Text in a JSP"

Quiz

1. What is the general syntax of the include directive?

   `<%@ include file="Relative_URL_and_Filename" %>`

2. When using the `include` directive, how is the text of the file included?

   The text is inserted into the JSP at translation time. If it is a JSP or an HTML document, the code is inserted at the location of the `include` directive.

3. How do you specify the filename and location of the included file?

   The `file` attribute of the `include` directive specifies the filename and location of the included file. Remember that it is a relative location—relative to the JSP, that is.

Answers for Hour 19, "Extending JSP Functionality with Tag Libraries"

Quiz

1. What is a tag handler?

   A tag handler is a server-side object that is executed at runtime to handle the interpretation of a JSP action tag.

2. What language is the tag library descriptor written in?

   The TLD is written in XML.

3. When you are using custom actions in a JSP, how does it know which tag library your custom action is defined within?

   When you use a custom action in your JSP, you specify the unique reference name, then a colon, then the name of the custom action. The unique reference name is the name assigned to the prefix attribute of the `taglib` directive. For example, `<friday:thankgoodness />`.

Answers for Hour 20, "Using Multiple JSPs to Handle the Request"

Quiz

1. What is the attribute that both the `include` and `forward` actions take?

   Both actions take a `page` for their attribute. The `page` attribute takes a relative path to the JSP that is going to be included or forwarded to.

2. What is the difference between the `include` action and the `include` directive?

   The `include` action includes the output of other JSPs. The `include` directive includes the code of the other JSPs into the current JSP.

3. What would the `forward` action tag look like if you wanted to forward to a JSP called `ForwardToMe.jsp` that was two subdirectories below your JSP, `forwardedFiles/anotherSubdirectory`?

   `<jsp:forward page="forwardedFiles/anotherSubdirectory/ForwardToMe.jsp />`

A

Answers for Hour 21, "Designing an Enterprise Application"

Quiz

1. What are the two ways to access a database with a JSP?

   A JSP can access a database directly or it can use a JavaBean to access it.

2. What are the two ways to send data from an HTML form to the server?

   An HTML form can use the POST or GET method in order to send data from an HTML form to the server.

3. Where would an application like this human resources Web site be found?

   This application would be found on a company's intranet. Many companies offer sites like this to get more interaction with the employees.

4. Why do you model your application before beginning to code?

   You should always model your applications before you begin coding in order to address all of your requirements. It is easier to catch problems in your application during the design phase, than it is to wait until the development cycle.

Answers for Hour 22, "Creating a Presentation Layer"

Quiz

1. What two directives were used in the PresentCompanyPolicies.jsp file?

   The include directive and the page directive. The include directive included the company banner and the site navigator; the page directive imported the appropriate classes for database access.

2. What is a benefit of including a file into a JSP via the include directive?

   The major benefit of including files via the include directive is that you only need to make changes in one place instead of all your files.

3. What action is used in the PersonalInfo.jsp file? How does this JSP action work?

   The PersonalInfo.jsp file uses the include action to insert the output of the other JSPs. The include action treats the included files as dynamic files and so it includes the output, not the code, of the files.

4. Many times a Servlet parses the user's request and uses a JSP to present the response. If you were to apply this philosophy to the Husky World Human Resources site, what JSP(s) would be replaced with Servlets?

   The JSP that could be represented by Servlets is `PersonalInfo.jsp`.

Answers for Hour 23, "Programming the Business Logic"

Quiz

1. What directive imported the appropriate files for doing database access?

   The `page` directive allows you to import Java packages into your JSPs.

2. What is a benefit of using the `include` directive?

   The `include` directive allows you to create HTML or static documents, and then dynamically insert their code into your JSPs. A common banner or copyright that appears on all your JSPs can be kept in a separate file, and any changes you make to it will propagate to all your JSPs.

3. When you execute an SQL statement on a database, what type of object is your data stored in?

   The data from the database is returned in a `ResultSet` object.

A

Answers for Hour 24, "Packaging and Deploying an Enterprise Application"

Quiz

1. What is a benefit of a Web archive file?

   A benefit of a Web archive file is portability. You can take the file and deploy it on any Servlet 2.2-compliant server.

2. What specification describes Web archive files?

   The Web archive files are described in the Servlet 2.2 specification.

3. What XML file is used to describe the Web application, and where is this file located?

   The `web.xml` file is used to describe the Web application; it is placed in the `WEB-INF` directory.

INDEX

SAMS Teach Yourself in 24 Hours

Sams Teach Yourself in 24 Hours *gets you the results you want—fast! Work through 24 proven one-hour lessons and learn everything you need to know to get up to speed quickly. It has the answers you need at a price you can afford.*

Sams Teach Yourself Java 2 in 24 Hours, Second Edition

Rogers Cadenhead
0-672-32036-3
$24.99 US/$37.95 CAN

Other Sams Teach Yourself in 24 Hours Titles

Sams Teach Yourself Adobe Photoshop 6 in 24 Hours
Carla Rose
0-672-31955-1
$24.99 US/$37.95 CAN

Sams Teach Yourself PHP4 in 24 Hours
Matt Zandstra
0-672-31804-0
$24.99 US/$37.95 CAN

Sams Teach Yourself Paint Shop Pro 7 in 24 Hours
T. Michael Clark
0-672-32030-4
$19.99 US/$29.95 CAN

Sams Teach Yourself SQL in 24 Hours, Second Edition
Ryan Stephens
0-672-31899-7
$24.99 US/$37.95 CAN

Sams Teach Yourself Macromedia Flash 5 in 24 Hours
Phillip Kerman
0-672-31892-X
$24.99 US/$37.95 CAN

Sams Teach Yourself Windows 2000 Professional in 24 Hours
Dan Gookin
0-672-31701-X
$19.99 US/$29.95 CAN

Sams Teach Yourself Active Server Pages in 24 Hours
Christoph Wille and Christian Kollier
0-672-31612-9
$19.99 US/$29.95 CAN

Sams Teach Yourself JavaScript in 24 Hours, Second Edition

Michael Moncur
0-672-32025-8
$24.99 US/$37.95 CAN

Sams Teach Yourself XML in 24 Hours

Charles Ashbacher
0-672-31950-0
$24.99 US/$37.95 CAN

SAMS

www.samspublishing.com

All prices are subject to change.

Other Related Titles

Installation Instructions

Windows 95/98/2000/ NT 4

1. Insert the CD-ROM into your CD-ROM drive.
2. From the Windows desktop, double-click on the My Computer icon.
3. Double-click on the icon representing your CD-ROM drive.
4. Double-click on the icon titled SETUP.EXE to run the installation program.

NOTE: If Windows is installed on your computer, and you have the AutoPlay feature enabled, the setup.exe program starts automatically whenever you insert the disc into your CD-ROM drive.

Linux and UNIX

These installation instructions assume that you have a passing familiarity with UNIX commands and the basic setup of your machine. Because UNIX has many flavors, only generic commands are used. If you have any problems with the commands, please consult the appropriate man page or your system administrator.

1. Insert the CD-ROM into the CD-ROM drive.
2. If you have a volume manager, mounting of the CD-ROM will be automatic. If you don't have a volume manager, you can mount the CD-ROM by typing

   ```
   mount    -tiso9660    /dev/cdrom    /mnt/cdrom
   ```
3. After you've mounted the CD-ROM, you can install files from the appropriate directories.

Read This Before Opening This Software